Ready for Takeoff?

DIRECTIONS IN DEVELOPMENT
Infrastructure

Ready for Takeoff?
The Potential for Low-Cost Carriers in Developing Countries

Charles E. Schlumberger and Nora Weisskopf

© 2014 International Bank for Reconstruction and Development / The World Bank
1818 H Street NW, Washington DC 20433
Telephone: 202-473-1000; Internet: www.worldbank.org

Some rights reserved

1 2 3 4   17 16 15 14

This work is a product of the staff of The World Bank with external contributions. The findings, interpretations, and conclusions expressed in this work do not necessarily reflect the views of The World Bank, its Board of Executive Directors, or the governments they represent. The World Bank does not guarantee the accuracy of the data included in this work. The boundaries, colors, denominations, and other information shown on any map in this work do not imply any judgment on the part of The World Bank concerning the legal status of any territory or the endorsement or acceptance of such boundaries.

Nothing herein shall constitute or be considered to be a limitation upon or waiver of the privileges and immunities of The World Bank, all of which are specifically reserved.

Rights and Permissions

This work is available under the Creative Commons Attribution 3.0 IGO license (CC BY 3.0 IGO) http://creativecommons.org/licenses/by/3.0/igo. Under the Creative Commons Attribution license, you are free to copy, distribute, transmit, and adapt this work, including for commercial purposes, under the following conditions:

Attribution—Please cite the work as follows: Schlumberger, Charles E., and Nora Weisskopf. 2014. *Ready for Takeoff? The Potential for Low-Cost Carriers in Developing Countries.* Directions in Development. Washington, DC: World Bank. doi:10.1596/978-1-4648-0282-9. License: Creative Commons Attribution CC BY 3.0 IGO

Translations—If you create a translation of this work, please add the following disclaimer along with the attribution: *This translation was not created by The World Bank and should not be considered an official World Bank translation. The World Bank shall not be liable for any content or error in this translation.*

Adaptations—If you create an adaptation of this work, please add the following disclaimer along with the attribution: *This is an adaptation of an original work by The World Bank. Responsibility for the views and opinions expressed in the adaptation rests solely with the author or authors of the adaptation and are not endorsed by The World Bank.*

Third-party content—The World Bank does not necessarily own each component of the content contained within the work. The World Bank therefore does not warrant that the use of any third-party-owned individual component or part contained in the work will not infringe on the rights of those third parties. The risk of claims resulting from such infringement rests solely with you. If you wish to re-use a component of the work, it is your responsibility to determine whether permission is needed for that re-use and to obtain permission from the copyright owner. Examples of components can include, but are not limited to, tables, figures, or images.

All queries on rights and licenses should be addressed to the Publishing and Knowledge Division, The World Bank, 1818 H Street NW, Washington, DC 20433, USA; fax: 202-522-2625; e-mail: pubrights@worldbank.org.

ISBN (paper): 978-1-4648-0282-9
ISBN (electronic): 978-1-4648-0283-6
DOI: 10.1596/978-1-4648-0282-9

Cover photo: © VivaAerobus. Used with the permission of VivaAerobus. Further permission required for reuse.
Cover design: Debra Naylor, Naylor Design

Library of Congress Cataloging-in-Publication Data has been requested.

Contents

Foreword		*xi*
Acknowledgments		*xiii*
About the Authors		*xv*
Executive Summary		*xvii*
Abbreviations		*xxiii*

	Introduction	1
Chapter 1	**The Low-Cost Carrier Business Model**	3
	Definition	3
	Key Elements of the LCC Business Model	3
	Are Low-Cost Carriers Really Low Cost?	15
	Conclusion	17
	Notes	18
	References	19
Chapter 2	**The Impact of Low-Cost Airlines**	23
	Empirical Evidence for the Impact of Air Transport	23
	The Impact of Low-Cost Airlines	25
	Conclusion	31
	References	32
Chapter 3	**Two Case Studies: Mexico and South Africa**	35
	The Mexican Wave: Growth and Innovation	35
	Now Anyone Can Fly—The Impact of Low-Cost Carriers in South Africa	44
	Conclusion	52
	Notes	53
	References	54
Chapter 4	**Transferability of the LCC Model to Developing Countries—A Framework**	59
	Demand Conditions	61
	Air Transport Infrastructure	63

	Air Transport Liberalization	67
	Labor	70
	Safety and Security	73
	Distribution	76
	Aircraft Financing	76
	Fuel	80
	Governance	81
	What Matters Most?	82
	To Enter or Not to Enter? A Market Entry Model for an LCC in Egypt	83
	Conclusion	87
	Notes	87
	References	88
Chapter 5	Opportunities and Challenges for LCC Development: The Case of East Africa	95
	Introduction	95
	East African Community (EAC)	95
	Demand	97
	Air Transport Infrastructure	123
	Air Transport Liberalization	138
	Safety and Security	143
	Labor	146
	Aircraft Financing	148
	Fuel Cost and Access	149
	Distribution	152
	Governance	156
	Conclusion	156
	Notes	159
	References	159
Chapter 6	Development Framework for Sustainable Air Transport	169
	Access to Markets	169
	Infrastructure and Physical Capacity	171
	Financing of Aircraft and Airport Infrastructure	173
	Safety and Security	174
	Regulation of Taxes and Fees	175
	Conclusions for Development of the LCC Sector and Role of Development Partners	177
	Notes	178
	References	179
Appendix A	Carrier Evaluation Methodology	181
Appendix B	Database of Low-Cost Airlines Classification	183

Appendix C	Selected Impact Studies	187
Appendix D	Freedoms of the Air	191
Appendix E	Major Airlines in EAC	193
Appendix F	Fare Comparison Methodology	197
Appendix G	Airports in EAC	199
Appendix H	Runway Capacity Estimation Methodology	205
Appendix I	Infrastructure Charges Methodology and Detailed Assessment	207
Appendix J	Accidents (2004–13)	217
Appendix K	Doing Business Report: Labor Regulations (2012)	223

Boxes

| 2.1 | Demand Stimulation—The Case of VivaAerobus | 29 |
| 3.1 | From Bus to Plane—LCC VivaAerobus Partnership with Grupo IAMSA Bus Operator | 39 |

Figures

1.1	Average Daily Aircraft Utilization by LCCs, 2011–12	8
1.2	LCC Average Stage Length, 2013	9
1.3	Online Distribution as Percentage of Total Distribution, 2011–12	12
1.4	Labor Productivity Comparison, 2011–12	13
1.5	Adherence to Low-Cost Model, 2011–12	14
1.6	Comparison of U.S. CASM, Network Carriers, and LCCs, 2005–11	16
1.7	Comparison of Network and LCC Fuel CASM	17
2.1	Flowchart of LCC Impact	27
B2.1	Traffic Evolution Pre- and Post-LCC Entrance, Monterrey–Verracruz	29
3.1	Domestic Passengers, Mexico, 2000–12	40
3.2	Domestic Total, Trunk, and Regional Passengers, 2004–08	41
3.3	Fare Comparison Mexico City–Cancun, April 2012	42
3.4	South African Airways International and Domestic Departures, 1990–94	45
3.5	Trends in Passenger Transport on Major Domestic Routes, 1986–96	47
3.6	Trends in Economy Class Fares on the Johannesburg–Cape Town Route, 1989–96	48

4.1	Flight Intensity, 2012	62
4.2	Air Transport Infrastructure Quality, 2012	64
4.3	Selected Lowest Economy Fare for African Routes, August 2012	67
4.4	Percentage of Firms Identifying Labor Regulation as a Major Constraint	73
4.5	Aircraft Financing: 2011 versus 2012	77
4.6	Cost Advantage by Element, 2011	83
5.1	Intra-EAC Traffic, 2004–13	98
5.2	Domestic Traffic Kenya and Tanzania, 2004–13	99
5.3	Domestic Traffic Uganda and Rwanda, 2004–13	99
5.4	Number of Carriers per Top Intra-EAC Routes, July 2013	101
5.5	Market Share per Carrier on Top Intra-EAC Routes, July 2013	102
5.6	Number of Flights per Aircraft Size, July 2013 (Intra-Regional and Domestic)	104
5.7	Comparison of Lowest Available Return Fare between Intra-EAC and Other International Routes (Including Taxes and Charges)	107
5.8	Distribution Fare Basis versus Taxation and Charges, 2013	108
5.9	Comparison of Lowest Available Domestic Fare (Including Taxes and Charges)	109
5.10	Distribution Fare Basis versus Taxation and Charges	110
5.11	GDP Growth in EAC Countries, 2008–12	111
5.12	Flight Intensity in EAC Countries, 2012	112
5.13	Poverty Headcount Ratio at $2 (PPP)	113
5.14	GINI Index for EAC	113
5.15	Wealth Distribution in EAC Countries	114
5.16	Forecasted GDP Per Capita Growth Rate in EAC Countries	115
5.17	Population Growth in EAC, 2007–12	116
5.18	Urban Population, 2007–12	116
5.19	Number of International Arrivals, 2006–10	117
5.20	International Tourism Receipts, 2010	119
5.21	Arrival by Mode of Transport	120
5.22	Air Transport Infrastructure Quality, 2012/13	124
5.23	Total Turnaround Charges for Domestic Daytime Flight	130
5.24	Total Turnaround Charges for Regional/International Daytime Flight	131
5.25	Total Turnaround Cost for Domestic Daytime Flight—Passengers versus Airlines	132
5.26	Total Turnaround Cost for Regional/International Daytime Flight—Passengers versus Airlines	132
5.27	Comparison of Airline Charges for Domestic Daytime Flight	133
5.28	Comparison of Passenger Charges for Domestic Daytime Flight	134
5.29	Comparison of Airline Charges for Regional/International Daytime Flight	135

5.30	Comparison of Passenger Charges for Regional/International Daytime Flight	136
5.31	Assumed Primary Cause of Accidents in EAC, 2003–13	144
5.32	Level of Implementation in Key Audit Areas	145
5.33	Percentage of Firms Identifying Labor Regulations as a Major Constraint—Comparison of EAC and Other Regions	148
5.34	Mombasa Refinery Output per Type of Product	151
5.35	EAC Internet Usage, 2006–11	153
5.36	Comparison of Internet Users with the United States, United Kingdom, Thailand, and Mexico, 2006–11	153
5.37	Mobile Cellular Subscriptions in EAC, 2008–11	154
5.38	Depositors with Commercial Banks, 2010	155
5.39	Governance Indicators for EAC	156
I.1	Daytime Landing Fees for Domestic Flights	209
I.2	Daytime Landing Fees for Regional/International Flights	210
I.3	Turnaround (Takeoff and Landing) Landing Fees for Nighttime Domestic Operations	210
I.4	Turnaround (Takeoff and Landing) Landing Fees for Nighttime Regional/International Operations	211
I.5	Approach and Overflight Charges for Domestic Daytime Flights	213
I.6	Approach and Overflight Charges for Regional/International Daytime Flights	213
I.7	Passenger Charges for Domestic Flights	214
I.8	Passenger Charges for Regional/International Flights	215
I.9	Passenger Charges at Other African Airports	215

Maps

4.1	USOAP Results, 2012	75
4.2	Ratification of Cape Town Convention	80
5.1	Route Network Map of EAC	100
5.2	Road Network: Major Primary Road by Type and Condition	121

Tables

2.1	Selected Air Transport Impact Studies	26
4.1	The Framework	60
4.2	Elements of Air Service Agreements	69
4.3	Intra-Regional Traffic by Type of Agreement	70
4.4	Accident Statistics and Accident Rates, 2012	74
4.5	Aircraft Financing Sources and Mechanisms	79
4.6	Key Results Entry Behavior Model	86
5.1	Passengers by Airport, 2012	97
5.2	Estimates of Bilateral Migrant Stock, 2010	119

5.3	Comparison of Bus Travel and Flight Times	123
5.4	Airfields in EAC	125
5.5	Potential Runway Capacity per Year (5 Minute and 10 Minute Lags) and Current Estimated Passenger Terminal Capacity	128
5.6	Major EAC Airport Operators	137
5.7	Main Elements of Yamoussoukro Decision	139
5.8	Bilateral Air Service Agreements between Tanzania and EAC Countries	142
5.9	Implementation of Yamoussoukro Decision (YD) in African RECs	143
6.1	Challenges and Measures for the Development of Sustainable Air Transport Markets in Developing Countries	177
A.1	Carrier Evaluation Methodology	181
B.1	Database Low-Cost Airlines Classification	183
C.1	Selected Impact Studies	188
D.1	Freedoms of the Air	191
E.1	Major Airlines in EAC	194
G.1	Airports in the East African Community	200
G.2	Airports in the East African Community: Features	202
J.1	Accidents 2004–13	218
K.1	Labor Regulations, 2012	224

Foreword

It gives me much pleasure to write a foreword for the research of Dr. Charles E. Schlumberger and Ms. Nora Weisskopf of the World Bank on the potential of low-cost carriers (LCCs) in developing countries. It is a timely publication that raises important issues about the challenges and potential these carriers can bring to a market. The authors discuss how these airlines successfully transformed inefficient and stagnant markets in developed countries and examine which industries benefited from the increased affordability of air travel. They find that the tourism sector, in particular, has experienced a strong impact, a sector that has great potential for further growth, especially in emerging countries.

LCCs have revolutionized the air transport industry. If deregulation shaped the last quarter of the 20th century, the first decade of the 21st century cannot be understood without reference to LCCs and the impact they have had on passengers, legacy carriers, and airports alike.

For many years, the topic of LCCs has been high on the agenda at many Airports Council International (ACI) meetings and conferences. For many of our members, this carrier segment represents a real business opportunity; for many others, it constitutes a serious challenge. Infrastructure planning, capital investment, airport charges, economic regulation, operational procedures, and commercial planning and marketing are just some aspects of the airport business that have been directly affected by the emergence of the LCC sector worldwide.

LCCs have clearly contributed to the increasingly competitive nature of the airport market. Today, airports compete to attract airlines that are free to choose where, when, and how they fly. LCCs have shown themselves to be nimble and can pull out of a market at a moment's notice while having a huge impact on the legacy carriers. Airports have had to react to this new reality and have taken on new risks by developing dedicated infrastructure, adapting their operational practices, and offering attractive financial incentive schemes—all without the guarantee of continuity.

Still, the possibility of increasing the number of passengers significantly at often quiet and remote regional airports has definitely got many airports interested in attracting LCCs. And when airports join forces with regional authorities and the private sector, the arrival of an LCC can have a very positive socio-economic impact on an airport's catchment area.

As the authors point out, the challenge is to ensure that LCCs represent a real opportunity for airports and the communities they serve, while also ensuring the sustainable development of the airport business and the air transport industry at large.

I highly commend this book to all those who are interested in the development of air service, the challenges and opportunities air carriers are experiencing in emerging markets, and the particularities of the low-cost airline industry.

Angela Gittens
Director General
Airports Council International

Acknowledgments

We would like to take this opportunity to express our gratitude to the people who have been instrumental in the successful completion of the research for this book.

First and foremost, we would like to give special thanks to Declan Ryan and James Muldowney from Irelandia Aviation who embarked with us on this project from day one and have been providing us with input and feedback throughout the two years of this research.

We would also like to show our gratitude for the invaluable assistance, support, and guidance we have received from experts within the airline industry to produce this book. We would, in particular, like to convey thanks to Anish Goel, Suzanne Raubenstine, and David Gamrath from the Boeing Company; Simon Pickup from Airbus; Phillippe Poutissou and Antonio Ficca from Bombardier; Hemen Shah from 8 Miles; Niko Herrmann from Oliver Wyman; and Niko Bezuidenhout from Mango Airlines. In addition, we would like to acknowledge the contributions of Elizabeth Kiguta and Alexey Smachtin.

We would also like to thank our colleagues at the World Bank who prepared important input or acted as peer reviewers, providing comments and suggestions for improving this research. These include Daniel Saslavsky, trade specialist, for his contribution of researching and authoring the section in chapter 4 on a market-entry LCC model in the Arab Republic of Egypt; Pierre Pozzo di Borgo, senior investment officer; Reindert Westra, senior urban transport specialist; Jean-Francois Arvis, senior economist; Vincent Vesin, transport specialist; Linda Tiemoko, knowledge management analyst, and Shruti Vijayakumar, air transport specialist, for their help throughout the publishing process. Furthermore, we wish to express our gratitude to Jose Luis Irigoyen, director of the Transport, Water and ICT Department, and Marc Juhel, sector manager, Transport, for supporting this research.

Finally we would like to thank our respective families, partners, and friends for their endless support and loving patience throughout the process of writing this book.

About the Authors

Charles E. Schlumberger is a lead air transport specialist at the World Bank in Washington, DC. In this function he is responsible for the Bank's policy and development priorities in the field of air transportation. Prior to his appointment to the World Bank he held the position of vice president at the Union Bank of Switzerland, was the chief executive officer of the Steinbeck Global Logistics Group in France, and worked as a lawyer on aviation-related matters in Switzerland. Schlumberger holds a law degree from Basel Law School in Switzerland, an MBA from Harvard Business School in the United States, and a doctorate in civil law from the Institute of Air and Space Law of McGill University in Canada.

Nora Weisskopf is an air transport specialist at the World Bank in Washington, DC. Her work covers a range of development-related air transport issues including airline/airport safety and security, airport finance and infrastructure, sustainability, aviation policy, and research. She has been involved, in particular, in the implementation of the World Bank's Pacific Aviation Investment Program, which aims to improve operational safety and oversight of international air transport infrastructure in the South Pacific. She holds a master's degree in international business from the University of Edinburgh in the United Kingdom, where she completed her dissertation on the sustainability of long-haul low-cost airlines.

Executive Summary

The emergence of low-cost carriers (LCCs) has been a key catalyst for the development of the aviation industry in the last decade. Indeed, extensive research has been undertaken to analyze the business model and impact on the aviation sector and beyond. Despite recent developments in the LCC markets in Asia and Latin America, much of the research has been focused on developed countries. Therefore, the purpose of this book is to identify the premises and prerequisites of the LCC model, and assess whether this business model could be successful in other less-developed countries, in particular the countries of Sub-Saharan Africa.

This book identifies various definitions that have been applied to describe the LCC business model. In essence the majority of researchers define LCCs as carriers which, through a variety of operational processes, have achieved a cost advantage over full-service carriers (FSCs). This cost advantage is, in most cases, translated to the consumers by a lower fare offering. Although many carriers are defined as LCCs, the LCC model has developed into many different variations since the original "Southwest Airlines model," the first U.S. LCC, which began operations in the 1960s.

There are a number of key characteristics that can generally be found in LCCs. These include (a) *simple service offering* focusing on the key service of transport and removal of all "frills" (for example, free baggage, on-board meals, assigned seating) or charging additional fees for them; (b) *short-haul, point-to-point route structure* rather than traditional complex and oftentimes expensive hub-and-spoke network; (c) *usage of secondary airports* with lower airport charges, higher availability of slots, and reduced congestion; (d) *high aircraft utilization* achieved through shorter turnaround times, longer routes,[1] or higher flight frequency; (e) *fleet commonality and generally newer, more fuel-efficient fleet* to minimize aircraft-specific expenditures (such as maintenance and personnel), increase purchasing power in aircraft procurement and reduce fuel costs; (f) *high-density one-class configuration* to maximize aircraft capacity; (g) *low-cost distribution* through online selling; (h) *high labor utilization* through a higher number of average block hours per employee and/or higher passenger-per-employee ratio.

Although these common operating practices can be identified across a range of low-cost airlines, there is no *one* particular LCC model or a single driving element responsible for its competitive advantage. The LCC business model has also been evolving rapidly in recent years with a considerable shift in operating practices. Many LCCs, particularly those in Europe and the United States have, for example, been "hybridizing" their models as more mature LCC competition, higher fuel prices, and powerful network alliances turn their focus to higher yield opportunities. Even airlines such as Southwest have shifted more toward traditional models that cater to business traffic by using primary airports and adjusting their schedules. Their network counterparts, under competitive pressures from the new entrants, have also become more cost sensitive. Furthermore fuel prices have had a considerable impact on this convergence, with LCCs losing their advantage of more fuel-efficient aircraft to the fleet renewal process currently under way at most traditional airlines.

It is well documented that the development of air transport services can have a substantial impact on the aviation market—as well as on other related and even unrelated industries (see for example ICAO 2004; Button and Taylor 2000; Oxford Economics 2011). These studies, varying in scope and methodology, have shown air transportation to have a considerable positive impact on employment, gross domestic product (GDP), trade, tourism, and productivity, among other factors.

Research on the impact of low-cost airlines has been scarce due to the difficulty of linking the impact of increased air transportation to a particular business model. However, a number of studies have confirmed the significant positive impact of LCCs on air transport and related markets. Although some anecdotal evidence from developing countries is available, research on LCC entrance is also almost entirely focused on developed countries, particularly in Europe and the United States. This is largely due to the more recent emergence of LCCs in developing markets and the required data often being unavailable.

Specific focus has been paid to the impact of LCCs on traffic stimulation through lower fares and their overall impact on competition and fare levels in the market. Coining the term "Southwest Effect," the U.S. Department of Transportation (DoT) researchers Randall Bennett and James Craun concentrated on three different aspects of how Southwest Airlines impacted the aviation market, namely through: (a) a direct competitive effect in terms of passenger growth and fare reduction on a given route where Southwest had entered; (b) the lowering of fares at surrounding airports through Southwest's entry; and (c) the role model effect, exhibiting the impact Southwest has on the business models of new entrants in other markets (Bennett and Craun 1993). Focusing on the California corridor, the study presented evidence that Southwest's entry had a significant impact on all three aspects outlined above. On the Oakland–Burbank route, for example, where Southwest entered in 1990, prices dropped by 55 percent, and passenger traffic increased sixfold between its entrance and the 3rd quarter of 1992 (Bennett and Craun 1993).

However, the effects of low-cost airlines go far beyond fare levels and passenger traffic. The aviation literature includes a particularly well-documented correlation between LCC entrance and tourism. The European Low Fares Airline Association (ELFAA) has grouped these benefits for tourism into three categories: (a) an increase in tourist destinations due to usage of secondary airports, for example, the London–Strasbourg route, previously used primarily for business travel, has proved a popular tourist destination with the entrance of Ryanair; (b) more even distribution of traffic throughout the year reducing "seasonality effects"; and (c) low off-peak fares, which have enabled mid-week holiday travel. This distributes traffic more evenly across the week and reduces congestion at airports (ELFAA 2004). A number of studies have also focused on other LCC impacts. Williams and Balaz (2007), for example, focused on the impact of LCCs on the flows of labor, migrants, knowledge, business connectivity/investment, and mobile markets including tourism.

The effects of reduced fares and traffic simulation could also be observed in developing countries, such as in the cases of Mexico and South Africa. Both countries have seen rapid LCC growth in the last decade, which has significantly benefited air travelers.

In Mexico, the emergence of LCCs has considerably stimulated traffic growth, with LCCs capturing almost 60 percent of the domestic market in 2012. They not only increased traffic from existing air travelers, but also attracted new flyers into the market (CAPA 2013). This was facilitated by the LCCs' considerably lower fares, as well as an expansion of the historically limited domestic network. VivaAerobus, a Mexican LCC, estimates that a quarter of its customers are actually first-time travelers (VivaAerobus 2012). Bus travelers, who had been enduring long rides on the country's dilapidated road infrastructure, proved to be a critical customer base for the airline.

Similarly, in South Africa, traffic was drawn from users of alternative modes of transport. On the Johannesburg–East London route, which takes more than eight hours by car, the entrance of LCCs increased air traffic by 52 percent between the second quarter of 2004 and the second quarter of 2006. This is seen to have been a major factor in revitalizing the region's tourism industry, resulting in a more than 50 percent increase in holiday packages. As one of the poorest regions in the country (US$1,400 per capita GDP), tourism is a key contributor to the region's economy. Estimates show that the 52 percent increase in foreign tourists translates into 62,000 additional tourists per year, resulting in 65.8 million South African rand (US$10 million) in tourism expenditures (ComMark Trust 2006).

The cases of both Mexico and South Africa offer some preliminary notions about the impact that LCCs can have in developing countries. However, the success of LCCs in these markets was dependent on certain market conditions. This book, which involved extensive research and stakeholder interviews, identifies the following key factors: (a) *economic growth and a sizable middle class to drive demand*; (b) *air transport liberalization and privatization of monopolistic state-owned carriers*; (c) *the availability of adequate, low-cost air transport infrastructure*; (d) *availability of qualified human resources*; (e) *appropriate safety and security standards*; (f) *low-cost distribution channels*; (g) *availability of cost-effective financing for aircraft;* (h) *fuel availability and cost;* and (i) *good governance* to provide a sound investment climate.

Based on this framework, the case of the East African Community was chosen for further study. Although a preliminary assessment, the analysis indicates that, given the limited traffic domestically and in the region, combined with numerous challenges—such as the lack of a significant middle class driving demand, stalled liberalization efforts, limited safety and security oversight, few navigational aids, and limited human and financial resources to create a low-cost airline—the emergence of profitable LCCs in the region may be premature. However, in light of traffic forecasts, projected economic development, and a growing tourism industry, considerable opportunities may arise in the near future.

In order for LCCs to capitalize on these opportunities, stakeholders in the aviation industry will have to proactively address some of the challenges highlighted above. Although an LCC model may not be suitable at this point in time, there are significant opportunities for lowering costs and fares, and consequently stimulating the development of a competitive air transport market. This will in turn create the proper environment for LCCs to emerge. In the case of the East African Community as well as other developing countries, measures which can be taken to capitalize on these opportunities include: (a) *the fostering of a competitive environment by removing any market distortions* (for example, monopolistic state-owned carriers, restrictive air transport policies, and bad governance); (b) *investments, where required, in air transport and air traffic control infrastructure,* in particular communications, navigation, and surveillance (CNS) infrastructure; (c) *improvements in safety and security oversight* through capacity building efforts in civil aviation authorities and airport operators (for example, training programs); and (d) *reduction in input costs* (for example, fuel and airport charges and taxes).

Note

1. Still within short to medium haul.

References

Bennett, R., and J. Craun. 1993. *U.S. Department of Transportation, The Airline Deregulation Evolution Continues: The Southwest Effect.* Office of Aviation Analysis, U.S. Department of Transportation.

Button, K., and S. Taylor. 2000. "International Air Transportation and Economic Development." *Journal of Air Transport Management* 6 (4): 209–22.

CAPA (Centre for Asia Pacific Aviation). 2013. "Mexico Returns to Double-Digit Domestic Growth in 2012, Boosting Outlook for Aeromexico and LCCs." *Centre for Asia Pacific Aviation* (online) 6 February 2013. http://centreforaviation.com/analysis/mexico-returns-to-double-digit-domestic-growth-in-2012-boosting-outlook-for-aeromexico-and-lccs-96464.

ComMark Trust. 2006. *Clear Skies over Southern Africa: The Importance of Air Transport Liberalization for Shared Economic Growth.* http://www.tourisminvest.org/Mozambique/downloads/Investment%20climate%20background/Infrastructure/Clear%20Skies%20over%20Africa.pdf.

ELFAA (European Low Fares Airline Association). 2004. *Benefits of LFAs.* http://www.elfaa.com/documents/ELFAABenefitsofLFAs2004.pdf.

ICAO (International Civil Aviation Organisation). 2004. *Economic Contribution of Civil Aviation.* http://legacy.icao.int/ATWorkshop/C292_Vol1.pdf.

Oxford Economics. 2011. *Economic Benefits of Air Transport Country Studies.* Available at: http://web.oxfordeconomics.com/OE_Cons_Aviation.asp#.

VivaAerobus. 2012. "Overview of VivaAerobus." Unpublished presentation.

Williams, A., and V. Balaz. 2007. "Low-Cost Airlines, Economies of Flow and Regional Externalities." *Regional Studies* 43 (5): 677–91.

Abbreviations

AADCP	ASEAN–Australia Development Cooperation Program
AAE	Air Arabia Egypt
ACARE	Advisory Council for Aeronautics Research in Europe
ACI	Airports Council International
ACSA	Airport Company South Africa
ADRS	Airport Development Reference Manual
ADS-B	automatic dependence surveillance-broadcast
AFIS	aerodrome flight information services
AICD	Africa Infrastructure Country Diagnostics
AIP	Aeronautical Information Publication
AKFED	Aga Khan Fund for Economic Development
AMU	African Monetary Union; Arab Maghreb Union
ANSP	air navigation service provider
ASA	air service agreement
ASAP	air service agreement projector
ASEAN	Association of Southeast Asian Nations
ASK	available seat kilometers
ASM	available seat miles
ATAG	Air Transport Action Group
ATC	air traffic control
ATM	air traffic management
ATNS	air traffic and navigation services
BEE	Black Economic Empowerment [program]
CAA	civil aviation authority
CAFE	Commercial Aircraft Finance Entity
CASK	cost per available seat kilometers
CASM	cost per available seat miles
CASSOA	Civil Aviation Safety and Security Oversight Agency

CEMAC	Communauté Économique des États de l'Afrique Centrale (Economic [and Monetary] Community of Central African States)
CET	Common External Tariff
CFI	certified flight instructor
CMA	continuous monitoring approach
CNS	communications, navigation, and surveillance
COMESA	Common Market for Eastern and Southern Africa
COSCAP	Cooperative Development of Operational Safety and Continuing Airworthiness Programs
CSA	comprehensive system approach
DOC	direct operating costs
DOT	Department of Transportation
EAC	East African Community
ECA	export credit agency
EETC	enhanced equipment trust certificates
ELFAA	European Low Fares Airline Association
ERA	European Regions Airline Association
ERR	economic rate of return
ETC	European Travel Commission
FIR	flight information region
FSC	full-service carrier
GDP	gross domestic product
GDS	global distribution system
GNSS	global navigation satellite systems
IATA	International Air Transport Association
ICAO	International Civil Aviation Organization
ICRG	International Country Risk Guide
ICT	information and communications technology
IFC	International Finance Corporation
ILO	International Labour Organization
ILS	instrument landing systems
IOC	indirect operating costs
IOSA	IATA Operational Safety Audit
KLIA	Kuala Lumpur International Airport
LACAC	Latin American Civil Aviation Commission
LCC	low-cost carrier
LOS	level of service
LSM	Living Standard Measure
MIT	Massachusetts Institute of Technology

NTC	National Transport Commission
NTPS	National Transport Policy Study
OAU	Organization of African Unity
OECD	Organisation for Economic Co-operation and Development
O/D	origin/destination
PAPI	precision approach path indicators
PAX	number of passengers
PFC	passenger facility charge
PPP	public-private partnership; purchasing power parity
PSC	passenger service charge
REC	regional economic community
RPM	revenue passenger mile
RSOO	regional safety oversight organization
SAA	South African Airways
SADC	Southern African Development Community
SCIA	Singapore Changi International Airport
SMS	safety management systems; short message service
UFIR	upper flight information region
UNPF	United Nations Population Fund
USAP	Universal Security Audit Programme
USOAP	Universal Safety Oversight Audit Programme
VAT	value-added tax
VFR	visiting friend(s) and relative(s)
VSAT	very-small aperture terminal
WAEMU	West African Economic and Monetary Union
WEF	World Economic Forum
WGI	Worldwide Governance Indicators
WHO	World Health Organization
WTO	World Trade Organization
YD	Yamoussoukro Decision
EUR	euros
K Sh	Kenya shillings
Mex$	pesos (Mexico)
US$	U.S. dollars
ZAR	South African rand

Introduction

The worldwide emergence of low-cost carriers (LCCs) has revolutionized travel, brought affordable air transport within economic reach of large segments of the population, and massively expanded the market for air travel. Although Southwest Airlines, considered to be the first airline to have made low cost a central element of its strategy, has been operating in this mode since the 1970s, it is only in the last two decades that LCCs have grown exponentially and internationally to become a market-shaping force.

Since 2000, the LCC market has virtually exploded, covering dense networks across international markets. Presently, around 128 airlines are defined as LCCs, representing over 26 percent of all globally available seats in May 2012. Initially bound to the air transport markets of developed countries, a significant push in LCC capacity growth has resulted from the entrance of LCCs in developing countries, particularly in Asia and Latin America. However, other regions, in particular Sub-Saharan Africa, still appear to lag considerably behind in the development of LCCs.

Recent research has found that the entrance of LCCs has not only brought lower fares to the air transport market, but has also made a substantial contribution to countries' economies. Tourism, for example, has been a key beneficiary of the emergence of LCCs, particularly for isolated island states, many of which are developing countries.

This book explores the characteristics of the LCC model and its impact on the air transport and related markets. Two case studies, Mexico and South Africa, will highlight some of the opportunities and challenges that LCCs have encountered. Using a defined framework, the authors then try to identify opportunities for LCC development in developing countries, focusing on the East African Community (EAC). Finally, the book outlines the role that international development agencies such as the World Bank Group can play in facilitating the development of LCCs in its client countries.

In consideration of the scope of such an endeavor, the purpose of this book is not to provide a holistic picture, but rather to build an initial foundation for further research into the development of LCCs in particular markets and regions.

CHAPTER 1

The Low-Cost Carrier Business Model

Definition

Various definitions for low-cost carriers (LCCs) exist today (Dietlin 2004; Kumar 2005; Doganis 2006; Hunter 2006; Holloway 2008). Although marginally different, most researchers define LCCs as carriers which, through a variety of operational processes, have achieved a cost advantage over full-service carriers (FSCs). However, these definitions often do not capture the effect of transferring cost advantages to consumers in the form of lower fares. It is therefore important to stress that in the context of this book, a low-cost carrier will be defined as a carrier which translates these cost savings into lower, more affordable fares for the travelling public. This chapter examines some of the main characteristics of LCCs in terms of service offering, network structure, marketing, and fleet and labor utilization, which have enabled them to achieve this cost advantage and consequently offer lower fares to customers.

Key Elements of the LCC Business Model

Service Offering

The key focus of the LCC business model is on the "atomization" of the product into the greatest possible number of discrete elements. LCCs are concentrated only on the most basic transportation function, which forms the core product. Other elements of the product are either not offered at all, or are offered separately, incurring additional charges for the customer. This results in cost reductions and/or creates opportunities for additional, so-called ancillary revenues for LCCs. The three most common "frills" removed from the LCC service offering are complimentary food and beverages, assigned seating, and free baggage allowances.

On most LCCs, food and beverages are very limited and often come at an additional charge. This not only decreases the cost and complexity of catering, but also reduces the need for the required facilities and extended galley space in the aircraft. Assigned seating is a similar "luxury" that very few LCCs offer. Following the model of Southwest Airlines, European-based carriers such as Ryanair have no preseating arrangements and operate on a first-come, first-served basis. Due to the importance attached to priority seating by customers, however, some airlines such as easyJet have started issuing "speedy boarding" tickets that can be purchased in advance. Other LCCs, such as Asian LCCs AirAsia and SpiceJet, have also introduced online advance seat purchase for customers wanting to choose their seats beforehand, while all other passengers are assigned seats at check-in. A further element of the business model concerns checked-in baggage. The majority of LCCs today charge passengers per piece of checked-in luggage, and some even apply strict rules on permissible luggage weights per passenger (Vasigh, Fleming, and Tacker 2008).

This pay-per-service approach is, to varying degrees, applied by most LCCs. There is, however, a broad spectrum between the minimalist approach, such as that offered by Ryanair, and other LCCs such as WestJet, where some or all of these services are complimentary. Furthermore, these operating practices are no longer unique to the LCC business model. Particularly in the North American market, network carriers have also started introducing these cost-saving measures. United Airlines and Air Canada, for example, have been charging customers for food on domestic flights and have introduced fees for the check-in of bags.

Network Structure and Scheduling
Point-To-Point versus Hub-and-Spoke Structures

The route structure that traditional airlines have adopted is a so-called "hub-and-spoke" system. "Spoke" flights concentrate the passengers in one or more "hub" airports and passengers transfer to an onward flight to either their final destination or, usually for transcontinental city pairs, to a further "hub" where they transfer to "spoke" flights to their final destination (Vasigh, Fleming, and Tacker 2008).

This is a very costly operation, as the often-expensive infrastructure at hubs such as runways, gates, and ground equipment has to be geared to short, very strong surges in traffic, which allow the rapid transfer of passengers between flights. The downtimes between these surges, however, lead to a low average utilization of the facilities. Furthermore, diseconomies of scale can arise because in peak times hubs have to deal with added congestion on the ground as well as in the air leading to delays and higher fuel and labor costs (Vasigh, Fleming, and Tacker 2008).

For many network airlines, particularly ones of considerable size with strong market presence or based at a strategic location, such as Emirates or Lufthansa, this model has been effective, as it enables many city pair choices and certain economies of scale. Most LCCs, however, try to avoid the complexities and costs of hub-and-spoke networks by operating a point-to-point route structure. Under this structure, the LCC serves a more widely spread route network offering nonstop flights between city pairs. Some LCCs still operate bases, which allow for economies of scale, but in contrast to traditional carriers, there are fewer peaks or downtimes. This allows for the continuous and improved utilization of facilities and employee services, thereby reducing costs.

Although most LCCs only offer point-to-point services, many still have so-called "focus cities," which serve a large network of destinations, even though there is no attempt to consolidate or connect passengers. There are also exceptions such as Jazeera Airways (Kuwait) that actually connects passengers through Kuwait International Airport hub, or Go-Air (India) that offers connections through its hub in Mumbai, India.

Due to the costs associated with traffic surges at hubs, efforts have also been made by network carriers to reduce peaks at hubs. Delta and Lufthansa, for example, have been spreading flights more evenly across the day at their hubs in Atlanta, Cincinnati, and Salt Lake City (Hirschmann 2004), and Frankfurt, respectively (Mederer and others 2008).

Usage of Secondary Airports

A commonly applied operating practice for LCCs is the usage of secondary or regional airports.[1] These airports generally have three main advantages in comparison to primary airports: lower airport charges, the availability of slots,[2] and reduced congestion.

In contrast to primary airports, secondary airports often offer lower airport charges to airlines. Due to their limited service offering in terms of airport infrastructure and, in the case of remote airports, lower input costs (for example, lower land rents), secondary airports often benefit from lower operating costs and increased efficiency (Forsyth 2003). In addition, due to the benefits that low-cost operations can bring to an airport and its surrounding area, some LCCs have been able to obtain favorable arrangements with local governments for the usage of secondary airports. In Rimini, Italy, for example, the respective airport authority subsidized Ryanair to start operations from their airport in 1998 (Calder 2002). However, when the airport's management changed a couple of years later, the arrangement had to be renegotiated and Ryanair cancelled its flights to Rimini. This is a good example of the bargaining power the airline had achieved.

Secondary airports have another advantage in that they often do not suffer from the type of congestion experienced at major airports, and consequently offer the required capacity for LCC development. With ever-rising air traffic, primary airports such as New York's La Guardia, London's Heathrow, and Amsterdam's Schiphol have experienced substantial challenges with regard to congestion and lack of capacity. Between June 2012 and 2013, for example, La Guardia Airport experienced over 12 percent in delays by airlines resulting from "national aviation system delays," which include nonextreme weather conditions, airport operations, heavy traffic volume, and air traffic control issues (RITA BTS 2013).

By contrast, most secondary airports across Europe and the United States were previously significantly underutilized. These secondary airports were historically built to serve low-frequency regional flights for travel onward from hubs to smaller- or medium-size towns. For example, Orio al Serio Airport in Italy was initially only meant to create a link between Rome and Bergamo. Until the arrival of low-cost airlines, the airport had not served any international routes. Other local airports used to have a military function but were abandoned over time. These have only now been recommissioned for civilian use with the entry of LCCs.

Despite only serving few destinations at a low frequency, many of these secondary or regional airports were of considerable size. Glasgow's Prestwick, for example, used approximately 1 percent of its capacity, and Belgium's Charleroi Airport received around 20,000 passengers per year (54 per day) before low-cost airline Ryanair entered the market (European Commission 2004).

Operating from these high capacity secondary airports has enabled LCCs to design the most efficient schedules to make the best use of their fleets and to avoid congestion (Barbot 2004). A study by Warnock-Smith and Potter (2005) showed that avoiding congestion often results in aircraft productivity gains of more than 50 percent for LCCs in comparison to network carriers.

LCCs in Europe and the United States have built up dense networks around secondary airports. Southwest Airlines, for example, serves secondary airports such as Manchester Boston Regional or Long Island Airport. The European LCC Ryanair uses almost exclusively minor airports to serve larger agglomerations. For example, Ryanair uses Hahn Airport located some 100 kilometers outside Frankfurt or Weeze Airports instead of Düsseldorf Airport (Ryanair 2013). However, with the extensive expansion of LCCs, there has been a shift in both carriers' networks to sometimes include a few select primary airports. Southwest now offers a high number of daily departures from Los Angeles International Airport (Southwest Airlines 2013), and Ryanair operates flights to Dublin, Gatwick, Birmingham, and Manchester (Ryanair 2013). In order to retain their cost advantage and reduce high charges at these airports, LCCs using primary airports often choose to avoid the rental of expensive ground facilities (for example, jetways) and use older facilities at the airport (De Neufville 2005).

A few LCCs also focus almost entirely on primary airports. Ryanair's rival easyJet, for example, has been serving primary airports such as Amsterdam's Schiphol, Paris's Charles De Gaulle, and Barcelona–El Prat. It also operates easyJet Switzerland, its subsidiary, from its base at Geneva International Airport. AirBerlin and the Spanish Airline Vueling follow a similar strategy. Alternatively, some U.S. LCCs, such as AirTran and JetBlue, base their operations at a prime international hub and serve secondary airports from this base.

In recent years, some primary airports have also been adjusting their offerings to attract LCCs and their high passenger volumes. Hong Kong International Airport, which serves a number of LCCs including AirAsia, Cebu Pacific (the Philippines), Oriental Thai (Thailand) and Jetstar Asia, caters to LCCs by offering them cheaper and better-arranged gates, and simplified procedures that reduce aircraft turnaround time. Some primary airports have even invested in so-called "low-cost terminals," specifically designed to suit the LCC business model omitting travelators, escalators, and aerobridges. Other primary airports also discount their aeronautical charges and reduce passenger facility service charges (Bentley 2009). Some good examples of LCC terminals (LCCTs) are Malaysia's Kuala Lumpur International Airport (KLIA), Zhengzhou Xinzheng International Airport (ZHCC) in China, and the budget terminal (BT) at Singapore's Changi International Airport (SCIA). The sustainability of this alternative to secondary airports remains to be seen (Zhang and others 2008).

High Aircraft Utilization

An important factor in the success of LCCs is the high daily level of utilization of their most capital-intensive asset, their aircraft. As research shows, there is a strong negative relationship between operating unit costs and aircraft utilization (Vasigh, Fleming, and Tacker 2008). Higher daily aircraft utilization is primarily achieved through shorter turnaround times, longer routes, or higher flight frequency (Vasigh, Fleming, and Tacker 2008).

Most low-cost airlines try to increase the daily utilization of their aircraft by minimizing turnaround time. This is achieved by abolishing seat allocation and consequently shortening boarding procedures, limiting or removing catering, and using less congested and more efficient secondary airports. Ryanair, for example, recorded an average scheduled turnaround time of approximately 25 minutes (CAPA 2013b). Southwest's turnaround time ranges between 10 and 25 minutes (Schlesinger 2011).

Some LCCs also increase their aircraft utilization by flying longer routes.[3] For example, JetBlue operations have an average stage length of 1,088 miles.[4] This is due to the fact that JetBlue operates a number of transcontinental flights, for example, between Los Angeles and Boston or between Long Beach and New York. Similarly, easyJet in Europe has extended its traditionally short-haul network to include medium-haul routes such as Geneva to Tel Aviv or Sharm-el-Sheikh to Manchester.

Some LCCs also increase their utilization by simply increasing the number of flights per day. By commencing their first flights very early in the morning, LCCs manage to operate a significant number of flights by utilizing their aircraft between 10 and 14 hours daily. Ryanair, for example, operates its first flight from London's Stansted Airport to Stockholm at 6:05 a.m. However, higher flight frequency has, in itself, not been proved to be a key success factor for LCCs (Dietlin 2004).

Figure 1.1 provides a comparison of average daily block hours per aircraft of a number of LCCs, showing that most LCCs operate long hours each day. Interestingly, Ryanair appears to tend more toward the lower end of the spectrum. According to aviation data provided by the Massachusetts Institute of Technology (MIT) Airline Data Project (MIT 2013) analyzing a sample of U.S. network carriers and LCCs, LCCs operate on average around an hour longer each day.

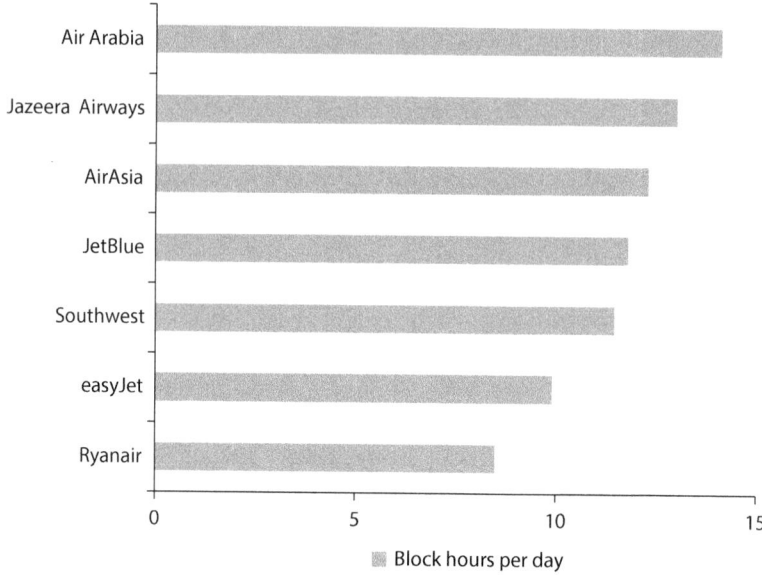

Figure 1.1 Average Daily Aircraft Utilization by LCCs, 2011–12

Sources: Based on information from airlines' annual reports and presentations, SEC filings, *Air Finance Journal*, and *Seat Guru*. (See appendix B.)
Note: Fiscal year may not be in line with calendar year for each airline and may vary in some cases. LCC = low-cost carrier.

Shorter Stage Lengths

Low-cost airlines operate in networks consisting predominantly of short-to-medium haul routes of fewer than 1,500 miles and/or fewer than six hours of flight time (see figure 1.2).[5] This contradicts traditional airline economics, where per mile costs for the same aircraft type are generally higher on shorter rather than on longer flights. Indeed, shorter routes traditionally result in higher costs due to more labor-intensive time spent on the ground due to multiple landings as well as fuel costs (particularly from the fuel-intensive ascent phase), which have to be spread over a shorter revenue generating distance in the air. Furthermore, landing fees and passenger processing costs are fixed, regardless of distance traveled (Dietlin 2004). This cost difference is particularly dramatic when extending a flight from short to medium haul, but becomes more linear with very long stage lengths.

Short-haul routes, although costlier, generally translate into higher unit revenues, however, due to the effects of scalability and market demand. Combined with LCCs' overall lower input costs and/or higher productivity this can be a significant competitive advantage over network carriers on short-haul routes. These relative cost advantages that LCCs have over network carriers on short flights resulting from lower distribution or ground handling costs would, however, diminish with increased stage length, as its percentage of the total cost shrinks (Dietlin 2004).

Figure 1.2 LCC Average Stage Length, 2013
miles

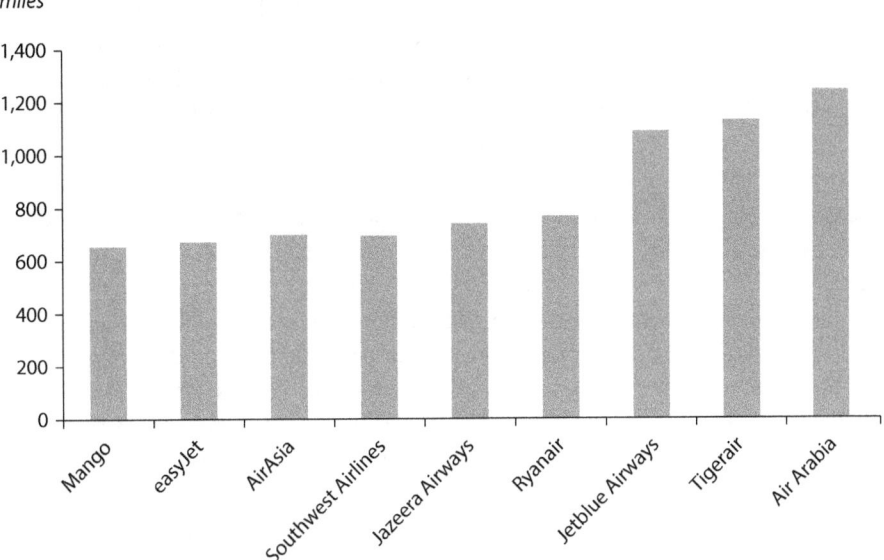

Source: Based on data from DiiO SRS Analyzer (2013).
Note: LCC = low-cost carrier.

Local demand for long-haul flights may also not generate sufficient traffic to sustain a point-to-point network structure. Furthermore, the low-cost airlines' purist "no frills" concept would have to potentially be adapted to include in-flight services, which would in turn increase turnaround times and decrease utilization hours. This being said, there have been some low-cost, long-haul airlines that have emerged recently but with varying degrees of success. AirAsia X is one of the few profitable ventures, which has adapted the original low-cost structure by introducing some elements of a network carrier in order to attract sufficient passenger volumes.

Fleet
Fleet Standard and Commonality
Another success ingredient of the LCC model is the use of a single aircraft type fleet. Fleet commonality can decrease costs considerably as it reduces the amount of ground support equipment, training, and spare parts inventories, and allows for standardized handling and maintenance processes as well as flexible crew scheduling. Furthermore, bulk purchases allow discounts from suppliers and economies of scale, as the LCC only has to invest once in fixed fleet costs (for example, specialized equipment) (Vasigh, Fleming, and Tacker 2008).

On the downside, fleet commonality can reduce flexibility to respond to market changes. Capacity changes are therefore only possible by adding or canceling flights. Moreover, dependency on one aircraft manufacturer may be restrictive.

The most typically used aircraft by LCCs are the Boeing 737 (B737) and the Airbus 320 (A320). Both airliners can accommodate anywhere from

110 passengers in low-density configurations to 220 passengers in high-density, single-class layout, and provide great range flexibility. Boeing's 737–800 has a range of up to 5,765 kilometers (3,113 nautical miles) (Boeing 2013). The A320 (with sharklets[6]) can even achieve up to 6,150 kilometers (3320 nautical miles) (Airbus 2013). Although it is difficult to compare unit costs across different aircraft as the cost depends largely upon the direct operating costs (DOC) of an airline, fuel efficiency and maintenance costs can be used as good indicators for LCCs in choosing these types of aircraft. Both models, particularly the newer 737–800 and the A321, perform well with regard to these criteria. Due to the late entrance of LCCs into the aviation industry, they were often able to invest in these newer aircraft types while traditional carriers were still operating with older models. The A320, for example, consumes between 11 and 25 percent less fuel per seat than Airbus's legacy aircraft, such as the Airbus 300 or 310 (World Bank 2011). Fuel costs are a crucial factor in both LCCs and network carriers, representing between 35 and 40 percent of operating costs (Boeing 2013).

The majority of LCCs have a single-type aircraft fleet, but there are some exceptions with SpiceJet and JetBlue having established a "two-type" model, with a fleet of slightly smaller aircraft such as the Bombardier Q400 and Embraer E-190 used for shorter distances.

Aircraft Configuration
A further element of the low-cost business model is a high-density, all-economy configuration. Narrow seat pitches of 28–29 inches are common in LCCs, compared to 31–33 inches in traditional airlines (Doganis 2006). Not all LCCs strictly adhere to this principle however, with LCCs such as Virgin Blue (now Virgin Australia), Southwest, and WestJet having seat pitches between 31 and 34 inches. Similarly, not all LCCs have a one-class policy, with Jazeera Airways and Vueling, for example, offering a business or economy premium class.

Marketing
Pricing
Traditionally airlines offer a range of fares in order to attract different customer demand segments in the market. Each of these demand segments are assumed to have differing time and price sensitivity, as well as what is called "willingness to pay."

This differentiated fare structure is justified to customers by offering varying levels of service amenities and fare restrictions. Service amenities may include bigger seat pitches and premium meals, distinctive separation of economy from business or first class, whereas fare product restrictions would relate to nonrefundability, cancellation fees, or minimum stays. The purpose of these restrictions is to make lower fares less attractive while still offering a viable option for more price-sensitive customers. The highest unrestricted economy class ticket, the so-called Y Fare, is in some cases almost five times that of the lowest discount fare with restrictions.

The entrance of low-cost airlines with a more homogenous product offering, accompanied by reduced corporate spending and the increased transparency of fares through the Internet, led to a shift in pricing strategy toward "fare simplification." This involved fewer fare levels, fewer restrictions, and a convergence of the highest and lowest fares offered. Restrictions for tickets on LCCs are in some cases just focused on time of booking, with fares tending to increase closer to the departure date.[7] In some cases, multiple fares are even filed with the same identical restrictions. Traditionally, airlines segment passenger demand by creating so-called "fences" with independent unique products by fare class. This has allowed them to forecast demand by fare class and then determine the right allocation against capacity. In the LCC fare simplification model, these fences do not exist and have allowed carriers to promote 100 percent "sell down" to the open fare class (Aircraft Commerce 2006). The benefits of fare simplification overall are still debated, as some network carriers such as Delta and American Airlines have failed in their attempts to simplify their fare structures.

Distribution
Since the early days of the Internet, airlines have implemented electronic, that is paperless, ticketing and have used their websites in order to provide reservation and ticketing capabilities. This development highlighted a break from the traditional and costly travel-agent system that was based on the payment of commissions. In the 1990s, commission payments cost airlines up to 13 percent of their passenger revenue (Belobaba, Odoni, and Barnhart 2009). Looking for a lower cost, competitive edge, low-cost airlines were at the forefront of introducing direct distribution channels through their websites and call centers. Southwest Airlines was the first major airline to develop a website and offer online booking (Southwest Airlines 2012). Cost per booking via an airline's own system is estimated at around US$1, whereas the cost per booking via a global distribution system (GDS) is between US$5 and US$12 (Perkins 2012).

Figure 1.3 shows that the percentage of online distribution of a sample of LCCs is generally between 75 and 99 percent, thereby reducing their costs significantly. However, the success of this strategy is highly dependent on the degree of Internet penetration in a particular region. Middle Eastern LCCs, such as Air Arabia or Jazeera Airways have much lower online distribution (around 30 percent), as overall Internet penetration is much lower (around 35 percent of population in comparison to around 60 percent in Europe). In some countries such as Saudi Arabia, Internet connections only arrived in 1999, and have experienced a slow process of adoption since then (Alterman 2000).

Some carriers, such as Ryanair, also follow the successful strategy of aligning themselves with a GDS provider in the beginning, but then ending their agreements, as their brands grow stronger. The advantage of this approach is that carriers initially have a wide distribution network and then narrow their distribution channels when shifting ticket sales toward their website (Field and Pilling 2005). Although initially providing a substantial competitive advantage for LCCs, high levels of online booking have become common today.

Figure 1.3 Online Distribution as Percentage of Total Distribution, 2011–12

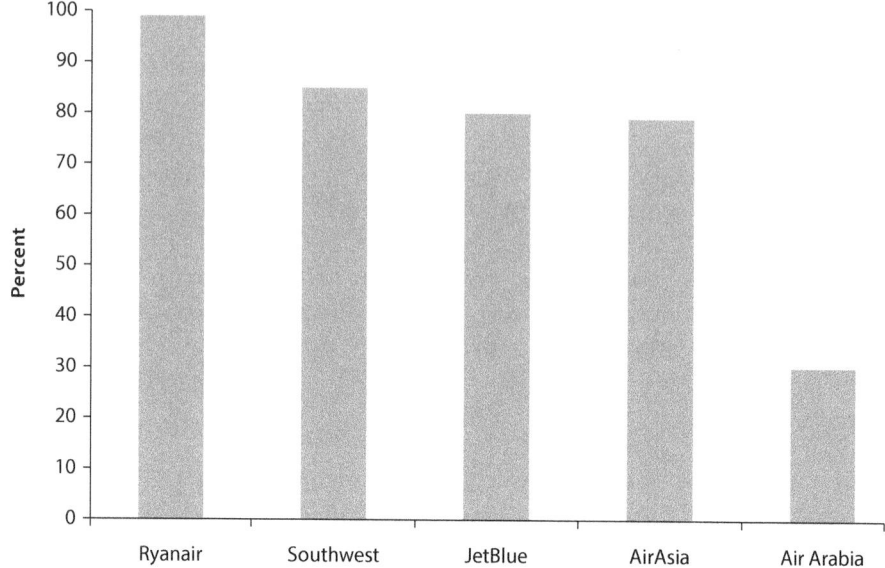

Sources: Based on information from airlines' annual reports and presentations, SEC filings, *Air Finance Journal*, and *Seat Guru*. (See appendix B.)
Note: Fiscal year may not be in line with calendar year for each airline and vary in some cases.

Labor

Labor represents a considerable expense in an airline's cost structure. In order to reduce this cost, LCCs are focused on increasing labor productivity by increasing airline "output" (available seat kilometers [ASK] or available seat miles [ASM] per employee).[8] This is generally achieved by a higher number of average block hours per employee and a higher passenger per employee ratio. Research by the MIT Airline Data Project in 2012 shows that in the United States, average block hours per pilot for LCCs were around 12 hours longer per month than for U.S. network carriers. An even larger difference is seen for flight attendants. Similarly, the number of passengers per flight attendant was more than double in its last estimate in 2012 (MIT 2013).

A more recent comparison of labor productivity in Europe by the Centre for Asia Pacific Aviation (see figure 1.4) shows that LCCs, particularly Ryanair, Vueling, Norwegian, and easyJet, have significantly higher ASK ratios per employee than network carriers, such as Air France or Lufthansa (CAPA 2013a).

In some research, it has been argued that low-cost carriers also pay significantly lower salaries. Harvey (2007), for example, highlights that, on average, pilot salaries at LCCs are 27 percent less than at their full-service airline colleagues. Some also believe that this is due to the lack of unionization in some LCCs, such as Ryanair, thereby allowing for longer hours and lower pay scales. There does not seem to be consensus with regard to this view however. Southwest, for example, a successful LCC with strong unionization, appears to prove the opposite.

Figure 1.4 Labor Productivity Comparison, 2011–12

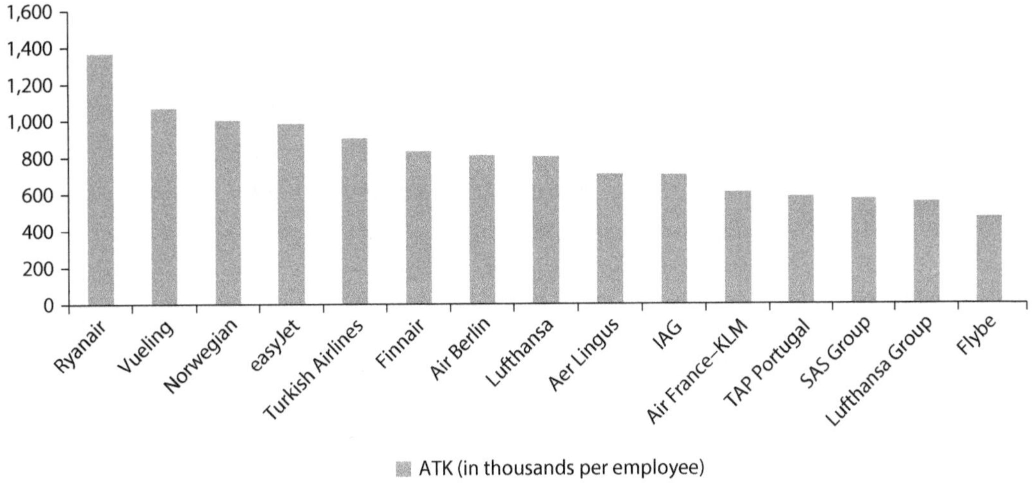

[Bar chart showing ATK (in thousands per employee) for airlines, approximately:
Ryanair ~1,370; Vueling ~1,070; Norwegian ~1,000; easyJet ~990; Turkish Airlines ~910; Finnair ~840; Air Berlin ~820; Lufthansa ~820; Aer Lingus ~720; IAG ~720; Air France–KLM ~630; TAP Portugal ~610; SAS Group ~600; Lufthansa Group ~580; Flybe ~490]

■ ATK (in thousands per employee)

Source: Based on data from the Centre for Asia Pacific Aviation (CAPA 2013).
Note: The measure Available Ton Kilometers (ATK) is used here to compensate for cargo-carrying carriers.

Different Types of LCC Models

A significant number of airlines are categorized as LCCs today. This definition, however, is, according to Chris Tarry from the airline magazine *Airline Business*, "the most over-used term in our industry" (Tarry 2010). As this research demonstrates—and has been established through previous research conducted by Oliviera (2008), Francis and others (2006), Graham and Vowles (2006), and others—even though some common operating practices can be identified across low-cost airlines, there is no one LCC model, nor is there a single driving element responsible for its competitive advantage. It is therefore necessary to distinguish between different subtypes of LCC models, as their scope for success and their impact on an aviation market may vary accordingly.

For this purpose, a small sample of LCC carriers was analyzed with regard to their adherence to the most common building blocks, as outlined above.[9] These include low unit cost per ASK;[10] presence of "frills" (baggage, food and beverages, assigned seating); use of secondary airports; point-to-point structure; high percentage of Internet-based sales; high daily aircraft utilization; homogenous fleet composition; presence of a one-class seating system; and high seating density. Based on previous work by Alamdari and Fagan (2005) and Weisskopf (2010), the authors use a point system to evaluate the extent to which each carrier applied the measures outlined above. (The data collected for each carrier and the point allocation can be found in appendixes A and B).[11]

As figure 1.5 shows, the level of "adherence" varies significantly, with supposed LCCs such as Virgin Australia operating with a similar business model as network carriers. This is in contrast to more purist LCCs, such as Ryanair and easyJet.

Figure 1.5 Adherence to Low-Cost Model, 2011–12

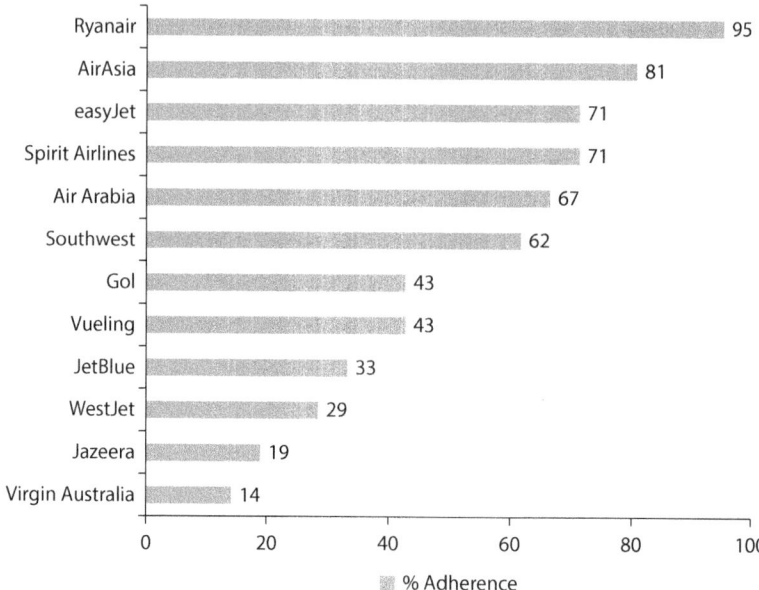

Sources: Based on information from Weisskopf 2010, airlines' annual reports and presentations, SEC filings, *Air Finance Journal*, and *Seat Guru*. (See appendixes A and B for details.)

Although the level of variability is still significant, in literature (Francis and others 2006; Graham and Vowles 2006; Oliveira 2008) LCCs are often clustered into different groups. For the purpose of this book, LCCs have been assigned to three groups, which are described below.

1. *The Purist model:* The Ryanair model is found to be the most "pure" LCC business model in the market. Based on the original Southwest Airlines model, the airline has perfected its lowest cost structure through a single fleet type; elimination of free in-flight services; high use of secondary airports; direct sales; e-ticketing; short-haul, point-to-point flights in dense markets with no interlining or transfer;[12] a simple network structure; absent or weak feed to long-range flights; single cabin layout; no frequent flyer program; and an optimal level of fleet utilization. With some modifications, easyJet, Spirit Airlines, AirAsia, VivaAerobus (Mexico) and Peach Aviation (Japan) can be seen as applying this model.
2. *The Southwest model:* Although the Ryanair model was based on the original Southwest model, Southwest Airlines' cost structure is, in reality, not as tightly managed as that of Ryanair. The airline offers complimentary refreshments aboard, does not charge for baggage, offers wider seat pitches, and actively promotes and sells connecting flights. Therefore, this model has more potential to attract other segments besides leisure travelers.

Varying types of spin-offs from the purist concept, as has been applied by Southwest Airlines, can also be seen with Air Arabia, Vueling, Nokair, Spicejet, and Gol.

3. *The JetBlue model:* This model is making significant moves away from the purist concept, with many frills offered, diversified fleets, and networks composed mostly of primary airports. The model's focus is on the low-fare business market by making use of multiservice operations with mini-hubs to provide convenient connections and more possibilities in terms of origin/destination (O/D) markets, as well as more complex fare structures including business or economy plus class. To varying extents, this model is used by Virgin Australia, Jazeera, Westjet, and Jetstar.

Although some research such as Alamdari and Fagan (2005) has shown that there is a moderate positive correlation between "adherence" and profitability, there does not seem to be one success strategy in the industry today and market conditions and even cultural factors play a significant role in how LCCs choose or are able to structure themselves.

It should also be noted that LCCs have not been static in their operating practices. As in every industry, LCCs have been adjusting to market conditions and competitive pressures over time, developing and refining their business models to best suit their market. Particularly in more mature markets, the continuing strength of network alliances across the globe has had a significant impact on the "hybridization" of existing and newer generation LCCs.

Are Low-Cost Carriers Really Low Cost?

All of the elements elaborated above comprise the essential difference between network carriers and LCCs—that is, the difference in cost. However, how much of a cost advantage do today's LCCs really have?

The most widely quoted metric to assess an airline's cost is cost per available seat miles (CASM; or cost per available seat kilometers [CASK]). CASM calculates the cost of operating one available seat per mile/kilometer. This metric can be used to compare a variety of costs, ranging from fuel to labor. Total CASM or CASK normally includes all DOC such as fuel, labor, maintenance, and other direct expenses (landing fees, capital equipment charges, and so on), as well as indirect or nonoperating costs (IOC), including station and ground expenses, passenger services, ticketing, sales, promotion, and general administration costs. IOC are fixed costs, whereas DOC are variable depending on the number of flights, stage lengths, type of aircraft used, and other factors (Vasigh, Fleming, and Tacker 2008). Although CASM is a valuable indicator when analyzing airlines, it can prove difficult to compare unit costs on a global level due to large differences in basic costs across regions. A network carrier in Asia may operate at a similar unit cost to a low-cost airline in Europe, making a comparison solely

Figure 1.6 Comparison of U.S. CASM, Network Carriers, and LCCs, 2005–11
U.S. cents

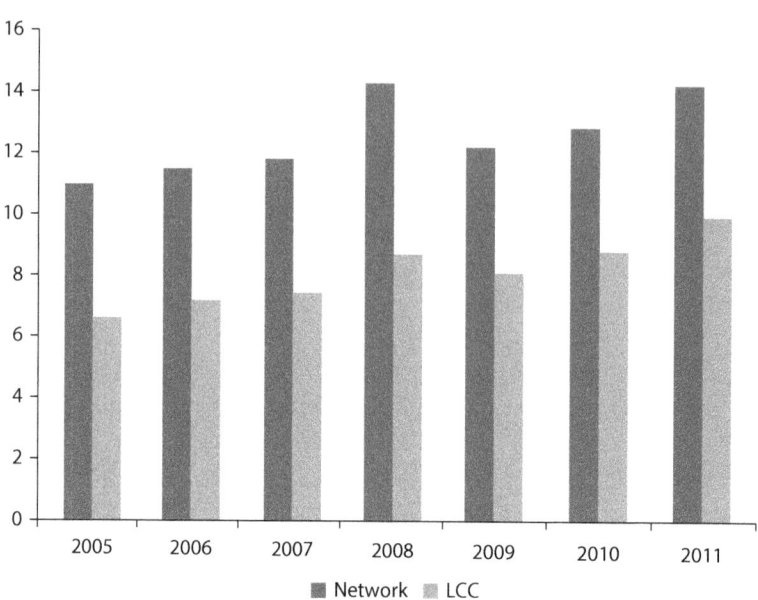

Source: Based on data from MIT Airline Data Project (MIT 2013).
Note: CASM = cost per available seat miles; LCC = low-cost carrier.

based on unit cost futile. This has to be taken into consideration when comparing LCCs and network carriers across regions.

Figure 1.6 shows a comparison of CASM of U.S. network carriers and LCCs between the years 2005 and 2011. As highlighted in the graph, LCCs have been operating with considerably lower unit costs in the past, with costs up to 40 percent lower than network carriers.

Figure 1.6 also demonstrates that this cost difference has been shrinking since 2005. In 2011, LCC unit costs were around 30 percent lower than those of network carriers, which have adapted their operating practices by introducing cost-reduction measures (for example, baggage and food charges and reducing distribution through travel agents). However, one of the main reasons for this cost convergence lies in the shrinking gap in fuel expenditures. As figure 1.7 shows, for U.S. carriers, the difference in fuel costs has been almost entirely eradicated. This is primarily related to the fact that as network carriers are modernizing their fleets, their fuel efficiency is reducing their costs. This removes one of the competitive advantages LCCs historically had over network carriers and has led some LCCs to adapt their business models to attract more higher yield passengers.[13]

In other markets, particularly in Europe, this convergence has not been as strong. This is primarily because of the presence of ultra–low cost airlines such as Ryanair and AirAsia gaining considerable cost advantages in other areas (Hazel, Stalnaker, and Taylor 2012).

Figure 1.7 Comparison of Network and LCC Fuel CASM

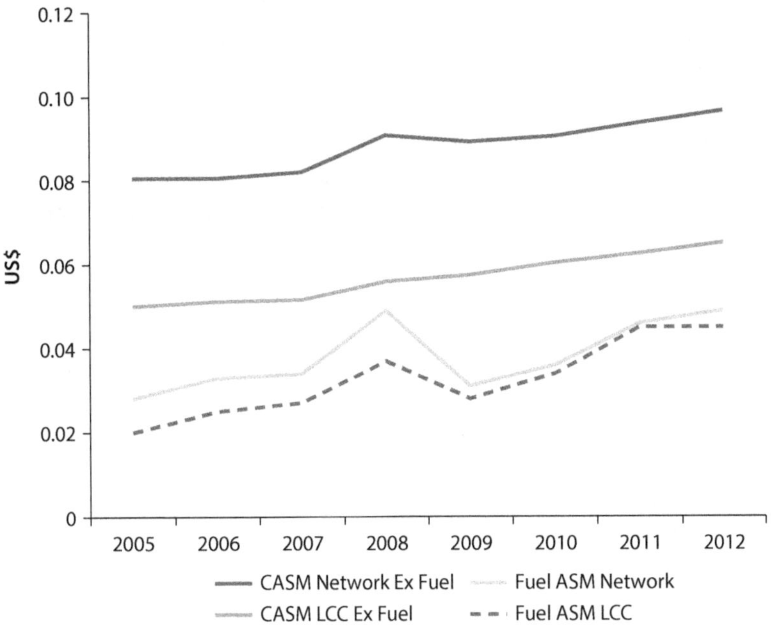

Source: Based on data from MIT Airline Data Project (MIT 2013).
Note: ASM = available seat miles; CASM = cost per available seat miles; LCC = low-cost carrier.

Conclusion

There are some common building blocks among LCCs, but there is no *one* low-cost model. As the analysis showed there are some challenges in defining exactly what constitutes the LCC business model. Although there are a number of elements that are common in most LCCs such as limited service offerings, the use of secondary airports, low distribution costs, and/or high labor utilization, there is a broad range of business models under the LCC umbrella. These models diverge considerably in their offering and operating practices. Industry characteristics and target markets, as well as cultural factors, have had a substantial impact on the respective business models.

Particularly in the United States, but also in Europe, many LCCs have been "hybridizing" their models as more mature LCC competition, higher fuel prices, and powerful network alliances have shifted the focus to higher yield opportunities. As the above analysis shows, there are numerous airlines such as JetBlue or Air Arabia that are operating a much more 'hybridized' LCC model. Even airlines such as Southwest have shifted more toward traditional models catering to business traffic by using primary airports and adjusting their schedules.

Low cost may not mean low cost anymore. A convergence in costs has occurred over recent years, as network airlines, under competitive pressures from their new counterparts, are becoming more cost sensitive. Fuel prices have had a considerable impact on this convergence as well, with LCCs losing their advantage of more fuel-efficient aircraft due to the fleet renewal process taking place among most traditional airlines.

Despite these recent developments, the lower fares that LCCs have been able to continually offer due to their cost advantages have significantly shaped the aviation market of today. Chapter 2 identifies some of the impacts that LCCs and the growth of aviation have had on the air transport industry and the economy as a whole.

Notes

1. Secondary airports are defined as airports complementary to a city's primary airport in a multiairport system (De Neufville 2005).
2. A slot is defined as a permission given by a coordinator to use the full range of airport infrastructure necessary to operate an air service at a coordinated airport on a specific date and time for the purpose of landing or takeoff (http://ec.europa.eu/transport/modes/air/airports/slots_en.htm).
3. Longer routes are determined as still within the short-to-medium haul frame, and do not refer to long-haul flights.
4. "Stage length" refers to the distance flown by an aircraft between a city pair.
5. A short/medium flight is usually domestic or regional in nature, typically lasting fewer than six hours in duration (per the Centre for Asia Pacific Aviation), or is between 200 and 1,500 miles (per the Economics of European Air Transport).
6. Sharklets are 2.4-meter-tall wingtip devices that provide operators with the flexibility of either adding an additional 100 nautical mile range or increased payload capability of up to 450 kilograms.
7. There has been some research disputing this monotonic relationship identifying that the volatility of fares increases four weeks prior to departure.
8. Available seat kilometers is the measure of a flight's passenger carrying capacity, calculated by multiplying the number of seats on an aircraft by the distance traveled in kilometers.
9. The sample included Ryanair, easyJet, AirAsia, Southwest, Air Arabia, Vueling, Westjet, Gol, Spirit Airlines, JetBlue, Jazeera, and Virgin Australia.
10. Unit costs were translated into PPP International Dollars to provide a more appropriate comparison across different countries.
11. The maximum number of points per element was set at 2. In some cases, 1 point was awarded when airlines only partially adhered to the pure LCC model, for example, in the use of secondary airports where some airlines have mixed strategies. Although the maximum number of points possible is set at 22, LCCs scoring 21 points are also classified as adhering 100 percent, as some data were unavailable.
12. Interlining is a voluntary commercial agreement between individual airlines to handle passengers traveling on itineraries that require multiple airlines.
13. "Yield" refers to a measure of passenger "unit revenue." "Higher yield passengers" normally refer to business class or first class passengers.

References

Airbus. 2013. "A320 Performance." http://www.airbus.com/aircraftfamilies/passenger aircraft/a320family/a320/performance/.

Aircraft Commerce. 2006. "Evolution from Legacy to Modern Revenue Management Systems." *Aircraft Commerce* (44): 43. http://airlinerevenuemanagement.com/uploads/ISSUE_44-REVENUES_1_.pdf.

Alamdari, F., and S. Fagan. 2005. "Impact of the Adherence to the Original Low-Cost Model on the Profitability of Low-Cost Airlines." *Transport Reviews* 25 (3): 377–92.

Alterman, J. B. 2000. *The Middle East's Information Revolution*. Center for Strategic and International Studies. http://csis.org/press/csis-in-the-news/middle-easts-information-revolution.

Barbot, C. 2004. "Low-Cost Carriers, Secondary Airports, and State Aid: An Economic Assessment of the Charleroi Affair." Centro de Estudos de Economia Industrial, do Trabalho e da Empresa. FEP Working Paper No. 159. http://wps.fep.up.pt/wps/wp159.pdf.

Belobaba, P., A. Odoni, and C. Barnhart. 2009. *The Global Airline Industry*. West Sussex, U.K.: John Wiley & Sons.

Bentley, D. 2009. *Low Cost Airport Terminals Report*. Centre for Asia Pacific Aviation (CAPA). http://centreforaviation.com/reports.

Boeing. 2013. "737-800 Technical Specifications." http://www.boeing.com/boeing/commercial/737family/pf/pf_800ERtech.page.

Calder, S. 2002. *No Frills: The Truth behind the Low-Cost Revolution in the Skies*. London: Virgin Books.

CAPA (Centre for Asia Pacific Aviation). 2013a. "European Airline Labour Productivity: CAPA Rankings." http://centreforaviation.com/analysis/european-airline-labour-productivity-capa-rankings-104204.

———. 2013b. "Ryanair SWOT Analysis—Michael O'Leary's Maniacal Focus on Being the Lowest Cost Producer." http://centreforaviation.com/analysis/ryanair-swot-analysis--michael-olearys-maniacal-focus-on-being-the-lowest-cost-producer-96465.

De Neufville, R. 2005. "Le Devenir Des Aéroports Secondaires: Bases D'un Réseau Parallèle De Transport Aérien?" *Les Cahiers Scientifiques du Transport* 47: 11–38.

———. 2006. "Accommodating Low-Cost Airlines at Main Airports." Paper presented at the Transportation Research Board. http://ardent.mit.edu/airports/ASP_papers/Accommodating%20Low%20Cost%20Carriers--%20revised.pdf.

Dietlin, P. 2004. *The Potential for Low-Costs in Asia*. Massachusetts Institute of Technology.

DiiO SRS Analyzer. 2013. DiiO Online Database. http://www.diio.net.

Doganis, R. 2006. *The Airline Business*. 2nd ed. Oxon: Routledge.

European Commission. 2004. "Commission Decision of 12 February 2004 concerning Advantages Granted by the Walloon Region and Brussels South Charleroi Airport to the Airline Ryanair in Connection with Its Establishment at Charleroi (notified in Number C(2004) 516)." *Official Journal of the European Union*.

Field, D., and M. Pilling. 2005. "The Last Legacy." *Airline Business* 21 (3): 48–51.

Forsyth, P. 2003. "Airport Competition and the Efficiency of Price Structures at Major Airports." Paper presented at the German Aviation Society, Research Seminar, Leipzig, Germany, November.

Francis, G., I. Humphreys, S. Ison, and M. Aicken. 2006. "Where Next for Low Cost Airlines? A Spatial and Temporal Comparative Study." *Journal of Transport Geography* 14 (2): 83–94.

Graham, B., and T. M. Vowles. 2006. "Carriers within Carriers: A Strategic Response to Low-Cost Airline Competition." *Transport Reviews* 26 (1): 105–26.

Harvey, G. 2007. *Management in the Airline Industry.* London: Routledge.

Hazel, B., T. Stalnaker, and A. Taylor. 2012. "Airline Economic Analysis." Oliver Wyman. http://www.oliverwyman.com/media/OW_Raymond_James_2012_FINAL.PDF.

Hirschmann, D. 2004. "How Hub 'De-Peaking' Would Work: Delta Plan Spreads Out Flights, Lengthens Connect Times." *Atlanta Journal Constitution.* http://archives.californiaaviation.org/airport/msg31841.html.

Holloway, S. 2008. *Straight and Level: Practical Airline Economics.* 3rd ed. Aldershot, U.K.: Ashgate.

Hunter, L. 2006. Low-Cost Airlines: Business Model and Employment Relations. *European Management Journal* 24 (5): 315–21.

Kumar, S. G. 2005. "Low-Cost Business Model." In *Low Cost Carriers—Concepts and Cases,* edited by R. Barath. Hyderabad, India: The ICFAI University Press.

Mederer, M., G. Klempert, and Lufthansa. 2008. "De-peaking des Lufthansa-Hub-Betriebs am Flughafen Frankfurt" In *Advances in Simulation for Production and Logistics Applications,* edited by M. Rabe. Stuttgart, Germany: Fraunhofer IRB Verlag.

MIT (Massachusetts Institute of Technology). 2013. *MIT Airline Data Project* (online). http://web.mit.edu/airlinedata/www/default.html.

Oliviera, A. 2008. "An Empirical Model of Low-Cost Entry." *Transportation Research Part A: Policy and Practice* 42 (4): 673–95.

Perkins, E. 2012. "Airlines Fight with Distribution Systems." *Chicago Tribune* (online). http://articles.chicagotribune.com/2012-10-10/travel/sns-travel-ed-perkins-airlines-fight-with-distribution-systems-20121010_1_gds-first-airline-fare-packages.

RITA (U.S. Research and Innovative Technology Administration) BTS (Bureau of Transportation Statistics). 2013. "Airline On-Time Statistics and Delay Causes." June 2012–June 2013. http://www.transtats.bts.gov/OT_Delay/ot_delaycause1.asp?display=data&pn=1.

Ryanair. 2013. http://www.ryanair.com.

Schlesinger, J. 2011. "10 Minutes That Changed Southwest Airlines' Future." CNBC News, July 15. http://www.cnbc.com/id/43768488.

Southwest Airlines. 2012. *South West Airlines One Report.* http://www.southwestonereport.com/2012/pdfs/2012SouthwestAirlinesOneReport.pdf.

Southwest Airlines. 2013. http://www.southwest.com.

Tarry, C. 2010. "Focus: Low-Cost Commodity." *Airline Business,* January 21. http://www.flightglobal.com/news/articles/focus-low-cost-commodity-337437.

Vasigh, B., K. Fleming, and T. Tacker. 2008. *Introduction to Air Transport Economics: From Theory to Applications.* Aldershot, U.K.: Ashgate.

Warnock-Smith, D., and A. Potter. 2005. "An Exploratory Study into Airport Choice Factors for European Low-Cost Airlines." *Journal of Air Transport Management* 11 (6): 388–92.

Weisskopf, N. 2010. *Global Expansion Strategies for Low-Cost Airlines*. Unpublished dissertation, University of Edinburgh.

World Bank. 2011. *Air Transport and Energy Efficiency*. Washington, DC: World Bank.

Zhang, A., S. Hanaoka, H. Inamura, and T. Ishikiura. 2008. "Low Cost Carriers in Asia: Deregulation, Liberalisation and Secondary Airports." *Research in Transportation Economics* 24 (1): 36–50.

CHAPTER 2

The Impact of Low-Cost Airlines

Research has provided well-documented evidence that the development of air transport services can have a substantial economic benefit for a country or region. The focus of this chapter is to highlight some of this research, particularly the benefits that the entrance of low-cost carriers (LCCs) have brought to air transport and related markets.

Empirical Evidence for the Impact of Air Transport

There is a wealth of studies assessing the economic impact of air services. The focus of these studies is primarily on the correlation between air transport and gross domestic product (GDP), trade, investment, productivity, employment and/or effects on related industries (ACRP 2008).

The majority of impact studies in current aviation literature are based on input-output analysis. Developed by the economist Wassily Leontief, input-output or interindustry analysis describes and quantitatively portrays the interdependency between different economic sectors (Leontief 1986). It normally measures the direct, indirect, and induced impact of an industry. In the case of aviation, input-output analysis looks primarily at (a) the employment and output in the aviation sector (direct impact); (b) employment and activity originating from aviation's supply chain (indirect impact); and (c) the employment or economic output resulting from household spending of directly or indirectly employed actors (induced impact) (Ishutkina and Hansmann 2009).

Studies using input-output analysis are particularly useful in mapping the impact of changes in demand. For example, increased demand for air services will consequently be matched by an increase in aviation services offered by airlines. This in turn benefits the industry's supply chain, as there is increased demand from airlines for aircraft, ground handling, and other products and services. Increased disposable household income, resulting from increased employment, will consequently be re-spent on goods and services. Input-output analyses try to quantify these impacts.

Due to data intensity, the focus of this type of study is often on a specific airport or region and mostly in developed countries. In the United States, for example, a multitude of studies have been commissioned by airports and regions to assess the economic impact of aviation (for example, the Texas Department of Transportation 2011; Association of Monterey Bay Area Governments 2003). Other examples of input-output studies include the "Economic Contribution of Civil Aviation" study by the International Civil Aviation Organization (ICAO 2004), and an economic impact study conducted by the Advisory Council for Aeronautics Research in Europe (ACARE) in 2003 (ACARE 2003).

Although prominently used in aviation literature, input-output analyses fail to capture the enabling or catalytic impacts of aviation and may therefore provide an incomplete picture. Catalytic impacts refer to the economic impact air transport can have on employment and income generated by economic activities which rely on the availability of air transportation (Ishutkina and Hansmann 2009).

Recent studies are increasingly trying to analyze the catalytic effect of air transport. Quantifying the enabling impact of air transport is very complex, however, as it is problematic to isolate the effects of air transportation from uncontrolled variables, such as institutional arrangements or globalization (Ishutkina and Hansmann 2009). Furthermore, it can be difficult to distinguish whether interrelationships are based on correlation or causality. Finally, obtaining the required data on investments and productivity can be challenging, particularly in developing countries.

Both Oxford Economics and Intervista Consulting have produced reports on behalf of aviation organizations such as Eurocontrol, the International Air Transport Association (IATA), and the Air Transport Action Group (ATAG). These studies estimate the enabling effects of aviation on tourism, trade, local investment, and productivity improvement. There are also a handful of academic studies that focus on the enabling effects of aviation (Button and Taylor 2000; Bel and Fageda 2005).

In addition, a number of research papers analyze the impact of changes in air transport policy or regulation of aviation services. The effects of air transport liberalization, domestically and internationally, and its influence on traffic volumes, prices, and networks, and consequently tourism, employment, and GDP, are of particular prominence in these types of studies. The consultancy Intervista, for example, has published a series of studies on the impact of air transport liberalization between 2006 and 2009 (Intervista Consulting 2006–09), as has Oxford Economics (Oxford Economics 2011). The former uses a gravity model that is able to forecast traffic between any two given countries. The model, developed in its core study (Intervista Consulting 2006–09), uses economic, trade, and geographic factors as well as the attributes of the respective air service agreements (ASAs) between the two countries as key variables to forecast traffic volumes. Cross-sectional data from over 800 country pairs were collected, based on the assumption that a specific relationship between traffic, liberalization, and socioeconomic conditions was valid in every market. The study then applied this model to a number of countries including Chile, Singapore, and Uruguay.

Although providing a rigorous generic framework for quantifying passenger traffic post-liberalization, the model is unfortunately not able to take into account certain market-specific factors. This limits its validity in certain cases (Ishutkina and Hansmann 2009).

To complement these more generic frameworks, there have also been multiple case studies analyzing the effects of liberalization in specific countries or regions. ComMark, for example, produced a report on the economic importance of air transport liberalization in the Southern African Development Community (SADC) in 2006, including country- and region-specific factors in their analysis (ComMark 2006).

The overall challenge with studies of this kind originates from the interrelationship between some of the variables used in impact studies. For example, export and trade figures are intrinsically linked to GDP. When including these variables in the regression analyses, used by most impact studies, it is difficult to isolate the impact of each individual variable on air traffic growth (Ishutkina and Hansmann 2009).

Economic impact studies in aviation are also increasingly highlighting the negative impacts of aviation growth including noise and pollution and the economic cost associated with these negative externalities.

An overview of the key impact studies is provided in table 2.1. A summary of all additional economic studies can be found in appendix C.

The Impact of Low-Cost Airlines

Building upon the research evidence above, the remaining part of this chapter will focus on highlighting some of the more specific effects that have been observed with regard to LCC market entry. These include not only the impact on the air transport market in terms of traffic and fare levels, but also on directly related and even unrelated industries.

Research on the impact of LCCs is still not as common as expected due to the difficulty of linking the impact of increased air transport to any one particular business model. However, a number of studies have identified some common effects related to the entrance of LCCs. Figure 2.1 graphically illustrates the sequence of these effects.

Unfortunately research on LCC market entrance is currently almost entirely focused on developed countries and regions, particularly Europe and the United States. This is mostly related to the fact that the more recent emergence of LCCs in new markets means that the required data are often unavailable.

Fares, Traffic, and Competition—The Southwest Effect

In 1993, the U.S. Department of Transportation (DoT) conducted a study on the impact of LCC entrants on the U.S. airline market. Coining the term "Southwest Effect," the DoT researchers Randall Bennett and James Craun focused on three different aspects of how Southwest Airlines impacted the aviation market, namely through (a) direct competitive effect in terms of passenger growth and

Table 2.1 Selected Air Transport Impact Studies

Title	Organization	Year	Key points
Aviation Benefits Beyond Borders	Air Transport Action Group (ATAG)	2012	• Quantitative assessment of the enabling impacts of air transportation for Africa, Asia-Pacific, Europe, the Middle East, Latin America and the Caribbean, and North America. • Study estimates aviation's global economic impact (direct, indirect, induced, and tourism catalytic) at US$2.2 trillion, equivalent to 3.5 percent of world gross domestic product (GDP). • Air transport industry generates a total of 56.6 million jobs globally (8.4 million direct jobs in the airlines, air navigation—service providers and the civil aerospace sectors; 9.3 million indirect jobs through purchases of goods and services from companies in its supply chain; 4.4 million induced jobs through spending; and 34.5 million jobs globally through tourism). • 2030 forecast suggests that there will be nearly 6 billion passengers and aviation will support almost 82 million jobs and US$6.9 trillion in economic activity.
The Economic Catalytic Impact of Air Transport in Europe	Eurocontrol	2005	• The data set covers 24 European countries over a time period of 10 years. • Focuses on the net economic effects (for example, on employment, income, government finances, and so on) resulting from the contribution of air transport to tourism and trade (demand-side effects) and the long-run contribution to productivity and GDP of growth in air transport usage (the supply-side performance of the economy). • Demand-side effects over the decade leading up to 2003 proved to be small, whereas supply-side effects have contributed up to 4 percent (by 2.0 percent in the EU as a whole, and by 4.6 percent in the 10 accession economies) of the European Union's GDP.
Aviation Economic Benefits, IATA Economics Briefing N.08	International Air Transport Association (IATA)	2007	• Analysis of the relationship between connectivity (range and economic importance of destinations, frequency of service, and number of onward connections available through each country's aviation network) and labor productivity. • In developing countries, clear positive relationship between higher levels of connectivity and higher levels of labor productivity—and hence higher GDP and living standards. Smaller incremental impact in developed countries once threshold level of connectivity as a proportion of GDP is reached. • Study assessed economic rate of return (ERR) of aviation investment. For example, Vancouver Airport's investment of Canadian $1.8 billion was estimated to have led to a 5.4 percent increase in connectivity and to have raised long-term productivity by 0.04 percent. Assuming constant number of hours worked, Canadian GDP rose by Canadian $348 million (19.3 percent ERR). In developing countries, for example Kenya, the rate of return was even higher (59 percent).
Economic Contribution of Civil Aviation	International Civil Aviation Organization (ICAO)	2003	• ICAO estimated that civil aviation contributed some US$370 billion in consolidated direct output to the world economy in 1998. • The air transport component of civil aviation is estimated to have generated a total output (direct, indirect, induced, and catalytic impact) of US$1,360 billion and 27.7 million additional jobs. It is estimated that each dollar of output produced in the air transport industry worldwide creates a demand of US$3.25 output in other industries, and that each job in air transport creates 6.1 jobs in other industries.

Figure 2.1 Flowchart of LCC Impact

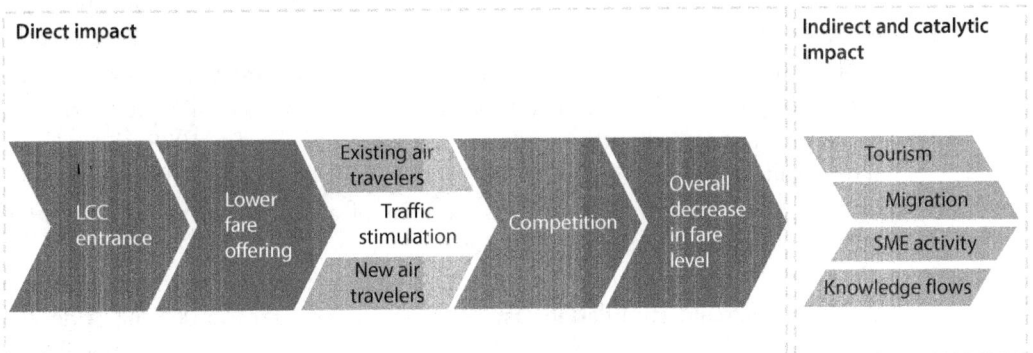

Note: LCC = low-cost carrier; SME = Small and medium enterprises.

fare reduction on a given route where Southwest had entered; (b) the lowering of fares at surrounding airports through Southwest's entry; and (c) the role model effect, exhibiting the impact Southwest has on the business models of new entrants in other markets (Bennett and Craun 1993).

Focusing on the California corridor, the study presented evidence that Southwest's entry had a significant impact on all three aspects outlined above. On the Oakland–Burbank route, for example, where Southwest entered in 1990, prices dropped by 55 percent, and passenger traffic increased sixfold between its entrance and the 3rd quarter of 1992 (Bennett and Craun 1993). The study confirmed some of the prior research that had been conducted by Whinston and Collins (1992), showing that the entry of low-cost airline People Express had resulted in a decrease in the mean fare level of 34 percent on 15 domestic routes between 1984 and 1985 (Whinston and Collins 1992).

Since then, numerous studies have been conducted focusing on the different areas (traffic, competition, and fares) of the Southwest Effect in the U.S. market (Windle and Dresner 1995; Dresdner, Lin, and Windle 1996; Richards 1996; Morrison 2001; Vowles 2001; Pitfield 2008; and Wu 2011). All of these studies confirm, to varying extents, the effect the entry of low-cost airlines has had on the air transport market.

Dresdner, Lin, and Windle (1996), for example, examined the effect of LCCs on other routes serving a specific airport, as well as on routes served by other airlines at surrounding airports. Using data of the top 200 origin/destination (O/D) markets, results indicated that the presence of LCCs contributed to lower yields and increased traffic on the route entered, as well as on competitive routes. Applying a regression analysis, the authors calculated that yields were reduced by approximately 53 percent on routes that Southwest had entered. The presence of LCCs in general resulted in a 38 percent yield reduction on average. On competitive routes originating in or terminating at surrounding airports, yields dropped between 8 and 45 percent if Southwest operated on that route, and between 0 percent and 41 percent if any LCC was present. Focusing on average fares and traffic, Windle and Dresner (1995) calculated an average price drop of 48 percent and a traffic increase of 200 percent on Southwest routes between 1991 and 1994.

The most comprehensive study on the Southwest Effect was completed by Morrison (2001). The author estimated that the entrance of Southwest on a route lowered fares by 46.2 percent. In his calculations for 1998, these lower fares resulted in direct savings of US$3.4 billion for passengers with an additional US$9.5 billion achieved through the effects of actual, adjacent, and potential competition from Southwest on other carriers' fares.

In Europe, the entrance of LCCs has also led to substantial fare decreases and attendant demand stimulation (Franke 2004; Dobruszkes 2006; and Alderighi and others 2012). According to Dobruszkes (2006), 50 percent of additional seats between 1995 and 2004 were provided by low-cost airlines. On the London–Barcelona route, for example, the entrance of LCCs easyJet and Debonair in 1995 increased traffic by 32 percent within one year of operation. This stands in comparison to a 7 percent growth rate in previous years (U.K. CAA 1998). In the Dublin–London market, between the entrance of Ryanair in 1986 and 2000, traffic demand quadrupled while yields dropped to one-fourth (Franke 2004).

In the European market, particularly low yields persisted over longer periods of time as network carriers such as British Airways responded with aggressive pricing. In some cases this even led to financial difficulties for LCCs, as they had to maintain lower fares for longer than initially intended. Ryanair's average fare decreased from approximately EUR60 in 2000 to EUR46.50 in 2003, representing a decline of 22.5 percent (Doganis 2006).

Due to the data intensity of this type of research, studies in other aviation markets have been more limited in number and scientific nature. In a study of the Republic of Korea island Jeju, Chung and Wang (2011) showed that LCCs accounted for 35 percent of total passengers in 2009 on the Seoul–Jeju Island route, corresponding to an average growth rate of 161.7 percent between 2005 and 2009. This stands in contrast to a negative growth rate of −0.3 percent for full-service carriers. Furthermore, a report issued under the Association of Southeast Asian Nations (ASEAN)–Australia Development Cooperation Program (AADCP) looked at the impact of LCCs in Southeast Asia. Referring to an article in *Asia Times* in 2004 (Raja 2004), the report highlights that the entrance of LCCs has led to an overall decrease in fare levels in the market. For example, network carriers such as Cathay Pacific and Singapore Airlines were required to cut fares by almost half in order to compete with Singapore-based LCC Valueair (Damuri and Anas 2005).

Research highlights the particular importance of the stimulation of new demand resulting from reduced fares. New demand refers to passengers who have, due to a variety of reasons, never flown before. Various studies (Lawton 2002; Campisi, Costa, and Mancuso 2010) emphasize that the traffic generated by LCCs is a result of demand stimulation rather than cannibalization of existing carrier passenger traffic. Box 2.1 highlights this demand stimulation by the example of VivaAerobus in Mexico.

Box 2.1 Demand Stimulation—The Case of VivaAerobus

In 2006, the low-cost carrier (LCC) VivaAerobus entered the Mexican market. Despite not being the first LCC in the market, VivaAerobus's "lowest cost" model had a tremendous impact on the country's aviation market. With fares of sometimes up to 50 percent lower than their network competitors, the carrier stimulated considerable new traffic (see figure B2.1). Furthermore, one-third of the carrier's approximately 50 routes were previously not served, creating new traffic and improving connectivity. According to the company's research, a quarter of its passengers are actually first-time travelers, which had previously relied on bus or other means of transportation. With similar average fares between VivaAerobus and domestic long-distance bus services, the airline estimated the potential bus-to-air trade-up market to be 300 million passengers in 2012.

Figure B2.1 Traffic Evolution Pre- and Post-LCC Entrance, Monterrey–Verracruz
number of passengers

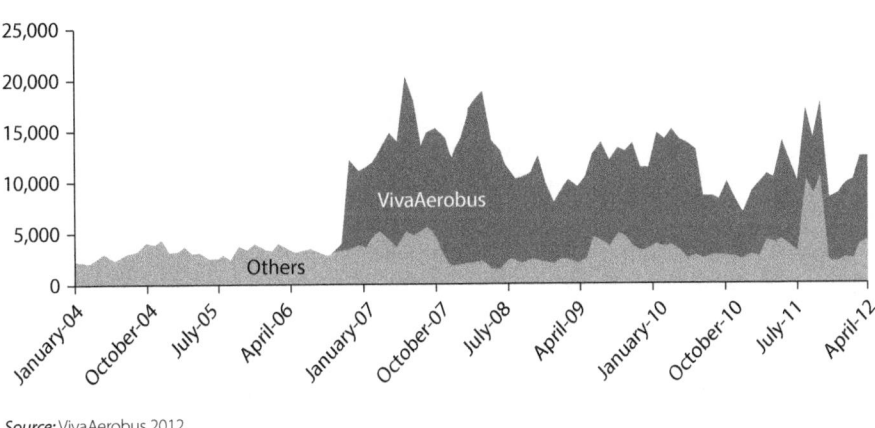

Source: VivaAerobus 2012.
Note: LCC = low-cost carrier.

Tourism

The effects of low-cost airlines go far beyond fare levels and passenger traffic. The correlation between LCC entrance and tourism is particularly well documented in aviation literature.

The European Low Fares Airline Association (ELFAA) has grouped these benefits to tourism into three categories: (a) an increase in tourist destinations due to the usage of secondary airports; for example the London–Strasbourg route, previously used primarily for business, has proved to become a popular tourist destination with the entrance of Ryanair; (b) a more even distribution of traffic throughout the year, reducing "seasonality effects"; and (c) low off-peak fares, which have enabled mid-week holiday travel. This has had the beneficial effect of distributing traffic more evenly across the week and reducing airport congestion (ELFAA 2004).

Although this area is still underresearched, the effects outlined above have been supported by a variety of reports and studies. The European Travel Commission (ETC), for example, has continuously recorded in its annual

Tourism Insight Report (ETC 2007) that LCCs have been the main driver for travel growth and tourism demand across Europe. The extension of the European Union (EU) Open Skies to the new EU member states in Eastern Europe in particular has resulted in a significant increase in LCC travel. According to Dobruszkes (2006), LCCs represented about 60 percent of new air services on west–east routes. This stimulated tourism in the region, in particular for cities such as Budapest, Warsaw, Krakow, and Prague, as well as for smaller towns and rural regions. For Krakow for example, the number of foreign tourists rose from 680,000 to almost 2.5 million between 2003 and 2007. In the same time period, foreign tourist arrivals by air increased from 19 percent to 63 percent. This has been driven significantly by the entrance of low-cost airlines, such as Ryanair (Olipra 2012).

Using a dynamic panel data model, Rey, Myro, and Galera (2011) showed that the entrance of LCCs has had a significant impact on tourism demand for the major six comunidades autónomas (CCAA; autonomous communities or provinces) in Spain from the top 10 EU countries in terms of income per capita. The study estimates that a 10 percent rise in the number of visitors using LCCs would increase tourist per capita figures from EU-15 countries by 0.2 percent. With the LCC share of passenger traffic having risen from 10 percent in 2000 to 53 percent in 2009, the projected impact is substantial.

Another study by Hoersch (2003) estimated the impact of Ryanair on the rural area around Frankfurt Hahn (Hunsrueck region). The author notes an increase from 2.17 million of total overnight stays in 1998 to 2.34 million in 2002 in Hunsrueck.

An analysis by the University of Santa Anna, Pisa (2003) estimated that in 2003, more than 480,000 passengers arrived in Pisa on low-cost airlines. Sixty-five percent of those passengers were foreign travelers, with 62.2 percent traveling for tourism and the remaining 37.8 percent for business. The per capita consumption for tourist and business travelers was estimated at around EUR497 (US$664) and EUR431 (US$575) respectively. In total, both tourist and business travelers generated almost EUR150 million (US$200 million).

The entrance of LCCs has particularly affected tourism on islands, as well as in smaller cities and in remote regions where secondary airports are located. This growth in tourism and consequent increase in employment and accommodation revenues has been analyzed by various authors (Signorini, Pechlaner, and Rienzner 2002; Gonçalves 2009; Donzelli 2010; Graham and Dennis 2010; Chung and Wang 2011; and Olipra 2012). Chung and Wang (2011), for example, attribute the growth in the number of tourists and accommodation revenues in Jeju Island almost entirely to the entrance of LCC Jeju Air. Research by Donzelli (2010) also showed that the opening of a new LCC route could result in EUR14.6 million in additional net income per year for locals in southern Italy, resulting largely from tourism income.

Furthermore, Aguilo and others (2007) and Donzelli (2010) highlight that the entrance of LCCs has not only impacted tourism numbers, but has also shifted traffic patterns, thereby reducing seasonality. This is assumed to be due to the flexibility of LCC schedules as well as the affordability of multiple shorter trips a year. However, results of studies estimating the effect on seasonality have been mixed, with some research finding only limited impact on seasonality in their markets (Chung and Wang 2011).

With regard to the impact of LCCs on domestic traffic and tourism, differing opinions have emerged. Whyte (2007), in his analysis of the Australian tourism market, finds that the entrance of LCC Virgin Blue has not resulted in an increase in domestic tourism in Australia, but has just shifted travelers from different transport modes to air travel. In the case of car-to-plane shifts, some smaller regional areas, which cars had previously been driving through, have suffered from the entrance of LCCs. Furthermore, the availability of lower international airfares has enabled people to travel abroad for their holidays.

Other Impacts

A number of studies have also focused on other impacts of LCCs. Williams and Balaz (2007) examined the impact of LCCs on flows of labor, migrants, knowledge, business connectivity/investment, and mobile markets (also looking at tourism in particular). In the absence of empirical evidence, the study shows how labor migration can be impacted in its composition due to the availability, frequency, and costs of air travel. A few other studies have also focused on the impact of LCC on migration. According to Button and Vega (2008), the reduced travel costs and increased accessibility that have been achieved through LCCs lower the overall cost of international labor migration. This includes not only the costs of transportation itself, but also the social costs resulting from the separation from families. As the authors observe, LCC entrance does not only reduce the cost of immigration, but can actually induce migration.

Murakami (2010) also looked at the effect of LCCs on social welfare in the United States. His empirical analysis showed that gains from lower fares can be substantial in some cases. Of these gains, 90 percent result from consumer surplus, with the rest originating directly from the profit of LCCs.

Conclusion

The development of air services can have a crucial impact on the aviation market, and consequently on other related and even unrelated industries. As the previous chapter highlights, there are a variety of studies, varying in scope and methodology, assessing the impact of air transport. These often focus on the direct, indirect, and induced impact of air transport—but more recently, also on the catalytic or enabling impact of air transport. They have shown air transport to have a considerable positive impact on employment, GDP, trade, tourism, and productivity, among others.

Although research is still limited, **LCCs have been proved to have a significant positive impact on air transport and related markets.** Research on the impact of low-cost airlines has been more scarce due to causality issues, but some organizations and scholars have quantified the impact of LCC entry.

Particular focus has been on the impact of LCCs on traffic stimulation through lower fares and their overall impact on competition and fare levels in the market. This type of research is still limited in developing countries however.

Tourism has been a key industry in the LCC equation. Due to the nature of LCCs, the key focus in most research has been on leisure travelers, and the effects on tourism, particularly for island states and remote regions. Research on the impact of LCCs in developing countries is, however, still sparse due to the lack of reliable data. This research and knowledge gap remains to be filled.

Having highlighted the positive impact LCCs can have in enabling access to air transport to a wider strata of society, the next chapters identify the opportunities that exist for the development of LCCs in developing countries. Chapter 3 outlines the experiences of two countries that have seen the emergence of LCCs in recent years. Based on the findings from the chosen case studies and complemented by stakeholder interviews, chapter 4 establishes a framework of key criteria that would enable the development of low-cost airlines in developing countries.

References

ACARE (Advisory Council for Aeronautics Research in Europe). 2003. *The Economic Impact of Air Transport on the European Economy.*

ACRP (Airport Cooperative Research Program). 2008. *Airport Economic Impact Methods and Models: A Synthesis of Airport Practice.* Transportation Research Board ACRP, Synthesis 7.

Aguilo, E., Rey, B., Rossello, J., and Torres, C. 2007. "Impact of the Post-Liberalisation Growth of LCCs on the Tourism Trends in Spain." *Rivista di Politica Economica* I–II: 39–60.

Alderighi, M., Cento, A., Nijkamp, P., and Rietfeld, P. 2012. "Competition in the European Aviation Market: The Entry of Low-Cost Airlines." *Journal of Transport Geography* 24: 223–33.

Association of Monterey Bay Area Governments. 2003. *Airports Economic Impacts Study for Monterey, San Benito, and Santa Cruz Counties.*

Bel, G., and Fageda, X. 2005. *Getting There Fast: Globalization, Intercontinental Flights and Location of Headquarters.* University of Barcelona.

Bennett, R., and Craun, J. 1993. *The Airline Deregulation Evolution Continues: The Southwest Effect.* Office of Aviation Analysis, U.S. Department of Transportation.

Button, K., and Taylor, S. 2000. "International Air Transportation and Economic Development." *Journal of Air Transport Management* 6 (4): 209–22.

Button, K., and Vega, H. 2008. "The Effect of Air Transport on the Movement of Labour." *Geojournal* 71 (1): 67–81.

Campisi, D., Costa, R., and Mancuso, P. 2010. "The Effect of Low-Cost Airlines Growth in Italy." *Modern Economy* 1: 59–67.

Chung, J., and Wang, T. 2011. "The Impact of Low Cost Carriers on Korean Island Tourism." *Journal Transport Geography* 19 (6): 1335–40.

ComMark. 2006. *Clear Skies over Southern Africa: The Importance of Air Transport Liberalisation for Shared Economic Growth.* http://www.tourisminvest.org/Mozambique/downloads/Investment%20climate%20background/Infrastructure/Clear%20Skies%20over%20Africa.pdf.

Damuri, Y. and Anas, T., 2005. *Strategic Directions for ASEAN Airlines in a Globalizing World—The Emergence of Low-Cost Carriers in South East Asia.* ASEAN–Australia Development Cooperation Program. ASEAN–Australia Development Cooperation Program. http://www.aadcp2.org/uploads/user/6/PDF/REPSF/04-008-FinalLCCs.pdf.

Dobruszkes, F. 2006. "An Analysis of European Low-Cost Airlines and Their Networks." *Journal of Transport Geography* 14 (4): 249–64.

———. 2009. "New Europe, New Low-Cost Air Services." *Journal of Transport Geography* 17 (6): 423–32.

Doganis, R. 2006. *The Airline Business.* 2nd ed. Oxon, U.K.: Routledge.

Donzelli, M. 2010. "The Effect of Low-Cost Air Transportation on the Local Economy: Evidence from Southern Italy." *Journal of Air Transport Management* 16 (3): 121–26.

Dresdner, M., Chris Lin, J.-S., and Windle, R. 1996. "The Impact of Low-Cost Carriers on Airport and Route Competition." *Journal of Transport Economics and Policy* 30 (3): 209–328.

ELFAA (European Low Fares Airline Association). 2004. *Benefits of LFAs.* http://www.elfaa.com/documents/ELFAABenefitsofLFAs2004.pdf.

ETC (European Travel Commission). 2007. *European Tourism Trends 2007.* http://www.etc-corporate.org/images/library/etc_tourism_insights_2007.pdf.

Franke, M. 2004. "Competition between Network Carriers and Low-Cost Carriers." *Journal of Air Transport Management* 10 (1): 15–21.

Gonçalves, S. 2009. *The Impact of Low-Cost Airlines on Madeira Islands.* ISCTE Business School.

Graham, A., and N. Dennis. 2010. "The Impact of Low-Cost Airline Operations to Malta." *Journal of Air Transport Management* 16 (3): 127–36.

Hoersch, S. 2003. *Low-Cost Airlines: A Veritable Chance for the Development of Small Airport and Regional Tourism?* Bournemouth University. http://www.du.se/PageFiles/5050/ETM%20Thesis%20Hörsch.pdf.

ICAO (International Civil Aviation Organization). 2004. *Economic Contribution of Civil Aviation.* http://legacy.icao.int/ATWorkshop/C292_Vol1.pdf.

Intervista Consulting. 2006–09. *The Impact of International Air Service Liberalization Country Studies.* [For example, Morocco, Singapore, Chile.] http://www.iata.org/policy/liberalization/agenda-freedom/Pages/studies.aspx.

Intervista Consulting. 2006. *The Economic Impact of Air Service Liberalisation.* http://www.transportstrategygroup.com/persistent/catalogue_files/products/06EconomicImpactOfAirServiceLiberalization_FinalReport.pdf.

Ishutkina, M., and Hansmann, J. 2009. *Analysis of the Interaction between Air Transport and Economic Activity.* Massachusetts Institute of Technology.

Lawton, T. 2002. *Cleared for Take-Off.* Surrey, U.K.: Ashgate Publishing Ltd.

Leontief, W. 1986. *Input-Output Economics.* 2nd ed. New York: Oxford University Press.

Morrison, S. 2001. "Actual, Adjacent and Potential Competition Estimating the Full Effect of Southwest Airlines." *Journal of Transport Economics and Policy* 35 (2): 239–56.

Murakami, H. 2010. *Time Effect of Low-Cost Carrier Entry and Social Welfare in US Large Air Markets.* Hideki Murakami, Graduate School of Business, Kobe University.

Olipra, L. 2012. "The Impact of Low-Cost Carriers on Tourism Development in Less Famous Destinations." Article as part of the project: The Impact of Air Transport on the Regional Labor Markets in Poland, financed by Polish Ministry of Science and Higher Education, Project no. N N114 180039.

Oxford Economics. 2011. *Economic Benefits of Air Transport Country Studies.* http://web.oxfordeconomics.com/OE_Cons_Aviation.asp#.

Pitfield, D. E. 2008. "The Southwest Effect: A Time Series Analysis on Passengers Carried by Selected Routes and a Market Share Comparison." *Journal of Air Transport Management* 14 (3): 113–22.

Raja, M. 2004. "No-Frills Flying Takes Off in Asia." *Asia Times*, May 22. http://www.atimes.com/atimes/South_Asia/FE22Df06.html.

Rey, B., Myro, R., and Galera, A. 2011. "Effect of Low-Cost Airlines on Tourism in Spain. A Dynamic Panel Data Model." *Journal of Air Transport Management* 17 (3): 163–67.

Richards, K. 1996. "The Effect of Southwest Airlines on U.S. Airline Markets." *Research in Transportation Economics* 4: 33–47.

Signorini, A., Pechlaner, H., and Rienzner, H. 2002. "The Impact of Low Fare Carrier on a Regional Airport and the Consequences for Tourism—The Case of Pisa." 52nd AIEST Congress Publication. In *Air Transport and Tourism*, edited by T. Bieger and P. Keller. St. Gallen, Switzerland: AIEST.

Texas Department of Transportation. 2011. *General Aviation in Texas: Economic Impact 2011.* http://ftp.dot.state.tx.us/pub/txdot-info/avn/tx_econ_tech.pdf.

U.K. CAA (United Kingdom Civil Aviation Authority). 1998. *Single European Aviation Market: The First Five Years.* CAP 685 report.

University of Santa Anna, Pisa. 2003. "Study on Low-Cost Airlines." European Low Fare Airlines Association Presentation at Annual Asia Pacific Low-Cost Airline Symposium 2005. http://www.elfaa.com/documents/ELFAAPresentation-2ndAnnualAsiaPacificLowcostAirlin.pdf.

VivaAerobus. 2012. *Overview of VivaAerobus.* Unpublished presentation.

Vowles, T. M. 2001. "The 'Southwest Effect' in Multi-Airport Regions." *Journal of Air Transport Management* 7 (4): 251–58.

Whinston, M., and Collins, S. 1992. "Entry and Competitive Structure in Deregulated Airline Markets: An Event Study Analysis of People Express." *The RAND Journal of Economics* 23 (4): 445–62.

Whyte, R. 2007. "Impacts of Low-Cost Carriers on Regional Tourism." Proceedings of the 17th Annual CAUTHE Conference, Sydney, Australia. http://eprints.jcu.edu.au/3189/1/3189_Whyte_2007.pdf.

Williams, A. and Balaz, V. 2007. "Low-Cost Airlines, Economies of Flow and Regional Externalities." *Regional Studies* 43 (5): 677–91.

Windle, R. J., and Dresner, M. E. 1995. "The Short and Long-Run Effects of Entry on US Domestic Air Routes." *Transportation Journal* 35 (2): 14–26.

Wu, S. 2011. "The Southwest Effect Revisited: An Empirical Analysis of the Effects of Southwest Airlines and JetBlue Airways on Incumbent Airlines from 1993 to 2009." *Michigan Journal of Business* 5 (2): 11–40.

CHAPTER 3

Two Case Studies: Mexico and South Africa

The Mexican Wave: Growth and Innovation

With a large population of over 100 million, an already sizable but ever growing middle-class, and vast travel distances, Mexico appears to be the ideal market for low-cost airlines (McMullan 2005). It is therefore surprising to discover that until less than a decade ago, Mexican low-cost carriers (LCCs) were unheard of.

Mexico's air transport sector has been defined by a long history of state involvement in the aviation industry. Its two main airlines, Aeromexico and Mexicana, although originally private enterprises established in the 1920s and 30s, became majority-owned by the Mexican government in the early 1980s. After a four-day strike of its staff in 1988, costing the airline an estimated US$7 million (Reuters 1988), Aeromexico declared bankruptcy. Shortly thereafter, both airlines were privatized again. Mexicana was acquired by a group headed by the Bremer Brothers, which promised to renew its fleet and retain the company's labor force. Aeromexico, free from financial and labor liabilities after its collapse, was purchased by a group of domestic investors. However, government participation never disappeared entirely, as 30 percent of capital stock in both companies was held by the state (Perez-Delgado, n.d.).

Although in organizational disarray and in need of fleet renewal, both airlines had reaped the benefits of temporary state involvement by obtaining the majority of permits to provide air services in the country. By the late 1980s, Aeromexico and Mexicana served around 90 percent of the market. Competitors, trying to gain permission to enter the market and compete with the two main carriers, faced significant hurdles (Ros 2010).

In 1991, after decades of protectionist policies, the government decided to finally initiate the deregulation of the air transport market. Liberalizing routes and fare levels, reducing entry restrictions, and improving the criteria for granting permits and concessions resulted in intense competition between the two legacy carriers—but also with new entrants (Perez-Delgado, n.d.). These new carriers included Transportes Aeros Ejecutivos (TAESA), Servicios Aéreos Rutas Oriente (SAERO), and AeroCalifornia, representing the first attempt at "lower-cost" carriers. Through their aggressive commercial practices, they quickly obtained considerable market share at the expense of the network carrier incumbents (Perez-Delgado, n.d.).

Partially due to new competitive pressures, Mexicana and Aeromexico found themselves in financial troubles by the mid-1990s. The purchase of 80 percent of Mexicana's shares by Aeromexico in 1993 (MacLeod 2004), initially hoped to alleviate some of the financial burden, failed and the airlines remained in financial difficulties. In order to prevent the airlines from entering bankruptcy, its major shareholders, principally Mexican banks, established the company Cintra (Corporacion International de Aviacion) in 1995. The newly founded corporation was to serve as a holding company for Mexicana and Aeromexico and its respective subsidiaries,[1] with their airline shareholders swapping shares for Cintra stock. Cintra would then own all of the financial assets of the two carriers and give the airlines the opportunity to restructure financially. Under the condition of establishing this arrangement temporarily until the airlines proved to be financially sound, Cintra was given the green light by the newly founded Comision Federal de Competencia (CFC) (Ros 2010).

The financial crisis in 1995, which led to the collapse of the Mexican peso, forced the government to eventually take a 66 percent stake in Cintra, making the state once again the principal shareholder of both carriers. Regardless of its stake in the airlines, however, Mexico further liberalized its air transport sector. In 1995, the government passed the laws of civil aviation and airports, "Ley de Aviacion Civil" and the "Ley des Aeropuertos" (Ros 2010). The latter initiated the privatization process of 35 of the country's 58 airports in 1998 (Ros 2010). Divided into four groups, the government offered concessions for 12 airports to Grupo Aeroportuario del Pacifico (GAP), 9 airports to Grupo Aeroportuario del Sureste (ASUR), 13 to Grupo Aeroportuario del Centro Norte (OMA), and Mexico City International Airport to Aeropueto Inernational de la Ciudad Mexico (AICM) (ICAO 2013).

Although Cintra was considered to be a temporary solution, the airlines Mexicana and Aeromexico remained under control of the government. Despite pleas by Cintra to sell off the two companies as one, the Competition Commission insisted that both carriers be sold individually. The argument that the Mexican market would only have space for one carrier was dismissed by the commission. It highlighted that new entrants in the early 1990s had grown below expectation, leaving sufficient potential capacity in the market. By 1999, Mexicana and Aeromexico were still capturing 80 percent of the market, which would, if sold together, give it complete control of the market. Despite their difficulties the airlines were only controlling 10 percent less than a decade ago and fares had remained high overall (Ros 2010).

In spite of the prevailing turmoil in the aviation industry, Cintra reported its first operating profit in 2004 (Ros 2010). Subsequently in 2005, the first of two long-awaited privatizations occurred. Mexicana with its newly rebranded regional low-cost subsidiary, "Click Mexicana" (previously Aero Caribe), was sold off to Grupo Posada, a Mexican hotel chain (Navarro 2005). Two years later, in 2007, Banamex, a Mexican bank, acquired Aeromexico, finally breaking the Mexican government's virtual lock on the domestic market. The government's exit signaled a new era for air transport, removing the (sometimes founded) belief by most new entrants that government intervention would squeeze them out of the market.

The New Kid(s) on the Block

In response to the changes in the air transport market, the establishment of Mexicana's Click was followed by the emergence of a new generation of LCCs. Between 2005 and 2007, a variety of low-fare carriers, which included Avolar, Interjet, Volaris, Aerolineas Mesoamericanas, Alma de Mexico, and VivaAerobus, entered the market.

There was certainly enough demand for the newly established low-cost business model. In spite of its geography and large distances, only 3–5 percent of Mexicans had been using air transport in 2007 (Reals 2007). Traditionally bus travel had been the primary mode of domestic transportation, with more than 55 million domestic trips being made on board the country's long distance buses in 2005.[2] Although travelers had to endure long hours, this mode was significantly cheaper and, for most of the population, the only affordable way to travel (Malkin 2005).

Furthermore, the economic conditions for the development of air travel were favorable. After years of economic turmoil marked by steep currency devaluations sending inflation and interest rates soaring, Mexico had finally achieved some macroeconomic stability (Smith 2006). This resulted in a 17 percent rise of its middle class between 2000 and 2010, and a consequent increase in discretionary spending (World Bank 2012).

Despite the promising pool of future air travelers, LCCs faced some significant challenges. One particular obstacle originated from the structure of Mexico's air transport network. In the Mexican air transport market, nine to ten city pairs accounted for 50–60 percent of traffic and were centralized in/to Mexico City (Reals 2007). Not only was Mexico City airport already highly congested, but newer regulations such as the Ley de Aviacion Civil and de Ley des Aeropuertos had failed to create explicit and transparent rules to allow for effective competition. Airport regulation, for example, delegated the decision of allocating takeoff and landing slots to a special committee, which oftentimes only included members of incumbent network carriers—but neither current nor potential competitors. This put new entrants at a distinct disadvantage, particularly at nearly saturated airports and in cases where incumbent carriers had already received preferential treatment through grandfathered clauses (Ros 2010). In addition, government regulation imposed a set of rules for the exchange or transfer of slots that hindered the creation of an active and transparent secondary market. Rules included, for example, the requirement to have used a slot for at least a year before exchanging or transferring it, and restrictions on transfer of slots for airlines with overdue debt. Worsening the imbalance, the regulation did not invoke a limit on the number of slots obtained by an airline (Benedetti and Comision Federal de Competencia de Mexico 2013). The country also suffered from particularly high airport and government taxes. This compromised the profit margin and sustainability of many LCCs. Airport and government taxes are in some cases between two to almost four times higher at Mexico City's Benito Juarez International Airport than in comparable airports in the United States, Brazil, and Colombia[3] (Aeropuerto International de la Ciudad de Mexico 2013; El Dorado International Airport 2013; Infraero 2013; U.S. Federal Aviation Administration 2013).

LCCs also struggled with finding low-cost distribution channels for the sale of their tickets. In 2005, Internet penetration in Mexico was only 17.2 per 100 users (World Bank 2013a) and, according to a study commissioned by Banco de Mexico, only 11.7 million credit cards had been issued by 2004 (Negrin 2005). LCCs followed a variety of innovative strategies in order to cope with these challenges (see box 3.1). Despite intense competition and still limited capacity, LCCs captured one-third of the domestic market by 2008. This occurred primarily at the expense of the country's legacy carriers whose market share had dropped from 64 percent in 2005 to 52 percent in 2008 (Ros 2010).

The global economic crisis of 2008, increasing fuel prices, the swine flu outbreak, and intense competition significantly impacted the Mexican air transport market. By 2009, five airlines,[4] including two LCCs, ceased operations (CAPA 2013a). In 2010, after years of battle with its rival Aeromexico, Mexicana, and with it LCC Click, also declared bankruptcy. Mexicana had long been struggling, having lost US$350 million between 2007 and 2010 (*The Economist* 2010). In the LCC segment, only Volaris, Interjet and VivaAerobus remained in the market, representing a new generation of more robust LCCs. All three carriers applied different models, with Interjet being more of a hybrid and Volaris and VivaAerobus providing more "purist" service offerings and operating practices. This allowed each of them to enter different niches of the market.

Notwithstanding fears of a resulting decline in overall domestic traffic, Mexicana's 27 percent of domestic market share was quickly taken over (CAPA 2013a). Between February 2010 and 2011, Interjet's domestic market share jumped from 12.6 percent to 23.5 percent, whereas VivaAerobus increased its share from 6.7 percent to 9.3 percent in the same period. Mexicana's rival, Aeromexico, had also been a beneficiary, increasing its domestic market share from 34.1 percent to 42.6 percent by 2011. Of particular importance were the sought-after slots at Mexico City Airport, allowing carriers such as VivaAerobus to enter high traffic routes (*Airline Leader* 2013).

Mexicana's fall also offered opportunities for growth in the international market, particularly in the United States. Mexico's LCCs had slowly entered the international arena in previous years with Volaris and Interjet offering flights to neighboring Central American countries, and VivaAerobus commencing flights to the United States with its route to Austin, Texas.

Box 3.1 From Bus to Plane—LCC VivaAerobus Partnership with Grupo IAMSA Bus Operator

When low-cost carrier (LCC) VivaAerobus entered the Mexican market in 2006, it faced a number of significant challenges. One particular challenge was finding a low- cost distribution network. The country's Internet penetration (around 19.5 internet users per 100 people at the time) and credit card usage were still low, making the common LCC distribution strategy of online selling more problematic. The airline therefore required an additional distributor, which could complement its online sales.

The airline partnered with IAMSA, the country's leading bus operator and co-founder of the airline. The bus company transported on average 300 million passengers a year. One of the many benefits of forming this strategic relationship with IAMSA was that VivaAerobus could circumvent traditional, more expensive distribution channels, thereby reducing its costs. VivaAerobus also benefitted from IAMSA's extensive experience in the bus market and its large network, including routes to and from airports. Low-cost ground transport is a significant decision factor in the choice of airport and flying generally.

Although VivaAerobus still primarily uses its Internet portal to sell tickets, sales through Grupo IAMSA at their bus stations or sales outlets have become an integral part of its distribution network. Tickets sold at Grupo IAMSA's bus stations account for 15–20 percent of the carrier's total sales today. Any fees payable to Grupo IAMSA are added directly to the ticket prices, and therefore paid directly by the airline's customers, without the airline incurring any additional distribution cost.

The strategic partnership also enables a multimodal offering to customers, which provides VivaAerobus with a unique channel through which they can convert bus travelers to air travel and grow their passenger base. Travelers purchasing bus tickets at Grupo IAMSA's bus stations are offered the alternative of purchasing an air travel ticket when applicable. This provides the airline with potential customer access at the point of purchase to the 300 million passengers yearly who travel by any of the bus companies within Grupo IAMSA. In many cases, the cost of traveling by air with VivaAerobus is comparable to the cost of a long distance bus ticket, and travel time is significantly reduced.

Bus travelers converted at the point of sale to airline travel are offered the opportunity to purchase a direct shuttle ticket to the origination airport, and upon flight arrival, from the destination airport to the destination bus station. This addresses the issue of access to airports, often common in developing countries, where public transportation to and from airports is not available. The combination of air and bus tickets enables VivaAerobus to quadruple its network to include nearly 100 destinations, which it would otherwise not be able to serve. This unique multimodal and ticket distribution relationship with Grupo IAMSA has provided a significant competitive advantage to the carrier.

Source: VivaAerobus 2012.

Increased Traffic from Stimulated Demand and Lower Fares

Since the entrance of LCCs in 2005, the Mexican air transport market has undergone substantial changes. The privatization of Mexico's state carriers in 2005 and 2007, the collapse of Mexicana and the resulting restructuring of the market, have increased domestic traffic significantly (see figure 3.1).

With the entrance of LCCs in 2005, with exception of a short-term decline in passenger traffic in 2008, the industry has been growing consistently. LCCs captured almost 60 percent of the domestic market in 2012 by increasing traffic on existing routes, and particularly by attracting new flyers into the market. The latter was facilitated by the LCCs' considerably lower fares, as well as an expansion of the historically limited domestic network. Through the offering of lower fares in a traditionally high price market, LCCs had been able to attract users of alternative modes of transport, particularly bus travelers who had been enduring long rides on the country's dilapidated road infrastructure. VivaAerobus, for example, estimates that up to a quarter of its customers are actually first-time travelers (VivaAerobus 2012).

Initially limited by slot restrictions at Mexico City Airport, LCCs also developed alternative route networks. As figure 3.2 shows, traffic growth could be seen particularly on domestic regional routes, many of which had not been served before LCC entry. This increased connectivity within the country. VivaAerobus, for example, initially entirely avoided Mexico City and opened new routes

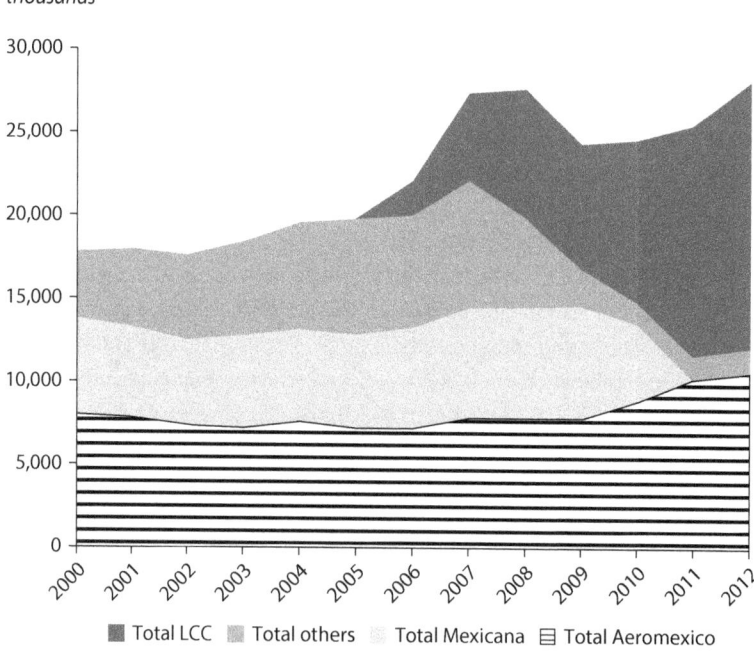

Figure 3.1 Domestic Passengers, Mexico, 2000–12
thousands

Source: Based on data from Dirección General de Aeronáutica Civil Mexico (2013).
Note: LCC = low-cost carrier.

Figure 3.2 Domestic Total, Trunk, and Regional Passengers, 2004–08
thousands

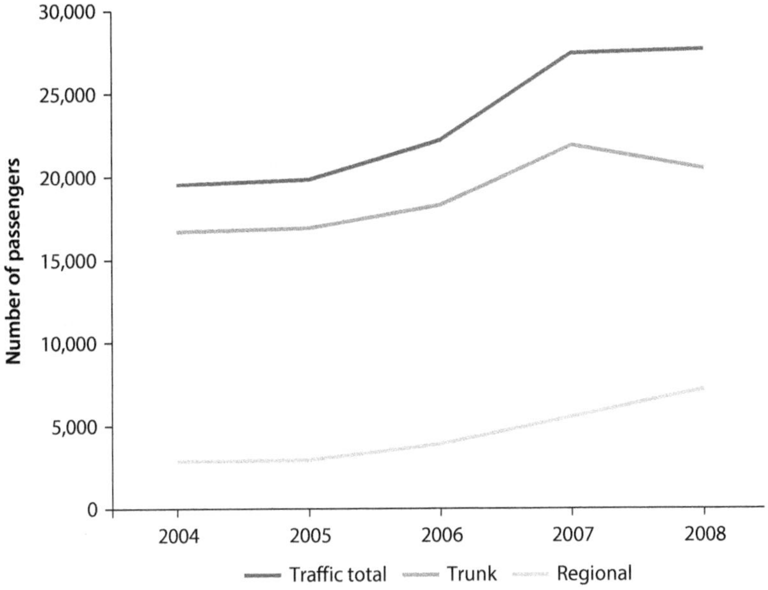

[Line chart showing three lines from 2004 to 2008: Traffic total rising from ~19,500 to ~28,000; Trunk rising from ~17,000 to ~21,000 (peaking in 2007 at ~22,000); Regional rising from ~3,000 to ~7,500]

Source: Based on data from Dirección General de Aeronáutica Civil Mexico (2013).
Note: Trunk Routes are routes with high flight frequencies.

such as the Monterrey–Oaxaca and later the Veracruz–Reynosa route. Alma de Mexico followed a similar strategy (Reals 2007).

Airfares within the Mexican domestic market also decreased considerably. In 2010, the Mexican government, in collaboration with the Organisation for Economic Co-operation and Development (OECD), commissioned a study to assess the competitiveness of the Mexican domestic air transport market. The study collected traffic and fare data on 500 point-to-point routes between April and August 2009. The analysis showed that LCC average prices per kilometer were 42 percent lower as compared with the average fare per kilometer of a traditional carrier. Using a variety of models and variables (for example, distance, total number of competitors, presence of Mexicana or Aeromexico, and gross domestic product [GDP] per capita), the results highlighted that on routes where one or more low cost airlines were present, prices dropped by 24–30 per cent (Ros 2010).

Looking at a specific example, figure 3.3 shows that on the Mexico City–Cancun route, Aeromexico's fares were between 30 and 117 percent higher than the LCC offerings. LCCs have also been matching and sometimes even undercutting bus fares. On the Monterey–Hermosillo route, for example, a journey of 2 hours by plane or 18.5 hours by bus, VivaAerobus has been able to offer equivalent fares to bus rides (VivaAerobus 2012).

The entrance of LCCs in the Mexican domestic market has been stimulating the country's tourism industry. Volaris, for example, has been focused on

Figure 3.3 Fare Comparison Mexico City–Cancun, April 2012
Mex$, thousands

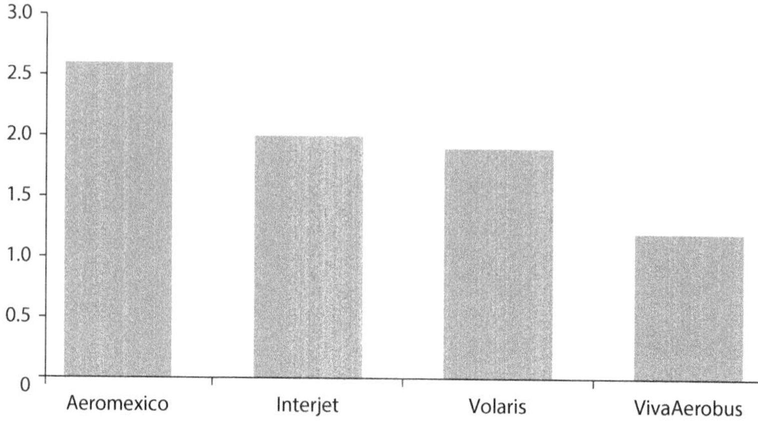

Airline	Fare (Mex$, thousands)
Aeromexico	~2.6
Interjet	~2.0
Volaris	~1.85
VivaAerobus	~1.15

Source: VivaAerobus 2012.
Note: Fares were compared for flights in the period between April 17 and 23, 2012. Mex$ = pesos.

providing additional flights to serve Mexico's tourist destinations. The Mexico City–Cancun route recorded a 39 percent growth in 2012, to 3.1 million passengers. The 900,000 additional passengers traveling on the route in 2012 represent one-third of the domestic market growth (CAPA 2013a).

Significant Opportunities, but Challenges Remain

Although Mexico's domestic air transport market grew almost 30 percent from 2005 to 2012, with 10 percent in 2012 alone, the country still has major opportunities for further development, particularly in the LCC market (CAPA 2013a). Domestic traffic is expected to grow by 5 percent per year between 2013 and 2032, with much of it expected to be generated by low-cost airlines (Airbus 2013).

Mexico's international traffic, specifically the U.S.–Mexico market, also represents considerable potential for LCCs. In 2012, U.S.–Mexico traffic represented 71 percent (19.2 million) of the international passenger market. This market is particularly attractive for LCCs due to the nature of cross-border travel, being migration-spurred visiting friends and relatives (VFR) travel and tourism. Although some LCCs have entered this market, it is currently still dominated by U.S. carriers (CAPA 2013a).

LCCs still face some important challenges however. One major issue in the expansion of air transport in the Mexican market has been the consistent increase in airport tariffs. As noted, Mexico's airport operators have been charging considerably higher fees than most of their Latin American counterparts. Presently comprising approximately 30 percent of average ticket prices at some airports, Mexican airport operators are planning further increases in airport charges in the near future. Operators have justified the increase by highlighting recent infrastructure investments undertaken at the country's airports. However, most airlines believe that these investments, which are required under the concession rules, are unwarranted. Airport operators, particularly OMA and GAP, also still rely heavily on aeronautical revenue, having developed few commercial income sources (CAPA 2011). In order to accommodate LCCs, however, some airports such as Monterrey Airport, which is the base of VivaAerobus, have established a separate LCC terminal. Simplified operations at LCC terminals have decreased airport costs, incentivizing LCCs to enter the market.

In addition to high airport charges, the Mexican government has also introduced additional fees for air travelers. The country currently charges a tourism tax of approximately US$20 for tourists entering the country, thereby negatively affecting fares on international routes.

Congestion at Mexico City Airport is another major problem for all carriers. In 2013, it was announced that the city's international airport had exceeded its hourly limit on landings and takeoffs, on average, once per week in 2012 (Rodriguez and Case 2013). As the quick entrance of LCCs showed (after Mexicana's demise), demand for slots at Mexico City airport clearly exceeds supply. The airport absorbed over 67 percent of traffic in 2009, with almost half of the slots held by incumbent carrier Aeromexico (Comision Federal de Competencia de Mexico 2013). Unfortunately, there have been few regulatory measures to address this imbalance, and the air transport sector still suffers from opaque slot allocation mechanisms.

Research by the Comision Federal de Competencia de Mexico and the OECD estimates that by addressing the challenges with current regulatory mechanisms for slot allocations, fares on routes from Mexico City could be reduced by up to 60 percent (Ros 2010). This would include an initial step of adopting economic criteria to effectively declare the presence of congestion (which currently does not exist). Once declared, the focus should be on measures such as the prevention of market foreclosure and the expansion of existing airlines during non-congested hours, as well as a defined fixed term for slots and the setting of limits to slot accumulation (Benedetti and Comision Federal de Competencia de Mexico 2013).

Although initially considered, an expansion of the airport appears to be unfeasible given the airport's location in a densely populated area. When proposed, expansion plans faced significant resistance from the local population, particularly farmers on the surrounding lands. Plans for investments in alternative airports, such as Toluca, 40 kilometers away from the downtown Santa Fe financial district, or the construction of a new airport at Texcoco, 34 kilometers east of Mexico City and 12 kilometers from the existing international airport have been announced (CAPA 2012). A new airport could potentially replace Mexico City's Benito Juarez International Airport (Rodriguez and Case 2013).

The case of Mexico illustrates the need for certain conditions to be in place in order for LCCs to emerge. These include (a) the liberalization of the domestic market; (b) the complete privatization of the state-owned carriers into two entities rather than a large conglomerate; (c) the large underlying demand for LCCs resulting from historically high fares and a large bus market; and (d) the availability of multiple airports with sufficient capacity (other than Mexico City). Although LCCs were able to engage in innovative ways to circumvent some of the difficulties they encountered in the Mexican market, challenges remain. Issues such as airport congestion at Mexico City and high airport charges will need to be addressed so as not to hamper LCC growth and future market development.

Now Anyone Can Fly—The Impact of Low-Cost Carriers in South Africa

With an unprecedented 62 quarters of uninterrupted economic growth between 1993 and 2007, South Africa has been the success story of economic development in Sub-Saharan Africa. Indicative of its success since the end of the apartheid regime in 1994, South Africa became part of the economically thriving conglomerate of BRIC countries in 2010,[5] and hosted both the 2010 International Federation of Football Association (FIFA) World Cup and the Durban Climate Change Conference.

The Road to Liberalization

The end of apartheid also brought significant changes to South Africa's air transport industry. Having fostered a strong state-owned carrier, South African Airways (SAA), with an extensive network, the end of colonization and the gradual emergence of independent states across the continent proved to be a significant threat to the country's air transport development. In opposition to its apartheid policies, many African states had closed their airports to SAA even for fuel stops (for example, Nairobi). Others repeatedly blocked access to busy air corridors connecting South Africa with the outside world (for example, Ethiopia, Algeria, the Arab Republic of Egypt, Libya, and Sudan).

Although SAA was able to maintain operations to Europe through Cape Verde and Luanda,[6] and through the investment in airport infrastructure in Upington in the Northern Cape, the airline still suffered significantly due to increased distances, higher fuel usage, and consequent higher fare levels, making air travel unattractive (Pirie 1990). Despite protests on the African continent as well as abroad, regular flights by international carriers also persisted and new routes were opened to the United States and Australia, thereby protecting South Africa from complete isolation.

In 1985, four major international airlines, Pan Am, Aerolinas Argentinas, SAS, and Iberia, ceased their services to South Africa. Although the high cost of aviation fuel in the country and subsequent low profitability was cited as the primary cause for their withdrawal, the political instability in the country played a significant role in the airlines' decision making. Shrinking passenger markets caused by political tensions had discouraged commerce and tourism, inflated the price of fuel, and resulted in the depreciation of the South African rand (ZAR), making overseas travel increasingly unaffordable for many South Africans (Pirie 1990). Marking only the beginning of turbulent years ahead, in 1986 the United States and Australia announced punitive actions against SAA following anti-apartheid protest activities at airports in New York and Sydney. The airline was given only a few days' notice to cease operations to the United States, and all U.S. aircraft were prohibited to land in South Africa. Various countries followed suit, announcing commercial sanctions against SAA (Pirie 1990). To worsen the situation, an official resolution by the International Civil Aviation Organization (ICAO) in 1986 urged carriers and governments to terminate air links with South Africa (Mackenzie 2010).

The end of apartheid in the early 1990s finally brought the lifting of international sanctions against the country. Flights to the United States and Australia resumed, and after 28 years, SAA operated for the first time via Sudan and Egypt (SAA 2013a). Between 1990 and 1998, the number of airlines operating to South Africa increased from 21 to 59 (Goldstein 2002), and SAA's international departures spiked between 1991 and 1993, marking the beginning of a new era of air transport (see figure 3.4) (Graham Muller Associates 2010).

The reinstatement of operations across the African market was accompanied by a general desire for a more harmonized liberalization across the continent. This was mainly driven by the challenges that most countries faced from dilapidated or, in some cases, nonexistent land transport infrastructure. Building upon existing bilateral air service agreements between individual African states that had evolved during the post-colonial years, most of the 54 states adopted the so-called Yamoussoukro Decision on November 14, 1999.[7] The Yamoussoukro Decision, stipulating the liberalization of access to air transport markets in Africa, entered into force and became fully binding on August 12, 2002, following an endorsement by the heads of states and governments of the Organization of African Unity (OAU) in July 2000 (Schlumberger 2010). Cross-continental implementation has unfortunately been slow, and although applied on a small

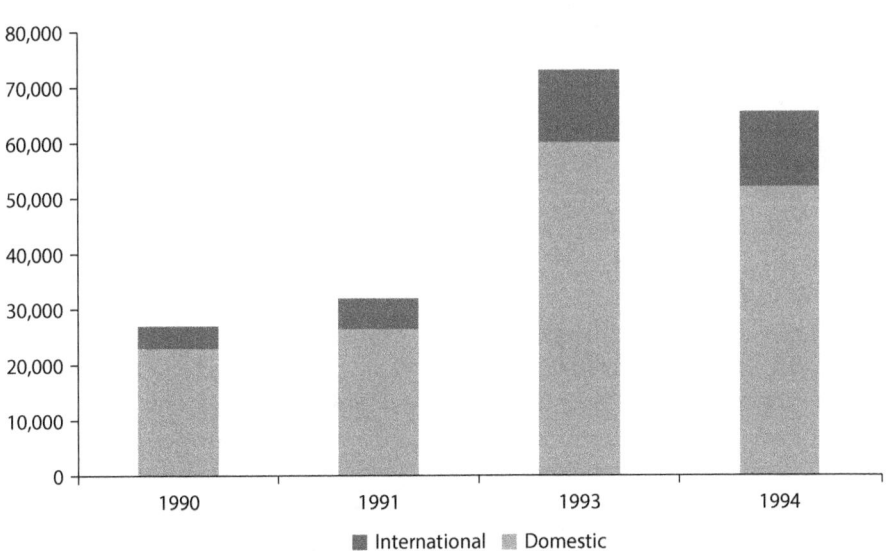

Figure 3.4 South African Airways International and Domestic Departures, 1990–94

Source: Estimates based on Graham Muller Associates 2010.
Note: No data available for 1992.

scale by some like-minded states, it has not led to the hoped-for "open skies" over Africa (ICAO 2010).[8]

As international liberalization was slowly moving forward, the looming end of apartheid in the 1990s had brought with it another significant milestone for air transport development: the liberalization of domestic air services.

By comparison with other countries in Sub-Saharan Africa, South Africa had a fairly well established domestic network with 53 out of 120 of the country's public airports receiving regular flights between 1987 and 1990. Connectivity was, however, still fairly poor, with 78 percent of total links (99 origin/destination) receiving fewer than 20 flights per week in 1988, which resulted in an average of two or fewer flights per route per working day. Not surprisingly, the majority of traffic was absorbed by the larger metropolitan airports of Johannesburg, Durban, and Cape Town (Smith 1998).

Based on the South African Air Services Act No. 51 of 1949 and the subsequent comprehensive air transport policy established by the National Transport Commission (NTC) in 1952, the domestic market was almost exclusively served by SAA until 1990. The policy prohibited the issuing of licenses for domestic services that would result in competition with an existing license, provided that the currently offered service was "satisfactory and sufficient" and "at reasonable charge" (Smith 1998). Of the total turnover for air transport services of around ZAR 720 million (around US$280 million,[9] 0.5 percent of GDP) in 1987/88, 81 percent was being generated by SAA (Victor and Booyse 1988). This represented around 95 percent (or 3.84 million passengers) of scheduled domestic air transport. The remaining domestic traffic (scheduled and unscheduled), which would not compete directly with SAA, was operated by the other 16–20 licensed airlines (Victor and Booyse 1988).[10]

A series of governmental investigations led to the monopoly finally being broken in 1990.[11] A revised domestic air policy deregulating the domestic market was enacted. The new Domestic Air Transport Policy promulgated an "even playing field" with all participants being treated equally with regard to licensing and passenger safety regulations.

After becoming an official Act of Parliament in 1991 (Government of South Africa, 1990), domestic deregulation triggered the entrance of a number of new airlines (for example, Flitestar, Sun Air, Nationwide, SA Express, SA Airlink), and allowed the few established airlines, such as Comair,[12] to apply for traffic rights on domestic routes previously only served by SAA. In seeking to expand its reach in the domestic market, SAA held shares in the newly founded regional carrier SA Express in 1994 (Walters 2010). The company was later acquired by Transnet, a fully government-owned parastatal, which was at that point still a parent company of SAA. A few years later, the state carrier formed a strategic alliance (governed as a franchise agreement) with SA Express as well as with SA Airlink to improve connectivity (SAA 2013b). SA Airlink was to mainly operate on the routes connecting to the main gateways such as Johannesburg, Durban, and Cape Town, where it would then connect with SAA's trunk and thinner secondary routes (Walters 2010).

The additional capacity in the domestic market in the years following deregulation resulted in a general increase in passengers, particularly from major hubs such as Johannesburg and Cape Town (see figure 3.5), but also on secondary routes from Port Elizabeth and East London. Despite newly arising competition, SAA and its alliance partners SA Express and SA Airlink remained the dominant players in the market. SAA still controlled around 70 percent of the domestic market by the end of the 1990s (Smith 1998).

Fare levels changed marginally in the first few years after deregulation. Only with the entrance of Flitestar and Comair on SAA's most popular routes did SAA reduce its prices and average fares. However, this overall reduction did not last long as new airline entrants attempting to compete with lower fares realized that SAA's well-established position made it difficult to gain the required market share to compete on a sustainable basis. SAA, aware of its market power, seemed to start raising its fares only to the point where undercutting by competitors was not viable over longer periods.

Fighting what seemed to be unfair competitive practices, Flitestar instigated an investigation with South Africa's Competition Board (the institutional overseer of the domestic deregulation). As part of their conclusion, the Board demanded that SAA reduce its capacity and increase fare prices in the market to allow for viable competition (Smith 1998). Despite these improvements, the harsh environment eventually led Flitestar, and subsequently other airlines,

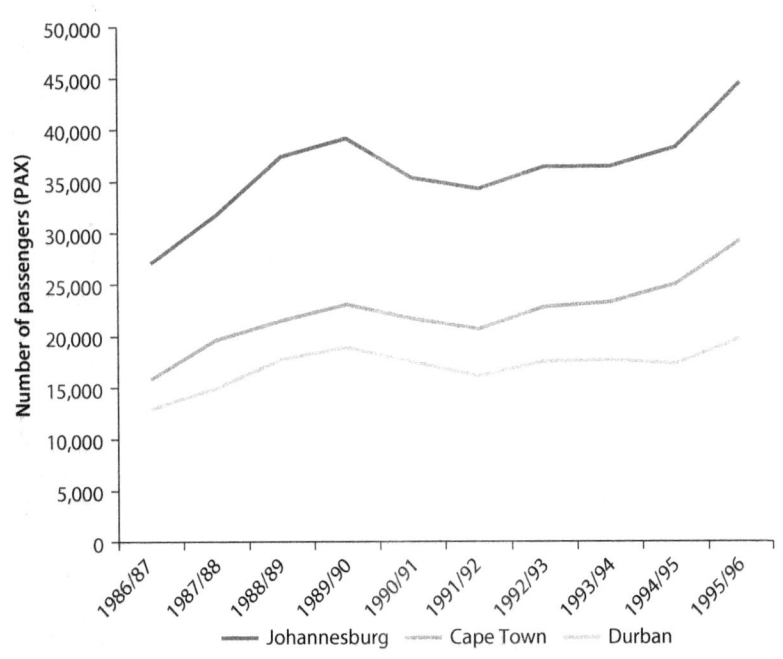

Figure 3.5 Trends in Passenger Transport on Major Domestic Routes, 1986–96
in hundreds

Source: Based on data from Smith (1998).

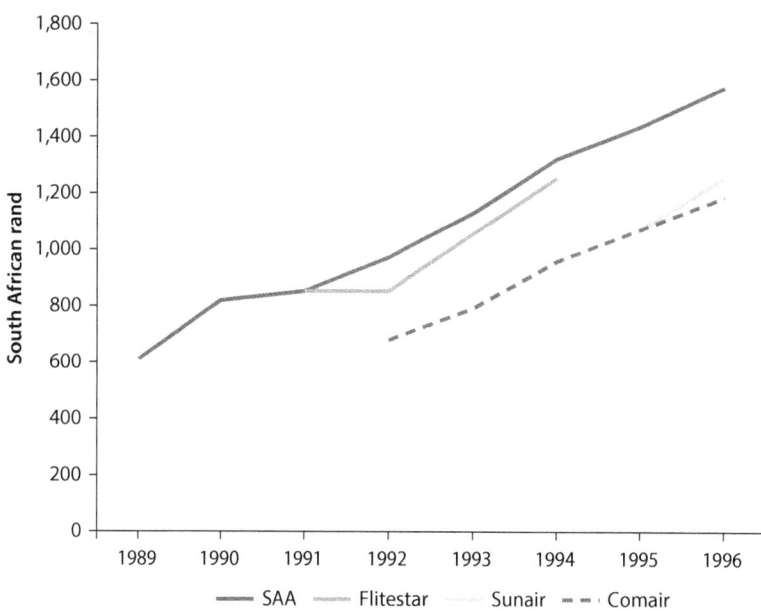

Figure 3.6 Trends in Economy Class Fares on the Johannesburg–Cape Town Route, 1989–96

Source: Based on data from Smith (1998).
Note: SAA = South African Airways.

to default. Thus, toward the end of the 1990s, there was an overall decrease in domestic traffic.

Using the example of the Johannesburg–Cape Town route (see figure 3.6), the only airline that managed to undercut SAA for longer periods of time was Comair, by leveraging its cost advantage from the franchising agreement it had with British Airways. However, the trend analysis shows that the carrier still had to increase fares over time (Smith 1998).

The Entrance and Impact of South Africa's LCCs

The 2000s finally marked a new era for aviation in South Africa. Following in the footsteps of the LCC revolution in the United States and Europe, South Africa's first low-cost airline, Kulula.com, entered the market. Wholly owned by Comair, the LCC based its operations on the successful easyJet business model, which had become, together with Ryanair, the dominating force of the LCC market in Europe. There was no assigned seating, no frequent flyer programs, a one-class configuration on its MD82 and B737-400s (Planespotters 2013), no complimentary onboard food and beverage, and a no-change policy.[13] In order to reduce its costs, the airline also avoided the usage of expensive distribution systems offered by Galileo and Amadeus by introducing a cost-efficient Internet reservation portal (Townsend and Bick 2011).

Kulula.com's entrance was well timed. South Africa's Black Economic Empowerment (BEE) program, initiated after the end of apartheid, had focused on reducing the inequality of the country's black population, which led to a significant growth of South Africa's middle class. Based on the "Living Standard Measure" (LSM),[14] the black middle class (LSM groups 6–8) had increased by 40 percent between 2001 and 2008. The lower-middle-income group, LSM 6, increased by 500,000 people during the same period. A consequent increase in disposable income led to a significant change in consumer traveling patterns (National Agricultural Marketing Council and Ministry of Agriculture, Forestry and Fisheries 2009).

Starting with three daily flights from Johannesburg's OR Tambo International Airport to Cape Town, the airline offered fares as low as ZAR 800 (around US$80 in 2001), and received 2000 bookings on its first day of operation. The carrier's increasing popularity filled its 750,000 available seats per year effortlessly, reporting average load factors above 80 percent (Townsend and Bick 2011). Building on its success, the airline added Port Elizabeth and George to its network in 2003 (Kulula.com 2013), contributing to a large extent to the 159 percent increase in passenger volumes on the Johannesburg to George route between 1998 and 2005 (ComMark Trust 2006). This is particularly significant in light of the fact that the municipality of George had a population of roughly 137,000 at the time (Government of South Africa, Statistics South Africa 2007), 48 percent of whom lived on less than ZAR 1,600 (US$246) a month (ComMark Trust 2006).

It was not long until other carriers began to realize the potential of the low-cost model. In 2004, LCC 1Time entered the market starting, as its rival Kulula had before, with the popular Johannesburg–Cape Town route with a three-time weekly service. Two years after beginning operations, the airline had expanded significantly, having added Durban, East London, George, and Port Elizabeth to its domestic destinations, and Zanzibar, Livingston, and Victoria Falls to its international network (1Time Holdings 2013). Passenger volumes increased drastically, particularly on routes where Kulula had not yet entered, and which were inconveniently located from the country's main entry point in Johannesburg. For example, on the Johannesburg–East London route (which takes more than eight hours by car), traffic increased by 52 percent between 2004 and 2006 (ComMark Trust 2006). This played a major role in revitalizing the region's tourism industry, resulting in a 50 percent increase in holiday packages. As one of the poorest regions in the country (US$1,400 per capita GDP), tourism is a key contributor to the region's economy. Estimates suggest that the 52 percent increase in foreign tourists translated into 62,000 additional tourists per year, and ZAR 65.8 million (US$10 million) in tourism revenues (ComMark Trust 2006).

Meanwhile, Kulula also entered the international market by opening its first routes from Johannesburg to Windhoek, Namibia, and Harare, Zimbabwe, as well as to Lusaka, Zambia.[15] Due to the restrictive air service agreement on the Lusaka route, Kulula entered a wet lease agreement with Zambian Airways,[16] which had ceased to operate on that route (Schlumberger 2010). In the time span of one year (comparing April–June 2006 accumulated traffic), passenger volumes increased by 38 percent and Kulula's low fares brought the price band of SAA on that route down by 33 percent from the top, and 38 percent from the bottom end. This brought the lowest available fare down to ZAR 1,988, around US$188. This success was, however, only possible due to the availability of unused capacity of Zambian Airways. Expansion without this condition would have made entry on the route impossible. This highlights the necessity of continued liberalization of regional routes to allow LCCs to establish larger regional networks (ComMark 2006).

The continued success of Kulula and 1Time forced SAA to rethink its strategy. The South African air travel market had grown by 50 percent between 2003 and 2006, with passenger numbers rising from fewer than 7 million in 2001 to 12 million in 2006 (Sobie 2006). LCCs, taking advantage of the growing economy and newly-emerged and continuously increasing black middle class, gained 30 percent market share in domestic traffic (Mtshalo 2007), leaving SAA with an ever-shrinking piece of the market. SAA, fearing a rapidly shrinking customer base, proposed the introduction of its own LCC.

In 2006, LCC Mango took to the skies, commencing operations on the busy Johannesburg–Cape Town–Durban triangle ("Golden Triangle"). Embarking on an aggressive pricing strategy, Mango offered a ZAR 200 (around US$32) one-way ticket on the Johannesburg–Cape Town route, thereby undercutting not only all of its competitors, but also the majority of luxury intercity buses. Over 10,000 tickets were sold on the first day alone (*The Star* 2006). Targeting the "unflown" segment enabled Mango to capture ten percent of the domestic market by 2007 (Phasiwe 2007).[17] In seeking to reach larger segments of the market—especially those not able to access the Internet or in possession of credit cards—Mango pioneered innovative distribution channels, such as supermarkets, allowing people to purchase tickets without credit cards. Kulula and others later followed this strategy.

With the entrance of Mango, competition became increasingly stiff, as the newest player started offering prices even below those of 1Time and Kulula. Mango's smaller network, however, allowed its competitors to match and sustain the same fare levels for at least short periods of time (Staisch 2007). Kulula, in a clever move, shifted some of its traffic from the Johannesburg to Cape Town route away from the city's busiest airport, OR Tambo, where Mango operated, to the secondary airport Lanseria in the northern part of the city. Mango only followed suit in 2011, leaving Kulula to reap the benefit of being the only LCC present for some time. In return, in a quest for routes that were not served by incumbent LCCs yet, Mango entered the Cape Town–Bloemfontein route, where it competed only with its parent company SAA.

With the entrance of Mango, the growth of 1Time and Kulula on domestic and international routes, and the stimulus from the 2010 World Cup, LCCs gained over 46 percent of market share by 2012 (CAPA 2013b).

The entry of LCCs has brought intense competition into the market, resulting in some "casualties" along the way. In 2011, for example, it took less than 12 months for newly entered LCC Velvet Sky to cease operations. A year later, despite trying to reduce its exposure to the very low fares within the domestic route network, and increase utilization of its aircraft by expanding its services beyond South Africa's borders to Zambia, Tanzania, and later Kenya (*allAfrica* 2012), 1Time was also forced to exit the market (Seggie and Vanek 2012). The newly started African LCC fastjet, at that point, voiced interest in potentially acquiring 1Time's share offering ZAR 1 (10 US cents) for its equity, and offering to take on the leases of three of the airline's aircraft (Jacobs 2012).

Challenges Ahead

Air transport liberalization in South Africa and the subsequent entrance of low-cost airlines have significantly impacted the country's air travel market. Introducing competition on domestic and international routes, and in particular on the highly popular routes of the Golden Triangle, has resulted in lower and more affordable fares and substantial growth in passenger numbers. Between 2002 and 2011, the percentage of South Africans traveling by air is estimated to have almost doubled from 4 percent to 7.4 percent.[18] Low-cost airlines have acted as a catalyst, growing at a considerably higher rate than network carriers. Even throughout the financial crisis, LCCs have proven to be more resilient, experiencing lower decline rates than network carriers. Furthermore, code-sharing agreements with British Airways have provided the needed connectivity to other African markets, such as Namibia and Tanzania. This has enabled not only tourism flows but also inter-regional business travel and trade, which were traditionally hindered by the inadequate capacity of the state-owned carriers and poor ground transportation links in the region (Ford 2005).

The South African air transport market is, however, still facing some considerable challenges. For example, economic regulation of air transport infrastructure is a challenge in South Africa. The country's airport operator, Airport Company South Africa (ACSA), had announced in 2011 a significant tariff increase of 34.8 percent for passenger services, landing, and aircraft parking. Additional increases of 30.6 percent in 2012, 5.5 percent in 2013, and 5.6 percent in 2014 were set resulting in a cumulative increase of 161 percent between 2010 and 2014 (Airports Company South Africa 2013). Fortunately these have not materialized. For the same period, an increase of 71 percent for air traffic and navigation services (ATNS) was planned (*Travel Pulse* 2011). Consequently Johannesburg, the country's main international airport, has become one of the most expensive airports considering its size. The reason for these increases is partially due to historic and planned infrastructure investments by ACSA. The company plans to invest ZAR 22.5 billion (US$3 billion) in airport infrastructure by 2015, with 60 percent going toward OR Tambo Airport. This includes the construction of an additional runway and the expansion of landside infrastructure. Further upgrades are also planned at Cape Town, potentially including a second runway (OSEC 2010).

Fortunately, it has been recognized by the Department of Transport that higher airport charges will most likely make low fares increasingly unsustainable. Options are being assessed as to how to alleviate the cost burden of increased charges. Government support programs and investments into secondary airports, as was done for Lanseria Airport, could help address this challenge (Ensor 2012).

Although deregulation has broken the monopoly held by the state-owned carrier, reducing its market share from around 95 percent to 34 percent in 2010, state-funded support for SAA is seen by many to have skewed the market and to have provided the airline with a competitive advantage. Furthermore, the fact that the state is competing with privately-owned airlines in a deregulated market presents the conundrum of the state wearing two hats, acting as both a "referee and a player in the market" (Walters 2010).

Another challenge is related to air transport liberalization. Much of South Africa's international traffic is still regulated by bilateral air service agreements. Although the government has been promulgating a more liberalized approach to bilateral negotiations, such as through its 2006 "Airlift Strategy," intended to ensure the needed capacity for future tourism (Government of South Africa, Department of Transport 2006), intra-African air travel, particularly on short- and medium-haul routes important to LCCs, is still restricted.

The process of pan-African liberalization that was formulated as part of the Yamoussoukro Decision has suffered from slow implementation, and the removal of restrictive regulations between African countries has been uneven (ICAO 2013).

Despite these challenges, however, South Africa is a very vital example of how low-cost airlines can stimulate air transport markets and reduce fares to increase accessibility. LCCs have been major contributors to tourism in the country, and in the region. In order for this growth to be sustainable, however, significant challenges such as liberalization, economic regulation, and government intervention will need to be resolved in the future.

Conclusion

As the two case studies illustrate, the development of LCCs has brought significant changes to the air transport market in South Africa and Mexico. Although the characteristics of their aviation sector vary significantly, a few key conclusions can be drawn.

Economic growth and the emergence of a sizable middle class have been key for the development of LCCs. Both Mexico and South Africa have undergone significant economic growth in recent years. The end of apartheid in South Africa, the opening of the country to the world again, and the establishment of the BEE program reducing inequality and enabling the growth of a middle class have been key determinants in enabling LCCs to attract a large part of society, and in particular segments that had previously not been targeted. Similarly in Mexico, after years of economic turmoil, resurgent economic and political stability coupled with the vast size of the country provided a solid customer basis for the emergence of VivaAerobus and other LCCs.

Liberalization and the privatization of state-owned carriers are fundamental to the entrance of LCCs. In South Africa, the liberalization of the domestic market in the 1990s allowed the air transport industry to flourish and encouraged the entrance of competition. The presence of a state-owned carrier in the market has been seen by other airlines as uncompetitive. Indeed, the multiple failures of LCCs in the market may point to a competitive disadvantage of private carriers.

However, the second LCC entrant, Kulula, is still growing strongly, having just secured financing to acquire another four B737-800 aircraft (Odendaal 2013). In Mexico, the breaking up and privatization of the Aeromexico and Mexicana monopoly and domestic liberalization has brought competition to the market, supporting the entrance of multiple LCCs with various business models. International liberalization, particularly in South Africa, is however still lagging behind. This issue will need to be addressed in order to create more regional LCC networks.

Airport charges are still a challenge. The costs of operations at some airports are still high in South Africa and Mexico and are bound to rise further. With government and airport operators increasing investments in infrastructure projects to alleviate congestion at the major hubs, and to comply with their concession arrangements, compensation is sought through airport charges. In addition, the economic regulation and in particular the allocation of slots in Mexico has been a considerable challenge. Only after the bankruptcy of Mexicana were LCCs actually able to access the congested Mexico City Airport.

Innovation is key. Both in South Africa and Mexico, airlines have to be able to adapt themselves to the market conditions. What worked in one country may not work in another, but flexibility has been key in the successful establishment of LCCs. The cooperation between IAMSA and VivaAerobus as well as the supermarket distribution channels of Mango allowed LCCs to overcome the lack of Internet and credit card usage, thereby reaching much larger segments of the market.

The case of both Mexico and South Africa give some preliminary notions about the development of LCCs, factors that have been conducive to their growth and their impact. Chapter 4 assembles some of these criteria and creates a framework of prerequisites that can be applied to other regions to assess the potential opportunities for LCC expansion in developing countries.

Notes

1. Aeromexpress, Aerolitoral, and Aeroperú for Aeromexico; and Aerocaribe, Aerocozumel, Aeromonterrey, and Aerolibertad for Mexicana.
2. This statistic focuses primarily on so-called "luxury" buses.
3. The authors compared airport charges per passenger for domestic flights from Atlanta International Airport, Sao Paulo Guarulhos International Airport, and Bogota El Dorado International Airport.
4. Avolar, Aero California, Alma, Azteca, and Aviasca.
5. "BRIC" is a grouping acronym that refers to the countries of Brazil, the Russian Federation, India, and China.
6. Nonstop flights from South Africa to Europe were not economically feasible then because fuel load would have to be substituted for passenger load with the existing combustion technology.
7. Only 44 properly ratified the Yamoussoukro Decision however (as some ratified but never deposited their instruments of ratification).

8. "Open skies" refers to an international policy concept that calls for the liberalization of the rules and regulations of the international aviation industry (a more detailed explanation is given in chapter 4).
9. Latest available exchange rate for 1990, 1 US$ = 0.85 ZAR, oanda.com.
10. Other scheduled domestic operators were Comair, Link Airways (later SA Airlink), and Bop Air (later Sun Air).
11. This included the "Report of the Commission of Inquiry into Civil Aviation in South Africa," better known as the Margo Commission in 1979, the National Transport Policy Study (NTPS) in 1981, and an additional independent study by the Civil Aviation (DCA) of the Department of Transport (DoT) in 1988.
12. Comair entered into a franchise agreement with British Airways and Sun Air, and formed an alliance with Virgin Atlantic in the mid-1990s. This allowed the airlines to price more aggressively as they could share state-of-the-art technology with foreign carriers.
13. This restriction was removed in 2003.
14. LSM is an index that was developed by the South African Advertising Research Forum (SAARF) in the 1980s, categorizing the population according to their standard of living based on a set of predefined criteria. It divides the population into 10 LSM groups, that is, from 10 (highest) to 1 (lowest). (Description available at http://saarf.co.za/LSM/lsms.asp.)
15. The Windhoek and Harare routes were later operated within a codeshare agreement with Comair, Kulula's parent company.
16. According to the Federal Aviation Authority, a wet lease is defined as "a lease agreement in which the aircraft and flight crew from one air carrier (lessor) is leased to another air carrier (lessee)."
17. "Unflown" refers to first-time flyers.
18. Estimate for 2011 is based on South African statistics (Government of South Africa, Statistics South Africa 2011) regarding South African residents' travel by mode and figures on South African population by the World Bank (World Bank 2013b).

References

Aeropuerto International de la Ciudad de Mexico. 2013. "Tarifas." http://www.aicm.com.mx/negocios/tarifas.

Airbus. 2013. "Global Market Forecast 2013–2032." http://www.airbus.com/company/market/forecast.

Airline Leader. 2013. "Country in Focus: Mexico." http://www.airlineleader.com/country-in-focus/mexico.

Airports Company South Africa. 2013. *Airport Tariffs*. http://www.airports.co.za/home.asp?pid=8532.

allAfrica. 2012. "Africa: Low-Cost Airline Expands Routes to African Countries." February 7. http://allafrica.com/stories/201202071304.html.

Benedetti, P., and Comision Federal de Competencia de Mexico. 2013. "Promoting Competition in the Mexican Air Transport Market." Presentation at the 12th Annual Conference of the International Competition Network. http://icnwarsaw2013.org/pre-icn/pre-icn-4c_Benedetti_-_Air_transport_Mexico.pdf.

CAPA (Centre for Asia Pacific Aviation). 2011. "Mexican Airports Continue Their Recovery." November 8. http://centreforaviation.com/analysis/mexican-airports-continue-their-recovery-62049.

———. 2012. "Mexico City Ponders a Second Airport, Again." February 8. http://centreforaviation.com/analysis/mexico-city-ponders-a-second-airport-again-67284.

———. 2013a. "Mexico Returns to Double-Digit Domestic Growth in 2012, Boosting Outlook for Aeromexico and LCCs." February 6, http://centreforaviation.com/analysis/mexico-returns-to-double-digit-domestic-growth-in-2012-boosting-outlook-for-aeromexico-and-lccs-96464.

———. 2013b. "South Africa's Mango, The Often Forgotten Budget Airline Subsidiary Starts to Pursue Faster Growth." July 4. http://centreforaviation.com/analysis/south-africas-mango-the-often-forgotten-budget-airline-subsidiary-starts-to-pursue-faster-growth-117288.

Castaneda, A. n.d. "Privatization and Regulation in Mexico." A Brief Recount and Agenda for the Future, Working Paper, http://kellogg.nd.edu/faculty/research/pdfs/castaned.pdf.

ComMark Trust. 2006. *Clear Skies over Southern Africa, The Importance of Air Transport Liberalization for Shared Economic Growth*. http://www.tourisminvest.org/Mozambique/downloads/Investment%20climate%20background/Infrastructure/Clear%20Skies%20over%20Africa.pdf.

Dirección General de Aeronáutica Civil Mexico. 2013. "Estadisticas." http://www.sct.gob.mx/transporte-y-medicina-preventiva/aeronautica-civil/inicio/.

The Economist. 2010. "A Clumsy Giant Stumbles: Mexicana's Bankruptcy Will Bring Welcome Turbulence to Mexican Skies." August 12. http://www.economist.com/node/16797757.

El Dorado International Airport. 2013. *Impuestos*. http://www.eldorado.aero/tramites.html.

Engineering News. 2011. "SA Could Have the World's Highest Airport Charges." *Engineering News*. http://www.engineeringnews.co.za/article/sa-could-have-the-worlds-highest-airport-charges-2011-10-14.

Ensor, L. 2012. "State Plans to Nurture Low-Cost Airlines." *Business Day Live* September 19. http://www.bdlive.co.za/business/transport/2012/09/19/state-plans-to-nurture-low-cost-airlines.

Ford, N. 2005. "Low-Cost Airlines Increase Market Share." *African Business*, December 2005.

Goldstein, A. 2002. "Infrastructure Development and Regulatory Reform in Sub-Saharan Africa: The Case of Air Transport." *The World Economy* 24 (2): 221–48.

Government of South Africa. 1990. *Air Services Licensing Act*. No 115. Pretoria: Government Printer.

Government of South Africa, Department of Transport. 2006. *Airlift Strategy*. Pretoria: Civil Aviation.

Government of South Africa, Statistics South Africa. 2007. *Community Survey, 2007 Basic Results: Municipalities*. http://www.statssa.gov.za/publications/p03011/p030112007.pdf.

Graham Muller Associates. 2010. *Socio-Economic Impact of an Air Transport Liberalisation Agreement in the Southern African Development Community*, Study commissioned by the Department of Transport, Republic of South Africa. http://grahammuller.files.wordpress.com/2011/09/air-transport-liberalisation-in-sadc.pdf.

ICAO (International Civil Aviation Organization). 2013. *Case Study on Commercialization, Privatization and Economic Oversight of Airports and Air Navigation Services Providers.* http://www.icao.int/sustainability/CaseStudies/Mexico.pdf.

———. 2010. "Liberalization of Air Services." Working Paper, ICAO General Assembly. Agenda Item 49: Liberalization of International Air Transport Services. http://legacy.icao.int/icao/en/assembl/a37/wp/wp211_en.pdf.

———. 2003. *Case Study: Background to Experiences of Liberalization in Africa.* http://www.icao.int/sustainability/CaseStudies/StatesReplies/AfricaBackground_En.pdf.

Infraero. 2013. *Tarifario.* http://www.infraero.gov.br/images/stories/Tarifas/2013/2407_2013/1_tarifario_port_2013_07.pdf.

Jacobs, R. 2012. "Fastjet Eyes Move into South Africa." *Financial Times,* December 19. http://www.ft.com/intl/cms/s/0/b15a1464-49da-11e2-a625-00144feab49a.html#axzz2QBTLg9kD.

Kulula.com. 2013. "Kulula.com Timeline." http://www.kulula.com/brand/timeline.

MacKenzie, D. 2010. *ICAO: A History of the International Civil Aviation Organization.* Toronto: University of Toronto Press.

MacLeod, D. 2004. *Downsizing the State: Privatization and the Limits of Neoliberal Reform in Mexico.* University Park: Penn State Press.

Malkin, E. 2005. "Mexico Discovers Low-Cost Airlines." *New York Times,* August 10. http://www.nytimes.com/2005/08/09/business/worldbusiness/09iht-peso.html?pagewanted=all&_r=0.

McMullan, K. 2005. "Low-Cost Take-Off." *The Economist,* March 23. http://www.economist.com/node/3795339.

Mtshalo, L. C. 2007. "Low Cost Airlines Still Flying High." *The Times,* July 11. http://www.sundaytimes.co.za./Business/Article.aspx?id=513168.

National Agricultural Marketing Council and Ministry of Agriculture, Forestry and Fisheries. 2009. *The South African Food Cost Review: 2008.* http://www.senwes.co.za/Files/SA_Food_Cost_Report_2009.pdf.

Navarro, C. 2005. "Government Agrees to Sell Mexicana Airlines to Mexican Investor Grupo Posadas; Aeromexico Sale Still Pending." *SourceMex.* University of New Mexico. December 7. http://www.thefreelibrary.com/GOVERNMENT+AGREES+TO+SELL+MEXICANA+AIRLINES+TO+MEXICAN+INVESTOR+GRUPO...-a0139569019.

Negrin, J. 2005. *The Regulation of Payment Cards: The Mexican Experience.* Paper for Research Conference at Federal Reserve Bank of New York. http://www.nyfedeconomists.org/research/conference/2005/antitrust/negrin_cards_regulation_mexico.pdf.

Odendaal, N. 2013. "Comair to Add Four New Aircraft to Kulula Fleet." *Engineering News,* May 27. www.engineeringnews.co.za/article/comair-to-add-four-new-aircraft-to-Kulula-fleet-2013-05-27.

OSEC. 2010. *Opportunities in Infrastructure. A Review of South and Southern Africa.* www.s-ge.com/en/filefield-private/files/6543/field_blog_public_files/7952.

Perez-Delgado, L. n.d. *Considerations Regarding the Decision of the Federal Competition Commission of Separately Selling the Companies Aerovias de México and Mexicana de Aviación.* http://www.martindale.com/members/Article_Atachment.aspx?od=984511&id=201990&filename=asr-201992.pdf.

Phasiwe, K. 2007. "South Africa: New Markets for 1Time as It Rethinks Strategy." *Business Day, allAfrica*. http://allafrica.com/stories/200708150172.html.

Pirie, G. H. 1990. "Aviation, Apartheid and Sanctions: Air Transport to and from South Africa, 1945–1989." *GeoJournal* 22 (3): 231–40.

Planespotters. 2013. *Kulula Fleet*. http://www.planespotters.net/Airline/Kulula.

Reals, K. 2007. "Mexican Revolution: Is There Room for Everyone in Mexico's Rapidly-Evolving Airline Sector?" *Airline Business*, December 17. http://www.flightglobal.com/news/articles/mexican-revolution-is-there-room-for-everyone-in-mexicos-rapidly-evolving-airline-sector-220280.

Reuters. 1988. "Aeromexico Files for Bankruptcy." *New York Times* archive (original article unavailable), April 18. http://www.nytimes.com/1988/04/18/business/Aeromexico-files-for-bankruptcy.html.

Rodriguez, C., and B. Case. 2013. "Pena Nieto Considering New Airport as Mexico City Reaches Limits." *Bloomberg*, June 18. http://www.bloomberg.com/news/2013-06-18/pena-nieto-considering-new-airport-as-mexico-city-reaches-limits.html.

Ros, A. 2010. *A Competition Policy Assessment of the Domestic Airline Sector in Mexico and Recommendations to Improve Competition*. Work Commissioned by OECD and Executive Branch of the Mexican Government under the program "Proceso para el fortalecimiento del marco regulatorio para la competitividad en México." http://www.oecd.org/daf/competition/45049588.pdf.

SAA (South African Airways). 2013a. "A Short History of South Africa Airways." http://www.flysaa.com/us/en/footerlinks/aboutUs/briefHistory.html.

———. 2013b. "Airlink History." http://www.flysaa.com/na/en/footerlinks/aboutUs/Airlink.html.

Schlumberger, C. 2010. *Open Skies for Africa*. Washington, DC: World Bank.

Seggie, E., and M. Vanek. 2012. "1Time Files for Liquidation." *Money Web*, November 2. http://www.moneyweb.co.za/moneyweb-south-africa/1time-files-for-liquidation.

Smith, E. 1998. "An Evaluation of the Impact of Air Transport Deregulation in South Africa." PhD thesis, University of Johannesburg.

Smith, G. 2006. "Piggybanks Full of Pesos." *Bloomberg Businessweek Magazine*, March 12. http://www.businessweek.com/stories/2006-03-12/piggybanks-full-of-pesos.

Sobie, B. 2006. "Three's a Crowd—South Africa Focus." *Airline Business*, December 20. http://flightglobal.comarticles/2006/12/20/211136/threes-a-crown-south-africa-focus.html.

Staisch, I. 2007. "A Strategic Analysis of the Latest Entrant into the South African Low-Cost Airline Industry—Mango." Working Paper, University of Stellenboach Business School.

The Star. 2006. "Ticket Frenzy as 10000 get New Cut Rate Airline Off to Soaraway Start." October 31. http://www.highbeam.com/doc/1G1-153684233.html.

Statistics South Africa. 2011. *Tourism 2011*. http://www.statssa.gov.za/publications/Report-03-51-02/Report-03-51-022011.pdf.

1Time Holdings. 2013. "History 1Time." http://www.1timeholdings.co.za/1timeair.htm.

Townsend, S., and G. Bick. 2011. *Kulula.com: Now Anyone Can Fly in South Africa. Emerald Emerging Markets Case Studies*. http://www.emeraldinsight.com/products/case_studies/pdf/kulula.pdf.

Travel Pulse. 2011. "IATA Urges South Africa to Bolster Air Transport Sector." http://www.travelpulse.com/iata-urges-south-africa-to-bolster-air-transport-sector.html.

U.S. Federal Aviation Administration. 2013. *PFC Monthly Reports*. http://www.faa.gov/airports/pfc/monthly_reports/media/airports.pdf.

Victor, W. C., and L. J. S. Booyse. 1988. *Characteristics of Air Transport in South Africa*. Pretoria: Van Wyk & Louw.

VivaAerobus. 2012. *Overview of VivaAerobus*. Unpublished presentation.

Walters, Prof. J. 2010. "An Overview of Developments in the Aviation Industry in South Africa with Special Reference to the Role of Low Cost Carriers." Presentation to the Leadership and Policy Seminar ITLS, University of Sydney, Sydney, Australia. http://sydney.edu.au/business/__data/assets/pdf_file/0012/70113/jackiew-presentation.pdf.

World Bank. 2012. "Mexican Middle Class Grows over Past Decade." World Bank Feature Story, November 13. http://www.worldbank.org/en/news/feature/2012/11/13/mexico-middle-class-grows-over-past-decade.

World Bank. 2013a. "Internet Users per 100 Persons in 2005." www.worldbank.org/data.

World Bank. 2013b. "Population (Total)." www.worldbank.org/data.

CHAPTER 4

Transferability of the LCC Model to Developing Countries—A Framework

Setting up an airline anywhere in the world is a significant challenge—start-up costs are high, competition is often fierce, and the risks are significant. Diligent and extensive analysis has to be undertaken by prospective carriers to determine the viability of entrance into a market. Assessing the industry and its players, cost of infrastructure, forecasting demand and evolving customer preferences, and examining regulatory mechanisms are just some of the factors that airline executives and their teams have to explore. Yet, even in seemingly good conditions, success is not guaranteed. Since the inception of commercial air transport, many airlines have entered the market and failed within short periods of time. The European Regions Airline Association (ERA) calculated that in the short time period between January 2008 and August 2009, 85 airlines had failed worldwide (Kjelgaard 2011).

Taking into account the significant complexity and unpredictability of assessing market potential, the focus of this chapter is to establish a number of factors conducive to low-cost carrier (LCC) growth that will provide a basis for assessing the opportunities for the LCC model in developing countries. For the purpose of creating this framework, the authors have conducted a series of interviews with industry participants, including operators, aircraft manufacturers, and leasing companies. Out of the discussions and in consideration of the breadth of LCC models and country experiences, this book collates what are deemed to be the key market characteristics that allow LCCs to realize the gains of their particular business model. This chapter describes each of these factors, how they can be measured, and indications of some of the preliminary challenges that may be encountered by LCCs in developing countries are delineated. A summary of the framework's indicators and measures can be found in table 4.1. In addition to framework, an empirical entry model was designed, which helps to provide an understanding of the factors and policies that are

Table 4.1 The Framework

Indicator		What does it measure?	Common measures (examples)	Common data sources (examples)
Demand	Existing	Existing air traffic market	Domestic and international traffic volumes, airlines, market shares, network structure	DiiO SRS Analyzer, International Air Transport Association (IATA), passenger and fare data from global distribution systems (GDS), airline and airport annual reports
	Potential	Potential traffic market	Economic growth, wealth distribution, population growth and urbanization, tourism patterns, availability and cost of alternative modes of transport, migration flows	World Bank development indicators, National Ministry of Tourism, World Tourism and Travel Council, World Bank migration database, National Ministry of Transport
Air transport infrastructure		Availability, quality, and cost of airport system	Airside and landside capacity (runway and apron capacity, terminal capacity) and quality (physical conditions, level of service), cost (aeronautical and nonaeronautical fees), ground access to airport	Online airport databases (AZ World Airports or Ourairports), International Civil Aviation Organization, civil aviation authorities, International Air Transport Association (IATA)
Air transport liberalization		Number and nature of bilateral agreements	Air service agreements, regional liberalization frameworks	National civil aviation authorities, governments, World Trade Organization Air Service Agreement Projector (ASAP) Tool
Labor		Availability, cost, and regulation of labor	Training facilities, labor regulations (working hours, overtime, social security and so on), unionization	World Bank *Doing Business* report and *Enterprise Survey*, labor unions, ministries of labor
Safety and security		Effective safety and security oversight	Number of accidents, safety and security audits	International Civil Aviation Organization, online accident databases (Aviation Safety Network)
Distribution		Availability of low-cost distribution channels	Internet penetration, mobile broadband, credit card penetration	World Bank development indicators, International Telecommunications Union
Aircraft financing		Access and cost of finance	Cape Town Convention, legislative system, credit ratings	International Civil Aviation Organization, aircraft leasing companies, World Bank *Doing Business* report
Fuel		Availability and cost of fuel	Jet fuel production, facilities, and cost	International Air Transport Association (IATA), Jeppesen
Governance		Effectiveness of governments	Rule of law, corruption, government effectiveness	World Bank *Worldwide Governance Indicators*, Economist Intelligence Unit, Transparency International

conducive to expansion of low-cost air transport on particular routes. The air transport market of the Arab Republic of Egypt served as a case study for the application of the model.

The framework is used in chapter 6 to look in more detail at one particular region, the East African Community (EAC), and assess the opportunities and challenges in that market. This will help in identifying concrete areas of intervention to facilitate LCC entry into developing countries.

Demand Conditions

For the development of air transport, as with any other industry, a certain level of existing or potential demand needs to be in place to allow new carriers to enter and succeed in the market. Although this appears to be a very obvious criterion, due to the traffic intensity needed for LCCs to operate profitably, the demand side of the equation requires particular attention and focus.

As elaborated in chapter 1, the key to success of the LCC model lies in its high level of productivity. This is achieved by maximizing the utilization of its most cost-intensive resources: aircraft and personnel. In order to achieve this utilization, LCCs rely on high output. This could be accomplished through high frequency, but is primarily achieved through high occupancy levels, or so-called load factors. In air transport, load factor is defined as "the number of revenue passenger miles (RPMs) expressed as a percentage of available seat miles (ASM), either on a particular flight or for the entire system. The load factor represents the proportion of airline output that is actually consumed" (MIT Airline Data Project 2013). The higher the load factor, the more efficiently an LCC's assets are utilized. The result is lower operating costs per passenger, consequently enabling LCCs to offer low airfares (Campisi, Costa, and Mancuso 2010). Another reason for the reliance on high load factors lies in the inability of LCCs to cross-subsidize to the same extent as network carriers. Network carriers are known to cross-subsidize within their class offering (economy, business, and first), and between short- and long-haul flights, where they are dominant due to high entry barriers (*Airline Leader* 2013).

In order to achieve high load factors, there is a commensurate need for high levels of existing and/or latent customer demand. Whereas levels of existing demand can be more easily identified by looking at current passenger flows, network structures, and incumbent carriers, potential demand is more unpredictable. It can be said, however, that latent demand is driven primarily by two factors: the ability of the overall population to afford air travel, and conditions that encourage the usage of air transportation.

As disposable income rises and a country's middle class grows, air travel becomes a more viable alternative for a broader part of society. Empirical studies such as those conducted by the International Air Transport Association (IATA) (IATA 2008) have highlighted that as households and individuals get more prosperous, they are likely to devote an increasing share of their incomes to discretionary spending, such as air travel.

According to the IATA study, the level of impact from increased income is not unilateral, meaning that there are substantial variations according to region and distance. In developing countries, for example, income elasticity for short-haul flights is higher than in more developed countries, demonstrating greater responsiveness to changes in income. The report also suggests that income elasticity becomes higher the longer the distance, as long-haul travel is seen as more "desirable" than commoditized short-haul travel (IATA 2008).

Figure 4.1 Flight Intensity, 2012

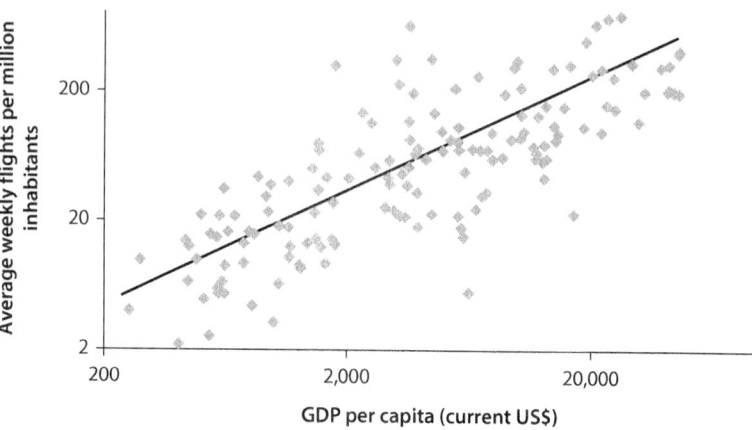

Sources: Based on World Bank (2013b) and DiiO SRS Analyzer data (2013).
Note: GDP = gross domestic product.

Gross domestic product (GDP) per capita has often been used as a metric for identifying the economic conditions of a country's population and the potential for air transport demand. As figure 4.1 shows, there appears to be a strong correlation between per capita GDP and average weekly flights per million inhabitants. Although GDP per capita can be a good indicator for the economic conditions of a country's population, the importance lies, not surprisingly, in the distribution of income and the level of inequality prevalent in a country. Particularly in resource-rich countries, GDP per capita can be a distorted indicator that does not capture the distributional effect of wealth. A recent report by the Africa Progress Panel analyzed the GDP per capita of different resource-rich countries in Sub-Saharan Africa. Although GDP per capita was generally higher, the revenues accrued from these resources have widened the gap between rich and poor significantly (Africa Progress Panel 2013).

In both the Asia and Central and Latin America regions, the growth of a strong middle classes has acted as an enabler for the emergence of LCCs. For example, Brazil's Real Plan, an economic plan implemented in 1994 to curb inflation and increase long-term financing allowing for increased household spending, was an important factor for the entry of the first low-cost airline, GOL (Franco and others 2002). Likewise, in Mexico, economic stability and a burgeoning middle class provided favorable conditions for the entrance of Mexican LCCs Click and Interjet (Euromonitor International 2012).

The World Bank Development Report 2009 also found that urbanization has been a key driver in middle-class growth (World Bank 2010). A direct correlation has been established by air traffic forecasts, such as those conducted by Airbus and Bombardier, between urbanization and an increased propensity to travel (Airbus 2012; Bombardier 2012). According to Mason Florence, executive director of the Mekong Tourism Coordinating Office (MTCO), "Asia's more sophisticated urban life will create demand for more specialized products, such as heritage and culture, 'edutainment' theme parks, soft adventure, luxury holidays, and sports tourism." Florence predicts that outbound travel from China and India, as well as from Indonesia and Vietnam—all countries with rapid urbanization—will grow further in the coming years due to increased purchasing power (Mason and Mekong Tourism Coordination Office 2011). Between 2001 and 2012, the region experienced an average annual growth in traffic (in passenger-kilometers performed) of 6.4 percent (ICAO 2012).

The second factor driving demand entails an environment conducive to the usage of air transport. This includes a number of conditions, for example: inexistent or poor quality ground transport infrastructure; tourism (existing and potential); or high levels of migration flows (work or education related). These drive demand in the traditional LCC target markets which have been seen to be predominantly leisure and so-called visiting friends and relatives (VFR) travelers (Mason 2000). Existing bus and train travel patterns, for example, can be a good indicator of potential VFR demand in a market. A number of studies (Dobruszkes 2009; Olipra, Pancer-Cybulska, and Szostak 2011) have shown that migration patterns in Europe have had a considerable influence on the LCC network structure.

As described in chapter 1, the target market of LCCs in developed countries has been changing, with the emergence of hybridized LCC models and reduced travel budgets by companies attracting business travelers (IATA 1997).[1] In this context, international businesses with a regional presence can also be a source of demand.

Air Transport Infrastructure

As elaborated in chapter 1, LCCs build their networks around airports with underutilized capacity, low levels of congestion, and low airport charges. This allows them to optimize their operations and minimize costs. In the European and U.S. markets, this has primarily been achieved through the usage of secondary airports and/or the usage of cheaper airport facilities. In addition, some primary airports have adjusted their offerings by operating, and, in some cases, even building low-cost terminals. However, in the context of developed countries, such a prerequisite would build on the assumption that the necessary infrastructure and efficient management are already in place. This is often not the case in developing countries. For an assessment of opportunities for LCCs in developing countries, the prerequisite has to be extended to include overall quality and management of airport systems. Although their simple service offering requires only very basic facilities, landside and airside infrastructure capacity and quality, including safety and security facilities, and equipment, as well as air traffic management, may pose a challenge in developing countries (Winston and de Rus 2008).[2]

There are various ways to assess the capacity of an airport, both of the airfield and passenger terminals. To estimate airfield capacity, most research typically focuses on its most constrained element, the runway(s). There are different approaches to defining and calculating runway capacity. One common definition applied is "maximum throughput," defined as "the expected (average) number of runway operations (takeoffs and landings) that can be performed within one hour without violating air traffic control (ATC) rules, assuming continuous aircraft demand." Another definition for determining the potential capacity of an airport is "declared capacity." Declared capacity is defined as a "declared limit on the number of aircraft movements that can be scheduled per unit of time (typically one hour) at an airport" (Odoni 2009). Declared capacity is normally set at 85 to 90 percent of saturation capacity. Both measures are influenced by a variety of factors, including aspects such as the number and layout of active runways, separation requirements, weather conditions, and the mix of aircraft.

The capacity of airport infrastructure is inherently linked to the quality of an airport, both on the airside and on the landside. There are unfortunately only a few current and reliable reviews of the overall quality of air transport infrastructure on a global scale, making a remote assessment more difficult. One useful but high-level indicator is produced by the World Economic Forum (WEF) as part of their Global Competitiveness Report. A survey is conducted each year assessing the competitiveness of 144 economies. It includes an evaluation of the quality of air transport infrastructure, focusing on airport quality and connectivity. As highlighted in figure 4.2, the results show that air transport infrastructure in many countries in Africa, Asia, and Latin America, and even in Eastern Europe, are still considered of poor quality (WEF 2012a).

Although useful as a general indicator of quality on a country level, a more detailed airport-level assessment is needed to understand the quality of a country's airport system—looking at not only the condition of the actual physical infrastructure itself (for example, the runway, equipment, passenger facilities, and so on), but also the quality of service provision. For airport terminals, for example, IATA and ACI have developed the Airport Development Reference

Figure 4.2 Air Transport Infrastructure Quality, 2012

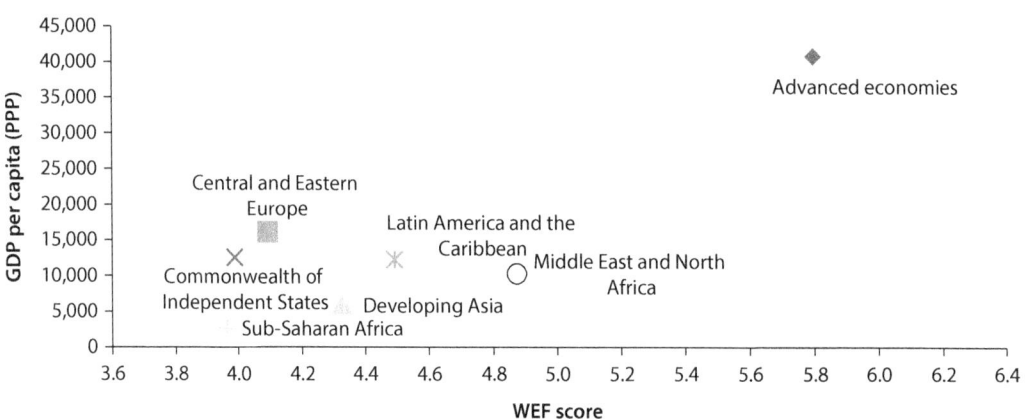

Sources: Based on data from World Economic Forum *Global Competitiveness Report*, Switzerland, 2012 (WEF 2012b); and International Monetary Fund *World Economic Outlook* (IMF 2013).
Note: GDP = gross domestic product; PPP = purchasing power parity.

Manual (ADRM), which categorizes airports in accordance with their level of service (LOS) taking into consideration a variety of elements. These include, for example, waiting times at key points such as security screening or passport control. Lower IATA classification of airports, meaning poorer LOS, is often related to airport capacity constraints and design, but can also be a result of poor management (for example, inefficient scheduling with uneven traffic distribution, a lack of adequate number of personnel, or inefficient processes at check-in or immigration).

A significant challenge of air transport infrastructure is related to facilities and equipment that ensure the safety of operations. This includes primarily communications, navigation, and surveillance (CNS) infrastructure. In many parts of the world, particularly in Africa, the lack of and/or insufficiently maintained ground-based navigation aids, has been an impediment to the development of air transport (Gwilliam and others 2011).

The reason for the dire state of airport infrastructure in many developing countries is related to the high levels of investment needed to improve and maintain airports. Funding for maintenance is often constrained by thin traffic and low passenger figures, as well as the inability of the central treasury to provide the needed capital. As a consequence, many of these countries are unable to meet basic international safety requirements (Winston and de Rus 2008).

For LCCs, reliance is also high on the efficient management of airport infrastructure. As elaborated in chapter 1, short turnaround times and consequently the maximization of aircraft usage are key for LCC profitability. In order to be able to achieve this, efficient processes need to be put in place by the airport operator (for example, the speed of ground handling or refueling) and ATC to manage operations smoothly. There are various methodologies available today that measure the efficiency and overall performance of airports, such as those established by the International Civil Aviation Organization (ICAO) or the Airports Council International (ACI). Many indicators are not applicable to smaller airport operations though and are not relevant for LCC operations generally. Some evidence has also been found that, inversely, LCCs can actually have a positive impact on airport performance. As airports become aware of the benefits gained from increased traffic, they adapt to LCC requirements (Botasso, Conti, and Piga 2012).

The level of airport charges, such as landing and passenger fees and other taxation, plays a major role in the development of affordable air services. Air travel charges are generally regulated by national laws. For domestic air travel, the national policy for charging taxes and fees is generally the only reference point. However, in domestic markets of states that belong to regional economic communities (RECs), such as the European Union, certain bloc principles on taxation may apply. The taxation of international air services is based on the principles of the "Convention on International Civil Aviation," the so-called Chicago Convention of 1944 (ICAO 1944). Article 15 of the convention regulates "airport and similar charges." However, the major part of the article only addresses impermissible price discrimination between national and foreign carriers. Nevertheless, the last sentence stipulates that charges should not be imposed solely for the right to enter and exit a territory on an aircraft. The underlying philosophy behind the rule is that international air transportation should not be taxed unreasonably, but can only be charged for services that are provided or for costs that are incurred from their operations.

Information on airport charges (aeronautical and nonaeronautical) for major airports can normally be found in a country's Aeronautical Information Publication (AIP) or, when not available, from international sources such as the ICAO and ACI.[3] Charges for smaller domestic airports are, in most cases, unavailable unless published by the respective civil aviation authority (CAA).

Airport charges can pose a significant challenge in developing countries. As secondary airports are less available, LCCs are forced to establish their operations at a country's primary airports. These airports experience not only higher levels of congestion, but also often demand higher airport charges as justified by the complexity of their operations and expensive, and sometimes unnecessary, infrastructure investments. In Senegal, for example, international airports have been charging an ever-increasing infrastructure development charge of EUR54 (US$72 in 2011) since 2005, which is used to finance the country's new airport, Dakar-Blaise Diagne International Airport, currently under construction (ICAO 2013a). Similarly in Zambia, the National Airports Corporation, a parastatal company, has recently introduced a new infrastructure and development charge to fund, develop, maintain, and manage four designated Zambian airports (Lusaka, Ndola, Livingston, Mfuwe) (*Lusaka Times* 2012).

In some cases, airports in developing countries can also prove to be an important source of foreign revenue for governments, and are therefore seen as "cash cows" (Winston and de Rus 2008). Furthermore, at smaller airports, the lack of landside infrastructure and limited opportunities for commercial revenue creates a larger dependency on aeronautical charges (Winston and de Rus 2008).[4] This can have a detrimental impact on ticket prices. As shown figure 4.3, charges and taxes on a sample of West African routes represent, in some cases, over 50 percent of the ticket price. Removing excessive charges and taxes can have a substantial positive impact on airfares, and the economy as a whole. According to a report by IATA (IATA 2013a), the removal of the infrastructure charge at Léopold Sédar Senghor International Airport in Senegal could increase economic benefits to Senegalese residents using air transport by US$31.5 million. It would decrease average round trip costs for foreign visitors by approximately 6.5 percent. Furthermore, the air transport industry's overall contribution to GDP would grow by more than US$37 million and support an additional 6,700 jobs in Senegal.

Although these reasons help to explain why airport charges may be higher in developing countries, such generalizations are difficult to make. Further assessments need to be made on a country-by-country basis.

In cases where secondary airports are available or primary airports are located far from cities, LCCs are dependent on the provision of low-cost ground access. Multiple studies have shown that airport accessibility is a key determinant in passenger choice of an airport (Kouwenhoven 2008). The dilapidated condition

Figure 4.3 Selected Lowest Economy Fare for African Routes, August 2012
U.S. dollars

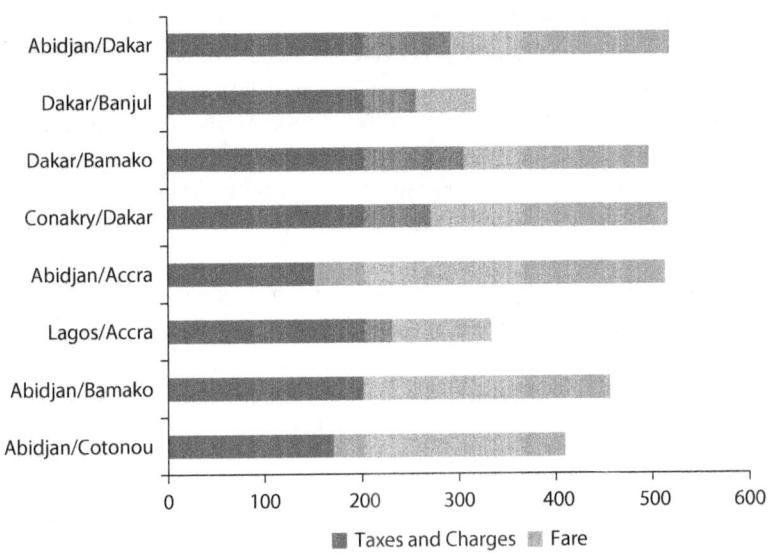

Sources: Analysis based on Senegal Airlines, Arik Air, and Air Cote d'Ivoire websites.
Note: Fares are for travel in August 2012.

of roads and the lack of public transport can therefore be a significant barrier in attracting consumers. In Europe, for example, Ryanair has recognized that costly ground access can act as a potential deterrent for customers using the airline. Therefore, it has developed a partnership with Terravision, a European coach operator (Ryanair 2008). In Mexico, the LCC VivaAerobus has been working in partnership with the bus company IAMSA to ensure accessibility (VivaAerobus 2012).

Air Transport Liberalization

Very few industries are as affected by regulation as the aviation industry. Other than market forces, government policy has been one of the most crucial components in shaping the operation and development of scheduled passenger air services. As in the case of Southwest Airlines and for most LCCs, deregulated domestic and international air transport markets have been a key prerequisite in their establishment.

In the air transport industry, regulation occurs on both a domestic and an international level, and covers a wide spectrum of responsibilities including safety, airspace policy, economic regulation, and consumer protection. These responsibilities traditionally lie with a country's designated governmental body, in most cases the CAA. Of particular importance in this context is their economic regulatory function involving the regulation of entry and exit of airlines, access to individual routes, determination of fares, as well as control over subsidies (Hooper 1997).

Historically, and in some cases still today, the involvement of a country's government in the aviation market extends even further through the presence of a state-owned national carrier, which is often supported by subsidies and fiscal incentives (Belobaba, Odoni, and Barnhart 2009). This would oftentimes have a strong influence on the way in which the air transport market is regulated, with preferential treatment being given in terms of route access and stringent or impossible entry criteria for new carriers.

Deregulation of domestic air transport was initiated in the United States in the 1970s. Since then domestic liberalization policies have also been implemented to varying degrees in many less developed countries. In recent years, liberalization policies have been introduced both in smaller domestic markets such as Papua New Guinea, Thailand, and Mongolia, as well as in larger markets with considerable scope for domestic services, such as Brazil, China and India (Hooper, Hutchinson, and Nyathi 1996). The privatization of national airlines is a particularly important factor in some developing countries, where state-owned carriers are still very common. This can partially be explained by the fact that government-owned carriers in developing countries are seen as a national asset and key for promoting economic and social development, particularly in countries with poor alternative modes of transport (Hooper 1997).

In larger developing countries, the opening of domestic routes has encouraged the development of efficient and affordable air services. For example, Brazil experienced a phased domestic liberalization from the 1990s onward, eliminating entry barriers to new airline enterprises and deregulating fare levels in order for new carriers, including low-cost airlines such as GOL, to enter the market (Franco and others 2002). Thailand is another example of a country that had historically protected its carrier Thai Airways by prohibiting private airlines from directly competing with the airline on its routes. Fares were also regulated according to route distances and types (trunk, local, and feeder routes). In the 2000s, however, Thailand gradually deregulated its domestic airline market by first allowing private carriers to enter domestic routes and subsequently removing fare restrictions—and even allowing for foreign ownership of up to 49 percent. Soon after deregulation, three new LCCs, Thai AirAsia, Nok Air, and One-Two-Go, started domestic operations and traffic increased by almost 40 percent in 2004 (Zhang and others 2008).

The regulation of international air transport is based on the Chicago Convention of 1944 (ICAO 1944). As a result of a disagreement on the regulation of air services at the time, a framework of bilateral air service agreements (ASAs) emerged regulating air transport between two countries on a country-by-country basis. Although multilateral agreements are becoming more common, most air transport today is still governed by bilateral ASAs. The convention also established the concept of "Freedom of the Air" with each freedom specifying the rights that the carrier of any country may have with respect to one another (see appendix D for the different freedoms of air) (Belobaba, Odoni, and Barnhart 2009). Depending on the type of freedom permitted between two countries, this may not only impact international, but may also affect domestic, traffic with the

Table 4.2 Elements of Air Service Agreements

Market access	Potential city pairs to be served under ASAs, as well as all freedoms beyond the third and fourth, which may be granted under the ASA.[a]
Airline designation, ownership, and control	Number of airlines from each state that have the right to provide service in each city pair included in the agreement, and the ownership criteria airlines must meet to be designated under the bilateral agreement. This clause sometimes includes foreign ownership restrictions.
Capacity	Frequency of flights and the number of seats that can be offered on each city pair.
Airfares (tariffs)	The manner in which passenger fares and/or cargo rate charges are determined, and any steps necessary for government approval of these fares.

Source: The Global Airline Industry (Belobaba, Odoni, and Barnhart 2009).
Note: ASA = air service agreement.
a. Third and fourth freedom rights allow basic international service between two countries. For an outline of all freedoms of the air, see appendix D.

highest level of freedom, cabotage, allowing carriers to move passengers within a foreign domestic markets (Belobaba, Odoni, and Barnhart 2009).[5] Table 4.2 below outlines the four critical aspects of an ASA.

The extent to which these rights are granted under an ASA range from traditional to open market or open skies, decreasing in restrictiveness. The least restrictive type of agreement, open skies, has been achieved in the United States and in Europe, but much of the developing world is still struggling with the implementation of such a liberalized regulatory framework.

Access to detailed ASAs is often difficult and has to be obtained directly from the respective CAA or ministry. The World Trade Organization (WTO) has been the only organization collecting information on ASAs worldwide. It has created an analytical tool, the air service agreement projector (ASAP), which measures the restrictiveness of a particular ASA between two countries. The degree of restrictiveness in the ASAP is based on the application of "standard provisions" (primarily third and fourth freedoms) under an ASA, but gives particular importance to the application of fifth freedom rights, liberal withholding/ownership provisions and multiple designations. The results for each ASA are categorized according to alphabetic letters, with A being the most and G being the least restrictive (WTO 2013).

According to the database, intra-regional, short- to medium-haul traffic, of particular importance for LCCs, is still highly regulated in most developing countries. Table 4.3 shows the number of intra-regional agreements by type in Africa, Latin America and the Caribbean, Asia Pacific, the Middle East, and the Commonwealth of Independent States (CIS). The only Asia Pacific intra-regional agreements that are categorized as Type G are between more developed countries, such as New Zealand, Australia, Singapore, and Brunei Darussalem.[6] In Latin America, the only fully liberalized intra-regional ASA is between Costa Rica and Chile. In the intra-African market, no such agreements exist. There are, however, a number of F type agreements between countries.

Table 4.3 Intra-Regional Traffic by Type of Agreement

Region	A	B	C	D	E	F	G	I	O
Intra–Asia Pacific	25	10	29	15	33	17	11	14	57
Intra–Africa	14	12	24	3	22	11	0	17	8
Intra–Middle East	7	7	3	0	7	0	0	2	0
Intra–CIS	1	4	0	0	0	0	0	5	6
Intra–Latin America	1	5	5	3	16	7	1	17	8

Sources: Analysis based on WTO (World Trade Organization) Quantitative Air Services Agreement Review (QUASAR) data.
Note: I refers to incomplete information available and *O* refers to combinations not covered in types *A* to *G*.
CIS = Commonwealth of Independent States.

Some progress has been achieved with the emergence of multilateral agreements in certain regions. In the Latin America and Caribbean region, for example, an effort has been made by the Latin American Civil Aviation Commission (LACAC) to enforce a "Multilateral Skies Agreement." In Africa, an open skies framework for intra-African air transport, the Yamoussoukro Decision, has been established and became binding for 44 countries. Unfortunately the framework has not been widely applied (Schlumberger 2010). This particular framework will be discussed in more detail in chapter 5.

RECs have played an important part in the liberalization of regional networks. The European Union has achieved complete liberalization between its member states, even including eighth freedom rights (Schlumberger 2010).[7] Member countries of the Association of Southeast Asian Nations (ASEAN) have also been gradually moving toward the implementation of an open skies agreement. It is planned that by 2015, an open skies agreement with unlimited 5th freedom rights—and without restrictions on frequency, pricing, and type of airlines—should be fully enforced. Monitoring current progress, however, this seems less likely to be achieved in this time frame (CAPA 2013a). There are also a number of RECs in Africa that have achieved some progress in liberalizing air transport, including the Arab Maghreb Union (AMU), the West African Economic and Monetary Union (WAEMU), and the Economic Community of Central African States (CEMAC) (Schlumberger 2010).

The implementation of regional agreements would be of significant benefit for LCCs, as it would open several secondary city pairs that are currently not served by network airlines and where LCCs could operate successfully with their business model. In the case of Southeast Asia, for example, many of the region's routes are short- to medium-haul, and can be operated by single-aisle aircraft such as A320 and B737 aircraft (Forsyth, King, and Rodolfo 2006; Zhang and others 2008).

Labor

As labor represents a substantial component of the LCC cost structure, the availability and cost of qualified staff, as well as a regulatory environment conducive to efficient labor utilization, are crucial to the development of LCCs.

The availability of qualified staff is a particular concern in developing countries where there is significant lack of experienced personnel, including pilots, crews, air traffic controllers, ground handling staff, aircraft maintenance, and many other vital human components of the air transport system. Many of these roles require a highly qualified workforce and a significant amount of training, which is often not available.

Even in more developed regions, a lack of pilots has become a particular concern. Boeing estimated in its "Pilot and Technician Outlook" that about one million new commercial airline pilots and maintenance technicians will be needed by 2031 (Boeing 2012). This includes 460,000 new commercial airline pilots and 601,000 maintenance technicians. Similar predictions have been made by ICAO, stating that with 151,000 aircraft expected to be in operation by 2030, 980,000 pilots will be required in the market—double the number there is today (ICAO 2011). This translates to 52,000 additional pilots per year, as compared with a total of 44,354 currently. The difference of 8,146 pilots a year will likely result in longer working hours, which may become a safety problem given pilot fatigue. This will be a particular issue for regions where air traffic is increasing rapidly, such as Asia Pacific (with a 9,048 shortfall per year), Latin America (4,305), and the Middle East (1,598). India alone is expected to require 1,150 new commercial planes over the next two decades (Boeing 2012), and China has just approved the building of 69 new regional airports by 2015 (CAPA 2013b). The impact of these shortages can already been seen in Asia, where delays and operational interruptions have been common due to pilot scheduling constraints. Similarly, there is an annual shortfall of maintenance and ATC personnel, although interestingly both the Latin America and the Africa regions currently appear to have a surplus of the latter (Coulter 2012).

A key reason for this shortage is the lack of adequate training facilities, and the high cost of training. In Asia, where demand is particularly high, the market for flight training facilities is still very fragmented with a significant number of smaller, mostly unsustainable flight schools. Many of these have already closed, and the ones still operating have a shortage of certified flight instructors (CFIs), airplanes, and appropriate equipment (Frost and Sullivan Market Insight 2007). Fortunately some larger independent flight schools are expanding rapidly across the region in response to the surging demand. Although these tend to reduce costs, they increasingly face training issues with regard to limited flying slots at larger airports and lack of air space. This hinders the development of large-scale local training programs, and forces aspiring pilots to rely on limited, often externally funded training opportunities abroad. These foreign-trained pilots often do not return to their country of origin because of more attractive working conditions abroad.

Unfortunately, the lack of pilots has also led to a rise in the number of unqualified aviation personnel taking to the skies. As a report issued by the Ministry of Transport in Tanzania highlighted, this shortage of pilots has increased the number of "unqualified pilot accidents," and in India several pilots' licenses had to be revoked in 2011 due to falsification of records (Arun 2011). Ensuring high quality standards is an issue that will need to be handled through better enforcement of regulations.

These problems have forced more established airlines in developing countries to find pilots abroad. Indonesia's Susi Air, for example, relies entirely on foreign pilots, which were able to be hired given the economic crisis in Europe and the United States. However, having recognized the issues this may pose in the future, the government is fostering the development of two new flight schools in addition to the 13 already in operation. The country's Ministry of Transport is also working with the private sector and the Indonesian National Air Carrier Association (INACA) to organize conferences on airport development, airline technology, and aviation training and education (Schonhardt 2012).

The limited supply of qualified staff and higher training costs often translate into higher cost for airlines. In some cases, this is further aggravated by unfavorable regulations and labor laws in developing countries. This could include, for example, limiting restrictions to working hours, the mandatory use of overly expensive social security systems, high labor taxes, or very high minimum wages. In Tanzania, labor costs often represent a high percentage of the overall operating costs of firms due to gaps in labor laws, for example, retrenchment procedures or remedies for unfair termination (Association of Tanzania Employers 2011).

In Europe, stringent labor regulations and high levels of government and union interventions have played an important role in the creation of LCCs. Both Ryanair and easyJet have purposely chosen to base their operations in England, despite the fact that most of their operations are located across Europe. The airlines have also been involved in legal battles in France where they have tried to avoid restrictive labor regulations by contracting all of their staff, including those based in France, under British labor law (Peanuts! 2007). French labor law is seen by many institutions, such as the Organisation for Economic Co-operation and Development (OECD) and the European Central Bank, as overly regulated, hindering the productivity of the labor market (Carnegy 2013). Although many LCCs have pointed to their general avoidance of unions as a factor in labor productivity, as highlighted in chapter 1, this has not been proved in the literature (Belobaba, Odoni, and Barnhart 2009).

The International Finance Corporation (IFC) and World Bank *Enterprise Surveys* has served as a good indicator for identifying overregulated labor markets. Based on a firm-level survey of a representative sample of an economy's private sector, the survey measures labor regulation across the world by quantifying the number of firms that identify labor regulation as a major constraint to their operations (World Bank and IFC 2013). Figure 4.4 shows that many developing countries still face constrained labor environments that could hinder the development of the private sector, and consequently the market for LCCs.

In addition, the World Bank's *Doing Business* report (World Bank 2013a) measures business regulations and their enforcement across 185 economies and selected cities at the subnational and regional level. As part of its country-level assessments, the report also measures flexibility in the regulation of employment

Figure 4.4 Percentage of Firms Identifying Labor Regulation as a Major Constraint

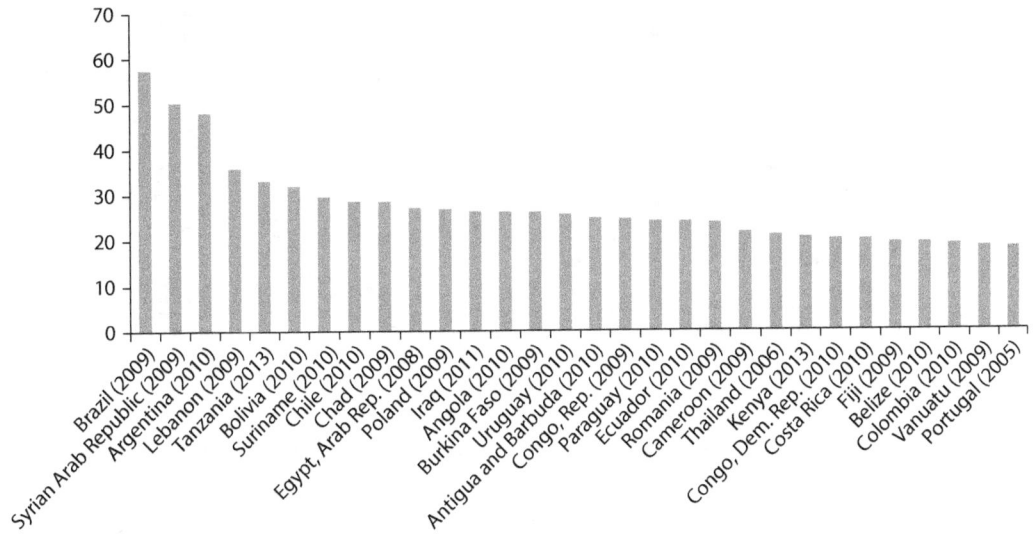

Source: World Bank and IFC *Enterprise Survey* 2013.

as it affects hiring and redundancy of workers and the rigidity of working hours—all of crucial importance for businesses.

Safety and Security

Adequate safety and security standards are of critical importance for air operations as technical malfunctions, human errors, and equipment failures can have catastrophic consequences. Due to the nature of air travel, the loss of human life is often greater per single occurrence compared to car or train accidents. The state of air transport safety and security in a country also plays a critical role with regard to aircraft financing and insurance as the cost of purchasing or leasing aircraft can be significantly higher when standards are perceived to be inadequate in the markets in which they operate (World Bank 2011). Indeed, aircraft manufacturers may be reluctant to sell aircraft due to reputational risk.

Although the aviation industry has come a long way to ensuring safe air travel, aviation safety still remains a major issue in the developing world, particularly in Africa and Asia (see table 4.4). While Africa only accounted for 5 percent of total accidents in 2012, 45 percent of all fatalities occurred in the region, and it still has the largest number of accidents per million passengers. Although the percentage of fatalities is followed closely by Asia, the region has a significantly lower overall accident rate.

The higher number of accidents can be attributed to various factors such as operational shortfalls, insufficient and defective equipment, inadequate maintenance of aircraft, poor oversight, and/or lack of properly trained staff.

Table 4.4 Accident Statistics and Accident Rates, 2012

UN Region	Accidents	Accident rate	Fatal accidents	Fatalities	Percent accidents	Percent fatal accidents	Percent fatalities
Africa	5	4.8	2	167	5	22	45
Asia	23	2.7	3	161	23	33	43
Europe	30	4.2	3	42	30	33	11
Latin America and the Caribbean	12	3.8	1	2	12	12	1
North America	29	2.8	0	0	30	0	0
Oceania	0	0.0	0	0	0	0	0
World	99	3.2	9	372	n.a.	n.a.	n.a.

Source: International Civil Aviation Organization (ICAO 2013b).
Note: n.a. = not applicable; UN = United Nations.

These derive primarily from a lack of adequate infrastructure, insufficiently trained human resources, and, most importantly, poor oversight.

The regulation of safety and security by the CAA plays an important role in verifying that the nationally registered carriers and airports comply with required safety and security standards. In order to assess the effectiveness of a country's safety and security oversight capacity, ICAO has established the Universal Safety Oversight Audit Programme (USOAP). Under the USOAP, so-called ICAO comprehensive system approach (CSA) audits are conducted by assessing eight critical elements which are considered essential for a state to establish, implement, and maintain an effective safety oversight system. These include

- *Primary aviation legislation:* the establishment of civil aviation legislation that supports the state's civil aviation system and regulatory functions in compliance with the Convention on International Civil Aviation (Chicago Convention).
- *Specific operating regulations:* the establishment of aeronautical regulations (rules) addressing all aviation activities, and implementing applicable ICAO provisions and standards and recommended practices (SARPs).
- *State's civil aviation system and safety oversight functions:* the establishment of a CAA or other authorities with safety regulatory functions, objectives, and safety policies, provided with sufficient financial resources and qualified staff.
- *Technical personnel qualification and training:* the establishment of minimum requirements for knowledge and experience of the technical personnel performing safety oversight functions, and the provision of appropriate training to maintain and enhance their competency at the desired level.
- *Technical guidance, tools, and the provision of safety critical information:* the provision of procedures and guidelines, adequate facilities and equipment, and safety critical information to the technical personnel to enable them to perform their safety oversight functions; this includes the provision of technical guidance to the aviation industry on the implementation of regulations and instructions.

- *Licensing, certification, authorization, and approval obligations:* the implementation of systems to ensure that personnel and organizations performing an aviation activity meet the established requirements before they are allowed to exercise the privileges of holding a license, certificate, authorization, and/or approval.
- *Surveillance obligations:* the implementation of a continuous surveillance program consisting of inspections and audits to ensure that aviation licenses, certificates, authorization, and/or approval holders continue to meet the established requirements and functions at the level of competency and safety as required by the state.
- *Resolution of safety concerns:* the implementation of processes and procedures to resolve identified deficiencies impacting aviation safety, which may have been residing in the system, and been detected by the regulatory authority or other appropriate bodies.

The audit looks across eight key areas for safety including legislation and regulation, civil aviation organization, personnel licensing and training, aircraft operations, airworthiness of aircraft,[8] aircraft accident and incident investigation, air navigation services, and aerodromes and ground aids (ICAO n.d.).

As map 4.1 shows, many developing countries still maintain poor safety oversight, with limited or negligible regulation. This allows carriers and airports to operate without complying with safety standards. Historically, the so-called CSA audits were conducted under USOAP only at a specific point in time and to be repeated after a number of years. Trying to monitor safety oversight performance on a more continuous basis, ICAO has now moved toward implementing a continuous monitoring approach (CMA).

Map 4.1 USOAP Results, 2012

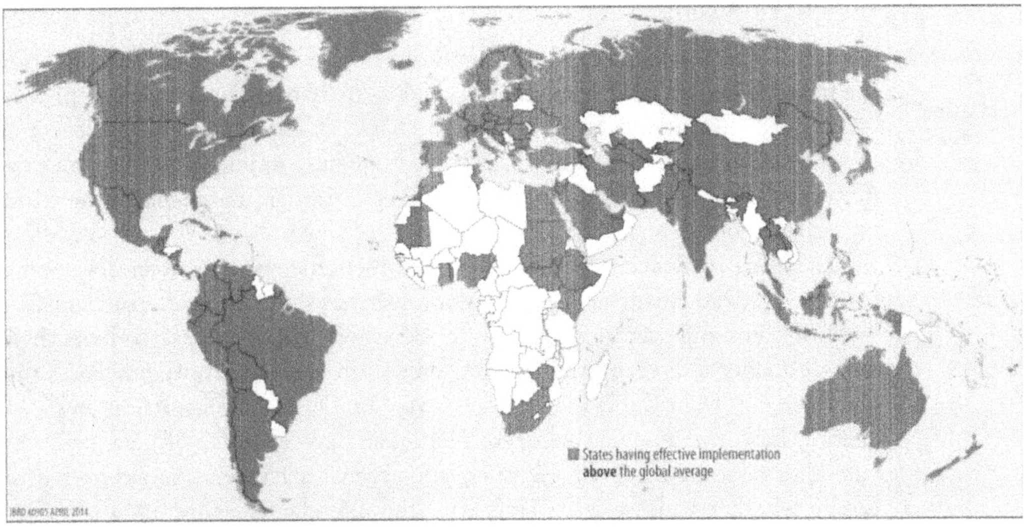

Source: International Civil Aviation Organization (ICAO 2013b).
Note: USOAP = Universal Safety Oversight Audit Programme.

To assess security oversight, ICAO has established a Universal Security Audit Programme (USAP), which measures the capacity of civil aviation authorities to oversee the enforcement of security standards. After decades of declining security challenges, the events of September 11, 2001, made security a renewed concern for some airports. The necessary infrastructure and principally the right training and enforcement, are required to ensure security at airports and on-board the aircraft.

Distribution

A cost-efficient network to advertise and sell air services is crucial for LCCs. Airline tickets are traditionally sold through travel agents, call centers, and global distribution systems (GDSs), all of which normally come at a considerable cost. As elaborated in chapter 1, LCCs try to avoid these expensive distribution channels and focus primarily on direct selling over the Internet. This represents a considerable cost saving. In order to realize the benefits of direct selling, the availability and quality of information and communications technology (ICT) infrastructure, as well as credit card market penetration, are major factors.

Internet penetration is still very low in most developing countries, and reliance is therefore much higher on costly travel and tourism agents. Although this has been identified as an important factor for LCC development, carriers have often found alternative ways of addressing this challenge. Nok Air in Thailand, for example, has used a mix of distribution channels including cash machines, convenience stores such as 7-Elevens, and even movie rental shops. Similarly, Mango in South Africa has used retail stores and bus operators as sales channels (Sobie 2006). This not only reduces costs, but also makes the purchasing process more accessible for customers.

Aircraft Financing

The financing of aircraft can be a significant hurdle for new carriers because of the required capital intensity and associated industry risk. Due to the complexity of aircraft financing mechanisms, only the basics of aircraft finance are covered here. The highlights of some of the most frequently applied financing mechanisms and their accessibility for developing countries are discussed below. Most importantly, however, this section examines the new policy measures to address the challenge of financing newer and more fuel-efficient aircraft in developing countries. Indeed, financing plays a major role in the setup and success of an LCC.

Most commonly, airlines have to decide whether to purchase or lease their aircraft. Under a direct purchase arrangement, the airline simply purchases the plane directly from the manufacturer or vendor. Due to the capital intensity of aircraft, however, many airlines resort to leasing agreements with leasing companies, or in some cases directly with aircraft manufacturers. An airline has to decide whether to lease an aircraft with the attendant responsibility of maintenance, registration, and insurance being with the lessee. This is a so-called dry lease, whereas a wet lease includes crew, maintenance, and insurance. There are various kinds of leasing agreements in the market today, the most common are finance leases and operating leases. Wet leases are normally operating leases, whereas dry leases can be either in the form of a finance or operating lease (Vasigh, Taleghani, and Jenkins 2012).

Finance leases are long-term, noncancellable lease contracts. The nature of a finance lease is such that the lessor typically agrees to transfer the title of the asset to the lessee at the end of the lease period at a nominal cost. The lessee normally bears the cost of maintenance, insurance, and repairs with only the title of the aircraft remaining with the lessor. In an operating lease, a lessor acquires or already owns an aircraft and leases it to an airline over a set period of time. This type of lease is mostly short term (less than 10 years), and allows carriers a certain level of flexibility in up- or downscaling their operations. There are also so-called "sale-and-lease-back" arrangements. In a sale-and-lease-back contract, an airline sells its aircraft and immediately enters into a leasing agreement with the purchaser (Vasigh, Taleghani, and Jenkins 2012).

Although some airlines have the capital available to pay for the direct financing or leasing of their aircraft in cash, over two-thirds of aircraft financing relies on other financing mechanisms (see figure 4.5) (PWC 2013).

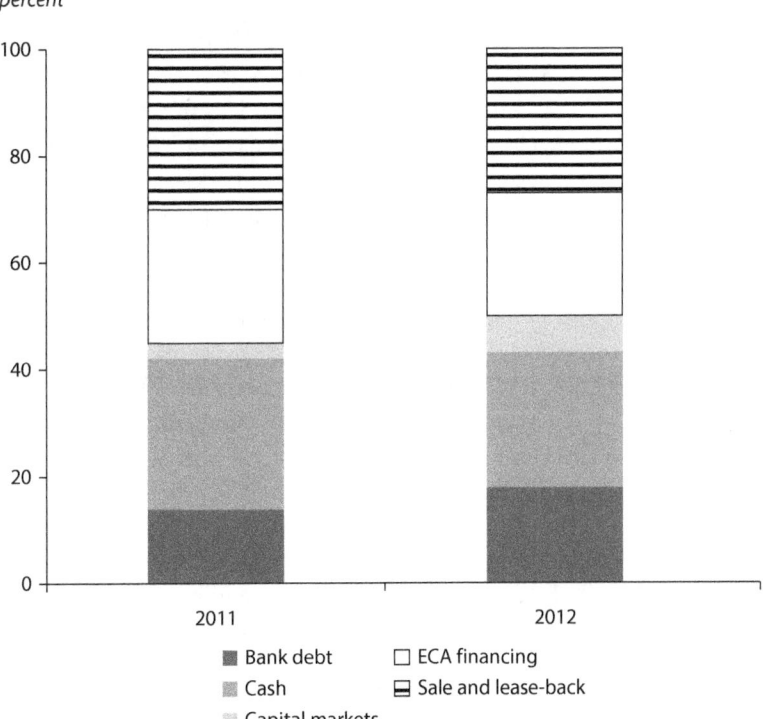

Figure 4.5 Aircraft Financing: 2011 versus 2012
percent

Source: Reproduced from PricewaterhouseCoopers, *Aviation Finance* (PwC 2013).
Note: The figure also captures sale and lease-back, which refers to a self-funding purchase by the lessors. ECA financing refers to financing obtained through export credit agencies (ECAs). Manufacturers' supported aircraft finance appears negligible and therefore is not shown in the graph.

The most common mechanisms for financing aircraft include bank loans/lease financing, export credit guaranteed loans and credits, manufacturer support, enhanced equipment trust certificates (EETC), Islamic finance, and loans from development banks such as the World Bank and other regional development banks. Table 4.5 summarizes some of the key elements, accessibility, and challenges of each financing type (Vasigh, Taleghani, and Jenkins 2012).

Any aircraft financier/investor, regardless of the mechanism applied, aims to minimize exposure to potential risk resulting from debtor failure (U.S. Department of Transportation 2004). This requires a legal system that has the ability to protect the financier's title, security interests,[9] and ensure enforcement (Bunker 1989). In the case of aircraft financing, this risk exposure is further aggravated by the mobility of aircraft being able to move across borders with varying legal systems.

The weakness of many legal systems, and the generally volatile environments in developing countries, increase this risk considerably. This leads aircraft financiers to restrict their exposure or to significantly increase financing costs for airlines in developing countries. The World Bank's *Doing Business* report (World Bank 2013a) serves as a good measure for the protection of lenders and borrowers in a given country. It provides a review of the legal rights of both parties in secured transactions as well as bankruptcy laws.

In addition to the high cost of financing, airlines in most developing countries face the disadvantage of a lack of economies of scale due to their smaller size operations, resulting in less favorable purchasing conditions. Larger LCCs, such as Ryanair, have been able to negotiate much lower prices due to their purchasing power. In 2013, Ryanair claimed that for its order of 175 Boeing 737 aircraft, the airline managed to negotiate its prices down to the level of its acquisition of a similar purchase arrangement in 2005. The carrier apparently only paid about 50 percent of the aircraft's list price in 2005 (Tobin 2013).

The most important initiative to address the challenge of aircraft finance has been the 2001 Cape Town Convention on "International Interests in Mobile Equipment," and the associated "Protocol to the Convention on International Interests in Mobile Equipment on Matters Specific to Aircraft Equipment." This Convention enables the financing of aircraft by "providing creditors with an internationally recognized set of rights in the event of a debtor's default or insolvency, and is allowing creditors to register their interests in an international register to guarantee the priority of their claim against other parties" (Government of Australia, Department of Infrastructure and Transport 2013). It includes, for example, the right of a lender to deregister aircraft and procure its export upon default of a debtor or to take possession or control of aircraft. As of March 2012, the protocol had 44 contracting states (see map 4.2).

The ratification of the Cape Town Convention should increase accessibility to funding and reduce associated costs for airlines. In the case of Boeing aircraft purchases, for example, the U.S. Export-Import Bank offers discounts on its exposure fees and longer-term finance for U.S. manufactured engines to airlines in countries that have ratified the Cape Town Convention. Furthermore, it

Table 4.5 Aircraft Financing Sources and Mechanisms

Finance mechanism type	Mechanism	Source	Accessibility for developing countries	Recent challenges
Commercial bank loan or lease finance	Commercial bank loan or lease financing with aircraft as collateral	Commercial bank	**Low** High interest rates due to high-risk environments of developing countries	Since the global financial crisis many banks, particularly in France, significantly reduced exposure to aircraft financing, perceived as a high-risk domain. The number of banks competing for aircraft financing fell globally from 15 down to 5 in some cases (Mueller 2012).
Export credit, insurance cover or guarantees (political and commercial)	Either direct credit from export credit agency (ECA) or guarantee/insurance to obtain loans from commercial sources	ECA	**High** Offer lower interest rates, as objective of ECA is to stimulate export financing for their national companies to realize export opportunities	ECAs replaced much of the aircraft financing of commercial banks since the start of the global financial crisis. In recent years, ECAs also increasingly finance more profitable carriers in developed countries. This led to claims that ECAs had distorted the aircraft financing market and stopped focusing on their intended purpose of helping weaker airlines. Consequently, the industry demanded that the ECA rates be increased. As part of the aircraft sector understanding (ASU), an agreement instigated by the Organisation for Economic Co-operation and Development (OECD) in 2011, ECA credit rates increased significantly. For airlines with BB and BB+ credit ratings, often encountered in developing countries, interest rates of up to 10 percent are common nowadays (Mueller 2011).
Manufacturer support	Support from aircraft manufacturer through direct finance, operating leases (rather than through costly lessors), or aircraft guarantees	Aircraft manufacturers, for example, Boeing Capital	**Low** High risk for aircraft manufacturer	Only little manufacturer support, less than 1 percent in 2012
Islamic finance	Interest free loans and lease finance (Ijara)	Islamic banks	**Medium** Accessible to carriers primarily in the Middle East	
Enhanced equipment trust certificate (EETC)	Special company set up by airlines that issue bonds to finance aircraft	Special purpose vehicles (SPVs)	**Low** Currently only used for U.S. carriers, but first non-U.S. airline, Emirates, financed through EETC	
Development bank loan	International development banks providing loans for aircraft finance	International Finance Corporation (IFC); regional development banks	**High** Affordable interest rates and special conditions	

Map 4.2 Ratification of Cape Town Convention

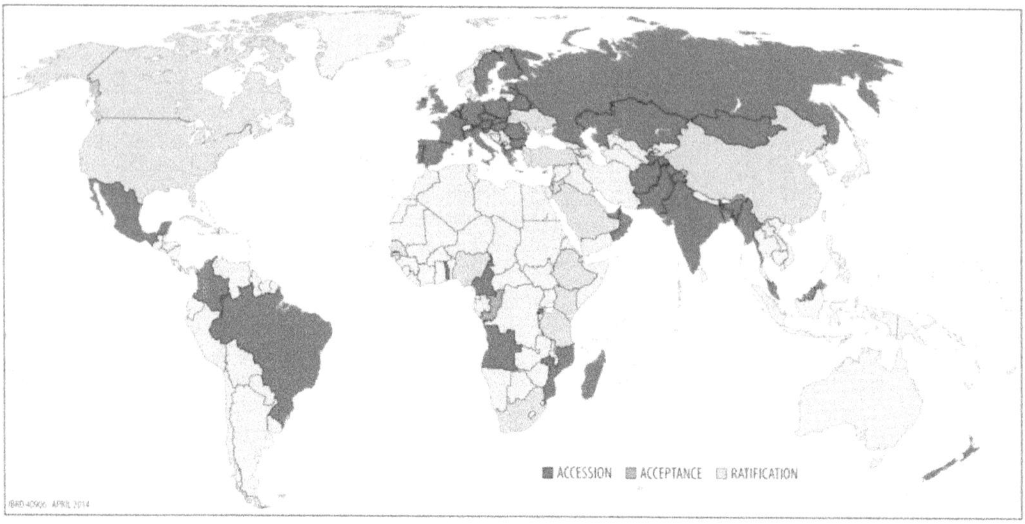

Source: Map based on information from Unidroit (International Institute for the Unification of Private Law n.d.).

provides favorable terms when both lessor and lessee country have endorsed the convention in their contractual frameworks (Hewitt 2009). Through ratification of the Cape Town Convention, EETCs are also expected to become more available to non-U.S. airlines in the future (Gewirtz 2011). This will particularly benefit developing countries, which have been unable to access commercial credit markets or have had to pay very high interest rates (U.S. Department of Transportation 2004).

Stronger carriers in developing countries also increasingly support smaller carriers in their region with regard to aircraft financing. Ethiopian Airlines has, for example, been involved with ASKY, a passenger airline in Togo, through a management contract. The contract provides the airline with managerial support and facilitates aircraft financing (Davidson 2012).

Fuel

The cost of fuel is a crucial, if not the most crucial factor impacting the profitability of low-cost airlines and the aviation industry in general. IATA estimated that the industry's fuel bill amounted to US$213 billion in 2013 (IATA 2013b). As fuel represents between 35 to 40 percent of direct operating costs, inflated fuel costs can therefore be detrimental (Vasigh, Fleming, and Tacker). Many of the factors influencing jet fuel prices, such as the cost of crude oil, increased international energy demand, and a stagnating supply of oil will impact airlines on a global level. However, these conditions can also vary on a local level due to taxation, government regulations as well as foreign exchange, geographic location, infrastructure, distribution channels, or local competition (Caltex Petroleum n.d.).

Landlocked countries, for instance, have faced higher costs and endured longer waits for fuel due to the lack of direct access to ports. Malawi, for example, imports all of its fuel through either Mozambique or Tanzania by rail and truck. Because of the high transport costs, as well as high levies, taxes, duties, and other costs, the inbound landed price for gasoline quadruples from the port in Dar es Salaam until it's sold (Mitchell 2011). Zambia has had to pay as much as 50 percent more for fuel than in other countries in the region, even before the recent oil price jumps (World Bank 2008).

Taxation and customs duties are other key factors, which can increase fuel costs. Under ICAO's policies on aviation fuel, it is clearly stated, "Aviation fuel used in the provision of international air transportation services is exempt from federal customs duties and excise taxes" (ICAO 2009). However, in accordance with Article 24 of the policy, this applies only to charging duty on aviation fuel already on board any aircraft that has arrived in a territory from another contracting state of the Chicago Convention. Furthermore, the exemption of airlines from national taxes and customs duties on a range of aviation-related goods, including parts, stores, and fuel is a principle that is anchored in most bilateral ASAs between individual countries.

However, many countries do not comply with this regulation. In India, for example, all fuel is subject to an 8.24 percent excise duty, and state fuel taxes of up to 30 percent on domestic flights, incurring considerably higher costs for airlines (Asiana Aviation 2012). In Africa, according to IATA, aviation fuel is about 21 percent more expensive than the global average, partly because of government taxation (IATA 2013c).

Governance

A final, very important criterion concerns an issue that is fundamental for every industry: good governance. Good governance has been defined in various manners by the World Bank and other institutions. The essence of good governance in the context of this book lies in creating an operating environment in which "the process of decision-making and the process by which decisions are implemented (or not implemented)" (UNESCAP 2013) are not an impediment to the establishment and growth of an industry or company.

The lack of good governance on a national, but also on an airport and airline, level has proved to hamper the development of air services in developing countries considerably. This has often resulted in hesitation of foreign companies to invest and bring the much needed managerial skills into the market. State ownership of the national airline and the resulting favorable conditions for the carrier have been a particularly prevalent example of bad governance in developing countries.

An often-cited example is the case of Virgin Nigeria. The joint venture between the now defunct Nigeria Airways and the Virgin Group started operations out of Lagos in 2004, but had to withdraw in 2008. The exit was triggered by a dispute over the relocation of the airline to the remote new Terminal 2, despite a clear memorandum of understanding granting the airline the rights to operate from the original terminal. The reasons for the failure of the carrier have often been linked to a nontransparent environment (Thome 2008).

Many organizations have produced measures for governance, covering various viewpoints and a wide scope of specific indicators. Some, such as the Economist Intelligence Unit (Economist Intelligence Unit 2013) or the Global Competitiveness Report (WEF 2013), predominantly measure indicators linked to economic development, whereas others, such as the International Country Risk Guide (ICRG) (PRS Group 2013), are concerned with challenges pertaining to businesses and investors. Many measures look at a multidimensional assessment of governance, whereas some focus on only one indicator such as the Perceived Corruption Index of Transparency International. The World Bank, together with the Brookings Institution, has developed its own measures, building upon some of the elements of the other indexes named above. The Worldwide Governance Indicators (WGI) Project looks at six different indicators including voice and accountability, political stability and absence of violence, government effectiveness, regulatory quality, rule of law, and control of corruption. A total of 215 economies have been assessed (World Bank 2013c).

What Matters Most?

All of the above-mentioned factors play a key role in the development of LCCs, but it is important to prioritize between the "make-or-break" and the potentially less essential market characteristics. Some elements are undeniably prerequisite—such as demand, deregulated air transport markets, and good governance. However, measuring the role of other, more operational, characteristics can be more complex and needs to take into account a multitude of country-specific factors. One approach to identifying their importance is to quantify the cost-reducing factors in the LCC business model discussed in chapter 1, and to link these directly to the elements outlined above. Based on information published by the consultancy KPMG's *Airline Disclosure Handbook* (KPMG 2013), figure 4.6 shows the typical breakdown of LCC cost advantages.

Figure 4.6 shows that fuel cost advantages still play a key role in the LCC cost structure, despite the convergence in fuel expenditures between network carriers and LCCs mentioned in chapter 1. Being able to obtain newer fuel-efficient aircraft and not being burdened by high taxation and stringent regulations on fuel is therefore crucial. The former is also intrinsically linked to safety oversight as it has a considerable impact on aircraft financing costs. The importance of aircraft type and its financing is further stressed by cost reductions related to depreciation, amortization, and operating leases.

Of equal importance are costs related to labor. The sample of LCCs shows that around 21 percent of their cost advantage comes from labor costs, making the required availability of human resources and favorable labor conditions paramount. This is followed by sales and marketing linked to inexpensive

Figure 4.6 Cost Advantage by Element, 2011
percentage of cost per available seat kilometers

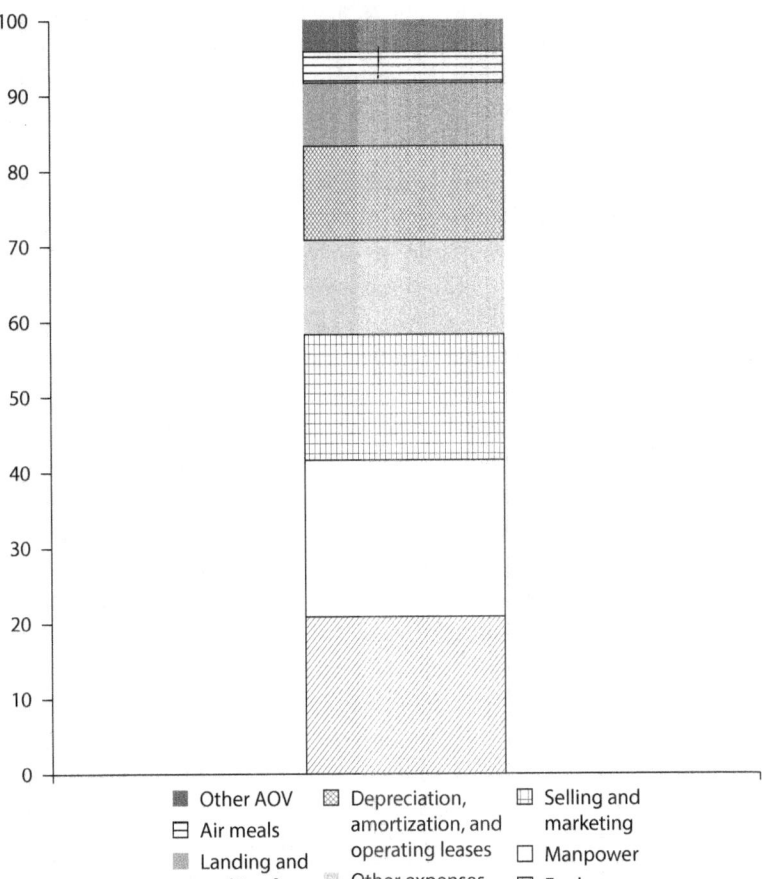

Source: Based on information from KPMG *Airline Disclosure Handbook* (Ramsay 2013).
Note: Airline operating variable (AOV) represents other operating costs. The sample compares 25 legacy carriers and 6 LCCs from Asia, Latin America, North America, the Middle East, and Europe.

distribution channels. Landing and parking fees can also comprise considerable cost savings. Interestingly, cost advantages derived from a reduced service offering, represented here as "air meals," are relatively low.

In order to assess the actual statistical significance of certain market criteria on a route rather than market environment level, the next section examines LCC market entry behavior through the example of the Arab Republic of Egypt.

To Enter or Not to Enter? A Market Entry Model for an LCC in Egypt

Airline networks are built upon a series of sequential decisions that involve market entry and exit. Along with other elements (for example, product type to be offered, value proposition to customers, competitive advantages over other carriers, organization of operations to deliver highest value at the lowest possible cost), the choice of geographical markets in which to operate is at the core of any carrier's competitive strategy (Holloway 2008). In making these decisions, management has to, among other things, assess the attractiveness of candidate markets. A simplified vision of this process assumes that the expected profitability in a particular market is a key determinant in an airline's entry decision. This may ultimately depend on demand conditions, intensity of competition, and the extent of sunk costs and barriers to entry.

Low-cost airline market entry behavior is well documented for U.S. LCCs. Evidence for the case of Southwest Airlines, for example, indicates that high passenger density, short distances, lower income areas, prior airport presence, and lack of within-route competition are core determinants of market presence (Boguslaski, Ito, and Lee 2004). However, LCC entry behavior in middle- and low-income countries has not been studied in great detail, with a few exceptions (for example, Brazil; see Oliveira 2008). In lesser-developed economies, market characteristics and regulations can radically depart from those found in high-income countries. To understand how LCCs have adapted (if at all) their entry strategies to cope with changing environments around the world is no longer a purely research-oriented question. In turn, this issue is key to understanding how the low-cost air transport market in developing countries can serve as a catalyst for higher economic growth.

Egypt presents an interesting case study for LCC entry behavior. With a total population of over 80 million inhabitants, more than 12 million tourist arrivals per year, and strong migratory, cultural, and business links with the Arab world, LCC penetration in Egypt is still a relatively new phenomenon. In June 2010, Air Arabia Egypt (AAE)—a joint venture between Air Arabia and a local travel company—started its low-cost operations out of the city of Alexandria (and previously from the cities of Luxor, Asyut, and Sohag). Its main destinations have been concentrated almost exclusively in the Middle East. Based on their observed route entry patterns, a city pair airline entry model was built following the empirical work put forward by Oliveira (2008); Müller, Bilotkach, and Huschelrath (2011); Lederman and Januszewski (2003); and Boguslaski, Ito, and Lee (2004).

The underlying theoretical framework assumes that an airline will enter a route if the expected net profits from serving that route are positive. In the model, a latent variable captures the expected profitability[10]—one that cannot be directly observed ex-ante—but instead inferred from other variables that can be directly observed. Hence, a probit regression estimates the likelihood of a positive outcome in the latent variable,[11] associated with LCC route entry in a particular airport pair. This probability is determined by market-specific characteristics at the airport, city, and country level, including demand factors, the extent of competition intensity, and barriers to entry, among others. Dummy variables by time period are used as well to control for any unobserved common shocks.[12]

The data set is constructed using monthly airline schedule information between 2007 and 2013, available from commercial vendors (DiiO SRS Analyzer 2013). The binary dependent variable takes a unitary value when AAE enters a route previously not served.[13] With regard to the explanatory variables in the model,[14] demand characteristics include GDP per capita at the destination airport (taken from World Bank development indicators), distance between origin and destination airports (CEPII bilateral data set; CEPII 2013), and dummy variables for seasonal and religious dates to specific destinations (for example, the *Hajj* or pilgrimage to Mecca). A dummy variable controlling for common ethnic and cultural ties at origin and destination was built using the CEPII bilateral data set. At the same time, bilateral migratory flows were obtained from the World Bank's Bilateral Migration Database. Meanwhile, for concentration measures like route-level and destination airport, Herfindahl indexes were put together using schedule data.[15] Finally, entry barrier measures, such as the level of slot coordination at destination airports, were obtained from IATA (n.d.).

The model aims to understand how different explanatory variables (size and type of demand, competition, barriers to entry, and so on) affect the probability of a positive outcome, that is, the entry of the carrier, as identified with AAE's market presence on a particular route. The most important results generated from the model are highlighted in table 4.6.

Regarding demand characteristics, results indicate that higher market density (proxied by scheduled capacity in seats) and higher purchasing power at the destination country (measured by per capita GDP) are positively correlated with AAE's city pair entry decisions. Longer distances, as found in similar studies, deter LCC entry. Meanwhile, other factors such as larger migratory flows (number of migrants living abroad), as well as the extent of cultural and ethnic ties between origin and destination, seem to increase the likelihood of low-cost airline entry. Furthermore, increased air travel demand associated with religious pilgrimage destinations (that is, Mecca in Saudi Arabia) is also positively linked to LCC presence.

With regard to competition and its effect on LCC market presence, route-level concentration is seemingly associated with low-cost operator route entry. A higher concentration may indicate less competition, and consequently higher margins and larger expected benefits from entry. However, capacity concentration at the destination airport acts as a deterrent for entry. The latter might be explained by, among other things, the higher likelihood of encountering a dominant incumbent carrier at the destination willing to react more aggressively to AAE's entry. Interestingly, the presence of other LCCs did not seem to discourage AAE from entering a route. Regression analysis also indicates that the availability of competing charter services greatly reduces the likelihood of LCC presence in the same market. At the same time, higher availability of flights connecting over EgyptAir's hub in Cairo reduces the likelihood of LCC presence when competing in the same origin and destination markets.[16]

Finally, sunk costs and other entry barriers seem to have an effect on an LCC's decision to operate a route, as observed from AAE's paradigm. In addition to the seemingly restricted access to the domestic market for LCCs, slot-controlled destination airports are also less likely to attract AAE, as they are usually more expensive to operate in, have longer turnaround times, and are more prone to delays.

Table 4.6 Key Results Entry Behavior Model

Time dummy	Year	Quarter	Month
GDP	0.0973*	−0.0405	0.0876*
	(0.0512)	(0.0498)	(0.0519)
Other LCC presence	0.611***	0.587***	0.634***
	(0.0776)	(0.0748)	(0.078)
Seat density	0.166***	0.156***	0.150***
	(0.0365)	(0.0353)	(0.0373)
Route concentration (HHI)	0.177*	0.183*	0.139
	(0.102)	(0.0995)	(0.105)
Destination airport concentration (HHI)	−0.514***	−0.501***	−0.536***
	(0.0528)	(0.0518)	(0.0539)
Route distance	−0.883***	−0.839***	−0.884***
	(0.0503)	(0.0492)	(0.051)
Connecting service EgyptAir (via CAI)	1.956***	1.751***	2.007***
	(0.139)	(0.134)	(0.145)
Volume connect service EgyptAir (via CAI)	−0.204***	−0.186***	−0.218***
	(0.0254)	(0.0249)	(0.0267)
Option of second airport at destination	−0.278	−0.331*	−0.282
	(0.18)	(0.179)	(0.185)
Internet penetration	−0.135	0.292***	−0.114
	(0.0876)	(0.0854)	(0.0894)
Migration volumes	0.00857	0.00432	0.0102[a]
	(0.00582)	(0.0057)	(0.00589)
Hajj pilgrimage	0.774***	0.764***	0.824***
	(0.22)	(0.218)	(0.228)
Holiday season	−0.0795	−0.00633	−3.995***
	(0.111)	(0.116)	(1.154)
Domestic services	−2.454***	−2.299***	−2.417***
	(0.252)	(0.245)	(0.255)
Common ethnicity between origin and destination	1.136***	1.176***	1.142***
	(0.102)	(0.0985)	(0.104)
Slot control at destination airport	−0.0217*	−0.0252**	−0.0197*
	(0.0113)	(0.011)	(0.0115)
Competing charter services on same route	−0.157**	−5.123***	−5.014***
	(0.0751)	(1.063)	(1.167)
Observations	14645	14645	14645

Source: Daniel Saslavsky, trade specialist, the World Bank.
Note: Standard errors in parentheses. CAI = Cairo International Airport; GDP = gross domestic product; HHI = Herfindahl-Hirschman Index; LCC = low-cost carrier.
***$p<0.01$, **$p<0.05$, *$p<0.1$.

As a final step, a prediction as to how likely an LCC following AAE's paradigm might enter a specific city pair can be computed using the same model.[17] This exercise takes all domestic and international routes flown into/out of Egypt and predicts the probability of entry in each case, depending on route and country-level conditions related to demand, competition, and other factors.

Routes such as: Taba–Aqaba, Egypt; Sharm el Sheik–Amman, Jordan; Sharm el Sheik–Jeddah, Saudi Arabia; Sharm el Sheik–Kuwait; Luxor–Doha, Qatar; Luxor–Medina, Saudi Arabia; Luxor–Dubai, the United Arab Emirates (UAE);[18] Hurghada–Kuwait; Asyut–Dubai, UAE; and Alexandria–Damman, Saudi Arabia, are the routes with the highest chances of being served by a low-cost operator based on AAE's observed route entry patterns.

Conclusion

Identifying a suitable framework for LCC market entry can be challenging. As market conditions are different across the globe, finding the one formula for success for LCCs has proven to be difficult. Therefore, throughout this chapter, a variety of conditions have been identified that should be taken into consideration when assessing if a country has the right conditions for LCCs to develop and succeed.

In developing countries, LCCs may face a significant number of obstacles to entry. As illustrated by means of a few examples, certain challenges can be significant to LCC growth in developing countries. Many regions of the world are still lagging behind in creating a sound environment for the development of air transport, and in particular for LCC entry.

Weighing the costs. The importance of each of these conditions varies significantly. Factors influencing fuel and labor costs play the most important role, followed by the availability of distribution channels and infrastructure conditions. LCCs have found various ways to circumvent restrictions, but will need to weigh the costs that these alternatives will incur. Empirical evidence for the market in Egypt provides an indication of the statistical importance of certain criteria for the entry of LCCs on a given route. Route concentration is, for example, positively associated with LCC entry. However, capacity concentration at the destination airport as well as the availability of competing charter services may deter entry of an LCC. Models, such as the one offered here, can be useful in identifying which factors and policies can lead to the growth of LCCs on certain routes.

Having identified some of the key factors in LCC development, chapter 5 assesses the market opportunities for LCCs in the EAC, and discusses some of the challenges that the region must overcome to enable their successful emergence.

Notes

1. "Hybridized" refers to the convergence between the LCC and the traditional network carrier model, which has created a number of carriers displaying both types of characteristics.
2. Landside infrastructure includes passenger services (terminal), food and beverage concessions, duty-free shopping, car parking, and so on. Airside infrastructure includes airfield, gates, air bridges, runways, aprons, and taxiways.

3. An Aeronautical Information Publication is defined by ICAO as a publication issued by or with the authority of a state and containing aeronautical information of a lasting character essential to air navigation.
4. Aeronautical charges include landing fees, terminal-area air navigation, passenger and cargo services, aircraft parking and hangars, security, airport noise, noxious emissions (air pollution), ground handling, and en route air navigation.
5. "Cabotage" refers to the right of a carrier from one country to operate within the domestic borders of another country.
6. Type G are ASAs that allow third, fourth, and fifth freedom rights, multidesignation of airlines, free pricing, substantive ownership, and free determination of capacity.
7. The unofficial eighth freedom is the right to carry passengers or cargo between two or more points within a foreign country and is also known as cabotage.
8. Airworthiness assesses an aircraft's suitability for safe flight.
9. A security interest involves the grant of a right in an asset which the grantor owns or in which he has an interest.
10. Latent variables are random variables, hypothetical constructs, whose realized values are hidden, and by definition, impossible to observe directly. Hence their properties must be inferred indirectly using statistical models linking them to observable variables.
11. A probit model is an econometric method used to estimate the probability of a positive outcome in a binary event (when only two mutually exclusive outcomes exist), based on a set of explanatory independent exogenous variables.
12. In econometrics, a dummy variable is a binary variable (0 or 1) utilized to indicate the absence or presence of some categorical effect that might shift a particular outcome in a regression.
13. A dependent variable or explained variable represents the output or the realization of a certain state, which can be explained by the explanatory or predictor variables.
14. An explanatory variable is a predictor variable. Intuitively, changes in the predictor variable will cause—all else being equal—a change in the dependent or explained variable.
15. The Herfindal Index is a measure of the size of firms in relation to the industry. It is an indicator of the amount of competition among them.
16. For instance, in the Alexandria (HBE)–Kuwait (KWI) market where AAE offers nonstop scheduled services (HBE–KWI) which directly compete with EgyptAir's connecting services via Cairo (HBE–CAI–KWI).
17. See Boguslaski, Ito, and Lee 2004.
18. Air Arabia operated from Luxor as late as 2012.

References

Africa Progress Panel. 2013. *Equity in Extractives: Stewarding Africa's Natural Resources for All*. http://africaprogresspanel.org/en/publications/africa-progress-report-2013/.

Airbus. 2012. *Global Market Forecast 2012–2031*. http://www.airbus.com/company/market/forecast/.

Airline Leader. 2013. "Virtual Alliances and Virtual Airlines." Issue 16. http://www.airlineleader.com/pdfs/Airline%20Leader%20-%20Issue%2016.pdf.

Arun, B. 2011. "These Dangerous Pilots." *Deccan Herald*. http://www.deccanherald.com/content/150955/these-dangerous-pilots.html#.

Asiana Aviation. 2012. "IATA Warns India on Fuel Tax." *Asiana Aviation*, March 15. http://www.asianaviation.com/articles/242/IATA-warns-India-on-fuel-tax.

Association of Tanzania Employers. 2011. *Business Agenda 2011–2014*. http://lempnet.itcilo.org/en/hidden-folder/ate-tanzania-business-agenda.

Belobaba, P., A. Odoni, and C. Barnhart. 2009. *The Global Airline Industry*. West Sussex: John Wiley & Sons Ltd.

Boeing. 2012. *Current Market Outlook 2013–2032*. http://www.boeing.com/boeing/commercial/cmo/.

Boguslaski, C., H. Ito, and D. Lee. 2004. "Entry Patterns in the Southwest Airlines Route System." *Review of Industrial Organization* 25 (3): 317–50.

Bombardier. 2012. *Market Forecast*. http://www2.bombardier.com/en/3_0/3_8/market_forecast/BCA_2012_Market_Forecast.pdf.

Botasso, A., M. Conti, and C. Piga. 2012. "Low-Cost Carriers and Airport Performance: Empirical Evidence from a Panel of UK Airports." *Industrial and Corporate Change* 22 (3): 745–69.

Bunker, D. 1989. *Canadian Aviation Finance Legislation*. Montreal: Institute and Centre of Air and Space Law, McGill University.

Caltex Petroleum. n.d. *Determining Fuel Prices*. www.caltex.com/global/resources/determining-fuel-prices.

Campisi, D., R. Costa, and P. Mancuso. 2010. "The Effects of Low Cost Airlines Growth in Italy." *Modern Economy* 1 (2): 59–67.

CAPA (Centre for Asia Pacific Aviation). 2013a. "ASEAN Single Aviation Market: Many Miles to Go." *Centre for Asia Pacific Aviation*, March 13. http://centreforaviation.com/analysis/aseans-single-aviation-market-many-miles-to-go-100831.

———. 2013b. "CAAC Outlines Support for Regional Aviation Development, 69 New Regional Airports by 2015." *Centre for Asia Pacific Aviation*, September 3. http://centreforaviation.com/news/caac-outlines-support-for-regional-aviation-development-69-new-regional-airports-by-2015-260720.

Carnegy, H. 2013. "France Battles with Labour Market Reform." *Financial Times*, January 9. http://www.ft.com/intl/cms/s/0/05b54c84-5a63-11e2-bc93-00144feab49a.html#axzz2ZGQU1vji.

CEPII (Centre d'Etudes Prospectives et d'Informations Internationales). 2013. *Base de Données. GeoDist*. http://www.cepii.fr/CEPII/fr/bdd_modele/bdd.asp.

Coulter, A. 2012. "Flying on Autopilot." *Routes*, August 23. http://www.routes-news.com/more-features/item/577-flying-on-autopilot.

Davidson, W. 2012. "Ethiopian Airlines Expansion Targets Five-Fold Revenue Increase." *Bloomberg*, September 7. http://www.bloomberg.com/news/2012-09-07/ethiopian-airlines-expansion-targets-five-fold-revenue-increase.html.

Dobruszkes, F. 2009. "New Europe, New Low-Cost Air Services." *Journal of Transport Geography* 17 (6): 423–32.

DiiO SRS Analyzer. 2013. *DiiO Online Database*. http://www.diio.net.

Economist Intelligence Unit. 2013. *Country, Industry and Risk Analysis*. http://www.eiu.com/default.aspx.

Euromonitor International. 2012. *Low-Cost Airlines Land in Mexico. Excerpt from Mexico Travel and Tourism Report.* http://www.marketresearchworld.net/content/view/1078/48/.

Forsyth, P., J. King, and C. L. Rodolfo. 2006. "Open Skies in ASEAN." *Journal of Air Transport Management* 12 (3): 143–52.

Franco, F., P. Santana, C. de Almeida, and R. de João. 2002. "Recent Deregulation of the Air Transport Sector in Brazil." Paper prepared by members of the Secretariat for Economic Monitoring of the Ministry of Finance.

Frost and Sullivan Market Insight. 2007. *Growing Asian Aviation Pilot Demand.* http://www.frost.com/sublib/display-market-insight-top.do?id=97586944.

Gewirtz, E. 2011. "The EETC in the Post–Cape Town Convention World." *Airfinance.* http://network.airfinancejournal.com/Post/The-EETC-in-the-Post-Cape-Town-Convention-World/4970/True.

Government of Australia, Department of Infrastructure and Transport. 2013. *The Cape Town Convention.* http://www.infrastructure.gov.au/aviation/international/consultation_cape_town.aspx.

Gwilliam, K., with H. Bofinger, R. Bullock, R. Carruthers, A. Kumar, M. Mundy, A. Nogales, and K. Sethi. 2011. *Africa's Transport Infrastructure.* Washington, DC: World Bank.

Hewitt, A. 2009. "A Practical Guide to the Cape Town Convention. Dentons Law Firm." http://www.lexology.com/library/detail.aspx?g=013fa7db-7a6f-4f00-b8f9-359336c6a3a7.

Holloway, S. 2008. *Straight and Level: Practical Airline Economics.* Aldershot: Ashgate Publishing, Ltd.

Hooper, P. 1997. "Liberalising Competition in Domestic Airline Markets in Asia—The Problematic Interface between Domestic and International Regulatory Policies. *Transportation Research Part E: Logistics and Transportation Review* 33 (3): 197–209.

Hooper, P., S. Hutchinson, and M. Nyathi. 1996. "The Challenge of Liberalising Domestic Airline Competition in a Less Developed Country." *Transportation* 23 (4): 395–408.

IATA (International Air Transport Association). n.d. Worldwide Slot Guidelines, Annex 10.12, Contact List for Level 2/3 Airports. https://www.iata.org/policy/slots/Pages/slot-guidelines.aspx.

———. 1997. "Cost Conscious Business Travelers Will Try Non Frills Airlines." *International Air Transport Association NewsRoom.* Press release: PS/13/9. January 27.

———. 2008. *Air Travel Demand: IATA Economics Briefing.* http://www.iata.org/whatwedo/Documents/economics/air_travel_demand.pdf.

———. 2013a. *IATA Economic Briefing: The Impact on Senegal of Removing the Infrastructure Development Charge at Dakar Airport.* https://www.iata.org/whatwedo/Documents/economics/Senegal_impact_assessment_final.pdf.

———. 2013b. "Products and Services Release: The Airline Industry for 2012." www.iata.org/pressroom/pr/Pages/2013-07-16-01.aspx.

———. 2013c. *Aviation: Strategic Driver of African Development. International Air Transport Association Newsroom,* April 16. http://www.iata.org/pressroom/pr/Pages/2013-04-16-01.aspx.

ICAO (International Civil Aviation Organization). 1944. *Convention on International Air Transport.* Montreal, QC: ICAO.

———. 2009. *ICAO's Policies on Taxation in the Field of International Air Transport.* Montreal, QC: ICAO.

———. 2011. *Global and Regional 20-Year Forecasts: Pilots, Maintenance Personnel and Air Traffic Controllers.* Montreal: ICAO.

———. 2012. "Robust Traffic Growth Expected until 2014." *International Civil Aviation Organization Newsroom*, July 5. http://www.icao.int/Newsroom/Pages/robust-traffic-growth-expected-until-2014.aspx.

———. 2013a. *Case Study on Commercialization, Privatization and Economic Oversight of Airports and Air Navigation Services Providers: Senegal.* International Civil Aviation Organization. http://www.icao.int/sustainability/CaseStudies/Senegal.pdf.

———. 2013b. *2013 Safety Report.* http://www.icao.int/safety/Documents/ICAO_2013-Safety-Report_FINAL.pdf.

———. n.d. *ICAO Universal Safety Oversight Audit Programme, Presentation.* http://www2.icao.int/en/usoap/Documents/USOAP-public.pdf.

IMF (International Monetary Fund). 2013. *World Economic Outlook.* http://www.imf.org/external/data.htm.

International Institute for the Unification of Private Law. n.d. "Status Cape Town Convention." http://www.unidroit.org/status-2001capetown.

Kjelgaard, C. 2011. "Start-up Airline Clearing for Take-off." *Airline Fleet Management*, January/February 2011. Issue 71. http://www.feelair.com/about/airline_fleet_management.pdf.

Kouwenhoven, M. 2008. "The Role of Accessibility in Passengers' Choice of Airports." International Transport Forum Discussion Paper 2008–14. http://www.internationaltransportforum.org/jtrc/discussionpapers/DP200814.pdf.

Lederman, M., and S. Januszewski. 2003. "Entry Patterns of Low-Cost Airlines." Working Paper, Massachusetts Institute of Technology, pp. 1–35.

Lusaka Times. 2012. "National Airports Corporation to Introduce an Infrastructure Development Levy on All Departing Passengers from Zambian Airports." August 11. http://www.lusakatimes.com/2012/08/11/national-airports-corporation-introduce-infrastructure-development-levy-departing-passengers-zambian-airports/.

Mason, F., and Mekong Tourism Coordination Office. 2011. "Urban Tourism: The Other Side of Responsible Tourism." Presentation, December 2011.

Mason, K. 2000. "The Propensity of Business Travelers to Use Low-Cost Airlines." *Journal of Transport Geography* 8 (2): 107–19.

MIT Airline Data Project. 2013. *Glossary.* http://web.mit.edu/airlinedata/www/Res_Glossary.html.

Mitchell, D. 2011. *Biofuels in Africa.* Washington, DC: World Bank.

Mueller, L. 2011. "The Export Credit Debate Explained." *Airline Business*, January 21. http://www.flightglobal.com/news/articles/focus-the-export-credit-debate-explained-352173/.

———. 2012. "What Will Money Worries Mean for Aircraft Financing?" *Pro News*, January 24. http://www.flightglobal.com/news/articles/in-focus-what-will-money-worries-mean-for-aircraft-financing-367272/.

Müller, K., V. Bilotkach, and K. Huschelrath. 2011. "The Construction of a Low Cost Airline Network." *ZEW-Centre for European Economic Research Discussion Paper 11-052*.

Odoni, A. 2009. "Some Performance Comparisons between U.S. and European Airports." Board meeting presentation, Massachusetts Institute of Technology. http://web.mit.edu/airlines/industry_outreach/board_meeting_presentation_files/meeting-oct-2009/Odoni%20Performance%20Comparisons.pdf.

Olipra, L., E. Pancer-Cybulska, and E. Szostak. 2011. "The Impact of the Migration Processes on the Low Cost Airlines' Routes between EU Countries and Poland after Its Accession to the EU, and on the Territorial Cohesion of Polish Regions." ERSA Conference Papers series. European Regional Science Association.

Oliveira, A. V. 2008. "An Empirical Model of Low-Cost Carrier Entry." *Transportation Research Part A: Policy and Practice* 42 (4): 673–95.

Peanuts! 2007. "Ryanair, EasyJet Told to Conform to French Labour Law." *Peanuts!* July 16. http://peanuts.aero/low_cost_airline_news/index.php?option=com_content&task=view&id=3952/50&Itemid=59.

PRS Group. 2013. *International Country Risk Guide.* http://www.prsgroup.com/icrg.aspx.

PwC (PricewaterhouseCoopers). 2013. *Aviation Finance: Fasten Your Seatbelt.* http://www.pwc.com/en_GX/gx/aerospace-defence/publications/assets/pwc-aviation-finance-fastern-your-seat-belts-pdf.pdf.

Ramsay, M., J. Stamp, J. Regueiro, D. Richards, and S. McGilvery. 2013. *Airline Disclosure Handbook.* KPMG Consulting. http://www.kpmg.com/Global/en/IssuesAndInsights/ArticlesPublications/Documents/airline-disclosures-handbook-2013-v2.pdf.

Ryanair. 2008. "Ryanair on the Road with Terravision." *Ryanair Press Release*, November 6. http://www.ryanair.com/en/news/ryanair-on-the-road-with-terravision.

Schlumberger, C. 2010. *Open Skies for Africa.* Washington DC: World Bank.

Schonhardt, S. 2012. "With Indonesian Airline's Expansion Comes Problem of Finding Enough Pilots." *New York Times*, August 2. http://www.nytimes.com/2012/08/03/business/global/03iht-airlineside03.html.

Sobie, B. 2006. "Nico Bezuidenhout: It's All about Distribution at South Africa's Mango." *Airline Business*, December 22. http://www.flightglobal.com/news/articles/nico-bezuidenhout-its-all-about-distribution-at-south-africas-mango-211098/.

Thome, W. 2008. "Branson's Virgin Nigeria Nightmare." *eTurboNews*, September 14. http://www.eturbonews.com/5010/branson-s-virgin-nigeria-nightmare.

Tobin, L. 2013. "Ryanair's Bargain Buy from Boeing." *The Independent*, May 29. http://www.independent.co.uk/news/business/news/ryanairs-bargain-buy-from-boeing-8635330.html.

UNESCAP (United Nations Economic and Social Commission). 2013. *What Is Good Governance?* http://www.unescap.org/pdd/prs/ProjectActivities/Ongoing/gg/governance.asp.

U.S. Department of Transportation. 2004. *Statement of Jeffrey Rosen General Counsel U.S. Department of Transportation before the Committee on Foreign Relations United States Senate on Advice and Consent to Ratification of the 2001 Cape Town Convention on International Interests in Mobile Equipment and Protocol on Matters Specific to Aircraft Equipment.* http://testimony.ost.dot.gov/test/pasttest/04test/Rosen2.htm.

Vasigh, B., K. Fleming, and T. Tacker. 2008. *Introduction to Air Transport Economics: From Theory to Applications.* Aldershot: Ashgate Publishing Limited.

Vasigh, B., R. Taleghani, and D. Jenkins. 2012. *Aircraft Finance: Strategies for Managing Capital Costs in a Turbulent Industry.* Midlothian: Ross Publishing.

VivaAerobus. 2012. *Overview of VivaAerobus.* Unpublished presentation.

WEF (World Economic Forum). 2012a. *Air Transport Infrastructure Quality.* http://www.weforum.org/issues/competitiveness-0/gci2012-data-platform/.

———. 2012b. *Global Competitiveness Report.* http://www.weforum.org/issues/global-competitiveness.

———. 2013. *Global Competitiveness Report.* http://www.weforum.org/issues/global-competitiveness.

Winston, C., and G. de Rus. 2008. *Aviation Infrastructure Performance: A Study in Comparative Political Economy.* Washington, DC: Brookings Institution.

World Bank. 2008. *Landlocked Countries: Higher Transport Costs, Delays, Less Trade.* World Bank News. http://web.worldbank.org/WBSITE/EXTERNAL/NEWS/0,,contentMDK:21805006~pagePK:64257043~piPK:437376~theSitePK:4607,00.html.

———. 2011. *Air Transport Safety.* http://web.worldbank.org/WBSITE/EXTERNAL/TOPICS/EXTTRANSPORT/EXTAIRTRANSPORT/0,,contentMDK:22441770~menuPK:3424213~pagePK:210058~piPK:210062~theSitePK:515181,00.html.

———. 2013a. *Doing Business.* http://www.doingbusiness.org.

———. 2013b. "GDP Per Capita." http://www.worldbank.org/data.

———. 2013c. *Worldwide Governance Indicator Project.* http://info.worldbank.org/governance/wgi/index.asp.

World Bank and IFC (International Finance Corporation). 2013. *Enterprise Surveys: What Businesses Experience.* http://www.enterprisesurveys.org.

World Trade Organization. 2013. *ASAP Analytical Tool.* http://www.wto.org/asap/index.html.

Zhang, A., S. Hanaoka, H. Inamura, and T. Ishikiura. 2008. "Low Cost Carriers in Asia: Deregulation, Liberalisation and Secondary Airports." *Research in Transportation Economics* 24 (1): 36–50.

CHAPTER 5

Opportunities and Challenges for LCC Development: The Case of East Africa

Introduction

After having established the key elements of the low-cost carrier (LCC) business model, and identifying the market environment that they can flourish in, chapter 5 provides insight into the potential development of LCCs in Sub-Saharan Africa, a region which still represents largely unexplored territory for the business model. Due to the region's vastness, complexity, and diversity, this chapter focuses on identifying opportunities and challenges using the example of the East African Community (EAC).

East African Community (EAC)

The EAC is a regional economic community (REC) formed between five East African countries: Uganda, Tanzania, Rwanda, Burundi, and Kenya. The region covers around 1.82 million square kilometers, and includes a population of 141.1 million (East African Community Statistics Portal 2013).

The history of the EAC goes back as far as 1917, when Kenya and Uganda formed one of the first cooperative entities in Africa by establishing a customs union. After assuming different shapes and forms—and even a temporary dissolution in 1977—the three major economies of Tanzania, Kenya and Uganda formed the EAC in 2000. In 2007, Rwanda and Burundi joined the EAC. Based on the EAC Treaty of 1999 (EAC 1999), which forms the legal basis of the community, its prime objective is to "develop policies and programs aimed at widening and deepening cooperation among the Partner States in political, economic, social and cultural fields, research and technology, defense, security and legal and judicial affairs, for their mutual benefit" (EAC 1999). To achieve these objectives, the EAC was to establish a customs union, a common market, and subsequently a monetary union, ultimately leading to a political federation (EAC 1999).

The EAC Treaty lays out a set of fundamental and operational principles that must govern the achievement of these objectives. The most significant fundamental principles include "mutual trust, political will, and sovereign equality," as well as "peaceful coexistence and settlement of disputes" (EAC 1999). The community's key operational principles are "the establishment of an export oriented economy for the Partner States in which there shall be free movement of goods, persons, labor, services, capital, information and technology" and the "principle of subsidiarity" of the EAC, which secures multilevel participation and the involvement of a wide range of stakeholders during the integration process (EAC 1999).

Air Transportation has been given particular attention in the EAC Treaty under Section 92. As its objective, EAC member countries are to "harmonize their policies on civil aviation to promote the development of safe, reliable, efficient, and economically viable civil aviation with a view to developing appropriate infrastructure, aeronautical skills and technology, as well as the role of aviation in support of other economic activities" (EAC 1999). There are also some specific provisions for different areas of the industry, which are outlined throughout this chapter.

Overall, the institutional framework of the newly established EAC is well defined and consists of all of the necessary elements for effective implementation of its goals, including economic cooperation and integration among its partner states.

In addition to the EAC, some of its member states are also part of other RECs. These may have different policies with regard to the air transport sector. Burundi, Rwanda, Kenya, and Uganda, for example, are also part of the Common Market for Eastern and Southern Africa (COMESA), a regional organization that has established a free trade zone between eastern, southern, and central African states.[1] Tanzania is also a part of the Southern African Development Community (SADC). SADC's objective is socioeconomic cooperation and integration, as well as political and security cooperation. It includes 15 members from the southern African region.

These dual/multiple regional bloc memberships of EAC states have, in some cases, slowed down decision-making processes due to the need for harmonization between individual RECs. To address this obstacle, EAC, COMESA, and SADC founded the COMESA-EAC-SADC Tripartite in 2005. The Tripartite decided to develop a road map for the harmonization of the three RECs at the Tripartite Summit of Heads of State in 2008. However, this has not been achieved yet. It has also been working toward the implementation of a comprehensive Trade and Transport Facilitation Programme, including providing support for various aspects of the air transport sectors (OECD and WTO 2011).

Demand

As established in chapter 4, the key factor for LCCs to flourish in a market is high utilization of their aircraft and personnel. This in turn requires high expected volumes of traffic. These volumes can be achieved by either targeting existing customers on high traffic routes to reduce market share of incumbent carriers, by stimulating new demand by attracting a larger segment of the population through a lower fare offering, or by opening previously unserved routes. In order to assess the opportunities in the EAC market, a short overview of the existing market, as well as an analysis of the potential for future growth opportunities, are provided below. This is by no means an exhaustive assessment, but serves as an overall indicator of trends in the market. A more detailed analysis would be required to assess actual route-level opportunities, and is beyond the scope of this research.

Existing Air Transport Market—Thin Routes and High Concentration

In order to provide a broad overview of the air transport market, this book primarily focuses on current air traffic capacity, as well as on the key participants in the market. Although some passenger data is available from the EAC Secretariat for an analysis of the existing EAC market, it is difficult to verify the data's accuracy. Therefore, this analysis relies on information from airline schedules as collated through the online database DiiO SRS Analyzer (2013), and a sample of passenger flow data for some African airports as provided by the Airports Council International. Using schedules data has the disadvantage that only capacity is provided rather than actual passengers flown. However, it does serve as an indication of overall traffic flows.

The current intra-EAC air transport market is still very small and the majority of domestic and regional traffic is still concentrated around the two major hubs of Nairobi, Kenya, and Dar es Salaam, Tanzania. These two airports absorb the largest number of passengers followed by Mombasa, Kenya, and Entebbe, Uganda (see table 5.1).

Table 5.1 Passengers by Airport, 2012

Airport	IATA	PAX
Jomo Kenyatta International Airport, Nairobi, Kenya	NBO	6,271,922
Julius Nyerere International Airport, Dar es Salaam, Tanzania	DAR	2,088,282
Moi International Airport, Mombasa, Kenya	MBA	1,347,908
Entebbe International Airport, Entebbe, Uganda	EBB	1,342,134
Abeid Amani Karume International Airport, Zanzibar, Tanzania	ZNZ	787,813
Kilimanjaro International Airport, Kilimanjaro, Tanzania	JRO	665,147
Kigali International Airport, Kigali, Rwanda	KGL	458,807
Mwanza Airport, Mwanza Tanzania	MWZ	392,298
Aéroport International De Bujumbura, Bujumbura, Burundi	BJM	291,838
Eldoret Airport, Eldoret, Kenya	EDL	103,729

Source: ACI 2012.
Note: IATA = International Air Transport Association; PAX = number of passengers.

As figure 5.1 shows, despite growth in recent years, the capacity for total traffic between the EAC member countries is still at less than 2.6 million available seats in 2013. This represents around 44 percent of total traffic within the region, highlighting the key role of domestic traffic, particularly in larger countries such as Kenya and Tanzania.

Some domestic markets have grown considerably in recent years, especially in Rwanda and Tanzania. After a period of decline between 2008 and 2010, Tanzania in particular has managed to increase its capacity significantly, reaching almost the same level of domestic traffic as Kenya, the largest domestic market in EAC (see figure 5.2).

Rwanda experienced a spike in domestic air transport starting in 2010 (see figure 5.3), with the country's national airline Rwandair increasing its weekly frequency between Kigali and Cyangugu sixfold between 2010 and 2013. After a short period of increased traffic, Uganda's domestic market has been declining considerably (see figure 5.3), with many of the domestic, probably largely unprofitable, routes being abandoned by 2010. Burundi currently has no scheduled domestic air transport.

As map 5.1 shows, the majority of traffic in East Africa can be broadly divided into three main categories: (a) a few high-frequency domestic routes in Tanzania and Kenya; (b) a small number of key intra-EAC routes with low frequency; and (c) a number of secondary, low-capacity intra-EAC routes. The top 15 routes amount to around 80 percent of the overall EAC market.

Figure 5.1 Intra-EAC Traffic, 2004–13

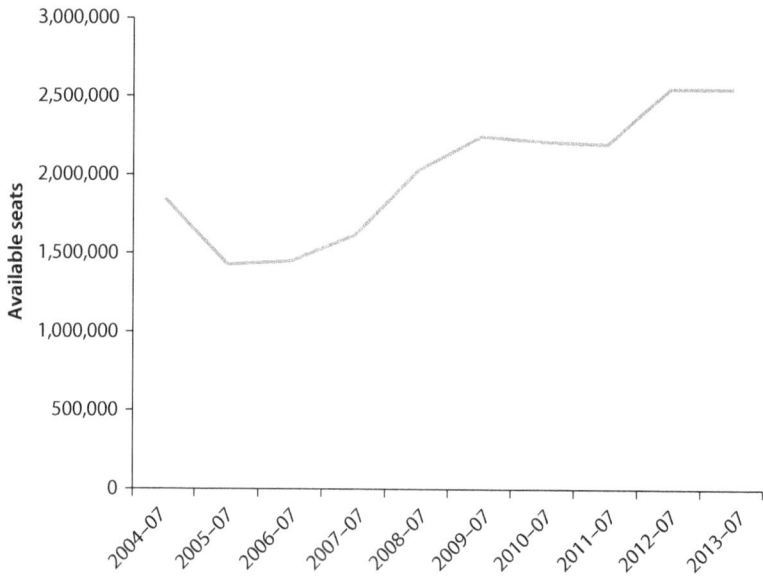

Source: Analysis based on data from DiiO SRS Analyzer (2013).
Note: Bi-directional traffic capacity. Number after year indicates month, 07 = July. EAC = East African Community.

Figure 5.2 Domestic Traffic Kenya and Tanzania, 2004–13

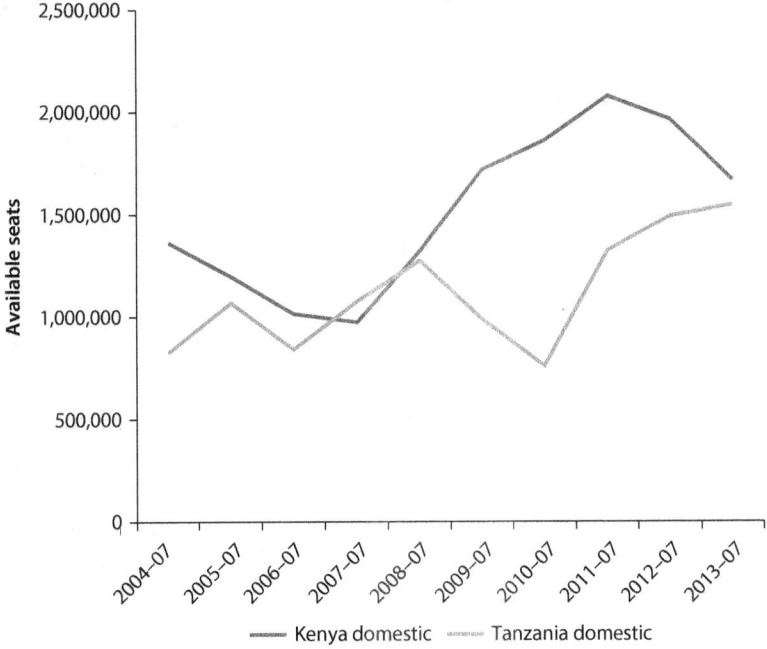

Source: Based on data from DiiO SRS Analyzer (2013).
Note: Bi-directional traffic capacity. Number after year indicates month, 07 = July.

Figure 5.3 Domestic Traffic Uganda and Rwanda, 2004–13

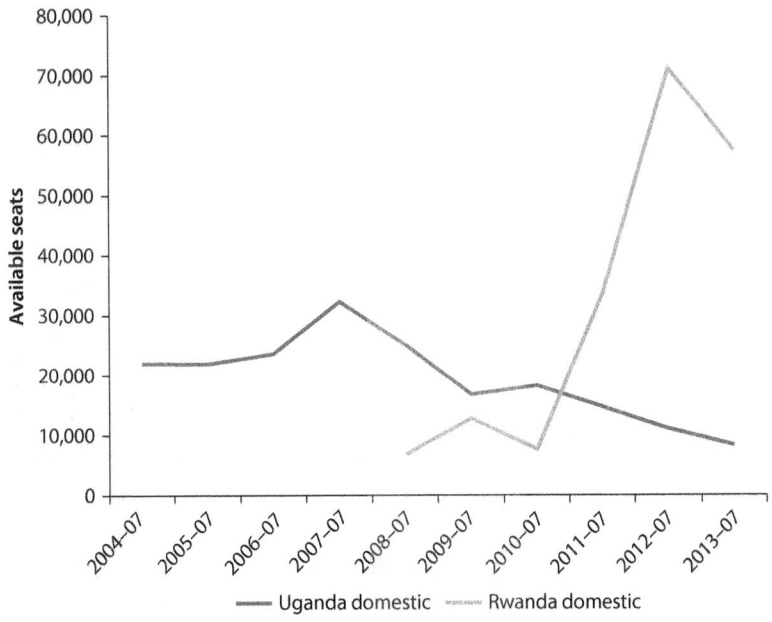

Source: Analysis based on data from DiiO SRS Analyzer (2013).
Note: Bi-directional traffic capacity. Number after year indicates month, 07 = July.

Map 5.1 Route Network Map of EAC

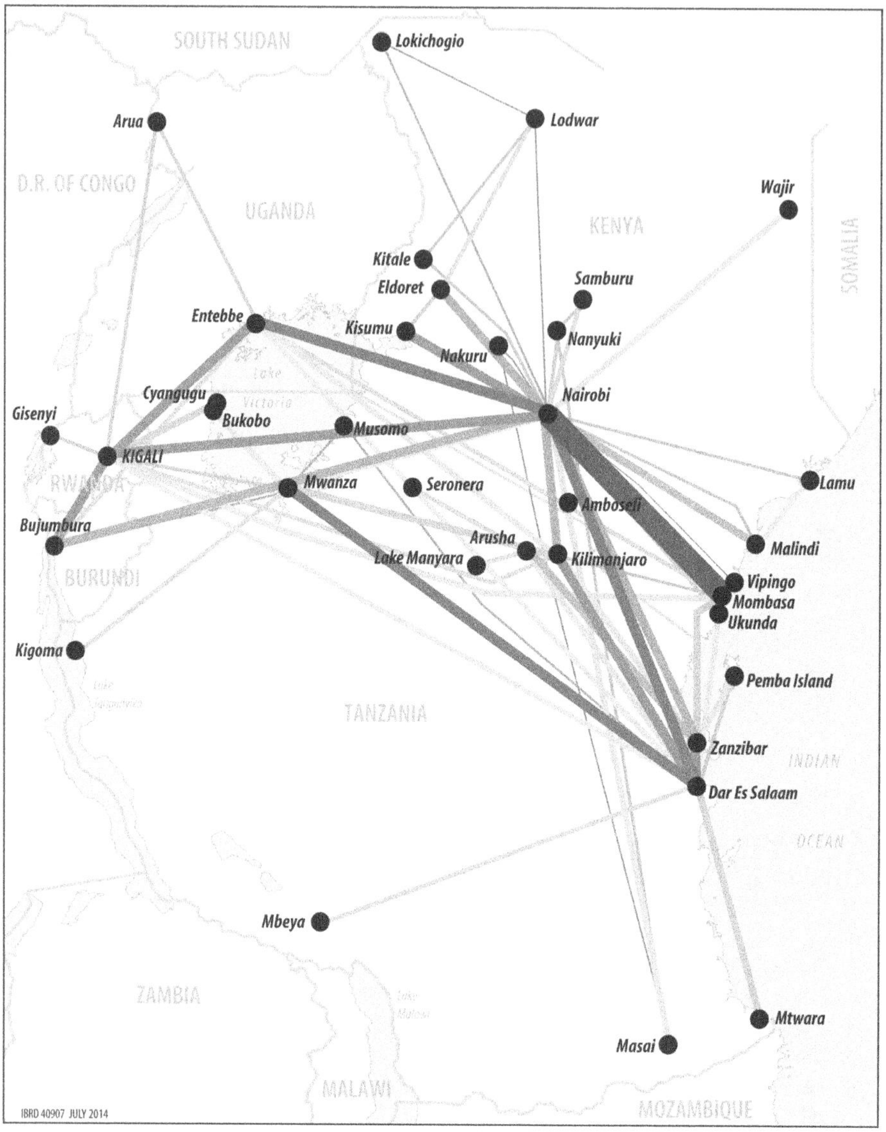

Source: Based on data from DiiO SRS Analyzer (2013).
Note: Thickness of a route indicates the level of traffic intensity (thick = high, thin = low). EAC = East African Community.

A few high frequency domestic routes represent a large share of overall traffic in the EAC. These are located primarily in Tanzania and Kenya, connecting their respective entry hubs in Dar es Salaam (DAR) and Nairobi (NBO) to their main economic and tourism centers. In Kenya, direct domestic traffic primarily links Nairobi (NBO) and Mombasa (MBA), Kenya's two largest cities and economic centers. There are 15–17 roundtrip daily flights connecting the two cities. High frequency domestic traffic also occurs between Dar es Salaam (DAR) and

Mwanza (MZW), Kilimanjaro (JRO) and Zanzibar (ZNZ). This feeds tourism traffic from the country's capital airport to popular tourist destinations.

International intra-EAC traffic is limited to a few key routes, primarily linking the EAC's large- and medium-size cities to the region's hub in Nairobi. In addition, key routes include services between capital cities such as Entebbe (EBB) and Kigali (KGL), and Kigali (KGL) and Bujumbura (BJM), as well as popular tourist destinations such as the route from Zanzibar to Mombasa. Together, the top 15 intra-EAC routes comprise almost 90 percent of all international intra-EAC traffic in 2013.

Some of these routes have grown consistently in recent years, such as the Nairobi (NBO) to Kigali (KGL), or the Entebbe (EBB) to Kigali (KGL) route. Others have undergone significant fluctuations, including the Nairobi (NBO) to Entebbe (EBB) route, or the Dar es Salaam (DAR) to Nairobi (NBO) route. The former experienced a considerable drop in capacity in 2005 and 2006, after Ethiopian Airlines suspended its flights on the routes in 2005. Trying to resume the flights in 2006, the Kenyan government refused to grant traffic rights to the carrier (*New Vision* 2006). This left Kenya Airways as the sole provider on the route for some time.

Intra-EAC traffic is dominated by few carriers and competition is very limited. As figure 5.4 shows, most intra-EAC routes are operated by one or two carriers. Even on routes where more than two carriers operate, such as the Nairobi (NBO) to Entebbe (EBB) route or the Nairobi (NBO) to Dar es Salaam (DAR) route, these routes are mostly dominated by one carrier (figure 5.5). However, a few routes from Kigali have been served by multiple carriers, with Ethiopian Airlines and South African Airways applying their fifth freedom rights.

Figure 5.4 Number of Carriers per Top Intra-EAC Routes, July 2013
percent

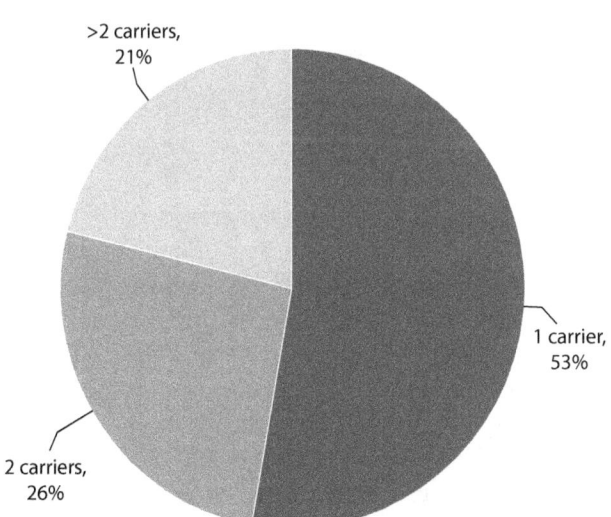

Source: Analysis based on data from DiiO SRS Analyzer (2013).

Figure 5.5 Market Share per Carrier on Top Intra-EAC Routes, July 2013
available seats (%)

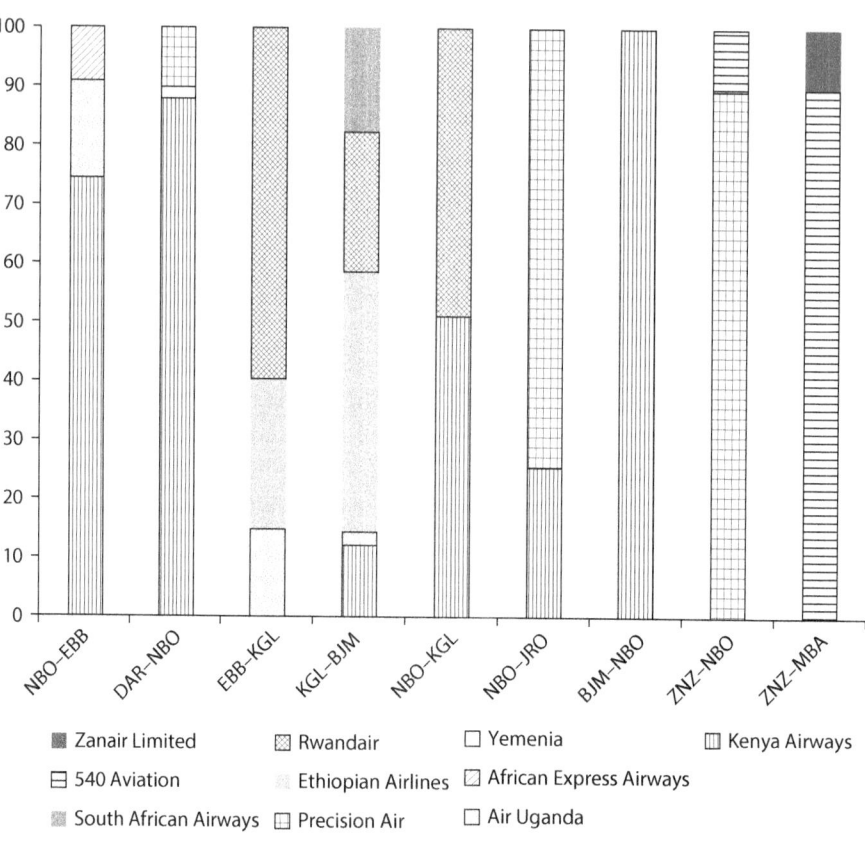

Source: Analysis based on data from DiiO SRS Analyzer (2013).
Note: BJM = Bujumbura International Airport, Burundi; DAR = Julius Nyerere International Airport (Dar es Salaam), Tanzania; EAC = East African Community; EBB = Entebbe International Airport, Uganda; JRO = Kilimanjaro International Airport, Tanzania; KGL = Kigali International Airport, Rwanda; MBA = Moi International Airport (Mombasa), Kenya; NBO = Jomo Kenyatta International Airport (Nairobi), Kenya; ZNZ = Abeid Amani Karume International Airport (Zanzibar), Tanzania.

In domestic markets, Tanzania appears to have the least concentration on its routes, with a handful of segments served by more than one carrier. In Kenya's large domestic market, many routes are still served only by Kenya Airways, although some key routes have seen the entry of competitors—driven by the country's move toward a deregulated domestic market. The entrance of the LCC Fly540 (discussed later), for example, has brought some competition to the more prominent domestic routes previously only served by Kenya Airways. Prior to the airline's entry, the domestic market appears to have been clearly divided between the more prominent domestic routes (for example, Nairobi to Mombasa or Eldoret) served by Kenya Airways, and the thinner routes by local carrier Air Kenya Express. This division occurred in recent years with the exit of domestic carriers, such as JetLink Express (which ceased operations in 2012) and African Express Airways from some these routes. In Rwanda and Uganda, the small domestic markets are monopolized by one carrier, Rwandair and Eagle Air. Considering the low traffic volumes in these markets though, the ability of another airline to operate profitably is in some cases questionable.

In addition, there are a number of domestic and some international so-called "milk-runs," or multistop routes, such as Nairobi (NBO) to Kisumu (KIS) to Eldoret (EDL) to Nairobi (NBO); and Nairobi Wilson Airport (WIL) to Samburu (UAS) to Nanyuki (NYK) to Masai Mara (MRE) in Kenya; or Kilimanjaro (JRO) to Zanzibar (ZNZ) to Dar es Salaam (DAR) in Tanzania. These all show very limited traffic however.

Airlines

Although still struggling with some unprofitable state-owned carriers such as Rwandair (Butera 2013) and Air Burundi—and in contrast to other regions in Sub-Saharan Africa—the market in the EAC has developed a few privately owned carriers. This includes, for example, Air Uganda which was created after the liquidation of the failing national carrier Uganda Airlines. The airline is part of the Celestair Group of African carriers, which is owned by the Aga Khan Fund for Economic Development (AKFED). Another private airline is Precision Air, the growing Tanzanian carrier, which posted a profit of around US$400,000 in 2012. However, in 2013, the airline had to report losses of US$18.9 million apparently due to "overly ambitious growth." The carrier expanded its network considerably in that year and leased three B737–800 aircraft (CAPA 2013a). The region has also witnessed the successful privatization of Kenya's national carrier Kenya Airways in 1995, the largest carrier in the region. In addition, there are a handful of smaller domestic scheduled and charter operators primarily in Kenya and Tanzania, such as Air Kenya Express, Regional Air, and Zanzair. A detailed list of the major carriers in the region can be found in appendix E.

Despite the positive progress in privatization, government intervention in the air transport sector may not have disappeared entirely. Kenya Airways' financial difficulties led to a recent news announcement stating that the government of Kenya is considering increasing its share in the carrier (Muiri 2013). This may serve as an indicator for a potentially more active involvement of the government in the air transport market. A small sign of intervention was already evident with the denial of traffic rights for Ethiopian Airlines in 2006, which left Kenya Airways as the only provider on the Entebbe (EBB) to Nairobi (NBO) route. The Ugandan government also announced recently that it was planning to re-launch its national carrier Air Uganda. The airline went into bankruptcy in 2001 after unsuccessfully trying to attract foreign investors (CAPA 2013b). Even the government of Tanzania is considering an equity stake in Precision Air (CAPA 2013a).

Due to limited traffic in the region, most airlines use smaller turboprop aircraft (for example, ATR-42 and 72, DHC-8), some regional jets (for example, CRJ Bombardier), as well as a very limited number of narrow-body jets (for example, B737, A320, Embraer E-Jet) for intra-regional routes. In addition, there are a number of small domestic and regional airlines such as Zanair operating with smaller piston engine aircraft (for example, Cessna 402).

Figure 5.6 Number of Flights per Aircraft Size, July 2013 (Intra-Regional and Domestic)
percent

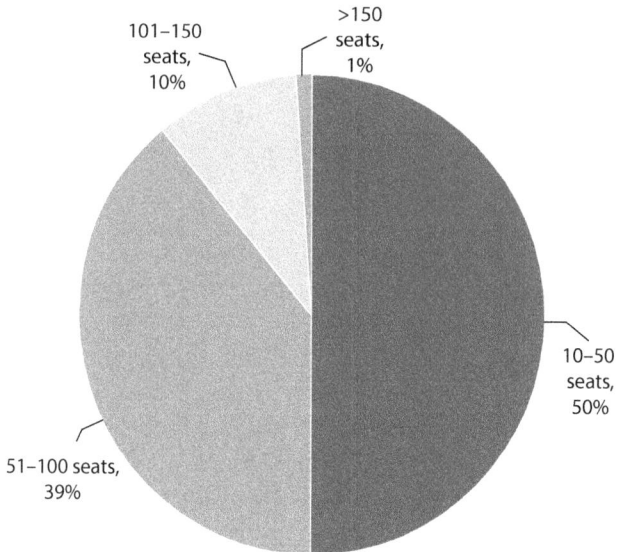

Source: Analysis based on data from DiiO SRS Analyzer (2013).

As figure 5.6 shows the frequent usage of aircraft with capacities below 100 seats is fairly common in the region. As a recent analysis by Bombardier shows, there has been a shift in the usage of aircraft in Africa to 75–100-seat aircraft, which more than doubled between 2007 and 2012 (Carrier 2013).

Even with smaller aircraft, airlines operating in Africa generally experienced lower load factors. A study by the International Air Transport Association (IATA) showed that in 2013, load factors were around 10 percent lower than in most other regions (IATA 2013). This signals that the usage of larger aircraft would most likely not be sustainable. The viability of regional jets for the LCC model is still questionable, however, due to generally higher unit costs (per available seat kilometer or mile: CASK or CASM) in comparison to the commonly used A320 and B737 narrow-body jets.

Fastjet—Successful LCC?

The region has already seen the emergence of its first low-cost airlines. In 2006, Fly540, a Kenya-based, low-cost airline was established. The carrier, owned by Five Forty Aviation Ltd., with a 49 percent investment stake by British company Lonrho Africa, introduced the first LCC model to the region. Based on its name, Fly540 offered a no-frills air transport service for 5,540 Kenya shillings (K Sh; approximately US$60) roundtrip fare. Starting with the high traffic Nairobi (NBO) to Mombasa (MBA) route with a 48-seat ATR42 aircraft, the airline expanded quickly adding new aircraft (two Dash 8–100s), and extending its route network to include Kisumu, Eldoret, Malindi, Lodwar, and Lamu in Kenya.

Later it also targeted international destinations in the Republic of South Sudan, Tanzania, the Democratic Republic of Congo, and Uganda by acquiring the Kenyan carrier East African Safari Air Express in 2010 (Thome 2010). Some of these expansion plans were later abandoned, however, primarily due to political and financial reasons (CAPA 2012). The company also set up its first franchise in Tanzania based at Mwanza Airport, operating flights to Zanzibar, Dar es Salaam, and Nairobi (CAPA 2012).

Building on its success in East Africa, Fly540 set up operations in Angola and Ghana in 2011. In Angola, Fly540 focuses on domestic operations between the country's capital Luanda and smaller cities, such as Soyo, Benguela, Cabinda, and M'banza Congo (*Fly540 Africa* 2013). The Angola operation commenced with a significant delay as the country had been under scrutiny by the International Civil Aviation Organization (ICAO) and the country's primary carrier had been blacklisted by the European Union due to safety concerns (CAPA 2011). In Ghana, services were initially operated to Tamale, Kumasi, and Takoradi domestically, and Abidjan and Freetown internationally. However, these services were discontinued, and according to the airline's website, the only operation remaining is between Accra and Kumasi, a wealthy mining city northwest of Accra. Although intending to become a regional hub, plans to develop services to Senegal and Equatorial Guinea were not realized. The airline also voiced ambitions to set up franchises in Rwanda, Zambia, and Zimbabwe, among other countries. By the end of 2011, the carrier recorded passenger figures of almost half a million (easyGroup 2013) across its operations with a fleet of 10 aircraft by June 2012 (CAPA 2012). In contrast, by its fourth year of operation in 2000, easyJet in Europe had recorded 5.6 million passengers (CNN 2000) with a fleet of 14 B737 aircraft (Planespotters 2013).

Despite this aggressive expansion strategy and increasing passenger growth, Lonrho Aviation's operations did not yield the desired results. In September 2009, it reported a loss (after tax) of US$7.5 million for the previous 12 months. This loss increased even further in September 2010 and 2011 to US$13.1 million and US$19.0 million, respectively. The 12 months ending September 30, 2009, showed a 24 percent negative operating margin, which increased to 35 percent the following year (September 2010), and then slightly decreased to 31 percent for the 15 months to December 31, 2011 (CAPA 2012). The airline's losses were primarily attributed to the establishment of its new franchises in Angola and Ghana, as well as unprofitable operations in Uganda. In addition, the carrier had been struggling with fuel-inefficient, small aircraft and insufficient utilization rates.

In 2012, Rubicon Ltd., a British investment company, purchased Lonrho's aviation arm and its investments in Fly540. The payment to Lonrho consisted of Rubicon shares for a total value of US$85.7 million, representing 73.7 percent of Rubicon's enlarged issued share capital. Another 5 percent of shares are owned by Sir Stelios Haji-Ioannou of easyGroup Holding Limited, the parent company of European LCC easyJet. Under a brand licensing agreement with easyGroup, the airline rebranded itself into fastjet (Lonrho Aviation 2012).

Fastjet has announced its transformation into a "real" low-cost airline, replacing the carrier's turboprop aircraft with Airbus 319s. In addition, it engaged in alternative distribution channels such as mobile distribution channels to avoid the expensive costs of global distribution system (GDS) providers. The airline was planning to increase its fleet to 15 A319 aircraft by the end of 2013 (CAPA 2013c). Its service offering is not entirely clear, but appears to be influenced by the LCC model of easyJet—attracting business and leisure travelers by offering food and beverages, priority boarding, and seating at a charge—and most importantly, providing connections to intercontinental carriers (CAPA 2012).

Focusing firstly on the East African market, the airline has encountered numerous challenges. It has an ongoing legal dispute with Five Forty Aviation, the previous owner of the Kenya Fly540 brand (and, although debated, still its majority shareholder) about operations into and within Kenya, as well as delays in obtaining international flying rights from Tanzania into other markets in the region. The airline has therefore been able to take over only Fly540's domestic operations in Tanzania. The delay in commencing operations in Kenya is particularly challenging as the launch of Kenya Airways' long-awaited LCC Jambo Jet seems to be coming closer. Trying to free up some much needed funds to recoup the cost incurred from these delays, the company has announced that it intends to reduce its 90 percent equity shareholding in Fly540 Tanzania (Peterson 2013).

While trying to salvage its position in East Africa, Fly540's West African operations in Angola and Ghana (in which fastjet owns 60 percent and 92.5 percent of shares respectively) have also significantly underperformed in 2012. Fly540 Angola has been struggling with bureaucratic hurdles, such as stringent regulations on transactions imposed by the Angolan Central Bank, and customs delays affecting the delivery of aircraft spares. Fly540 Ghana has faced intense competition on its Accra (ACC) to Kumasi (KMS) route with the entrance of two new LCCs, Starbox and Africa World Airlines. The carrier's cost structure has also been severely affected by excessive passenger taxes, airport services charges, and fuel price increases (CAPA 2013d).

As a result, fastjet posted a loss of US$56 million for the 18 months leading up to December 31, 2012. The auditors, KPMG, voiced concerns about the company's stocks' ability to continue to be traded on the London Stock Exchange. Losses in West Africa have been particularly detrimental, amounting to US$17.8 million (CAPA 2013d).

However, since the beginning of 2013, the company has demonstrated success in the Tanzanian market, with high average load factors on the routes between Dar es Salaam (DAR) and Kilimanjaro (JRO), and Dar es Salaam (DAR) and Mwanza (MWZ), where 38 percent of passengers were first-time flyers. Recently, Fly540 Ghana has also experienced increased bookings. In May 2013, it recorded an 11 percent increase from April 2013 and 52 percent from May 2012. Web-based sales in the country have experienced a large increase of nearly 400 percent, reducing the company's distribution costs. In addition, the airline has managed to finalize a license-based joint venture with a South African investment company, Blockbuster, to enter the South African domestic market. This finally succeeded

Opportunities and Challenges for LCC Development: The Case of East Africa

after a variety of attempts to enter the market, including the proposed purchase of bankrupt South African carrier 1Time (CAPA 2013d). Despite this promising outlook, the overall viability of the carrier still remains to be seen.

Fares

In order to provide an assessment of fare levels in the EAC market, two comparisons are made; one for domestic and one for intra-EAC routes, with routes in other regions that are currently operated by LCCs (see appendix F for detailed methodology and sample airports chosen).

As figure 5.7 shows, the lowest available return fares on comparable routes are significantly lower than on intra-EAC routes. Particularly routes originating from Morocco and Cambodia prove to be significantly lower. The route between

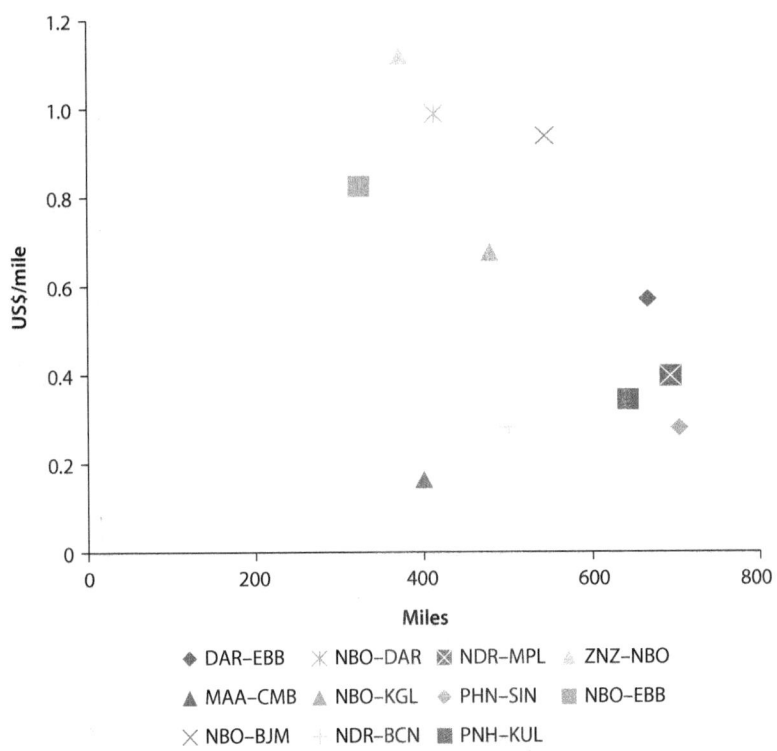

Figure 5.7 Comparison of Lowest Available Return Fare between Intra-EAC and Other International Routes (Including Taxes and Charges)

Sources: Analysis based on airline websites, Air Uganda, Jet Airways, Kenya Airways, Precision Air, Rwandair, Ryanair, AirArabia Maroc, Jetstar Asia, Air Asia, and Fly540; and DiiO SRS Analyzer (2013).

Note: BCN = Barcelona el Prat Airport, Spain; BJM = Bujumbura International Airport, Burundi; CMB = Bandaranaike International Airport (Colombo) Sri Lanka; DAR = Julius Nyerere International Airport (Dar es Salaam), Tanzania; EAC = East African Community; EBB = Entebbe International Airport, Uganda; KGL = Kigali International Airport, Rwanda; KUL = Kuala Lumpur International Airport, Malaysia; MAA = Chennai International Airport, India; MPL = Montpellier Méditerranée Airport, France; NBO = Jomo Kenyatta International Airport (Nairobi), Kenya; NDR = Nador International Airport, Morocco; PNH = Phnom Pen International Airport, Cambodia; SIN = Singapore Changi Airport; ZNZ = Abeid Amani Karume International Airport (Zanzibar), Tanzania.

Nairobi (NBO) and Dar es Salaam (DAR), for example, is over 100 percent more expensive than the route between Kuala Lumpur (KUL) and Phnom Penh (PNH). The fare from Nairobi (NBO) to Zanzibar (ZNZ) is almost three times higher than from Chennai (MAA) to Colombo (CMB).

In looking at the distribution of cost versus taxation and charges, it is clear that taxation and charges comprise a large percentage of total fares on intra-EAC markets (see figure 5.8). There are also some cases where the base fare is much higher, such as on the Nairobi (NBO) to Bujumbura (BJM) route, which could be directly linked to the limited competition on this segment.

As figure 5.9 shows, fares on domestic routes in Kenya are generally more expensive than the routes in the chosen sample. Interestingly, on the routes where LCC Fly540 is present in Kenya, Kenya Airways actually undercuts the LCC by a small margin on the chosen dates, thereby displaying some sign of fare convergence in the market. The competition with the LCCs seems to have brought down fares to a similar level than on comparable sectors for some routes, such

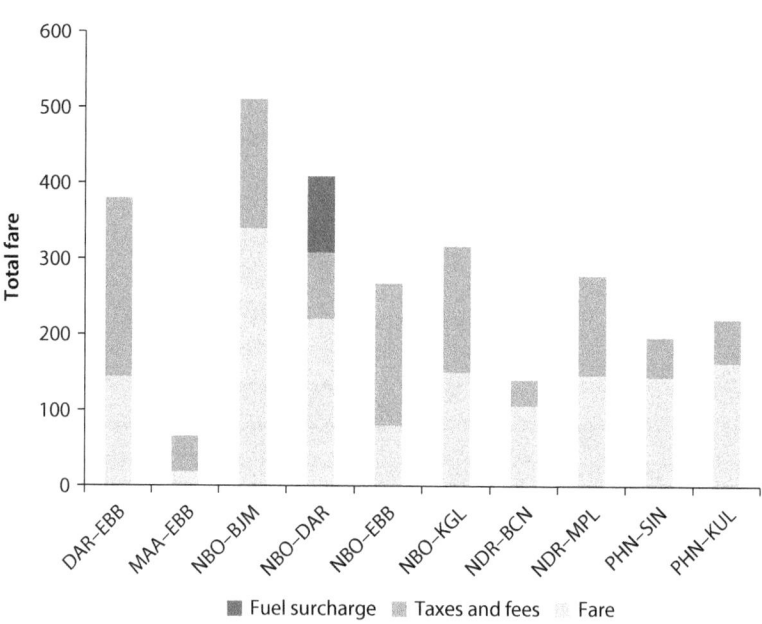

Figure 5.8 Distribution Fare Basis versus Taxation and Charges, 2013
US$

Sources: Analysis based on airline websites including Air Uganda, Jet Airways, Kenya Airways, Precision Air, Rwandair, Ryanair, AirArabia Maroc, Jetstar Asia, Air Asia, and Fly540; and DiiO Analyzer (2013).
Note: ZNZ-NBO had to be excluded as website did not provide for a breakdown of the fare. BCN = Barcelona el Prat Airport, Spain; BJM = Bujumbura International Airport, Burundi; CMB = Bandaranaike International Airport (Colombo) Sri Lanka; DAR = Julius Nyerere International Airport (Dar es Salaam), Tanzania; EBB = Entebbe International Airport, Uganda; KGL = Kigali International Airport, Rwanda; KUL = Kuala Lumpur International Airport, Malaysia; MAA = Chennai International Airport, India; MPL = Montpellier Méditerranée Airport, France; NBO = Jomo Kenyatta International Airport (Nairobi), Kenya; NDR = Nador International Airport, Morocco; PNH = Phnom Pen International Airport, Cambodia; SIN = Singapore Changi Airport; ZNZ = Abeid Amani Karume International Airport (Zanzibar), Tanzania.

Figure 5.9 Comparison of Lowest Available Domestic Fare (Including Taxes and Charges)

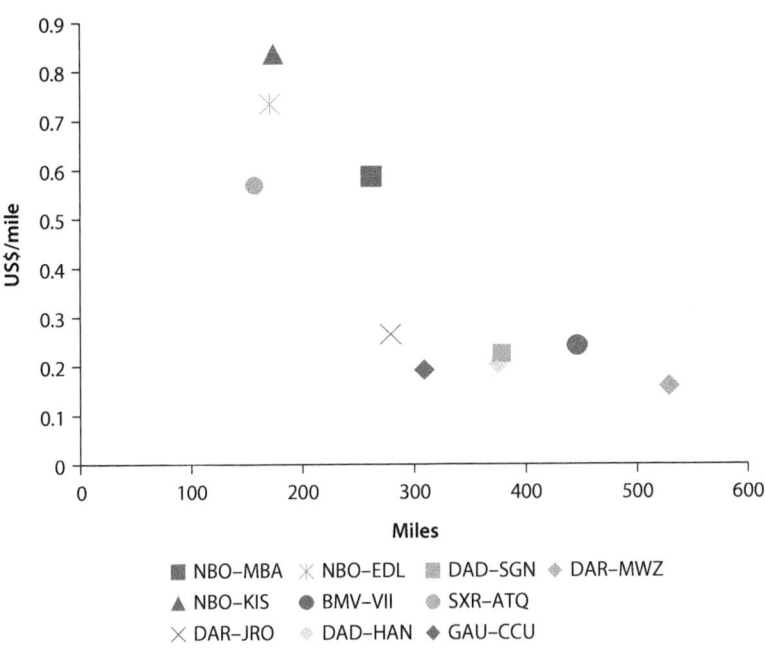

Sources: Analysis based on airline websites including Kenya Airways, Precision Air, Fastjet, Jetstar Pacific, and Spicejet; and DiiO SRS Analyzer (2013).
Note: ATQ = Sri Guru Ram Dass Jee International (Amritsar), India; BMV = Buon Ma Thuot Airport, Vietnam; CCU = Netaji Subhas Chandra Bose International Airport (Kolkata), India; DAD = Da Nang International Airport, Vietnam; DAR = Julius Nyerere International Airport (Dar es Salaam), Tanzania; EDL = Eldoret International Airport, Kenya; GAU = Guwahati Airport, India; HAN = Noi Bai International Airport (Hanoi), Vietnam; JRO = Kilimanjaro International Airport, Tanzania; KIS = Kisumu International Airport, Kenya; MBA = Moi International Airport (Mombasa), Kenya; MWZ = Mwanza Airport (Mwanza) Tanzania; NBO = Jomo Kenyatta International Airport (Nairobi), Kenya; SGN = Tân Sơn Nhất International Airport (Ho Chi Minh City), Vietnam; SXR = Srinagar International Airport, India; VII = Vinh Airport, Vietnam.

as the Nairobi (NBO) to Mombasa (MBA) route, but not on others such as the Nairobi (NBO) to Eldoret (EDL) and the Nairobi (NBO) to Kisumu (KIS) routes.

In Tanzania, the entrance of LCC fastjet appears to have lowered fares considerably on par with similar routes in India and Vietnam. One reason for the lower fares offered by fastjet is its removal of the added fuel surcharge of US$80 that its competitor, Precision Air, adds to the ticket price. The exception appears to be the Dar es Salaam (DAR) to Zanzibar (ZNZ) route (not depicted in figure 5.9), which has very high fares per mile. Some of the difference in fare may likely be a result of the enlarged distance on some routes, particularly for the Buon Ma Thuot (BMV) to Vinh City (VII) route in Vietnam.

When comparing the distribution of costs between the actual fare and taxes (see figure 5.10), an interesting result can be seen. With the exception of the two routes chosen in the Indian domestic market, base fares in Vietnam are at similar levels or even higher than fares in Kenya and Tanzania. As with international routes, taxation and fees are the key drivers of higher fares.

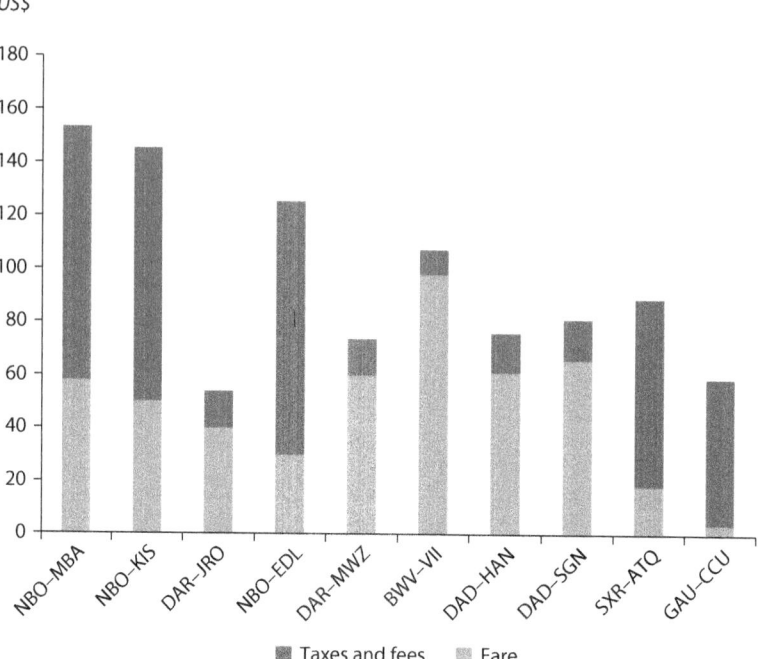

Figure 5.10 Distribution Fare Basis versus Taxation and Charges
US$

Sources: Analysis based on airline websites, including Kenya Airways, Precision Air, Fastjet, Jetstar Pacific, and Spicejet; and DiiO SRS Analyzer (2013).
Note: ATQ = Sri Guru Ram Dass Jee International (Amritsar), India; BMV = Buon Ma Thuot Airport, Vietnam; CCU = Netaji Subhas Chandra Bose International Airport (Kolkata), India; DAD = Da Nang International Airport, Vietnam; DAR = Julius Nyerere International Airport (Dar es Salaam), Tanzania; EDL = Eldoret International Airport, Kenya; GAU = Guwahati Airport, India; HAN = Noi Bai International Airport (Hanoi), Vietnam; JRO = Kilimanjaro International Airport, Tanzania; KIS = Kisumu International Airport, Kenya; MBA = Moi International Airport (Mombasa), Kenya; MWZ = Mwanza Airport (Mwanza) Tanzania; NBO = Jomo Kenyatta International Airport (Nairobi), Kenya; SGN = Tân Sơn Nhất International Airport (Ho Chi Minh City), Vietnam; SXR = Srinagar International Airport, India; VII = Vinh Airport, Vietnam.

The identification of potential comparable routes revealed that LCCs in countries in Asia with similar gross domestic product (GDP) per capita and population (allowing for a considerable margin) are almost always connected to a large economic hub such as Singapore or Kuala Lumpur internationally. These not only provide the high feed into those routes, but also have a significantly larger GDP per capita. No examples could be found where countries with similar GDP per capita to EAC countries have LCC services between them at such distances and population numbers. A more extensive analysis over a specific time period would need to be done to validate these results.

Potential Demand

As noted, the EAC air transport market is still at its early development stages with few routes of significant traffic and a high concentration of carriers, which include state-owned and, in some cases, possibly "government favored" airlines. The industry has, however, seen a new breed of private carriers such as Precision

Air and Air Uganda, as well as the development of an LCC. Despite current limited traffic, leading aircraft manufacturers project significant growth in Africa's air transport market. Airbus has forecast average annual growth rates for traffic to and within Africa to reach 5.7 percent between 2012 and 2031, well above the global growth of 4.7 percent. Between 2012 and 2031, domestic and intra-regional traffic, of crucial importance for LCCs, is expected to grow at 6.2 percent per year (Airbus 2013).

In order to assess the opportunities for growth in air travel demand, this section elaborates on some of the factors that could influence potential underlying demand, and which could provide the basis for increased air transportation, in particular LCC development in the EAC region.

Positive Economic Growth but High Inequality

Spurred by overall political and macroeconomic stability as well as pro-market reforms, the countries of the EAC have seen considerable economic growth in the last decade.

As figure 5.11 shows, all EAC countries have experienced positive GDP growth rates since 2008, in particular Rwanda, Uganda, and Tanzania with average growth rates between 6.4 percent and 8.2 percent. Burundi, plagued by years of civil conflict, has experienced a more stagnant level of growth and Kenya,

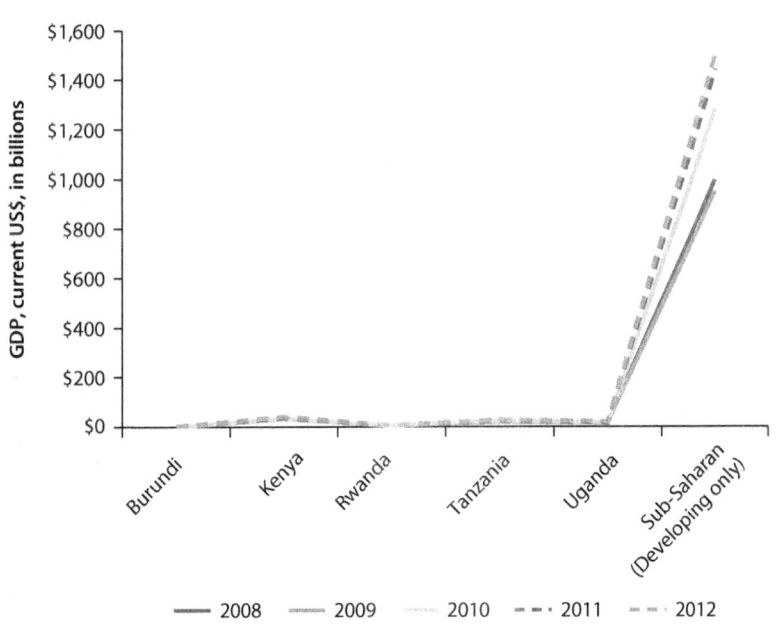

Figure 5.11 GDP Growth in EAC Countries, 2008–12

Source: World Bank 2013c.
Note: EAC = East African Community.

the largest economy in the region, has showed fluctuating growth levels, with particularly low levels of growth in 2008/2009. The fluctuations were caused by its exposure to the global financial crisis, including reduced flows of remittances and the depreciation of the shilling (McKormick 2008). Overall, GDP growth for most EAC countries appears to be in line or above the average GDP growth rate of 4.1 percent experienced across Sub-Saharan developing countries.

With strong GDP growth, per capita incomes have also been increasing steadily. According to the International Monetary Fund, average per capita income (weighed by population in year 2000 dollars) in EAC had reached US$411 in 2010, close to the US$425 average for Sub-Saharan Africa (excluding South Africa and Nigeria). However, wide variations remain within the region with Kenya displaying an average per capita income of US$464 in comparison to US$147 in Burundi (McAuliffe, Saxena, and Zabara 2012).

Figure 5.12 shows air transport intensity (domestic and international) in relation to GDP per capita. As indicated, EAC countries, when compared with countries with similar GDP per capita, display a comparable or higher number of weekly flights per million inhabitants. The exception is Uganda, which has a significantly lower number of weekly flights per million inhabitants. This indicates that, all other things being equal, the air transport market in Uganda still has room for growth at current income levels.

Despite good GDP per capita growth across the region, the emergence of a strong and large middle class has been slow. Poverty levels are still very high in the region, in particular in Burundi where over 90 percent of the population lives below US$2 (purchasing power parity [PPP])[2] a day (see figure 5.13). Similar figures can be seen for Rwanda and Tanzania. This puts air transport, even at a lower fare, out of reach for the majority of the population. Indicators measuring inequality, such as the GINI index, are a direct reflection of this (figure 5.14).

Figure 5.12 Flight Intensity in EAC Countries, 2012

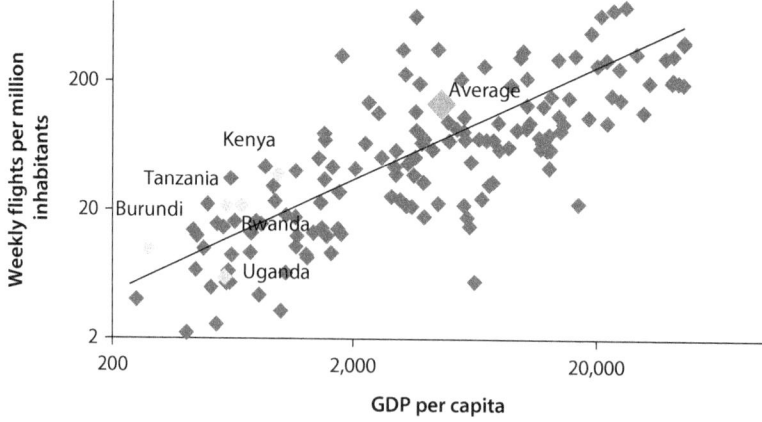

Sources: Analysis based on DiiO SRS Analyzer (2013) and World Bank (2013c).
Note: EAC = East African Community.

Figure 5.13 Poverty Headcount Ratio at $2 (PPP)
percent

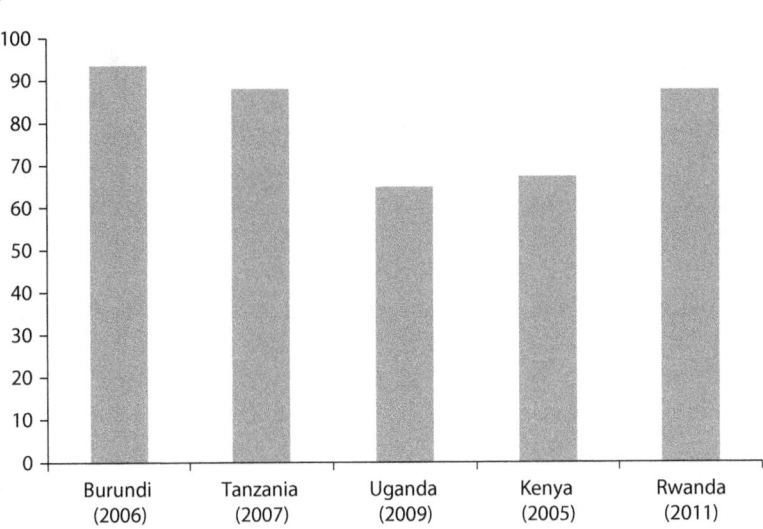

Source: World Bank 2013c.
Note: PPP = purchasing power parity.

Figure 5.14 GINI Index for EAC
percent

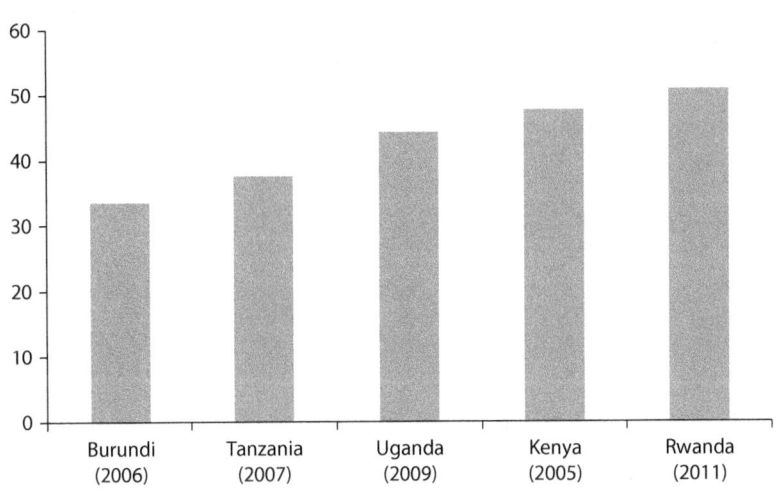

Source: World Bank 2013c.
Note: EAC = East African Community.

The Gini coefficient (in figure 5.14, shown as the GINI index) is the most commonly used measure of inequality. The coefficient varies between zero, which reflects complete equality, and one, which indicates complete inequality (that is, one person has all the income or consumption, all others have none). As figure 5.14 highlights, GINI coefficients for Rwanda, Kenya, and Uganda are particularly high.

Another measure indicative of the levels of inequality is income share distribution (see figure 5.15). In contrast to the GINI coefficient, this gives a clearer picture of where shifts are occurring within the different income classes over time. Due to the lack of data for EAC countries, however, figure 5.15 is only able to display a snapshot of the most recent data. Still, it clearly indicates a strong unequal distribution of wealth in EAC countries. In Rwanda, Kenya, and Uganda, for example, the top 20 percent of the population holds over 50 percent of the country's income. In Uganda, where two data points are available, this inequality appears to be increasing further since 2006.

According to an analysis of the region undertaken by the International Monetary Fund (IMF), in order to achieve significant poverty reduction and middle-income status, the region's real GDP per capita will have to grow at an average rate of 5.5 percent until the end of this decade. This is around two percentage points faster than between 2005 and 2010. Kenya is probably closest to achieving middle-income status, whereas Uganda, Tanzania, and Rwanda would have to grow their per capita income by 7–8 percent a year. For Burundi, this is expected to take much longer.

Current IMF forecasts (IMF 2013) show a positive outlook for the economies of the EAC (see figure 5.16). However, its countries will have to focus on reducing poverty and inequality in order to establish a middle class that can afford air transport.

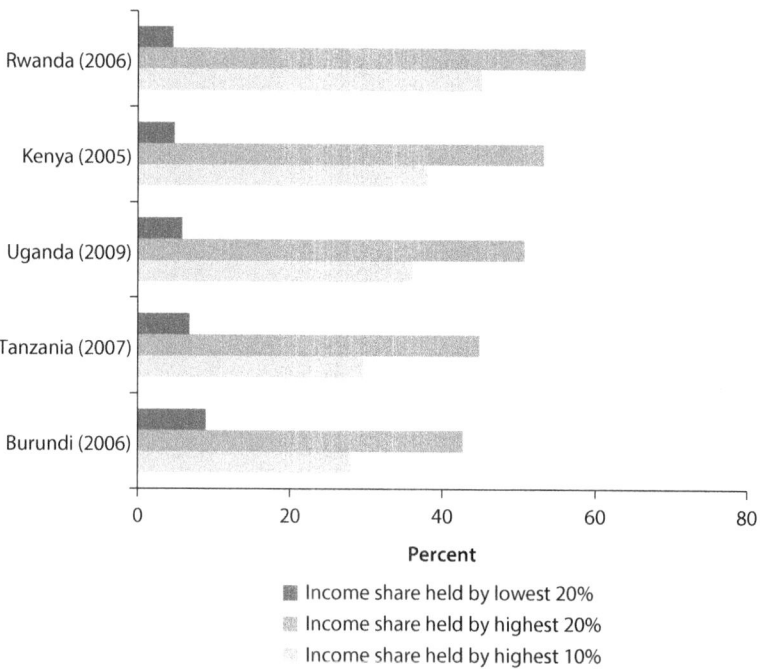

Figure 5.15 Wealth Distribution in EAC Countries

Source: World Bank 2013c.
Note: EAC = East African Community.

Figure 5.16 Forecasted GDP Per Capita Growth Rate in EAC Countries

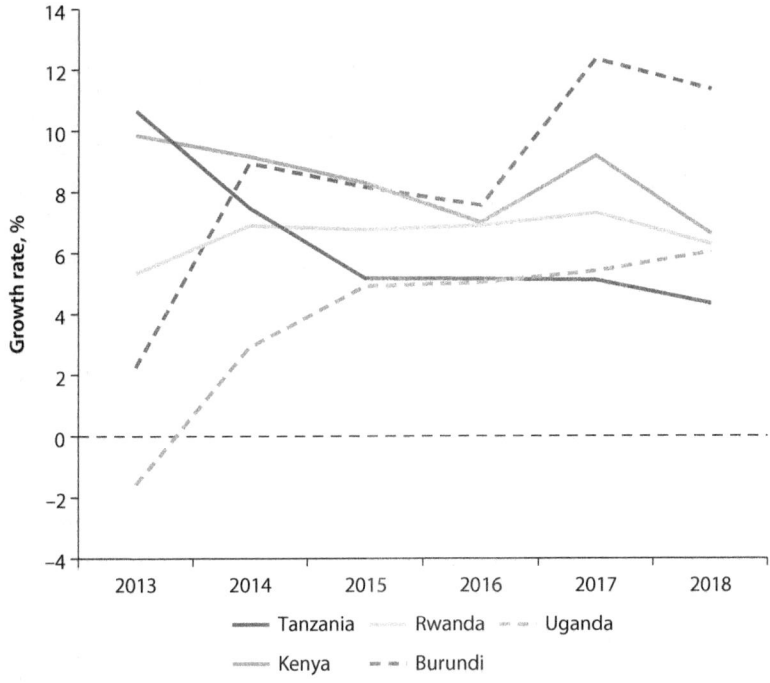

Source: Calculation based on International Monetary Fund (IMF 2013).
Note: Base gross domestic product (GDP) in current prices, U.S. dollars. Year when estimate starts varies by country: Tanzania, 2006; Kenya, 2010; Rwanda, 2010; Burundi not applicable. EAC = East African Community.

Population and Urbanization

Population in the EAC has been continuously growing in recent years, with average growth rates ranging from 2.6 percent to 3.4 percent between 2007 and 2012 (see figure 5.17). Uganda and Burundi achieved the highest growth rate, with Uganda having the second highest fertility rate globally. Some organizations, such as the United Nations Population Fund (UNPF), have voiced concerns about this development, given that EAC countries still face challenges in providing the required education and employment for a growing younger generation (Emorut 2012b).

Population growth will be accompanied by a shift in migration from rural to urban environments. Urbanization has increased consistently between 2007 and 2012 (see figure 5.18). Tanzania's urban population represents over a quarter of its total population, with 8 percent of the population found in Dar es Salaam. Urbanization in Burundi is still low at 11 percent, with 90 percent of the population consisting of self-subsistence farmers. Similarly, Uganda has large populations in rural lands tending to the agricultural exports (for example, coffee, cotton, tea) of the country. The primary sector employs 75 percent of the country's work force (Uganda Bureau of Statistics 2007).

Figure 5.17 Population Growth in EAC, 2007–12

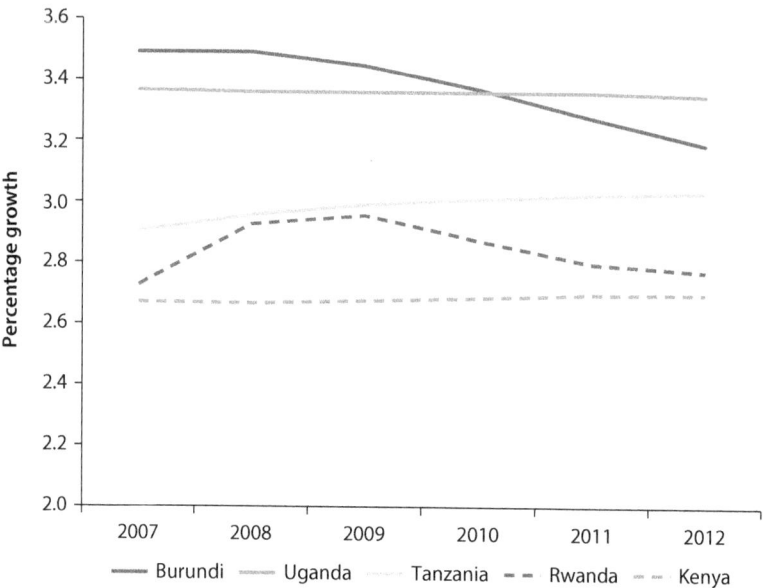

Source: World Bank 2013c.
Note: EAC = East African Community.

Figure 5.18 Urban Population, 2007–12

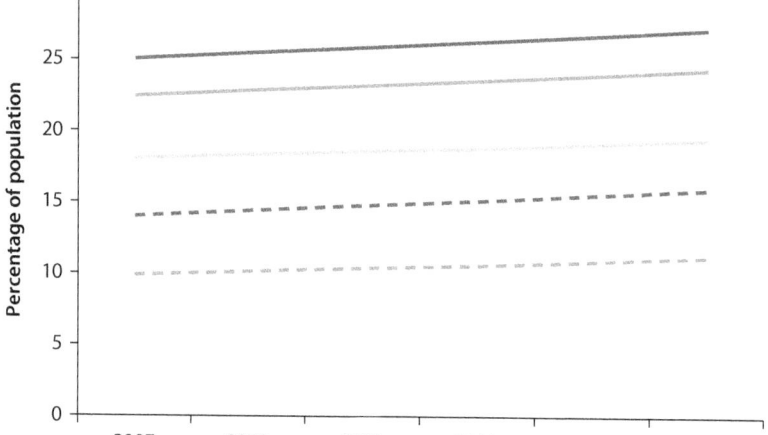

Source: World Bank 2013c.

Urbanization has been seen as a key driver for economic growth, and consequently the development of air transport markets, particulary in Kenya and Tanzania. In both markets, urbanization is expected to grow, with forecasts for Kenya showing that by 2033, its population will be equally distributed between urban and rural areas (World Bank 2011b). Much of this urbanization will however be concentrated in few locations, particularly in Kenya where Nairobi and Mombasa represent the only cities with a population above one million and Kisumu, the third largest city, recording a population of only 400,000.

Leisure Markets—Tourism and Visiting Friends and Relatives Travel

As outlined in chapter 4, LCCs primarily target leisure travelers, who are cost sensitive but more amenable with regard to service offerings and scheduling. This allows LCCs to operate with greater flexibility and limits operational complexity. The leisure category includes in particular tourist and visiting friends and relatives (VFR) travelers.

East Africa with its national parks, mountain ranges, and scenic beaches has become a popular destination for tourism. As figure 5.19 shows, the number of international arrivals has grown considerably in most EAC countries.

Uganda has shown particularly high growth, which can be attributed to the increase of tourists from Asia to its famous national parks, and its relative political stability and security (Emorut 2012a). Both Tanzania and Rwanda have also experienced increasing visitors between 2006 and 2010. Rwanda, after having restructured its tourism sector in 2001, has been particularly focused on attracting high-end customers. This has been reflected in the major private investments that have been made to upgrade accommodations in the market. Both Marriott and Sheraton hotel chains are constructing 5-star facilities for US$160 million and employing about 200 people (Rwigamba 2013). Kenya's tourism industry experienced a large drop in arrivals in 2007 and 2008 due to the outbreak of violence and political instability, triggered by the events following the 2007 Kenyan elections. The industry is recovering, however, and

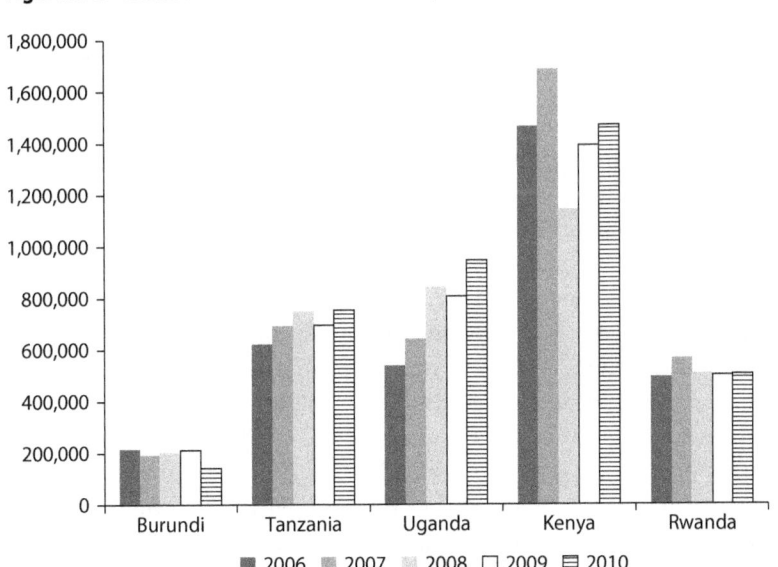

Figure 5.19 Number of International Arrivals, 2006–10

Source: World Bank 2013c.

recorded almost 1.5 million international tourists in 2010 (UNWTO 2011). Burundi is still lagging considerably behind due to years of civil strife and limited tourism infrastructure.

EAC tourism is dominated primarily by European and American visitors. In Kenya, for example, the Kenya Tourism Board found that in 2010 almost half of its tourists originated from only five countries (the United Kingdom, the United States, France, Italy, and Germany) (Kenya Ministry of Tourism 2010). In Tanzania, a survey by the Tanzania National Bureau of Statistics and the Bank of Tanzania also showed that arrivals from Italy, the United States, the United Kingdom, and Germany dominate the tourism market (Tanzania National Bureau of Statistics 2012). More recently, intra-African and intra-EAC tourism have also been recorded. In Kenya, recorded tourist arrivals from Uganda and Tanzania were 33,900 and 30,264 visitors respectively (Kenya Ministry of Tourism 2010) and in Rwanda around 40 percent of visitors originated from the region in 2010. Only 5 percent traveled for tourism purposes however (Rwanda Development Board n.d.). Similarly, in Uganda arrivals from Africa seem to dominate its market but only 5 percent are tourists (Uganda Bureau of Statistics 2010), while European visitors primarily dominate the tourism market (Balinda 2013). No equivalent information could be found for the tourism market in Burundi.

According to the World Tourism and Travel Council, tourism is forecast to grow considerably in the region. Between 2013 and 2023, international tourist arrivals in Kenya are set to grow to 2.6 million visitors (World Travel and Tourism Council 2013a). Similarly, for Rwanda this growth rate is forecast at around 4.6 percent (World Travel and Tourism Council 2013b). Expected growth is even higher in Uganda (World Travel and Tourism Council 2013c) and in Tanzania (World Travel and Tourism Council 2013d), at about 5.6 percent and 5 percent respectively.

This growth will be of particular importance, as tourism plays a crucial role in the economies of the EAC. As figure 5.20 shows, for Rwanda and Uganda, tourism comprises a large percentage of their exports.

Significant efforts have therefore been made to facilitate intra- and inter-regional tourism. The EAC Secretariat is trying, for example, to remove restrictive customs and border control processes to facilitate travel in the region. To this end, all EAC member states met in July 2013, to outline new milestones for the introduction of a common EAC tourism visa, as well as a common passport for EAC member countries. The proposal has been deliberated since 2005, but has experienced significant delays resulting from security concerns, poor infrastructure, and disagreement over visa fee schedules and revenue-sharing frameworks. Leaving time to resolve these issues, the changes are now planned to be introduced by the end of 2014. In an initial step, all EAC countries have agreed to align their immigration laws and to put into place the technology needed for integrating their information network systems (Ramah 2013). These changes will also be a key factor for another known source of LCC demand, the so-called VFR travel resulting from intra-regional migration flows.

Figure 5.20 International Tourism Receipts, 2010
percentage of total exports

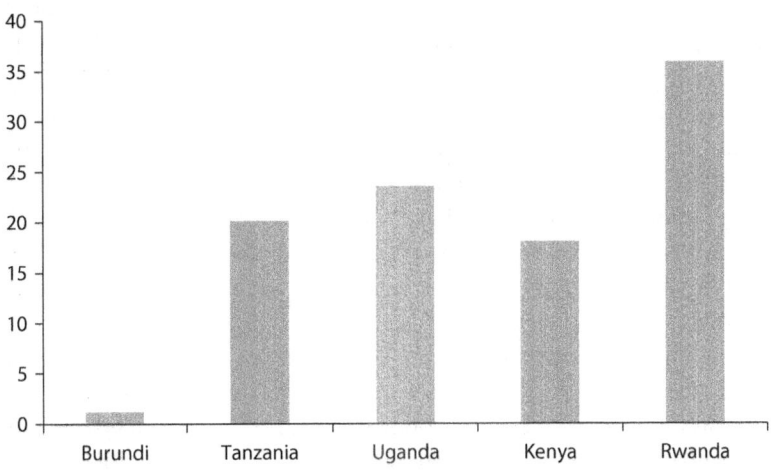

Source: World Bank 2013c.

Table 5.2 Estimates of Bilateral Migrant Stock, 2010

	Destination				
Source	Burundi	Kenya	Uganda	Tanzania	Rwanda
Burundi	—	0	101,826	151,313	44,785
Kenya	0	—	41,065	91,146	0
Uganda	0	531,218	—	30,110	20,737
Tanzania	7,608	92,527	71,833	—	6,037
Rwanda	33,540	0	123,860	49,536	—

Source: Migration and Remittances Factbook (World Bank 2011b).
Note: — = not available.

According to a 2011 World Bank study, more than 50 percent of migration in East Africa actually occurs within the region (Ratha and others 2011). Table 5.2 shows the migration stocks of EAC member countries as collated in the World Bank's Migration and Remittances Factbook 2011 (World Bank 2011c). Unfortunately, data on migration in Africa are often missing, out-of-date, or inconsistent with definitions used in other countries. Therefore, such data should be interpreted with caution. For example, it is surprising to see that no migrants have been recorded from Burundi to Kenya.

Migration within the EAC has occurred because of several reasons. These are primarily economic (for example, employment and education) and/or political (that is, civil unrest, political instability). Assessing various patterns of migration within the region is very complex and would be outside the scope of this book. However, a few key developments that may potentially have an impact on future air travel demand are reviewed below.

One important factor for migration within the EAC has been the economic integration and free movement of labor in the region through the EAC Treaty.

This has been particularly attractive for smaller, less developed, and historically unstable countries, such as Burundi and Rwanda. For example, Rwandese nationals, spurred by forced migration during the Rwanda Genocide in 1994, have a substantial presence in Uganda, Tanzania, and neighboring Burundi. Movements are further facilitated by language, cultural, or historical ties. Emigrants from Burundi and Rwanda, for example, often speak the same language as or have historical ties with the native populations in Uganda and Tanzania (Ratha and others 2011). High levels of migration have also been observed between Uganda and Kenya, potentially contributing to the increased traffic on the Entebbe (EBB) to Nairobi (NBO) route. The economic integration of the region and the introduction of a common passport are expected to further increase this growth.

Alternative Modes of Transport

Inefficient ground transport has been a key driver for the development of air transport and LCCs in developing countries. Figure 5.21 compares the numbers of visitors arriving by each mode of transport. It shows clearly that in Rwanda and Uganda, and to a lesser extent in Tanzania and Kenya, arrivals are often by land transport. The more detailed statistics for Rwanda show that land access is particularly prevalent for tourists. In 2011, 61 percent of arrivals by passengers traveling for tourism purposes entered by land (Rwanda Institute of Statistics 2012).

Kenya displays a high share of arrivals by air, mostly due to traffic through the region's hub in Nairobi (Kenya National Bureau of Statistics 2010).

In order to understand the market opportunities for "converting" land-based transport users to air travelers, it is important to look at the availability, quality,

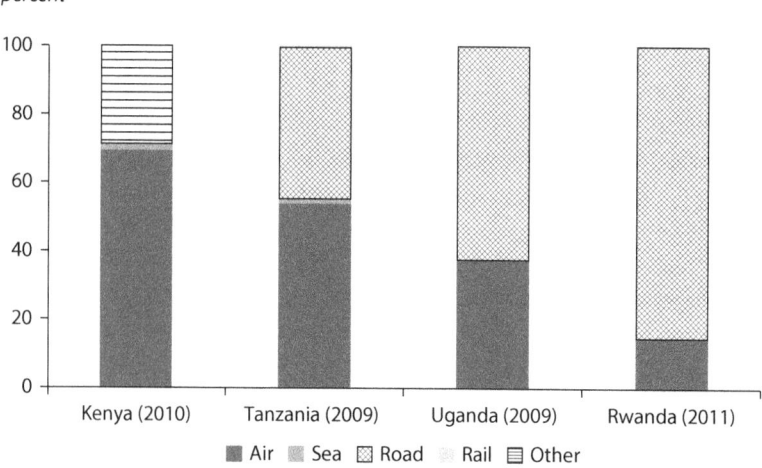

Figure 5.21 Arrival by Mode of Transport
percent

Sources: Analysis based on data from Kenya National Bureau of Statistics (2010); Uganda Bureau of Statistics 2010; National Institute of Statistics Rwanda 2012; and Tanzania Ministry of Natural Resources and Tourism 2010.
Note: Definition of mode may vary. In Kenya "other" includes rail and road transport.

and cost of these means of transport. To assess this, the book draws upon an extensive analysis of transport infrastructure in the region conducted by the World Bank in 2011 (Ranganathan and Foster 2011).

Road Transport

As map 5.2 shows, EAC regional corridors are typically paved (around 73 percent of all roads are paved) and almost 80 percent of regional roads are in good or fair condition. Although few, there are some road segments of poor quality and significant unpaved stretches, as for example on the Dar es Salaam to Bujumbura route or on the Kampala to Kigali route. The poor condition of these roads slows traffic considerably.

Generally, all EAC members except Uganda show good maintenance records on their portions of the regional network. The EAC, together with development partners such as the African Development Bank, the Japanese Bank for International Cooperation, and the World Bank have focused on improving road conditions under the East African Road Network Project and other programs (NEPAD–OECD Africa Investment Initiative 2008).

Generally road infrastructure between larger cities in the EAC is in good condition, but the quality of rural roads providing access to primary roads, still

Map 5.2 Road Network: Major Primary Road by Type and Condition

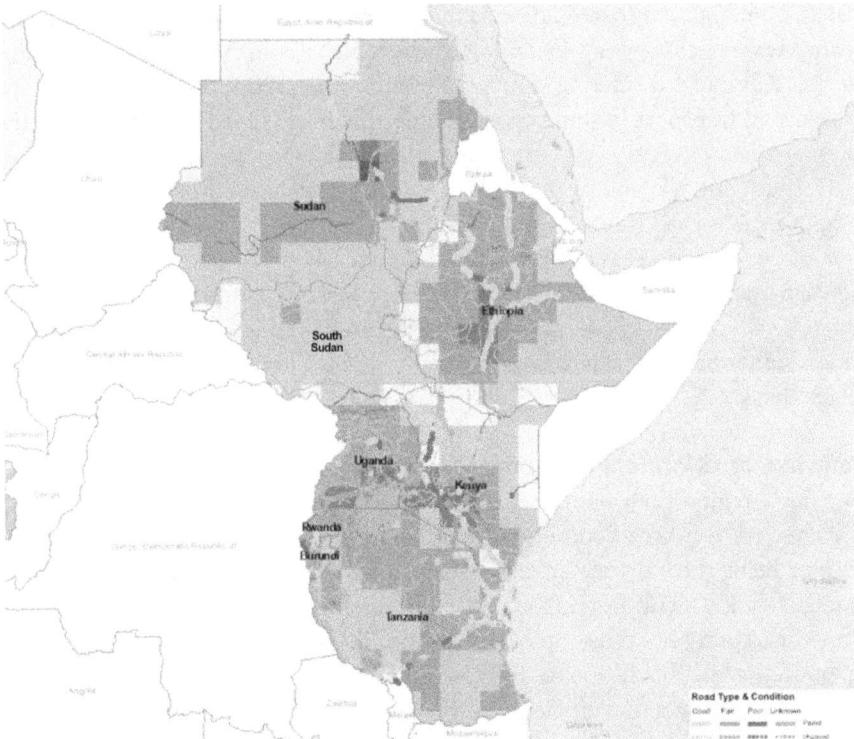

Source: World Bank's *East Africa Infrastructure Report* (World Bank 2011a).

varies significantly. A rural road condition assessment by the Africa Infrastructure Country Diagnostics (AICD) program (in Gwilliam and others 2011) shows that the quality of rural roads in the region is still poor. Among EAC states, Rwanda's rural network is assessed the worst—with poor quality, rural roads across its entire network. In Uganda, over 50 percent of rural roads (by length) are still considered to be of inferior quality, whereas in Tanzania, Kenya, and Burundi, the share of poor quality rural roads falls below 50 percent. Kenya is the country with the most high quality roads in the region, followed by Burundi.

The use of passenger cars is still low in the EAC. In Rwanda, there were only 0.5 cars per 1,000 inhabitants in the year 2007, 2 in Burundi, 4 in Tanzania and 3 in Uganda. Kenya has the highest rate with 14 passenger cars per 1,000 inhabitants in 2010. This compares to 423 cars per 1,000 inhabitants in the United States and 457 in the United Kingdom for the same year. As access to passenger cars is still limited, reliance is high on other forms of ground transport, including buses and trains. There are various companies providing bus services in the region, primarily connecting major cities. A prominent provider is Scandinavia Express, offering high frequency bus service to 18 destinations within Tanzania, Kenya, Uganda, and Zambia. A one-way fare from Dar es Salaam to Nairobi costs around US$23, and between Kampala and Nairobi about US$30 (Scandinavia Express 2013). Two other Kenyan companies, Mash and Easy Coach primarily offer bus operations within Kenya and to Kampala. According to the Easy Coach website, a fare between Nairobi and Kampala is offered at US$27 (Easy Coach 2013). Some bus companies, such as the Riverside shuttle, have been particularly geared toward connecting incoming tourism at Nairobi Airport to destinations such as Kilimanjaro, offering competitive fares of US$20 for a one-way trip. This makes land transport in some cases, and on this route in particular, an attractive alternative and a significant competitor for LCCs.

Despite the availability of alternative modes of ground-based transport on certain routes, road safety is still a large concern in Africa. In 2010, the World Health Organization (WHO) estimated that nearly 8,484 people were killed on Kenyan roads in 2010 (WHO 2013). This translates into a death rate of 20.9 per 100,000 people. In contrast the United States and the United Kingdom, with much higher usage of cars, have death rates of 11.4 and 3.7 per 100,000 people respectively.

Railways and Maritime Transport

The EAC region does not have a truly integrated rail network, and only three railway lines run across more than one country, with the one linking Kenya to Uganda being the only one linking EAC countries. The quality of railways in EAC is relatively low, with little maintenance having been undertaken. Moreover railway infrastructure is only capable of light and slow-moving trains, and regional operations are difficult due to differing railway gauges in each country.

There are only a few efficient railway operators in the region. Tanzania's two operators, Tanzania Railways Limited (TRL) and Tazara, have been showing some signs of success in past years, but both operators are still lagging behind

Table 5.3 Comparison of Bus Travel and Flight Times

Route	Bus time (approx.)	Flight time
Nairobi–Mombasa	8 hours	1 hour
Nairobi–Kampala	12 hours	1 hour, 8 minutes
Nairobi–Dar es Salaam	13 hours	1 hour, 25 minutes
Nairobi–Kigali	24 hours	1 hour, 22 minutes
Entebbe–Kigali	9 hours	50 minutes
Nairobi–Kisumu	5 hours, 30 minutes	50 minutes
Dar es Salaam–Arusha	9 hours	1 hour, 25 minutes

Source: Flight schedules and bus websites.

the Rift Valley Railways (RVR) consortium that operates between Kenya and Uganda. The railway concession, financed by various donors including the African Development Bank and the International Finance Corporation (IFC) (Evans 2011) carried around 1.5 million tons in 2012 in comparison to less than half a million for both TRL and Tazara.

On the Dar es Salaam to Zanzibar route—a main gateway for tourism, air transport also competes with maritime transport. The route has a modern ferry service running four times daily with economy class fares of US$35.

Despite the availability of alternative modes of transport on certain routes, air travel has a significant advantage over each of them, that is, speed. Table 5.3 shows the travel times by bus and by plane between major cities in EAC. This excludes any delays, such as customs hold ups or journey interruptions, which could potentially add to total transport time.

A bus journey from Dar es Salaam to Nairobi takes around 13 hours, and almost a whole day between Nairobi and Kigali (Scandinavia Express 2013). In Kenya, the bus from Nairobi to Mombasa takes around 8 hours, and until the Uganda–Kenya railway is modernized, the rail journey takes around 15 hours (Evans 2011).

Air Transport Infrastructure

As elaborated in chapter 4, the availability—but most importantly the quality, capacity, and cost of air transport infrastructure—plays a crucial role for the development of LCCs and air transportation in general. This section provides an analysis of airports in the EAC region, focusing in particular on availability, quality, and capacity of airside,[3] landside,[4] CNS (communications, navigation, and surveillance) infrastructure, and ground handling, as well as airport management and usage costs. In addition, factors relating to airport access will be reviewed.

Airport Infrastructure
Overall Quality

With the exception of the World Economic Forum's annual quality of air transport infrastructure report, there are few indexes that measure the overall quality of air transport infrastructure. As figure 5.22 shows, Kenya's air transport

Figure 5.22 Air Transport Infrastructure Quality, 2012/13

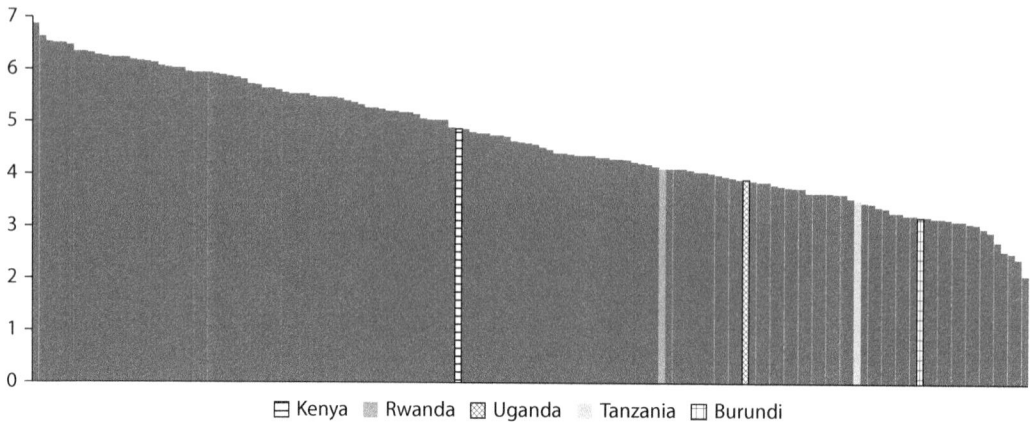

Source: World Economic Forum *Global Competitiveness Report 2012–2013*, Switzerland (WEF 2013).
Note: 7 – high quality, 1 – low quality.

infrastructure is ranked the highest among EAC states, followed with a significant margin by Rwanda and Uganda. Tanzania and Burundi appear to have the lowest ranking air transport infrastructure.

Although this gives an indication of the overall quality of air transport infrastructure, large differences prevail between individual airports, requiring a more detailed assessment.

Airside—Runways, Taxiways, and Aprons

The EAC has a considerable number of airfields, particularly in Kenya and Tanzania. However, the majority of airfields have unpaved runways, and are, with few exceptions, unsuitable for commercial operations. For July 2012–13, only 10 percent of total airports actually received scheduled services and less than 40 percent are both paved and have the required runway length to accommodate regional jets, such as the fuel-efficient Embraer ERJ-170-100 (see table 5.4). In order not to impose major limitations, however, the sample chosen focuses on all airports which currently receive scheduled services, as well as other airports with paved and sufficiently long runways for operations of regional aircraft (based on ERJ-170-100). A list of all airports assessed and detailed information can be found in appendix G.

The majority of EAC airports receiving scheduled services, with the exception of some airports in Kenya (for example, Mara Serena Airport in Kenya), and Tanzania (for example, Bukoba Airport), have paved runways, taxiways, and aprons. Assessing their conditions remotely, however, is a difficult task. It is often based on a few high level indicators that can be evaluated from satellite imagery. This includes any patching that has been undertaken to cover previous pavement failures, which, when observed over a period of time, may be linked to ongoing condition issues. It is, however, in most cases impossible to identify any major signs of pavement failure, such as cracking, rutting or chip loss.

Table 5.4 Airfields in EAC

Country	Number of airfields	Scheduled service (July 2013)	Paved	Unpaved	International	ERJ-170-100 capable (approx. 5,400 ft at maximum take-off weight)
Burundi	3	1	1	2	1	1
Kenya	194	17	15	179	5	4
Tanzania	106	14	11	95	6	5
Rwanda	7	3	4	3	2	1
Uganda	46	2	5	41	1	3
Total	**356**	**37**	**36**	**320**	**15**	**14**

Sources: AZ World Airports 2013a; CIA 2013; and DiiO SRS Analyzer 2013.

There are few reports available on runway conditions in the EAC. A report produced by the AICD program previously assessed the runway quality of major airports in Africa. It identified that the airports in the region receiving the highest volumes of traffic, for example Nairobi and Dar es Salaam, generally have higher quality runways of standard length for larger jet aircraft operations (AICD 2009).

Communications, Navigation and Surveillance Infrastructure

CNS infrastructure in the EAC is still largely insufficient, but some progress has been achieved in recent years. The installation of ground-based navigation aids for en route and approach navigation is patchy, with only a bit more than half of the airports assessed having any installations. This often requires pilots to fly under visual flight rules (VFR), whereby pilots rely on the "see and avoid" rule and are dependent on clear weather conditions to ensure visibility. Most airports that have any ground-based navigation aids are equipped with simple nondirectional beacons (NDBs) or in some cases with additional, more sophisticated VHF omnidirectional range (VOR) systems. Few VOR installations are complemented with distance measuring equipment (DME), which aids aircraft pilots in determining the exact distance from the land-based navigation aids, further improving navigation precision. Installations for aircraft approach and landing such as instrument landing systems (ILS), precision approach path indicators (PAPI), and more sophisticated lighting systems are common only at major airports such as Nairobi, Dar es Salaam, or Entebbe.

Radar installations for surveillance and air traffic management (ATM) are rare due to high equipment and maintenance costs. Some airports such as Dar es Salaam and Nairobi have secondary radar installations, and Mombasa can use radar procedures if required (Gwilliam and others 2011). Uganda installed a new secondary radar for EUR7 million in 2006.[5] The radar is also able to monitor parts of the airspace in neighboring Rwanda, the Democratic Republic of Congo, Kenya, and Tanzania—but does not provide any services to aircraft operating in those airspaces (Kazooba 2007).

Whether or not all of these installations are actually operational is unknown. This is related to the fact that the necessary information for pilots that would indicate the failure of any equipment, so-called NOTAMS (notices to airmen), are not being issued consistently or are not publicly available.

The lack of ground-based navigation aids and radar is still a critical weakness at this point in time. However, it is seemingly becoming a smaller issue due to the development of satellite-based navigation and surveillance systems. Although NDB and VOR remain common in developed countries, most modern aircraft rely now on global navigation satellite systems (GNSS). GNSS approaches are already being used at the major airports in Dar es Salaam and Nairobi. A pilot study to introduce GNSS procedures throughout the EAC has been undertaken with U.S. government funding in 2006. The EAC has formulated a plan to introduce GNSS procedures at three airports of each community member, which has yet to be implemented (EAC n.d.).

GNSS also provides the basis for modern surveillance technology, such as the automatic dependent surveillance-broadcast system (ADS-B). ADS-B is a more advanced and cost-effective substitute to today's radar system, and is currently being implemented in the United States, Europe, Australia and a few other countries. It has also been considered in the EAC, with Tanzania recently announcing the implementation of ADS-B at its air traffic control (ATC) center in Dar es Salaam (Comsoft 2013).

Communications infrastructure (ground-to-air and ground-to-ground) has improved considerably, and all EAC countries have benefited from regional communications projects such as the SADC Very-Small Aperture Terminal (VSAT) Network, which covers Tanzania, Rwanda, and Burundi, as well as the North Eastern African Indian Ocean VSAT (NAFISAT) network covering Tanzania, Uganda, and Kenya (Air Traffic and Navigation Services 2013). VSAT is a technology used to define two-way satellite communications, to transmit and receive data from a relatively small satellite dish on earth, and communicate with an orbiting geostationary satellite.

The management of air traffic lies with a designated provider in the respective flight information region (FIR). The EAC region is divided into five FIRs (Nairobi FIR, Dar es Salaam FIR, Entebbe FIR, Kigali FIR, and Bujumbura FIR) each with a designated ATM provider. With the exception of the Bujumbura FIR that relies on Dar es Salaam to provide ATM for its upper air space, each of the respective ATM providers is responsible for upper and lower air space.[6] Rwanda, whose upper air space was historically also managed by Tanzania, has recently announced that it will be taking over control of its upper air space (Muson 2009). Currently ATM services are provided by the specialized departments of the respective civil aviation authority (CAA) in each country. The respective CAA also provide approach and aerodrome control at major airports, as well as aerodrome flight information services (AFIS) on some secondary airports.

Multiple initiatives have been introduced to improve CNS capabilities in the region. COMESA has launched an integrated air space project with the financial support of the African Development Bank. The project's objective is to develop (a) a legal and regulatory framework for a unified upper airspace in the COMESA Region; (b) an adequate institutional framework for providing and regulating regional air traffic services; and (c) public-private partnership arrangements to finance, build, and operate the regional communications, navigation, and surveillance systems for air traffic management (CNS/ATM) infrastructure (African Development Bank 2011a). Simultaneously, the EAC Secretariat has been working toward a regional upper flight information region (UFIR) governing the upper air space of all EAC members, thereby enhancing safety and efficiency and allowing for a seamless flow of traffic (CASSOA 2013). Trying to integrate all of these efforts within the region, the COMESA-EAC-SAD Tripartite has been developing a strategy for the seamless integration of all upper air space between the three RECs (OECD and WTO 2011).

Landside

There is often little public information available about the condition of landside infrastructure, especially passenger terminals, in EAC. Many airport facilities in the region have relatively old (for example, Entebbe or Dar es Salaam), limited, or in some cases no passenger facilities (for example, Lodwar Airport). Many of the smaller airports also do not have any or only part-time customs or immigration facilities required for international traffic. Whereas outdated and deteriorated infrastructure may be a significant issue at the country's main gateways, smaller airports with little traffic do not, in most cases, require any lavish airside facilities as long as safety and security standards can be ensured.

As described in chapter 4, most large airports in developed countries use various metrics to determine the level of service (LOS). These include aspects such as waiting and processing times and available space. This often relies on data-intense and costly primary research, for example through surveys, which are unavailable for this case.

When unable to obtain the needed data to quantitatively assess the quality of landside infrastructure, customer reviews provide for an alternative qualitative, albeit less scientific view. Skytrax, for example, a commonly known source for airport rankings, covers some of the larger airports in the region such as Nairobi, Mombasa, Dar es Salaam, Entebbe, or Kigali. As the number and timing of reviews vary and are subject to personal opinions, caution is warranted. However, the ranking serves as an interesting indicator of passenger perception. Both Entebbe and Kigali rank high in their reviews (achieving 7.3 and 8 out of 10 points), whereas Bujumbura, Jomo Kenyatta, and Mombasa achieve low scores, particularly due to slow processing times and the general quality of facilities (Skytrax 2013).

Airport Infrastructure Capacity

A crucial factor in assessing the current quality of infrastructure and prospects for the development of air services is available capacity. As outlined in chapter 1, LCCs avoid highly congested airports because of the costs associated with delays and inflexible scheduling. In order to assess the current utilization of airports and

Table 5.5 Potential Runway Capacity per Year (5 Minute and 10 Minute Lags) and Current Estimated Passenger Terminal Capacity

Airport	Current capacity (available seats)	Potential runway capacity yearly (5 minute lag, PAX)	Potential runway capacity yearly (10 minute lag, PAX)	Current terminal passenger capacity (estimated)
NBO	Ca. 8.5 million	12,467,232	6,233,616	2.5 million
DAR	Ca. 3.0 million	9,198,000	4,599,000	1.5 million
EBB	Ca. 1.8 million	10,659,168	5,329,584	2.5 million
MBA	Ca. 1.5 million	9,534,384	4,767,192	0.9 million
KGL	Ca. 1.5 million	9,702,576	4,851,288	0.4 million
JRO	Ca. 1.0 million	3,048,480	1,524,240	0.5 million
ZNZ	Ca. 880,000	4,982,688	2,491,344	3.0 million (by end of 2013)
MWZ	Ca. 550,000	2,743,632	1,371,816	1.0 million (90 percent completed)
BJM	Ca. 500,000	8,062,704	4,031,352	—
KIS	Ca. 330,000	4,860,924	2,430,462	0.5 million

Sources: Calculation based on DiiO SRS Analyzer (2013), and AZ World Airports *Passenger Capacity* (2013b).
Note: BJM = Bujumbura, Burundi; DAR = Dar es Salaam, Tanzania; EBB = Entebbe, Uganda; JRO = Kilimanjaro, Tanzania; KIS = Kisumu, Kenya; KGL = Kigali, Rwanda; MBA = Mombasa, Kenya; MWZ = Mwanza, Tanzania; NBO = Nairobi; PAX = passengers; ZNZ = Zanzibar, Tanzania; — = not available.

potential for growth, it is necessary to look at both airside and landside capacity of a given airport.

Table 5.5 shows the current and potential estimated capacity of the region's largest airports by movement (see appendix H for methodology on runway and terminal capacity estimations). Setting aside constraints posed by apron capacity, the estimates show that almost none of the airports in this sample have reached their potential runway capacity when assuming a five-minute time lag between each flight. When assuming a longer time lag of ten minutes between operations, the only airport that has already exceeded runway capacity is Jomo Kenyatta Airport in Nairobi. Thus, additional runway capacity appears not to be required for most airports. Instead, the focus should be on rehabilitation of current infrastructure, and on possible apron extensions, as well as on more effective scheduling and potential relocation of taxiways to enable a more efficient flow of traffic. It should be noted that these estimates are based on the current average capacity per operation, and runway extensions required for the operation of larger aircraft may be warranted if traffic increases dramatically.

Although the figures show that runway capacity does not pose a major challenge for airport operations, passenger terminal capacity appears to be greatly constraining air traffic. Most passenger terminals were not built to handle the increase in passengers, as experienced at some airports, particularly in Nairobi, Dar es Salaam, Kigali, and Zanzibar.

Expansion Projects Underway

Recognizing the constraints of landside facilities, major investment projects have been initiated in the region. This includes the expansion of Jomo Kenyatta Airport, partially financed by the World Bank, which includes a new terminal and possibly a new runway, increasing the number of potential movements.

The Kenyan government has also been upgrading smaller airports, such as the Mandan Airstrip in Lamu, which included the construction of a two-kilometer runway, a new terminal building, additional water supplies, and fencing, as well as a new fire station (*Ventures* 2013).

Tanzania is currently refurbishing and upgrading 10 regional airports under a US$67.5 million infrastructure project (Mbalamwezi 2011), and is investing US$170 million to build Terminal 3 for Julius Nyere Airport in Dar es Salaam. The existing international Terminal 2 will then be used for domestic flights (*allAfrica* 2013). Under the World Bank's Tanzania Transport Sector Support Project, the country is also paving and rehabilitating the runway at Kigoma and Tabora Airports, and extending, rehabilitating, and paving the runway, apron, terminal, and car parking at Bukoba Airport.

In Rwanda, the government is finalizing talks with a Chinese firm to construct the Bugesera International Airport, which will serve as a complementary airport for Kigali, located 25 kilometers east of the capital (Ssuuna 2013). Kigali, having reached its maximum capacity according to authorities, is also currently being upgraded to cater to higher passenger volumes.

Finally, the government of Uganda has announced, in its 20-year civil aviation master plan in 2013, a US$400 million project to modernize Entebbe airport facilities as well as smaller domestic airports such as Kasese, Gulu, Arua, and Kotido (Muchira 2013). These are just a few examples of ongoing projects, which are increasing the capacity of the aviation system in EAC.

Ground Handling Services

The provision of ground handling services varies significantly across EAC countries. Kenya has a competitive ground handling services industry with 15 different passenger and cargo ground handling providers, both local and international. Although companies provide varying offerings, competition appears to exist across almost all service categories (for example, ramp, passenger services, load control and support, and so on), with the notable exception of fueling services (Airline Update n.d.). This has significantly driven costs down, but could be unsustainable in the long term (World Bank 2005). Tanzania, after years of a ground handling monopoly with the firm Swissport Tanzania (previously Dahaco), has finally allowed competition to enter the market in 2009 (Tanzania Civil Aviation Authority 2013a), although a few licenses have been granted a quasi-monopoly and high charges have remained. Similarly in Rwanda, the government has finally allowed a second ground handling provider to enter the market, with Rwandair Express having been the only service provider for many years (Airline Update n.d.). In Uganda, ground handling is managed by two companies, with airlines complaining about the high cost of service and potentially uncompetitive practices between Uganda's CAA and one of the ground handling providers ENHAS (Muhumuza 2012). In Burundi, there is currently only one ground handling provider, Asjetflow (Airline Update n.d.). However, considering the low volumes of traffic, more ground handling providers may be not feasible.

Infrastructure Charges

As seen in the case studies of South Africa and Mexico, high levels of airport charges can pose a considerable challenge for the development of LCCs. The analysis here assesses current infrastructure charges at EAC countries, and benchmarks these against similar airports in the region and globally (see appendix I for methodology including base case scenario and more detailed charges assessment).

The level of airport charges at EAC airports varies considerably in relation to destination and type of charge (passenger borne or airline borne). Figure 5.23 compares airport charges for a sample of airports in EAC for domestic operations. As the analysis shows, airport charges for domestic operations are particularly high in Rwanda, driven strongly by high passenger facility charges/service charges (PFC/PSC).

Figure 5.23 Total Turnaround Charges for Domestic Daytime Flight
US$

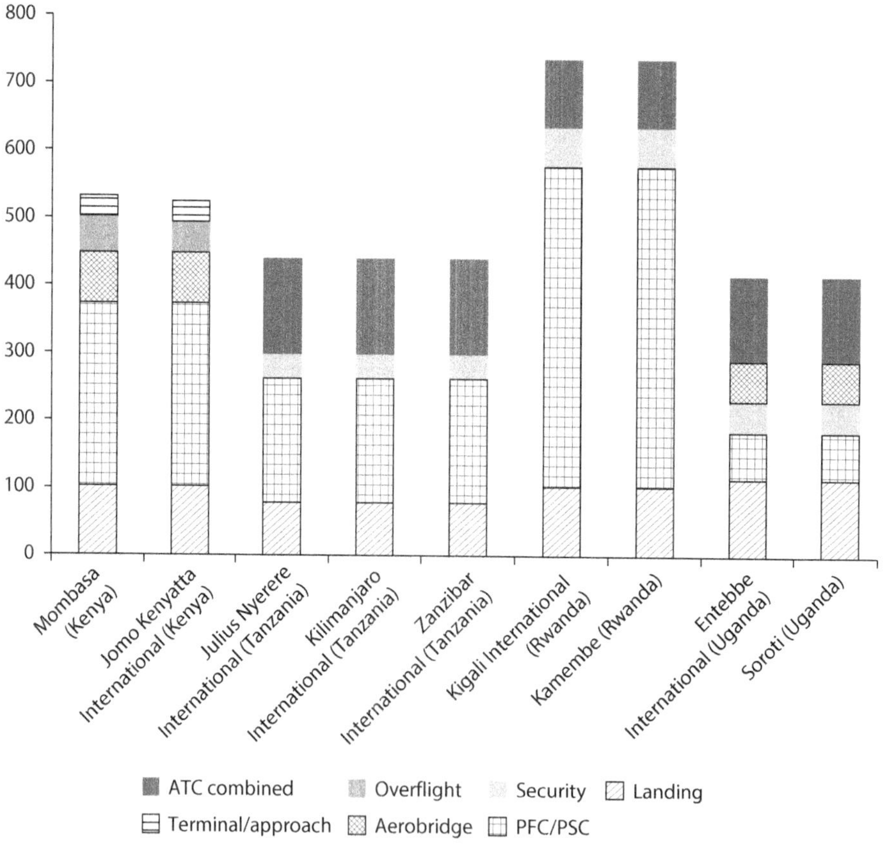

Sources: Analysis based on aeronautical information publications from Kenya, Rwanda, Tanzania, Uganda, Burundi, and airport websites.
Note: Domestically registered ATR72-500, maximum takeoff weight 23 tons, 74 passengers at 80 percent load factor, turnaround time two hours. The methodology and data sources used for the calculations of charges are described in more detail in appendix I. ATC = air traffic control; PFC = passenger facility charge; PSC = passenger service charge.

Figure 5.24 Total Turnaround Charges for Regional/International Daytime Flight
US$

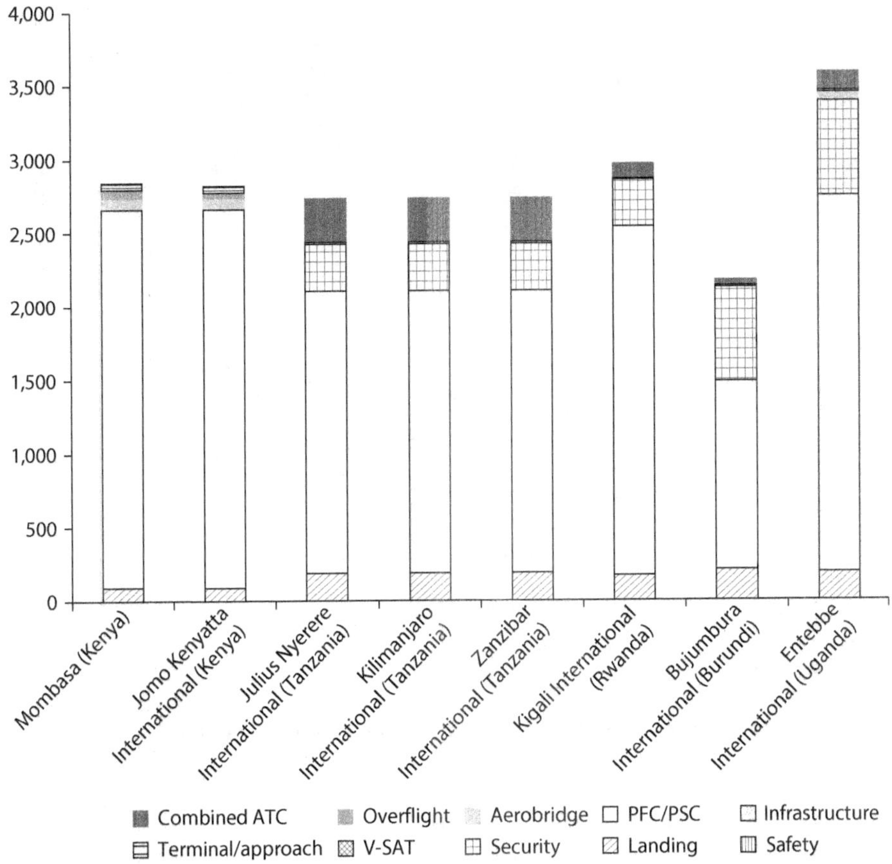

[Bar chart showing total turnaround charges across airports: Mombasa (Kenya) ~2,850; Jomo Kenyatta International (Kenya) ~2,830; Julius Nyerere International (Tanzania) ~2,780; Kilimanjaro International (Tanzania) ~2,760; Zanzibar International (Tanzania) ~2,760; Kigali International (Rwanda) ~3,000; Bujumbura International (Burundi) ~2,200; Entebbe International (Uganda) ~3,620. Categories include: Combined ATC, Overflight, Aerobridge, PFC/PSC, Infrastructure, Terminal/approach, V-SAT, Security, Landing, Safety.]

Sources: Analysis based on aeronautical information publications from Kenya, Rwanda, Tanzania, Uganda, Burundi, and airport websites.
Note: Internationally registered ERJ-170, maximum takeoff weight 37 tons, 80 passengers at 80 percent load factor, turnaround time two hours. ATC = air traffic control; PFC = passenger facility charge; PSC = passenger service charge; V-SAT = Very Small Aperture Terminal (satellite communications).

For regional or international operations, figure 5.24 shows that Entebbe has the highest turnaround cost of the sample, charging over US$3,500 per aircraft. Airport charges in Tanzania and Kenya appear to be at a similar level of around US$2,700, and slightly lower in Burundi at approximately US$2,100.

In order to weigh the cost for airlines versus passengers, all costs are aggregated for each category. Figure 5.25 shows that for domestic operations, charges are more equally distributed between passenger and airline charges in Kenya and Tanzania, whereas in Uganda the majority of charges are absorbed by the airline. In Rwanda, by contrast, the majority of costs are borne by passengers.

For international operations, passenger charges significantly outweigh charges paid by airlines (see figure 5.26). For LCCs this means that load factors have little impact on their overall charges level, and the profitability of airlines is less sensitive to load factors (IFC 2013). Total turnaround charges vary

Figure 5.25 Total Turnaround Cost for Domestic Daytime Flight—Passengers versus Airlines
US$

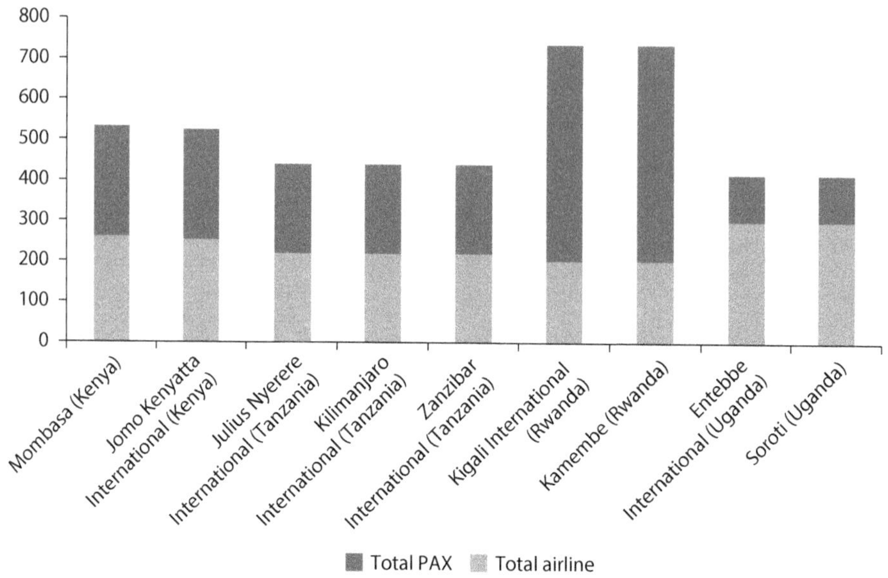

■ Total PAX   ■ Total airline

Sources: Analysis based on aeronautical information publications from Kenya, Rwanda, Tanzania, Uganda, Burundi, and airport websites.
Note: Domestically registered ATR72-500, maximum takeoff weight 23 tons, 74 passengers at 80 percent load factor, turnaround time two hours. PAX = passengers.

Figure 5.26 Total Turnaround Cost for Regional/International Daytime Flight—Passengers versus Airlines
US$

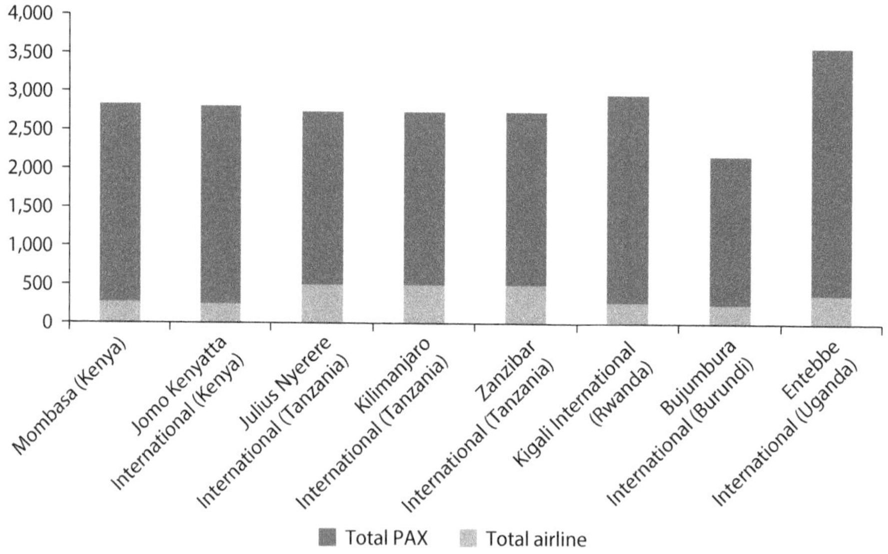

■ Total PAX   ■ Total airline

Sources: Analysis based on aeronautical information publications from Kenya, Rwanda, Tanzania, Uganda, Burundi, and airport websites.
Note: Internationally registered ERJ-170, maximum takeoff weight 37 tons, 80 passengers at 80 percent load factor, turnaround time two hours. PAX = passengers.

between approximately US$2,100 at Bujumbura International to approximately US$3,600 at Entebbe International.

Comparison with Other Countries

Although this analysis provides an indication of the level of charges in the intra-regional and domestic EAC markets, it gives little indication as to whether these charges are comparable to other airports or countries in the region or even

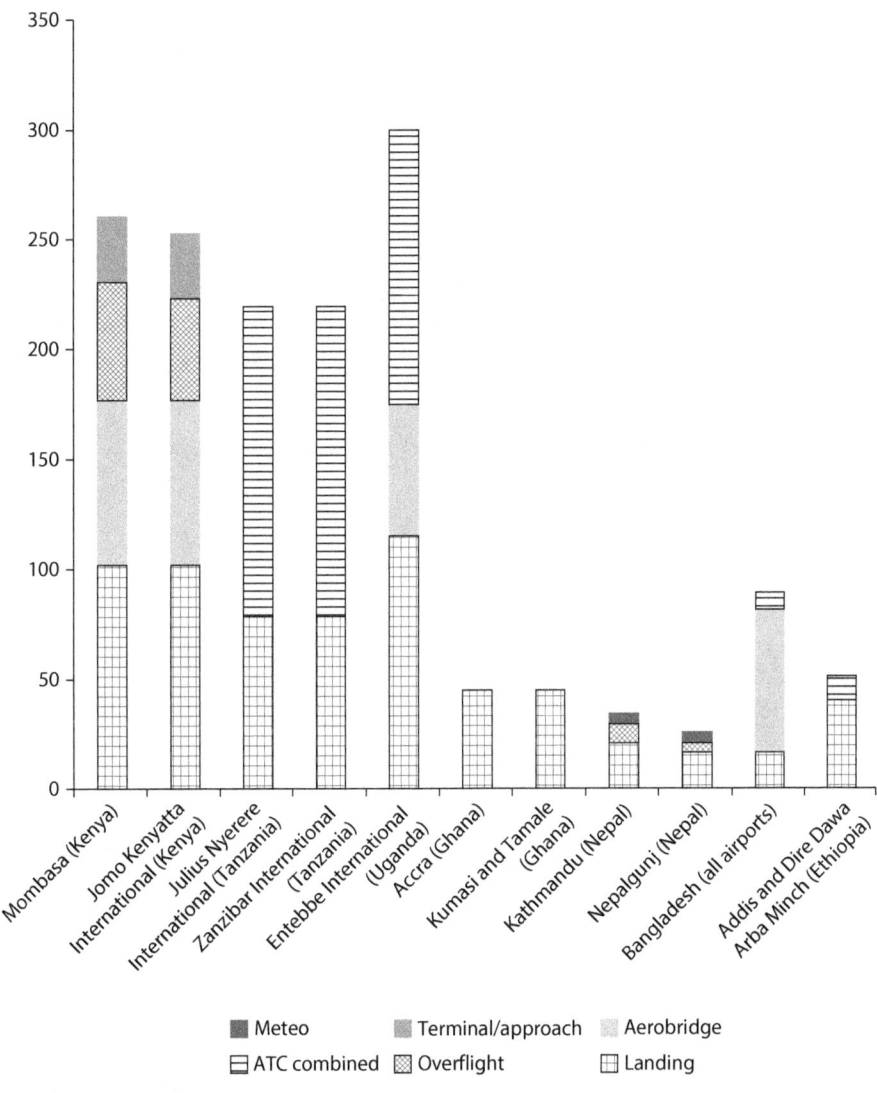

Figure 5.27 Comparison of Airline Charges for Domestic Daytime Flight
US$

Sources: Analysis based on aeronautical information publications from Bangladesh, Burundi, Ethiopa, Ghana, Kenya, Nepal, Tanzania, Uganda, and airport websites.
Note: Domestically registered ATR72-500, maximum takeoff weight 23 tons, 74 passengers at 80 percent load factor, turnaround time two hours. ATC = air traffic control.

globally. Comparing domestic and even regional charges on a more global scale is difficult because of the differing characteristics of each market, something that applies even to comparisons within the EAC region. It is also important to recognize that aeronautical charges are, in many cases, set as a form of cost-recovery or on a cost-plus basis. Airports with recent infrastructure investments, as for example in Senegal, are required to repay high debt services costs and therefore charge much higher aeronautical charges.

As figure 5.27 shows, charges that are levied on airlines are relatively lower in other domestic markets. As expected, smaller countries such as Ghana, Ethiopia, Bangladesh, and Nepal charge much lower overall fees, driven particularly by lower or nonexistent ATC charges. This cannot, however, be entirely credited to geographical size, as Uganda still charges high ATC fees.

With regard to passenger charges, the distinction is less obvious, with passenger charges for Tribhuvan International Airport in Kathmandu, Nepal being similar to airports in Tanzania. Uganda, Bangladesh, and Ethiopia have the lowest overall passenger charges for domestic travel, between US$1.06 and US$1.95 respectively (see figure 5.28).

When comparing charges between airports of similar size for regional/international traffic within a short-haul radius, airports in EAC actually charge much lower fees to airlines in comparison to some of their African counterparts, and even select Asian and Latin American airports. Only charges for Cusco in Ecuador are similar to Kenyan airport charges at around US$280. The highest fees for

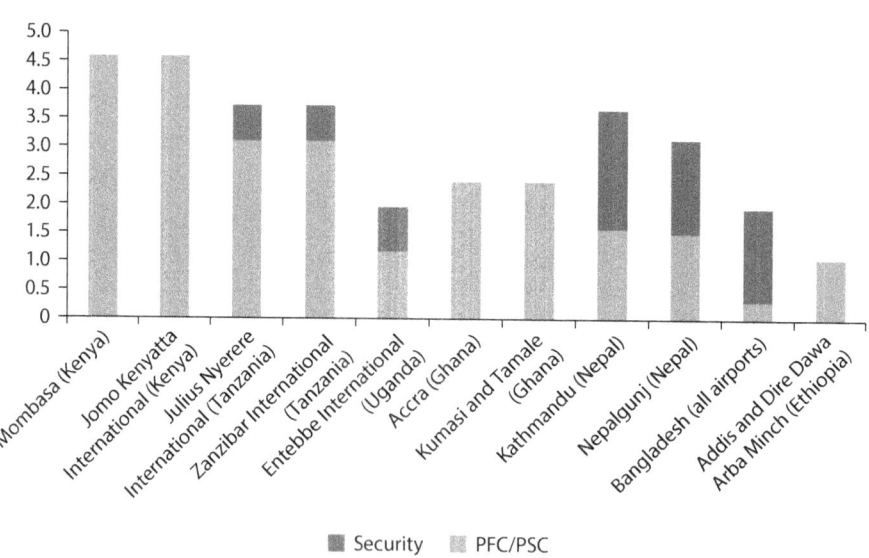

Figure 5.28 Comparison of Passenger Charges for Domestic Daytime Flight
US$

Sources: Analysis based on aeronautical information publications from Bangladesh, Burundi, Ethiopa, Ghana, Kenya, Nepal, Tanzania, Rwanda, Uganda, and airport websites.
Note: Domestically registered ATR72-500, maximum takeoff weight 23 tons, 74 passengers at 80 percent load factor, turnaround time two hours. PFC = passenger facility charge; PSC = passenger service charge.

Figure 5.29 Comparison of Airline Charges for Regional/International Daytime Flight
US$

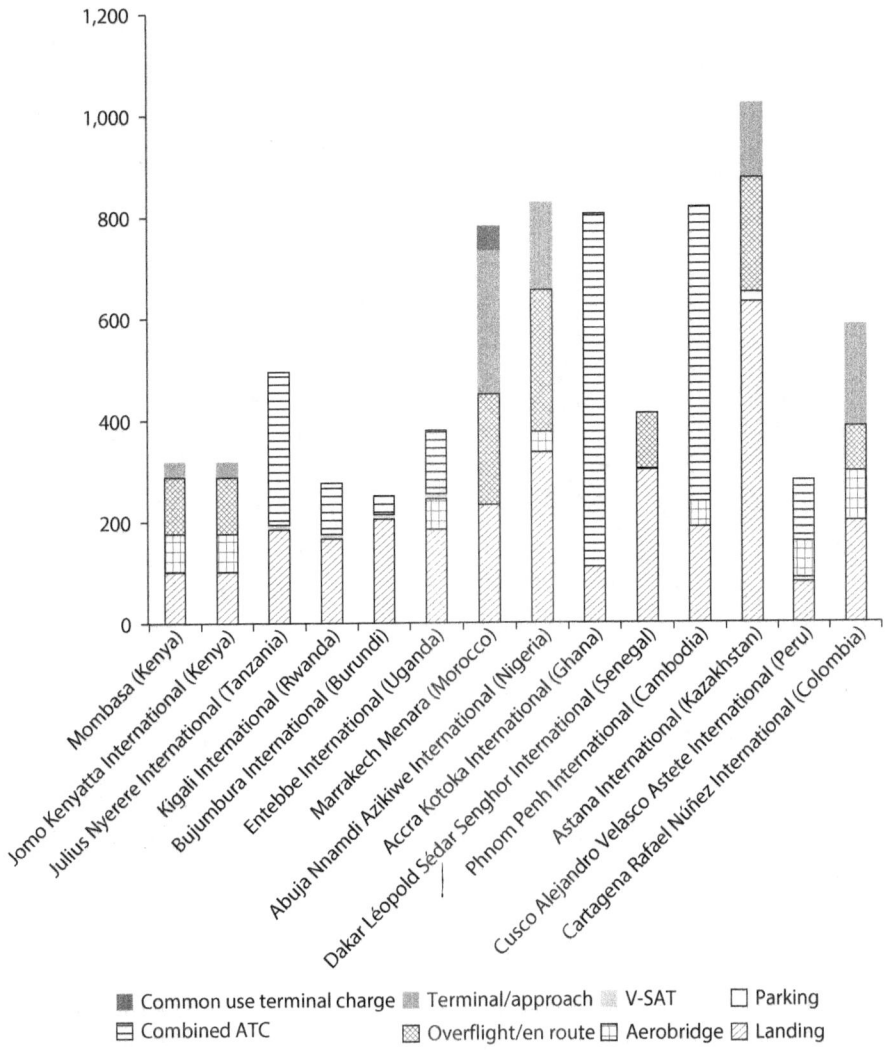

Sources: Analysis based on aeronautical information publications from Bangladesh, Burundi, Cambodia, Colombia, Ethiopia, Ghana, Kazakhstan, Kenya, Morocco, Nepal, Nigeria, Peru, Rwanda, Senegal, Tanzania, Uganda, and airport websites.
Note: Internationally registered ERJ-170, maximum takeoff weight 37 tons, 80 passengers at 80 percent load factor, turnaround time two hours. See appendix I for methodology and sources. ATC = air traffic control; V-SAT = Very Small Aperture Terminal (satellite communications).

airlines are charged at Astana International Airport in Kazakhstan at US$1,021 (see figure 5.29).

When looking at passenger charges, however, charges at other airports outside of Sub-Saharan Africa charge considerably lower rates (see figure 5.30). Cusco or Marrakech airport only charge a PSC of US$10 and US$7.50 respectively. In comparison to other airports in Africa, however, such as Dakar, Senegal, levies in EAC are still much lower. Dakar has introduced several additional charges, for

Figure 5.30 Comparison of Passenger Charges for Regional/International Daytime Flight
US$, departing

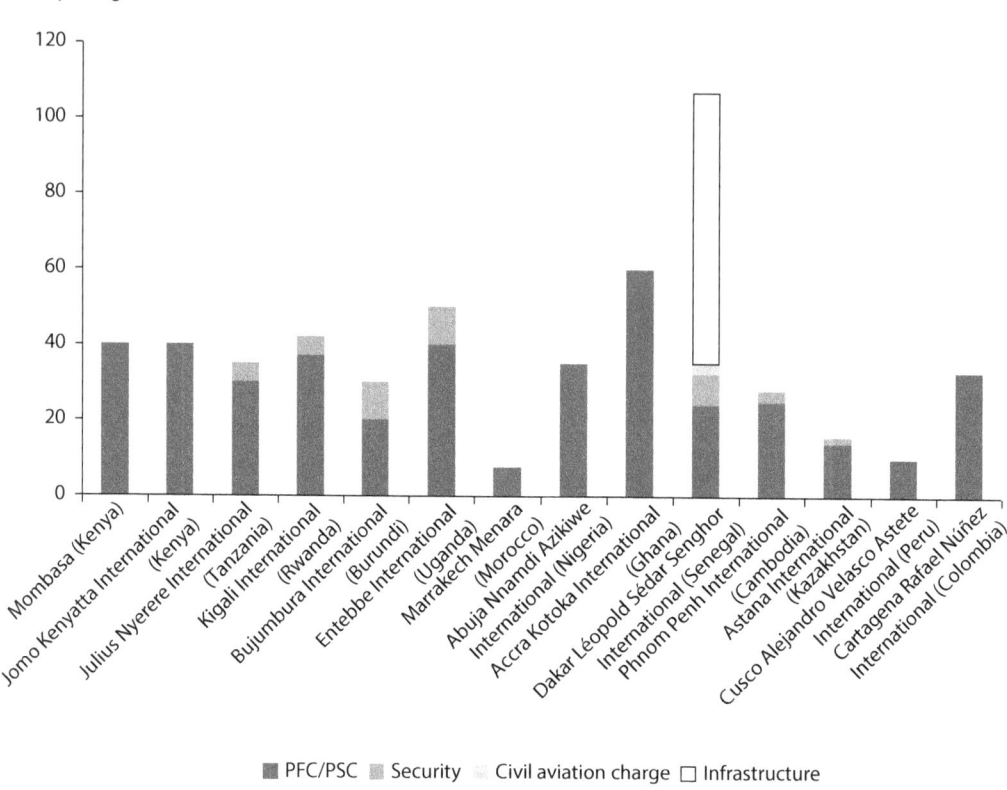

Sources: Analysis based on aeronautical information publications from Bangladesh, Burundi, Cambodia, Colombia, Ethiopa, Ghana, Kazakhstan, Kenya, Morocco, Nepal, Nigeria, Peru, Rwanda, Senegal, Tanzania, Uganda, and airport websites.
Note: Internationally registered ERJ-170, maximum takeoff weight 37 tons, 80 passengers at 80 percent load factor, turnaround time two hours. See appendix I for methodology and sources. PFC = passenger facility charge; PSC = passenger service charge.

example, an infrastructure and civil aviation charge, assumed to finance its new greenfield airport.

Management and Operational Performance

Many of the airports in Africa are government-owned and operated. Table 5.6 shows the major airport operators in the region and highlights that this is also the case for most airports in EAC. There are a few exceptions though, with public-private partnerships (PPP) becoming more popular across the continent.[7] Kilimanjaro Airport, for example, was operating under a concession arrangement with the Kilimanjaro Airport Development Company Ltd, a locally registered firm set up by the global airport operator Mott MacDonald (U.K.), Inter Consult of Tanzania, and the government of Tanzania. The government has since acquired the other participant's stake in the consortium however (Momberger Airport Information 2012). The government of Uganda has also been in

Table 5.6 Major EAC Airport Operators

Operator	Airports covered	Government/private
Kenya Airports Authority	Ownership of major airports and service contract by government to maintain remaining airports	Government
Tanzania Airports Authority	All airports excluding Kilimanjaro and Zanzibar	Government
Kilimanjaro Airport Development Company	Kilimanjaro airport	Privatized
Zanzibar Airports Authority	Unguja and Pemba Island Airports	Government
Autorité de l'Aviation Civile Burundi	All	Government
Rwanda Civil Aviation Authority	All	Government
Uganda Civil Aviation Authority	All	Government

Sources: Kenya Airports Authority (2013); Tanzania Airports Authority (2013); Kilimanjaro Airport Development Company (2013); Autorité de l'Aviation Civile Burundi (2013); Rwanda Civil Aviation Authority (2013); and Uganda Civil Aviation Authority (2013).
Note: All airports not listed, such as many domestic airfields in Kenya for example, appear to be operated by the respective civil aviation authorities or responsible government entities.

ongoing conversations for some time about a possible concession arrangement for Entebbe Airport. Changi Airport Group (CAG), the operator of Singapore Changi Airport, and the United Arab Emirates–based firm Dodsal Infrastructure Development, were seen as the main contenders. However, major resistance from trade unions has stalled progress (CAPA 2010). Seeing the opportunities arising for private sector participation, the Rwandese government announced in 2011 that it would seek expressions of interest for a private sector investor and/or operator for the new airport in Bugesera. Some airports have also allowed for the concession of specific airport services, such as Swissport's passenger counter services in Dar es Salaam airport, as well as cargo handling by private contractors at smaller airport such as Mwanza (Gwilliam and others 2011).

The effect of state ownership on the performance of airports in developed countries has been researched extensively (for example, Vasigh and Haririan 2003; Vogel 2006; Mueller, Ulku, and Zivanovic 2009). There is, however, no consensus among researchers if and to what extent government ownership actually impacts an airport's performance. Nonetheless, it has to be noted that in the EAC region, the management of airport operations by CAAs such as those in Rwanda and Uganda can pose a conflict of "self-regulation." ICAO therefore clearly stipulates the separation of airport management and regulatory bodies. In addition, the presence of state-owned airports in conjunction with airlines that are partially or fully state-owned, such as Rwandair, Air Burundi, or even Kenya Airways, would not appear to be favorable for the development of a competitive aviation sector.

As mentioned in chapter 4, what is of primary concern for LCCs is inefficiencies that can increase time on the ground and consequently cost. However, this is very difficult to measure and the causes of delays are difficult to attribute to any particular party in the aviation system. In the United States, for example, detailed data are available on the timing of gate push-off, taxi time, and "wheels up" time, providing an indication of the cause and source of delay. This information is not available for any airports in the EAC.

Access to airports can pose a considerable challenge due to limited public transport, high levels of congestion, and high costs. This is particularly significant where airports are located far away from towns. Most larger airports in the EAC such as in Nairobi, Entebbe, and Dar es Salaam have cheap public buses, connecting the airports to the city center. However, smaller airports rely on private means of transportation or more expensive taxis. In Kenya, there is also the option of *matatus*, privately owned minibuses, which charge a fairly low fare.

Air Transport Liberalization

As highlighted throughout this book, the basis for the development of LCCs has in most cases been linked directly to the deregulation of the domestic and international air transport markets, as well as to a transparent and competitive market without protected state-owned carriers. In the case of the EAC, the book examines the regulation of the region's larger current and potential domestic markets in Kenya, Tanzania, and Uganda, as well as the regional implementation of the pan-African air transport liberalization framework, the Yamoussoukro Decision (YD). In addition, some liberalization frameworks within the different RECs in the region are highlighted.

Air Transport Liberalization in Africa—The Yamoussoukro Decision

Air transport liberalization on the African continent is delineated under the so-called YD, which entered into force in the year 2000, after having evolved from an earlier agreement, the Yamoussoukro Declaration of 1988.

The Yamoussoukro Declaration had established a new African air transport policy, which focused primarily on airline cooperation and integration. It committed all representative governments to make all necessary efforts to integrate their airlines within eight years (UNECA 1988). The eight-year period was subdivided into three phases: In the first phase (two years), the focus was to be on maximizing capacity usage between carriers. This was to be achieved by exchanging technical and capacity data, preparing for the designation of gateway airports, and promoting cooperation among national carriers in order to eventually merge them into larger and more competitive airlines. The second phase (three years) would have committed the airlines to joint operations on international routes. In addition, certain airline operations would have been conducted jointly to achieve better economies of scale and deeper integration by, for example, instituting a common insurance mechanism and computer reservation system, purchasing spare parts and aircraft, undertaking promotion and marketing, providing training, and maintaining equipment. The last phase (three years) was to be used to strive toward achieving the complete integration of airlines by establishing joint airline operations or entities (UNECA 1988).

Despite its already overly ambitious objectives and its low likelihood of implementation, the Yamoussoukro Declaration set in motion further initiatives aimed at liberalizing the African air transport market. In 1994, having evaluated the steps required to implement the Yamoussoukro Declaration, the African ministers in charge of civil aviation met in Mauritius and agreed on a set of measures to facilitate the granting of third, fourth, and fifth freedom rights to African carriers. Most remarkable was the understanding that fifth freedom rights should be granted on routes where third and fourth freedom flights did not yet exist (UNECA 2004).

Eleven years later, in 1999, African ministers responsible for civil aviation revisited the topic of the liberalization of air services. Based on the objectives of the Yamoussoukro Declaration and the resolutions discussed in Mauritius, the meeting aimed at accelerating implementation of the Yamoussoukro Declaration. This was partially a result of the recommendation of the 11th Conference of African Ministers Responsible for Transport and Communications held in Cairo in November 1997. It called for a regional meeting of African ministers to find ways to implement the Yamoussoukro Declaration (UNECA 2004). The conference in Yamoussoukro ended with the adoption of the "Yamoussoukro Decision Relating to the Implementation of the Yamoussoukro Declaration concerning the Liberalization of Access to Air Transport Markets in Africa," which became known as the YD. The YD was then formally adopted during the Assembly of Heads of State held in Lomé, Togo, on July 10–12, 2000 (Schlumberger 2010). The YD came into force on August 12, 2000, 30 days after its signature by the chair of the Assembly of the African Economic Community (UNECA 2004). The main elements of the YD are summarized in table 5.7.

Table 5.7 Main Elements of Yamoussoukro Decision

Area	Provision	Yamoussoukro Decision
Traffic rights	Article 2	Free exercise of first, second, third, fourth, and fifth freedom rights on both scheduled and nonscheduled passenger and freight (cargo and mail) air services performed by an eligible airline.
Tariffs	Article 4	No approval is required by the aeronautical authorities of state parties for any tariff increase. An increase in tariffs only has to be filed with competent authorities 30 working days before they enter into effect; while a lowering of tariffs takes immediate effect.
Capacity and frequency	Article 5	No limit on the number of frequencies and capacity offered in air services linking any city pair combination between state parties concerned. No state party shall unilaterally limit the volume of traffic, the type of aircraft to be operated, or the number of flights per week unless there are environmental, safety, technical, or other special considerations.
Designation and authorization	Article 6	Each state party can designate at least one airline to operate intra-African air transport services on its behalf. States can designate any eligible airline from another State party to operate air services on its behalf, including an eligible African multinational airline in which it is a stakeholder. There is no limitation on the number of designated carriers as long as the eligibility criteria are met. Eligibility is based on compliance with minimum standards with regard to the carrier's legal and physical establishment, its licensing and operating capacity, its insurance coverage, and its capacity to comply with international standards.
Safety and security	Article 6.12	Obligation for all parties to comply with the established civil aviation safety and security standards and practices of the International Civil Aviation Organization (ICAO).

Source: Schlumberger 2010.

The YD is a relatively ambitious framework that aims to open air services between all African states. Indeed, it is a relatively progressive and radical move away from regulating air services between states on the basis of restrictive bilateral agreements. However, implementation of the decision has encountered two divergent realities. Implementation in terms of carrying out public policy has seen little progress at the pan-African level. Many of the key policy elements are still missing or exist only on paper. At the same time, in terms of operational implementation, many examples can be seen of countries opening up by applying the YD at the bilateral level. Given the current structure of the air transport sector in many African countries, one can assume that about two-thirds are willing to apply the YD because they see little value in protecting their own markets from outside competition (Schlumberger 2010).

Implementation of the Yamoussoukro Decision in the EAC

As highlighted, the EAC Treaty of 1999 outlines the modalities of cooperation in infrastructure and services by partner states with particular focus on civil aviation and civil air transport (Article 92). The Treaty provides a list of concrete steps to reach these goals (EAC 1999) including (a) the adoption of common policies to develop civil air transport in collaboration with other relevant organizations; (b) liberalizing the granting of air traffic rights for passenger and cargo operations; (c) harmonizing civil aviation rules and regulations; (d) establishing an upper area control system, that is, a system of ATC for the upper flight levels; (e) coordinating the flight schedules of designated carriers; (f) applying ICAO guidelines to determine user charges for scheduled air services; and (g) adopting common aircraft standards and technical standards.

Some of these steps match elements of the YD, which was signed the same year as the treaty of the EAC. The latter is, however, limited to liberalizing the granting of air traffic rights for passengers and cargo operations and does not specify further the extent of liberalization. Even though the EAC Treaty did not incorporate all of the principles of the YD, the EAC's Sectoral Council on Transport, Communications, and Meteorology worked continuously on several key measures of the YD. The most important was the formulation of a liberalized air transport policy for scheduled air services. Whereas other RECs developed specific regulations that liberalized air services within their REC (for example, the West African Economic and Monetary Union), the EAC chose to focus on amending the bilateral agreements between the partner states. The 11th Meeting of the EAC Council of Ministers formally approved several projects pertinent to air transport and issued the necessary directives, namely (East African Community Secretariat 2006):

- The amendments to the bilateral agreements between the EAC states toward full implementation of the YD on air transport liberalization are approved and must be incorporated into the respective bilateral agreements.
- The amendments include full liberalization of air services between any points within the territory of the EAC. Following the principles of the YD,

no restriction shall be posted on the frequency, capacity, or types of aircraft operated by designated EAC carriers.
- The EAC Secretariat is to inform the Economic Commission for Africa, with copies to COMESA and SADC, that the EAC is fully compliant with the YD. The latter two organizations are urged to "expedite the move towards continental implementation of the Yamoussoukro Decision."
- The EAC Air Transport Subcommittee for implementation of the YD will be staffed by an official responsible for administering the bilateral agreements, and with officials from the civil aviation authorities, airport authorities, and the attorneys' general chambers of each partner state.
- The heads of civil aviation and airport authorities of each partner state are authorized and instructed to renegotiate the funding for civil aviation safety and airport projects with their respective ministers of finance and to seek other resources for such projects.

Thus, the EAC has displayed great interest in and motivation toward liberalizing and developing air services within its territory. As a relatively small REC, the EAC relies mainly on mutual consent with respect to major decisions and program implementation. The notion of cooperation among partner states has a long history in the region and must be regarded as the best way forward. The approach of agreeing to bilateral accords that conform to the principles of the YD is therefore the most appropriate manner of implementation.

However, the key element of the EAC's approach toward implementing the YD, that is, amending the bilateral agreements between EAC states, is still pending. The most recent update from the EAC Secretariat that could be obtained with regard to the implementation of the YD in EAC (from January 2013) announced that the development of the framework for the implementation was progressing well and a draft was to be considered by the end of May 2013. However, no information could be found to verify its implementation (Ssenyonga 2013).

Currently, the existing bilateral regime between EAC states is more restrictive than that established by the YD framework. Air service agreements (ASAs) that could be found for Tanzania (see table 5.8) show that in its current bilateral ASA with Kenya, for example, there are generally no limitations on capacity or types of aircraft. However, limits on frequencies, and in the case of Kenya, the destinations to be served in both countries, are delineated. In addition, there are no provisions for fifth freedom traffic (Munyagi 2006).

The World Trade Organization's air service agreement projector (ASAP) tool only has information on three ASAs in the region, that is, between Rwanda and Tanzania, Tanzania and Burundi, and Kenya and Uganda. From the information available, the ASA between Rwanda and Tanzania appears to be the most liberal, achieving comparatively high scores in all four areas ("standard," fifth freedom, designation, and ownership). This is followed by the agreement between Tanzania and Burundi (Category E). The ASA between Uganda and Kenya appears to have the lowest score (Category C), with single designation and capacity constraints (WTO 2013).

Table 5.8 Bilateral Air Service Agreements between Tanzania and EAC Countries

Country	Designation	Frequency/type of aircraft	Date of last review	Operating carriers
Kenya	Multiple	Unlimited frequencies on any point in Kenya to Zanzibar 42 on Nairobi–Kilimanjaro (reciprocal) 42 on Nairobi–Dar es Salaam (reciprocal) 14 on Kisumu–Mwanza (reciprocal) 14 on Mombasa–Kilimanjaro Unlimited from any point in Tanzania to Mombasa 14 on Nairobi–Mwanza (reciprocal) 35 on Zanzibar–Nairobi Any aircraft size	Feb. 28, 2011 (MoU)	Kenya Airways Air Kenya Express Five Forty Aviation Safari Link Jetlink Express Precision Air
Uganda	Multiple	As many as commercially viable Any aircraft size	March 4, 2003 (MoU)	Air Uganda Precision Air
Burundi	Multiple	Up to 14 per week No frequency and capacity restrictions on cargo	Signed April 2009	No airlines operate
Rwanda	Multiple	Up to 14 per week Any aircraft size	Signed April 2006	Rwandair

Source: Tanzania Civil Aviation Authority 2013b.
Note: EAC = East African Community; MoU = memorandum of understanding.

COMESA, which includes all EAC member states with the exception of Tanzania, has also been working toward the liberalization of air transport. The REC even decided to go beyond the principles of the YD by allowing COMESA carriers to operate between any destinations within COMESA countries (Schlumberger 2010). The implementation of this had been hinging on the establishment of a competition authority, which was initiated in 2008 jointly with both EAC and SADC under the COMESA-EAC-SADC Tripartite. However, the consolidation of efforts with other RECs has slowed implementation significantly.

The Tripartite, as part of its efforts to integrate air transport policies between the three RECs, has also been working toward the harmonization of all liberalization efforts across the region. Considering the varying scope of liberalization efforts, this may delay implementation. This is further illustrated in table 5.9 outlining the individual efforts to date by each REC, and grading it in accordance with its application to the YD (Schlumberger 2009). Among the RECs, the Bangul Accord Group (BAG), the Economic and Monetary Community of Central African States (CEMAC), and the Economic Community of West African States (WAEMU) seem to have advanced the most significantly. Full implementation of the YD is a crucial step in the development of air services in the region.

Although it is of paramount importance that restrictions on capacity, frequency, and designation be removed, the additional benefit of applying more extended traffic rights, in particular fifth freedoms, is questionable in the current market. There could potentially be significant advantages to the air transport market in EAC in the future, but the impact in the current competitive context would appear to be minimal as traffic is still very limited.

Table 5.9 Implementation of Yamoussoukro Decision (YD) in African RECs

REC	General status of YD implementation	Status of air services liberalization	Score
AMU	No implementation.	No liberalization within AMU initiated, but need is recognized.	1
BAG	Principles of YD agreed upon in a multilateral air service agreement.	Up to fifth freedom granted, tariffs are free, and capacity/frequency is open.	4
CEMAC	Principles of YD agreed upon in an air transport program. Some minor restrictions remain.	Up to fifth freedom granted, tariffs are free, and capacity/frequency is open. Maximum of two carriers per state may participate.	5
COMESA	Full liberalization decided ("Legal Notice No. 2"), but application and implementation remain pending until a Joint Competition Authority is established.	Incomplete. Once applied, operators may be able to serve any destination (all freedoms), tariffs and capacity/frequency will be free.	3
EAC	EAC Council has issued a directive to amend bilateral agreements among EAC states to conform with YD.	Air services are not liberalized, as the amendments of bilateral agreements are pending.	3
SADC	No steps taken toward implementation, despite the fact that Civil Aviation Policy includes gradual liberalization of air services within SADC.	No liberalization within SADC initiated.	2
WAEMU	Within WAEMU, the YD is fully implemented.	All freedoms, including cabotage, granted. Tariffs are liberalized.	5

Source: Schlumberger 2009.
Note: AMU = African Monetary Union; BAG = Bangul Accord Group; CEMAC = Economic and Monetary Community of Central African States; COMESA = Common Market for Eastern and Southern Africa; EAC = East African Community; REC = regional economic community; SADC = Southern African Development Community; WAEMU = West African Monetary Union; YD = Yamoussoukro Decision.

Liberalization of Domestic Markets

Liberalization in domestic markets has occurred to varying degrees, with Tanzania being probably the most advanced in the region. The country's domestic liberalization has allowed competition in its market to flourish, and has supported the establishment of a strong private operator in addition to the state-owned carrier, Air Tanzania. In Kenya, the reform of its air transport policies in the 1990s allowed for some competition, although implementation has since been slow. Only recently has progress been seen with the entrance of its first LCC, Fly540. This has been driving down fares in the domestic market. The most important milestone has been the privatization of Kenya Airways, which removed government control from day-to-day operations. As noted, however, a recent announcement by the government of an increasing stake brings into question whether government intervention has really been eliminated.

Safety and Security

Air transport safety records are still poor in Africa. Despite only representing around 5 percent of global scheduled seat capacity, 43 percent of all fatalities from air transport occurred in the region in 2012 (ICAO 2013a). Only 25 airlines in the region are certified through IATA's Operational Safety Audit (IOSA), and many are listed on Europe's airline blacklist (European Commission 2013).

Unfortunately, the EAC is no exception. In the last decade, the region has experienced 41 accidents, of which 13 resulted in fatalities. An analysis of accidents in the region in figure 5.31 (see appendix J for full details of each accident) shows that the majority of accidents or incidents have occurred due to two reasons: (a) human error, such as loss of control, deviation from original flight plans, aircraft overloading, or unlicensed personnel; and (b) aircraft failure, such as engine fires or issues with undercarriage. Some accidents, particularly in the mountainous areas of Kenya, were also linked to the lack of appropriate navigational aids in place. Although these causes are not only present in the developing world, the frequency of accidents, considering the limited traffic, is very high, and points to a systemic deficiency in the air transport system.

According to the IATA, the main determining factors for accidents in Africa are related to the lack of three things: (a) effective regulatory oversight; (b) data collection to perform flight data analysis (FDA); and (c) safety management systems (SMS) implementation (Matschnigg 2013).

Poor oversight has been particularly critical, with Africa performing significantly worse than other regions. Although the Universal Safety Oversight Audit Programme (USOAP) results for each critical element (CE) are not publicly available, the level of implementation for each audit area, based on the country's latest safety audit, is published. In the case of the EAC, the audit results show that implementation in EAC varies between countries and across key areas. Kenya, for example, performs above the global average in most areas, whereas Tanzania displays unsatisfactory implementation in legislation, flight operations,

Figure 5.31 Assumed Primary Cause of Accidents in EAC, 2003–13

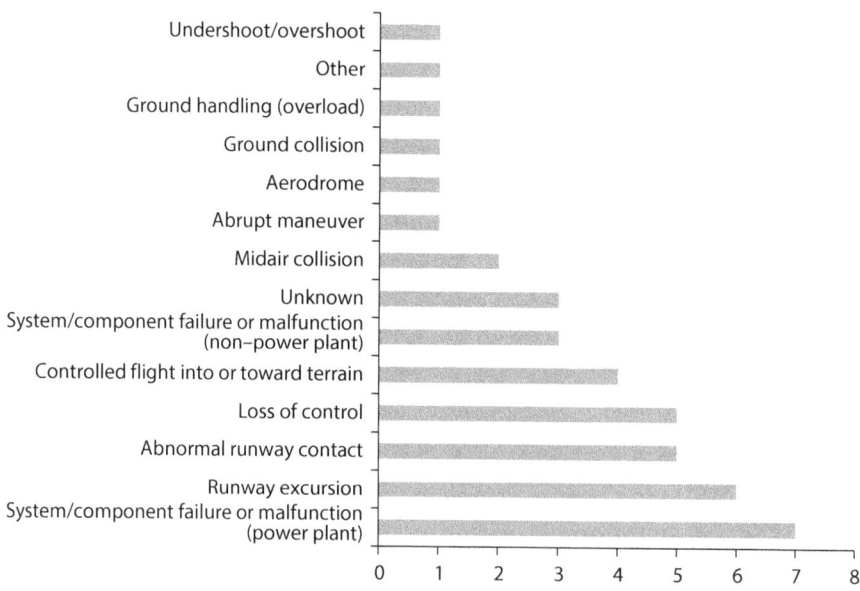

Source: Analysis based on the Flight Foundation's *Aviation Safety Network* (2013).
Note: EAC = East African Community.

and air navigation services. Similarly, Rwanda's level of implementation for many areas is above the global average, but nonexistent in the areas of accident investigation and air navigation services (see figure 5.32).

As promulgated in the EAC's treaty, the region has, with the support of the U.S. Department of Transportation's Safe Skies for Africa initiative, created a regional safety oversight organization (RSOO) in 2007. The Civil Aviation Safety and Security Oversight Agency (CASSOA), has the mandate to (a) promote the safe, secure, and efficient use and development of civil aviation within and outside the partner states; (b) assist the partner states in meeting their safety and security oversight obligations and responsibilities under the Chicago Convention, including its appendixes; and (c) provide the partner states with an appropriate forum and structure to discuss, plan, and implement common measures required for achieving the safe and orderly development of international civil aviation through the implementation of international standards and recommended practices relating to the safety and security of civil aviation (CASSOA 2013).

One of CASSOA's major achievements has been the harmonization of regulations and the development of guidance materials between Tanzania, Kenya, and Uganda. The harmonization of regulations of the newer members Rwanda and Burundi is, however, still ongoing. As voiced by CASSOA's board chairman at the 2nd East African Community Civil Aviation Safety and Security Oversight Agency (EAC-CASSOA) conference, inadequate funding mechanisms as well as attracting and retaining qualified staff has proved to be a considerable challenge (*News of Rwanda* 2013). There is an attempt to address funding issues through the introduction of an additional passenger surcharge in the amount of US$0.70. This would, however, put more pressure on airlines (Ihucha 2012).

Figure 5.32 Level of Implementation in Key Audit Areas

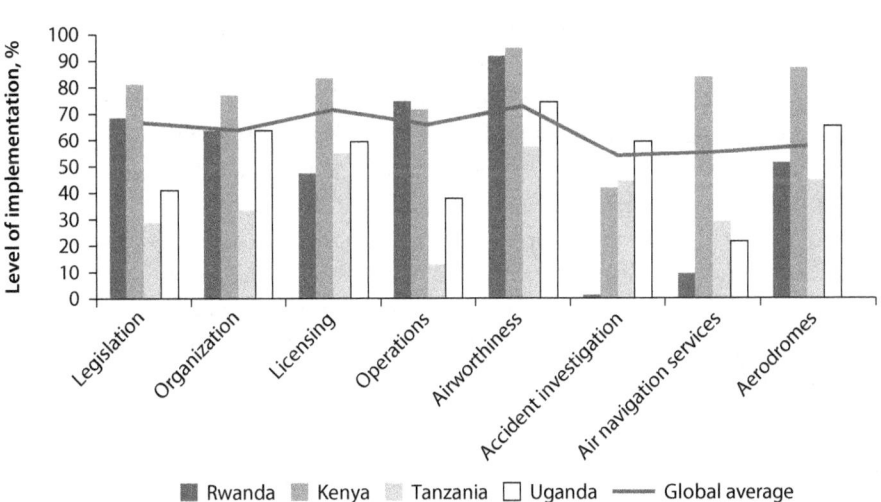

Source: ICAO *Safety Audit Information* (2013b).
Note: Information is in accordance with the last scheduled audit for the region in November 2008. For Rwanda and Kenya, a follow-up audit was conducted in 2012 and 2013, respectively.

ICAO has also set up multiple cooperative programs called Cooperative Development of Operational Safety and Continuing Airworthiness Programs (COSCAP) in the region, including one in the SADC REC. COSCAP is an agreement between participant states, which aims at enhancing the safety of air transport operations in a subregion by providing technical services in safety oversight to its member states.

Aviation security is also increasingly becoming a challenge in the region. Industry stakeholders have shown concern due to the increasing levels of drug and human trafficking, as well as terrorism and proliferation of small arms. Kenya has become a particular target with recent terrorist attacks and instability and prevalent militant groups in neighboring Somalia. Various proposals have been made to address the security challenges in the EAC, including the establishment of an antiterrorism task force at the EAC Secretariat, joint training for aviation security personnel, an intervention force, as well as the implementation of corrective action plans resulting from security audit programs such as the ICAO's Universal Security Audit Programme (USAP) (*News of Rwanda* 2013).

Labor

The availability of qualified aviation staff is still a major challenge across the African region. Indeed, deficiencies are apparent across the whole aviation sector, including pilots and flight attendants, but also maintenance engineers and technicians and regulatory staff.

Kenya's flag carrier Kenya Airways is facing a shortage of experienced pilots to support its expansion plan. The carrier has been struggling with unions to allow for the hiring of 40 expatriates to fill the void. Kenya is said to need 2,000 more pilots to meet its current requirement of 5,000 pilots (*News of Rwanda* 2013). Likewise, the director general of the Tanzanian CAA highlighted in an interview in 2012 that local pilots and engineers represent only 40 percent of the total requirement, with 60 percent of staff coming from outside the country. In addition, the Tanzanian CAA has been facing a shortage of adequate inspectors to conduct the necessary audits (*Tanzania Daily News* 2012). Similarly, in 2007, ICAO's USOAP for Rwanda identified a lack of qualified aviation personnel as a major deficiency in many areas (*In2EastAfrica* 2011).

The reasons for these deficiencies vary. Primarily, they are both inadequate and underfunded training centers and civil aviation authorities, and "brain drain."[8] In addition, there appears to be a gap between academia and the airline industry, with limited on-the-job training and practical experience offered to students. In the EAC, regional training schools, such as the East African School of Aviation located in Kenya, and the East African Civil Aviation Academy (EACAA) at Soroti Airport in Uganda, have been able to promote the development of aviation professionals in the region. They have been struggling to achieve the necessary economies of scale, however, which has resulted in high costs. In 2011, the estimated cost for training an air traffic controller was K Sh 3.5 million (Ndegwa 2012).

In spite of the Kenyan CAA spending US$15 million over the last 10 years to improve training and capacity at the East African School of Aviation, the sector is fighting an endless battle against brain drain (Kagwe 2011b). Middle Eastern carriers in particular have been attracting newly-graduated aviation staff from the region's training centers, offering significantly higher salaries and better opportunities.

Although salaries offered outside of the African market are considerably higher, wages for aviation personnel, particularly airline crews are by no means low in the EAC. The shortage of adequate human resources and the high cost of training have translated into a doubling of salaries for pilots between 2008 and 2011 (Maina 2011).

Various international efforts have been made to address these challenges. Examples include the Initiative on Human Resources Development by the African Civil Aviation Commission (AFCAC), the African Union's specialized agency for civil aviation matters; and ICAO's Next Generation of Aviation Professionals (NGAP) Initiative offering courses and seminars aimed at the development of human resources in the region.

In addition to the shortage and high cost of qualified human resources, airlines and businesses in developing countries often face considerable challenges with regard to labor regulations and laws. However, overall labor regulation in Sub-Saharan Africa is seen as less of an impediment when compared with aggregated survey results for Latin America and the Caribbean, and the Middle East and North Africa regions (see figure 5.33). In the EAC region, Tanzania and Kenya appear to be facing higher regulatory constraints than their neighbors. This is surprising in light of the historically anchored labor laws in the region. Kenya, Uganda, and Tanzania's labor laws are all anchored in British Common Law, which is sometimes seen as more favorable for investors than other legal systems (Astier 2012). Rwanda on the other hand was long governed under the Belgian Civil Law System and is only now gradually moving toward a Common Law system (Uwanyiligira 2012).

A closer analysis of the EAC labor markets indicates some further challenges related to specific labor regulations in the region. The results from the World Bank's *Doing Business* report for the EAC countries (World Bank 2013a) (see details appendix K) highlight a few potentially restrictive labor regulations that could affect an airline:

- In Tanzania, fixed-term contracts are prohibited for permanent tasks, reducing the flexibility of employees and airlines hiring for seasonal flight destinations, for example additional flights during holiday seasons.
- In Burundi, the additional percentage for night work is 35 percent, which would apply for airlines operating at airports that are sometimes open 24 hours per day.
- In Tanzania, Kenya, and Burundi, notification of a third party is required for the dismissal of a person; in Tanzania, this dismissal even needs to be approved by the third party.

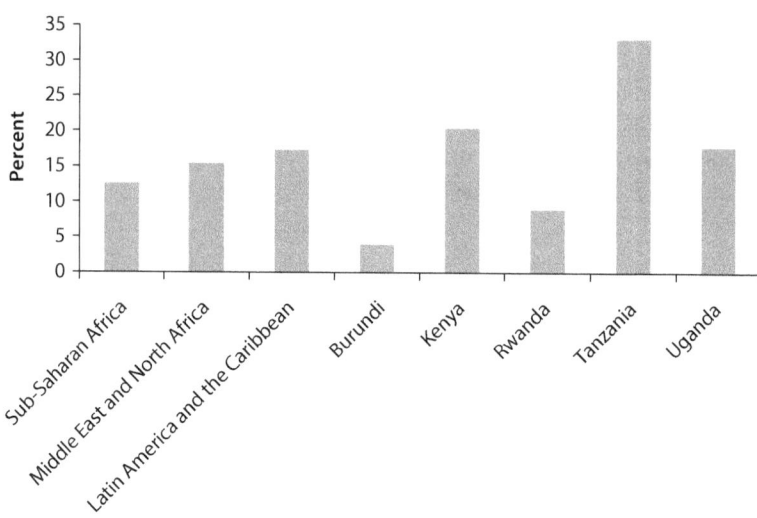

Figure 5.33 **Percentage of Firms Identifying Labor Regulations as a Major Constraint—Comparison of EAC and Other Regions**

Source: World Bank and IFC *Enterprise Surveys* (2013).
Note: Year of data capture—Burundi (2006), Kenya (2013), Rwanda (2011), Tanzania (2013), and Uganda (2013). Regional averages vary depending on different years of data capture of each country in the region.
EAC = East African Community.

- Contributions to social security are very high in Tanzania (20 percent of salary) (PwC 2013). In addition, in Tanzania a "skills and development" Levy of 6 percent of the wage bill is charged, of which only a third goes to the Vocational Education Training Authority (VETA), while the remaining two-thirds is remitted to the treasury (Association of Tanzania Employers 2011).

The presence of unions, sometimes representing a significant challenge for businesses, is relatively low in the region. The latest figure by the International Labour Organization (ILO) estimates the density of trade unions for Kenya at 4.1 percent, Uganda at 1.1 percent, and Tanzania at 2.2 percent (Hayter and Stoevska 2011). No data could be obtained for labor activities by unions.

Aircraft Financing

Aircraft financing has proved to be a considerable impediment to the development of air services in Africa. This is primarily related to the high cost of capital for aircraft finance and to the fact that African airlines, with few exceptions, are unable to reach the economies of scale needed for lower aircraft prices and superior purchasing conditions. Historically African carriers have been reliant on export credit agencies, and operating leases for older aircraft from airlines from developed countries. However, these sources of finance are becoming continuously scarce or more expensive (see chapter 4). This problem is further aggravated by the high rate of accidents, poor safety and security oversight, lack of adequate maintenance facilities, and challenges in the legal protection of borrowers and lenders alike across the continent.

Although deficiencies in other areas such as safety and security still persist, most countries in the region have made progress toward the legal protection of borrowers and lenders. In the 2013 *Doing Business* report for the EAC (World Bank 2013a), Kenya displays the highest score for protection of lenders and borrowers, followed by Uganda, Tanzania, and Rwanda. Burundi has the lowest score (3 out of 10). Kenya and Tanzania have both ratified the Cape Town Convention, and Rwanda has acceded to the convention. Adherence to the convention is greatly facilitating the countries' access to aircraft finance.

Development institutions, such as the African Development Bank and the IFC, as well as other private and public institutions, have also played a crucial role in providing financing for airlines in the region. AfriExim, a public-private consortium with the purpose of financing, promoting, and expanding intra-African and extra-African trade, has also been involved in the region providing a US$1.9 billion financing package for Kenya Airways, fleet expansion (Gichane 2012). The IFC has invested US$25 million in equity in the airline (Mutegi 2012; Ngigi 2012) and is currently also reviewing a potential investment in Precision Air. In 2011, the African Development Bank also provided a US$40 million second lien corporate loan to Ethiopian Airlines to support the purchase of five Boeing 777-200LR passenger aircraft (African Development Bank 2011b).

In addition, various initiatives across the continent have been put forward to alleviate the burden of high aircraft financing costs. One of them is the Commercial Aircraft Finance Entity (CAFE), which aims to provide access to infrastructure and related finance on a public-private-initiative basis for aircraft leasing and financing (Tierny 2012).

Fuel Cost and Access

Access to fuel and the cost of fuel are intrinsically linked to the survival of an airline, especially for LCCs. Jet fuel prices in Africa are considered a major hurdle for the development of air transport. Prices are influenced by high taxation, regulations, and the lack of adequate storage facilities, as well as the often-monopolistic market structure of the oil industry in the region. In addition, many African countries are faced with the geographic challenge of being landlocked, resulting in delays and inflated prices for jet fuel due to higher transport costs in the region.

Publicly available data on jet fuel prices at the airport level is very difficult to obtain. For EAC countries, the book's authors were only able to obtain information for Kenya. Kenyan airports charge US$1.1 per liter (approximately US$130.9 per barrel), which is around US$6 higher than the average global jet fuel price in 2013 (IATA n.d.). No direct information could be found for jet fuel prices at Tanzanian airports. However, in an interview in 2012, the CEO of Precision Air, Alfonse Kioko, stated that "aircraft operators in Tanzania are badly hurt by rising jet fuel, which almost doubled in the past year, forcing some aircraft to fly to neighboring Kenya for refueling at prices 30 percent lower than Tanzania," (Tairo 2012) hinting that the situation in Tanzania is not more favorable.

Airline websites, where charges and taxes are individually listed, can be a good indicator of fuel prices. A look at Precision Air's website shows that for a one-way ticket between Dar es Salaam and Nairobi, a US$50 fuel service fee is applied. On a flight from Dar es Salaam to Entebbe, the surcharge is US$55 for a one-way ticket. For domestic flights, there is a fuel service surcharge of US$40.

There are a variety of reasons for the higher cost of fuel, including government taxation and custom tariffs. As indicated in chapter 4, ICAO's policies on aviation fuel clearly state that aviation fuel is to be exempt from customs duties and excise taxes or any other form of taxation (ICAO 2009). This not only excludes domestic aviation (which faces a value-added tax [VAT] in some countries), but is also far from being implemented in most African countries. EAC countries have, however, been complying, to varying extents, with these regulations, with no excise or other taxes being applied to jet fuel, at least for international transport.

Uganda has made a special provision for fuel imported by registered airlines and companies with designated storage facilities or contracts with airlines, and Tanzania has abolished all excise duties for jet fuel (PwC 2013). Some countries, such as Rwanda and Kenya, however, still apply VAT and other taxes for domestic usage of jet fuel. According to PricewaterhouseCoopers, Kenya charges a US$0.06 excise duty for kerosene-type, and US$0.22 duty for spirit-type jet fuel per liter—in addition to a US$0.004 petroleum development levy per liter. The new VAT Act in Kenya, which was approved in 2013, also limits the exemption of jet fuel from VAT to three years under a "transitional period" (Kenya Revenue Authority 2013).

Under the EAC Common External Tariff (CET) regulations, to be applied by all countries, customs duties on jet fuel (both kerosene- and spirit-based) are to be removed. The application of the CET has not been uniform, with exceptions being applied on a country basis. Uganda, Rwanda, and Burundi have all produced a list of goods to be exempted from the CET. In some cases, resistance is high, as income from taxation represents a large part of a country's revenue. Rwanda, for example, lost revenues of US$9.8 million when it abolished customs duties on petroleum products (Rwanda Revenue Authority n.d.). In addition, Tanzania, as part of SADC, has committed to the implementation of both CETs, which poses a considerable challenge. Similar issues have arisen in the other EAC members, which are also a part of COMESA (Makame 2012).

Regional production facilities are also few and comparably small in scope, limiting local supply. Of the EAC countries, the only country that currently appears to have a refinery producing jet fuel is the Kenya Petroleum Refineries near the port of Mombasa. The Mombasa refinery is one of the largest petroleum refineries in the region with a capacity of 90,000 barrels/day (bbl/d) and a throughput of almost 35,000 bbl/d as of 2011. It processes heavy crude, imported solely from the United Arab Emirates. In order to meet local demand, the country also imported around 56,000 bbl/d of refined oil products, primarily from Asia and the Middle East. Together with kerosene, this represents about 22 percent of its total fuel production (see figure 5.34) (U.S. EIA 2011).

The Kenya Pipeline Company (KPC), responsible for transporting the fuel from the refineries, has two aviation fuel depots at Jomo Kenyatta and Mombasa's Moi International Airports, and an additional two smaller depots at Eldoret and Kisumu (KPC 2013). Jet fuel throughput was around 970,000 cubic meters in 2011 (KPC 2012). In order to meet growing demand KPC has been seeking financing of US$1 billion to boost its capacity (*New Times* 2013).

Jet fuel produced in Kenya is transported via the company's pipeline network from Mombasa to Nairobi and farther to Nakuru, Kisumu, and Eldoret. From there it is trucked to neighboring Rwanda, Uganda, and Burundi. The comparatively poor road conditions and the resulting high transport costs between Eldoret and Uganda, and Rwanda and Burundi, are assumed to have a considerable impact on the retail cost. The dependence on Kenya has also made the countries vulnerable to any political and economic shocks, as occurred during the 2008 political instabilities in Kenya. Uganda is lobbying for a new pipeline to extend from Eldoret to Entebbe, but is also considering its own facilities. In 2010, the country discovered commercially viable oil deposits estimated at around 3.5 billion barrels. A local refinery with jet fuel production is to commence operations soon (Sskika 2013). This can be considered a positive development for airlines serving Entebbe airport, as dependency on jet fuel imports and

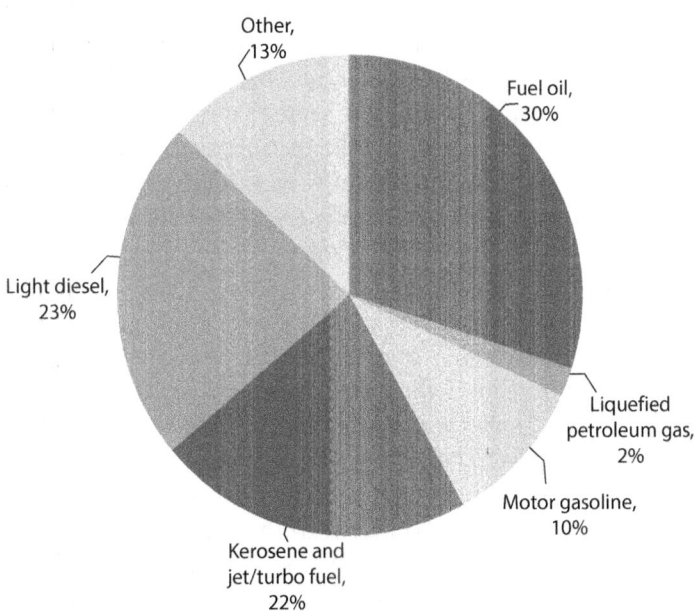

Figure 5.34 Mombasa Refinery Output per Type of Product
percent

Source: United States Energy Information Agency (2011) based on data from Kenya Petroleum Refineries (U.S. EIA 2011).

inadequate inventory planning have created some challenges, with various incidents of fuel shortages at the airport (*eTurboNews* 2011). Carriers were required to divert to other airports or reduce passenger loads to carry additional fuel. Similar scarcity has also occurred at Malindi Airport in Kenya, forcing aircraft to divert to Mombasa and leaving tourists stranded (*Daily Nation* 2010).

The lack of adequate facilities at some airports still poses a challenge for regional operations. Many of the smaller airports in the region do not have any refueling facilities; for example Tanzania's Iringa and Mbeya Airports, which both have scheduled services. In Kenya, over half of the airports in the chosen sample do not have any facilities for refueling. In Rwanda and Uganda, the respective airports in Entebbe and Kigali are the only ones with refueling facilities (Jeppesen 2013). The lack of fueling facilities has a considerable impact on airlines, as aircraft have to take on additional fuel rather than passengers, thereby increasing costs substantially.

Competition between fuel suppliers is still limited at the region's airports, creating quasi-monopolies in the market. Airlines have been trying to accommodate the higher fuel costs by adjusting their maintenance routines, or by hedging part of their fuel purchases, as seen at Kenya Airways. The region's larger airlines including Kenya Airways, Precision Air, and Rwandair have also joined forces with six other African airlines to jointly purchase jet fuel, thereby increasing their purchasing power (Okulo 2012).

Distribution

In order for LCCs to establish low-cost distribution channels, a solid information and communications technology (ICT) infrastructure and corresponding payment methods are required. With the exception of Burundi, Internet usage has been growing considerably in EAC countries, particularly in Tanzania, Uganda, and Kenya (see figure 5.35). Kenya has been at the forefront of Internet penetration with 28 per 100 people using the Internet as of 2011. The country has invested significantly in ICT infrastructure, particularly in fiber-optic cables in 2010, resulting in a doubling of Internet users within one year (Ombok 2011). Uganda also experienced an over 80 percent average increase in Internet users between 2006 and 2011.

Although the number of Internet users has been growing, it is still far below that of developed countries such as the United States or the United Kingdom—and even behind other developing countries such as Thailand and Mexico (see figure 5.36). This is primarily caused by poor infrastructure, the high cost of services, a lack of access to electricity, and unreliable power grids. In addition, computer literacy is still low in most African countries.

EAC countries also have similar issues with respect to Internet access and usage. According to the International Telecommunications Union (ITU), only 3.6 percent of households had a computer in Kenya in 2009. In Rwanda, it was only 2 percent in 2011 (ITU 2013a). In Tanzania, only 14 percent of the population had access to electricity in 2010, as compared with 8 percent in Uganda

Figure 5.35 EAC Internet Usage, 2006–11

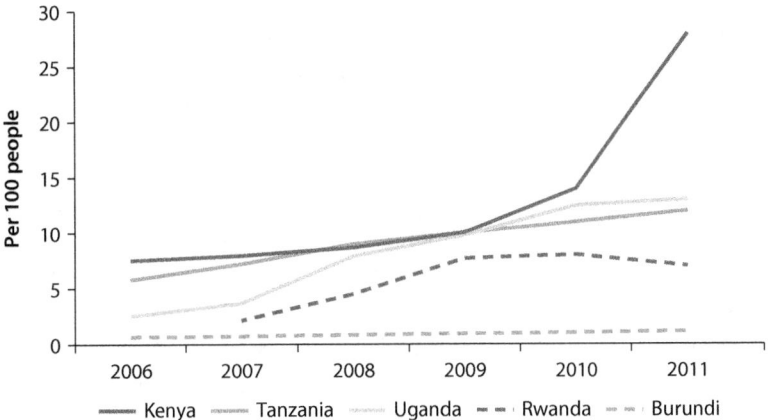

Source: World Bank 2013b.
Note: EAC = East African Community.

Figure 5.36 Comparison of Internet Users with the United States, United Kingdom, Thailand, and Mexico, 2006–11

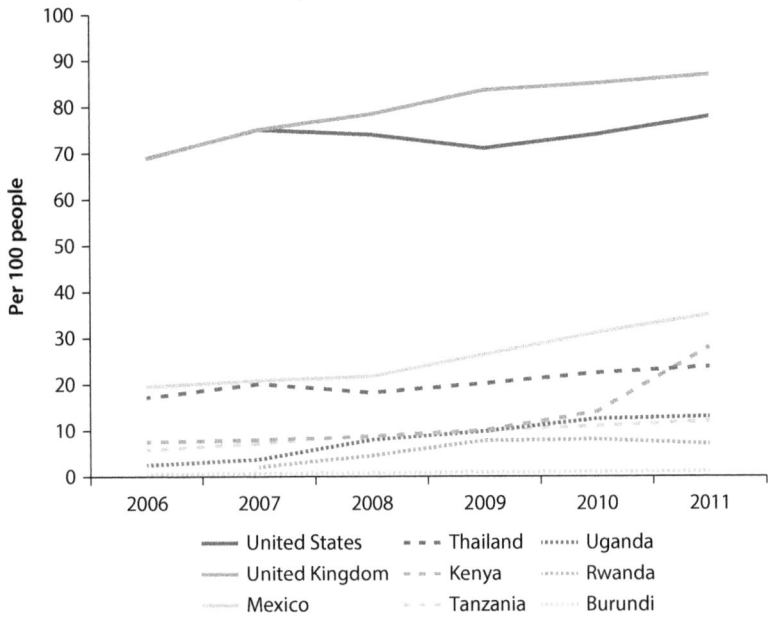

Source: World Bank 2013b.

and 18 percent in Kenya. This is further aggravated by limited power availability, with frequent blackouts in larger cities (for example, in Dar es Salaam).

Even where Internet access is available, the speed of fixed broadband is still very slow. By early 2012, the entirety of Kenya's fixed broadband ran at less than two megabits per second (Mbit/s). In comparison, the most prevalent speed in developed countries is between two and ten Mbit/sec, and in most European countries it is above ten Mbit/sec (ITU 2013b). The low speed further discourages usage, and makes online LCC booking processes particularly difficult.

Nevertheless, opportunities arise from the rapidly increasing use of mobile technology in the region. As the cost of mobile devices and usage prices decline, and coverage increases, mobile cellular subscriptions have seen a substantial rise of up to 100 percent in some markets (figure 5.37).

This new development gives LCCs the opportunity to facilitate bookings through three channels: short message service (SMS), interactive voice response, and Internet on mobile broadband. For the first two channels, all that is required is a mobile phone with texting and voice calling functionality. Both are available in almost all modern mobile phones. SMS bookings have already been used in other regions of the world, as for example in India with Kingfisher Airlines offering SMS booking by sending a simple text including data, origin, and destination, with a response for the requested schedule via SMS. Similarly for interactive voice response, all that is needed is an automated voice recording guiding a customer through to purchase.

Access to mobile broadband has helped fill the gap arising from the lack of fixed broadband infrastructure, and has enabled many customers to book their airline tickets via mobile Internet browsing and dedicated airline applications. According to a study by Deloitte Consulting and the GSM Association (Deloitte and GSMA 2012), 3G services are now available in all EAC countries. In Tanzania, operator Smile has even launched a faster 4G service for Dar es Salaam. This has considerably increased Internet access via mobile platforms. In Kenya, for example, over 27 percent of Internet browsing is done through mobile devices. The increased usage of smartphones is expected to further support

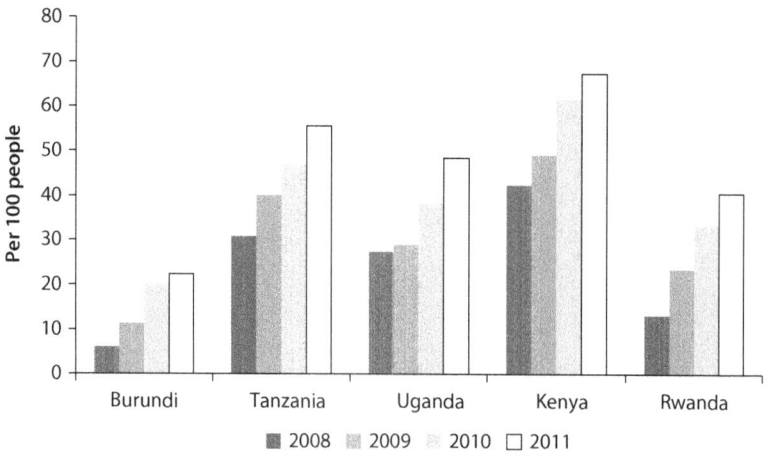

Figure 5.37 Mobile Cellular Subscriptions in EAC, 2008–11

Source: World Bank 2013b.
Note: EAC = East African Community.

access to mobile broadband in the future. The study estimates that by 2017, the penetration of smartphones in Kenya and Tanzania will be at 28 percent and approximately 22 percent respectively. Decreased costs for smartphones have made the devices more accessible, with the launch of a US$50 smartphone in 2013. Some providers, such as the Tanzanian mobile company Tigo, have even created systems that allow for access to Internet via SMS at a cost of US$0.06 per day (Kazonta 2012).

Mobile markets have increasingly become a solution for coping with the challenge of formal electronic payment methods, such as credit cards. Credit card penetration is still very low in Sub-Saharan Africa, at around 3 percent in 2012 (Togan-Egrican, English, and Klapper 2012), because of a lack of access to financial services, particularly in rural areas. With the exception of Kenya (no data were available for Tanzania), the majority of the population does not deposit their money with commercial banks. In Burundi, only 27 out of 1,000 people use commercial banks for deposits (see figure 5.38).

The mobile payment (M-Pay) market has grown considerably in Africa. M-Pay allows users to make their transactions via their mobile devices, without the need for a bank account. It therefore has the ability to capture a much larger share of the market. EAC countries have been at the forefront of introducing M-Pay initiatives. Kenya has become the global leader in mobile money transfer services through their M-PESA system. Provided by Safaricom, the country's leading mobile network operator in 2007, personal accounts are held by the operator and transactions are made and recorded using SMS. The conversion of cash into electronic value is done through retail stores. M-PESA had 15 million customers in 2012 (Clayton 2012), and was used by LCC Fly540 for airline bookings (Kagwe 2011a). Zain, a leading mobile telecommunications provider in the Middle East and Africa, launched Zap in 2009, providing a platform for transactions in Tanzania, Kenya, and Uganda (Grail Research 2010).

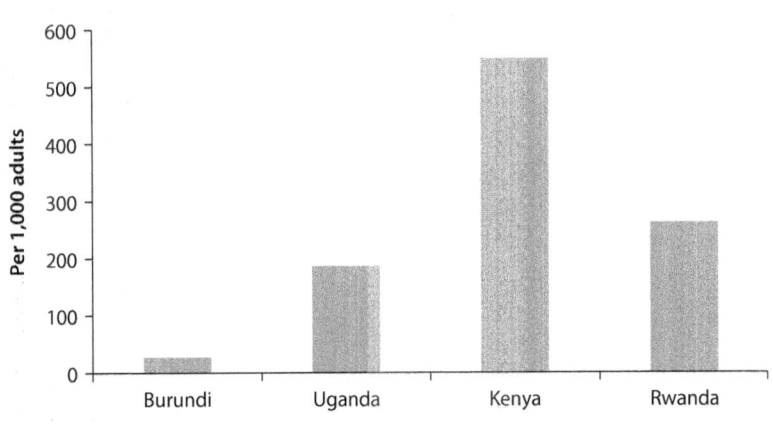

Figure 5.38 Depositors with Commercial Banks, 2010

Source: World Bank 2013b.

Figure 5.39 Governance Indicators for EAC

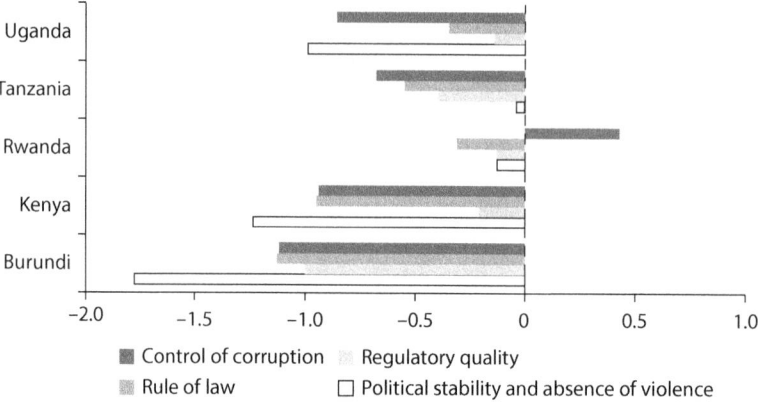

Source: World Bank's *Worldwide Governance Indicator Project* (World Bank 2013c).
Note: Estimate of governance ranges from approximately −2.5 (weak) to 2.5 (strong) governance performance. EAC = East African Community.

Governance

Good governance is the key for a competitive and transparent market in any country. The World Bank's *Worldwide Governance Indicator Project* (World Bank 2013c) has developed a holistic assessment of governance in most countries around the world. For the EAC countries, the study examines governance in light of four out of the six key indicators, which are particularly important in this context: political stability and the absence of violence, regulatory quality, rule of law, and control of corruption. The data set gives an estimate of the level of governance within a range of −2.5 (weak) to 2.5 (strong) as a measure of governance performance.

In four of the five EAC countries, the perceived level of governance is negative for all four indicators (see figure 5.39). The exception is Rwanda, which is perceived to have stronger governance with regard to the indicators for corruption and regulatory quality.

Political stability appears to be one of the key concerns in the region, particularly in Uganda, Kenya and Burundi. All three countries have undergone political unrest and conflict in the past, with Burundi emerging from a civil war in 2005. Kenya has been in political turmoil since its election in 2008. The re-emergence of the Lord Resistance Army (LRA) insurgency, an ongoing guerilla campaign in Uganda in 2008, has been another significant challenge. Corruption is also perceived to be rife across Burundi, Kenya, Tanzania and Uganda—and rule of law is perceived as weak in most countries.

Conclusion

Chapter 5 provides an overview of the EAC market in light of the LCC framework developed in chapter 4. While this represents a preliminary assessment and further research, particularly of the air transport market, is required to identify the viability of this business model for the EAC market, initial conclusions can be drawn that will give an indication as to whether the environment is conducive to LCC growth.

The air transport market in EAC appears to still be in the early stages of development. Traffic is primarily concentrated around Nairobi and Dar es Salaam, with little intra-regional traffic and only a few high frequency domestic routes. Competition varies on a route basis, but many intra-regional routes are served by only one or two carriers. However, considering the limited traffic, this may be as much as the markets can absorb at this time. Due to limited traffic, the types of aircraft used are primarily 60–80 seaters, which generally have higher unit costs than the A320 or B737 aircraft commonly used by LCCs. Airline operating costs are driven up even higher by airport taxes, fees, and charges in the region. Although still struggling with some unprofitable state-owned carriers such as Rwandair and Air Burundi, the market in the EAC has developed a few privately-owned carriers. The market has also seen the emergence of its first LCC Fly540—later renamed Fastjet. Though overall fare levels are still very high, the presence of the LCC has had a significant impact on fare levels in some markets, particular in Tanzania. The airline has, however, been ridden by financial difficulties in the past, making its future prospects doubtful.

Although economic growth, tourism opportunities, rising urbanization, and the state of transport infrastructure in some EAC countries are all factors conducive to LCC operations, inequality is still very high. Only Kenya appears to have a considerable middle class forming in the near future. Therefore, a lack of sufficient demand will make it difficult for LCCs to fill its planes and utilize its resources efficiently.

Airside infrastructure is generally not the problem. There is still plenty of airside capacity for growth at most EAC airports. In the medium term, some airports may require additional apron space and taxiway layouts must be adjusted in some cases. However, good maintenance routines of existing airside infrastructure may be more effective and cost-efficient than newer runways.

Landside infrastructure may in some cases constrain growth in the future. The size of passenger terminals, particularly in Nairobi, has compromised the quality of service at larger airports. To address this, a considerable number of expansion projects across EAC have been initiated by the World Bank and other donors.

CNS infrastructure is still limited, compromising the safety of operations. Newer GNSS-based technologies such as ADS-B are expected to provide a low-cost CNS solution, enabling countries to avoid costly radar installations.

Aeronautical fees are still high in some cases, but relatively moderate when contrasted with other African countries, such as Angola or Senegal. The burden has mostly been on passengers, however, which significantly influences the level of fares LCCs can charge.

Liberalization of air transport is under way. Progress has been made toward the liberalization of air transport in EAC. However, the required amendment of bilateral agreements in accordance with the YD is still pending. In addition, the frameworks promulgated under other RECs, of which EAC member states are also a part, have slowed progress considerably.

The removal of capacity and frequency restrictions is expected to stimulate air transport significantly. In effect, it will provide more opportunities for emerging carriers to provide intra-EAC routes, which is of particular importance for LCCs. Given the current traffic levels, however, it is questionable whether the application of fifth freedom traffic rights would actually have a significant impact. For LCCs that provide point-to-point traffic, this is generally less relevant.

Safety and security is still a challenge in EAC countries. The region experienced a significant number of accidents in the last decade, which were rooted in poor safety oversight and inadequately trained staff. ICAO audits show that in many audit areas, EAC countries still underperform. The regional body, CASSOA, has been trying to harmonize and improve safety standards in the region, but lacks the necessary financial and human resources.

The lack of human resources and training facilities is a general problem across EAC, with only a few sufficiently funded and cost-efficient training schools in the region. Trained pilots and maintenance engineers frequently get solicited by carriers from other regions, such as the Middle East, which offer better and higher paid opportunities. The lack of aviation personnel has driven costs up in the region, placing a high burden on an airline's operating costs. In addition, labor regulations in some countries, such as Rwanda and Tanzania, drive up costs by excessive social security contributions and additional labor-related levies.

Aircraft financing is still very expensive, with the cost of finance and the inability to reach economies of scale making it difficult for airlines to finance their aircraft. In addition, the safety standards and the lack of legal protection in some countries make aircraft manufacturers and leasing companies shy away from selling their aircraft to the region. Various initiatives have tried to address this. As a first step, Kenya, Tanzania, and Rwanda have become party to the Cape Town Convention providing lenders with a certain degree of protection in case of failure of the airline.

Taxation of fuel and the lack of appropriate facilities have been an impediment to growth. Most EAC countries have abolished their excise duty. However, Kenya still taxes jet fuel through an excise and a development levy. In addition, tariffs for the import of jet fuel and the high transport cost between Eldoret via road to Uganda, Rwanda, and Burundi drive costs even higher.

Mobile technology and mobile payments are providing for new low-cost distribution channels. The high penetration of mobile technology and the expected rise in smartphones provide important distribution channels for airlines. The EAC has also been at the forefront of developing mobile payment systems to address the lack of credit cards in the region. This is of particular importance to LCCs, as it provides a low cost and accessible means of promoting their product.

Good governance is still an issue in the region. Corruption levels are still perceived to be high in almost all countries, with the exception of Rwanda.

Rule of law and regulatory quality have both been compromised in EAC countries, posing a substantial challenge to investments.

This preliminary analysis has shown that LCCs will face a considerable number of hurdles in the EAC market. Challenges include (a) a limited existing network; (b) high levels of economic inequality hampering demand; (c) in some cases high infrastructure costs; (d) limited human resources; (e) high fuel costs; and (f) restrictive ASAs. This renders it difficult for a business model that relies on low input costs and high utilization to survive. The removal of these impediments would considerably accelerate and foster the development of air transport in the region. However, it is questionable whether the LCCs could flourish and sustain profitability at this point in time.

Notes

1. The member states (effective December 21, 1981, unless another date is shown) are Angola, Burundi, the Comoros, the Democratic Republic of Congo, Djibouti, the Arab Republic of Egypt (January 6, 1999), Eritrea (1994), Ethiopia, Kenya, Libya (June 3, 2005), Madagascar, Malawi, Mauritius, Rwanda, the Seychelles (2001), Republic of South Sudan, Swaziland, Uganda, Zambia, and Zimbabwe.
2. Purchasing power parity is the ratio between the currencies of two countries at which each currency, when exchanged for the other, will purchase the same quantity of goods as it purchases at home, excluding customs duties and costs of transport.
3. Airside infrastructure is defined as the part of an airport nearest the aircraft, the boundary of which is the security check, customs, and passport control. This includes part of the terminal, airfield, gates, air bridges, runways, aprons, and taxiways.
4. Landside infrastructure is defined as the part of an airport farthest from the aircraft, the boundary of which is the security check, customs, and passport control. It includes part of the terminal, passenger services, food and beverage concessions, duty-free shopping, car parking, and so on.
5. Secondary radar is a radar system used in air traffic control, which detects and measures the position of aircraft and requests additional information from aircraft, such as identity and altitude.
6. Upper airspace is airspace above Flight Level 245 (24,500 ft).
7. PPPs, public-private partnerships, are agreements between a government and one or more private sector partners (which may include the operators and/or the financiers), according to which the private partners deliver the service in such a manner that the service delivery objectives of the government are aligned with the profit objectives of the private partners—and where the effectiveness of the alignment depends on a sufficient transfer of risk to the private partner.
8. "Brain drain" refers to qualified staff emigrating from a vicinity or place for better jobs.

References

ACI (Airports Council International). *Air Traffic Report Africa*. 2012.

African Development Bank. 2011a. "AfDB and COMESA Sign Airspace Integration Project Grant Agreement." African Development Bank Press Release, February 15.

http://www.afdb.org/en/news-and-events/article/afdb-and-comesa-sign-airspace-integration-project-grant-agreement-7754/.

———. 2011b. "AfDB Approves USD 40 Million Loan to Ethiopian Airlines." African Development Bank Press Release, March 24. http://www.afdb.org/en/news-and-events/article/afdb-approves-usd-40-million-loan-to-ethiopian-airlines-7857/.

AICD (Africa Infrastructure Country Diagnostics). 2009. *Air Transport: Challenges to Growth*. http://siteresources.worldbank.org/EXTAIRTRANSPORT/Resources/515180-1262792532589/challenges.pdf.

Airbus. 2013. *Global Market Forecast 2013–32*. http://www.airbus.com/company/market/forecast/.

Airline Update. n.d. *Airline Ground Handling in Kenya*. http://www.airlineupdate.com/content_subscription/gha/africa/kenya.htm.

Air Traffic and Navigation Services. 2013. *VSAT Networks—Cape Town to Cairo and Beyond*. http://www.atns.co.za/commercial-services/vsat.

allAfrica. 2013. "Tanzania: Dutch Win Dar es Salaam Terminal Three Contract." April 29. http://allafrica.com/stories/201304291884.html.

Association of Tanzania Employers. 2011. *Business Agenda 2011–2014*. http://lempnet.itcilo.org/en/hidden-folder/ate-tanzania-business-agenda.

Astier, C. 2012. *Exponential Growth of African Business Law and the Spread of Common Law*. Hogan Lovells Africa. http://www.hoganlovellsafrica.com/_uploads/Publications/Information_sheet_-_African_business_law_growth.pdf.

Autorité de l'Aviation Civile Burundi. 2013. "Décret portant organisation et fonctionnement de l'AACB." http://www.aacb.bi/spip.php?article16.

AZ World Airports. 2013a. *Runway Surface*. http://www.azworldairports.com/cfm/homepage.cfm.

———. 2013b. *Passenger Capacity*. http://www.azworldairports.com/cfm/homepage.cfm.

Balinda, B. 2013. "Driving Tourism in Africa (The Uganda Case)." Presentation at Routes Africa Strategy Summit, Uganda Tourism Board, Kampala, Uganda.

Butera, S. 2013. "Rwandair May Offer Shares after Returning to Profit in Two Years." *Bloomberg*, February 11. http://www.bloomberg.com/news/2013-02-12/rwandair-may-offer-shares-after-returning-to-profit-in-two-years.html.

CAPA (Centre for Asia Pacific Aviation). 2010. "Singapore Aviation Outlook: A Key Asia Pacific Market with Key Asia Pacific Airlines." March 24. http://centreforaviation.com/analysis/singapores-aviation-outlook-a-key-asia-pacific-market-with-key-asia-pacific-airlines-22861.

———. 2011. "Fly540 Targets Continued Growth in Under-Served African Market." January 10. http://centreforaviation.com/analysis/fly540-targeting-continued-growth-in-underserved-african-markettargeting-18-country-network-by-2012-43164.

———. 2012. "Opportunities and Challenges as Fly540, First Pan-African Airline, Adopts Stelios Fastjet Brand." June 14. http://centreforaviation.com/analysis/opportunities-and-challenges-as-fly540-first-pan-african-airline-adopts-stelios-fastjet-brand-76040.

———. 2013a. "Precision Air Reports a USD18.9 Million Loss for FY2013 Due to Overly Ambitious Growth." September 7. http://centreforaviation.com/analysis/precision-air-reports-a-usd189-million-loss-for-fy2013-due-overly-ambitious-growth-127300.

———. 2013b. "Uganda Plans to Relaunch Airlines and Invest USD400 Million in Airport Development." August 1. http://centreforaviation.com/analysis/uganda-plans

-to-relaunch-uganda-airlines-and-invest-usd400-million-in-airport-developments-121503.

———. 2013c. "Fastjet Pushed Ahead with African Expansion in 2013 but Faces Protectionist Hurdles." March 12. http://centreforaviation.com/analysis/fastjet-pushes-ahead-with-african-expansion-in-2013-but-faces-protectionist-hurdles-100841.

———. 2013d. "Fastjet Posts USD56 Million Loss but Remains Optimistic about African Success." June 8. https://centreforaviation.com/analysis/fastjet-posts-usd56-million-loss-but-remains-optimistic-about-african-success-113205.

Carrier, C. 2013. "Regional Aircraft as a Solution to Network Growth in Africa." Presentation at Routes Africa, Bombardier, July 8. http://www.routesonline.com/library/479/routes-africa-strategy-summit-2013/479/regional-aircraft-as-a-solution-to-network-growth-in-africa-charles-carriere/.

CIA (Central Intelligence Agency). 2013. "The World Factbook." https://www.cia.gov/library/publications/the-world-factbook/.

CASSOA (Civil Aviation Safety and Security Oversight Agency). 2013. *Report of the Second Aviation Symposium.* http://www.cassoa.org/docs/FINAL%202ND%20SYMPOSIUM%20REPORT%20-%20June%202013.pdf.

Clayton, N. 2012. "More to African Mobile Payments than M-Pesa." *Wall Street Journal*, October 29. http://blogs.wsj.com/tech-europe/2012/10/29/more-to-african-mobile-payments-than-m-pesa/.

CNN (Cable News Network). 2000. "Easyjet Values Itself at $816 Million; Sets IPO Price Range." http://cnnfn.cnn.com/2000/10/31/europe/easyjet/.

Comsoft. 2013. "Tanzania CAA Choose COMSOFT for Tandem Delivery of ADS-B and AMHS." June. http://www.comsoft.aero/press-media-events/press-releases/press-releases/?tx_ttnews%5Btt_news%5D=169&cHash=fff0fbe28f568386afc1fb691d5ab664.

Daily Nation. 2010. "Malindi Airport Hit by Jet Fuel Scarcity." January 7. http://www.nation.co.ke/business/news/-/1006/838254/-/view/printVersion/-/iftxanz/-/index.html.

Deloitte Consulting and GSMA. 2012. *Sub-Saharan Africa Mobile Observatory 2012.* http://www.gsma.com/publicpolicy/wp-content/uploads/2012/03/SSA_FullReport_v6.1_clean.pdf.

DiiO SRS Analyzer. 2013. DiiO Online Database. http://www.diio.net.

EAC (East African Community). n.d. *Proposal for the Partnership Funding: Global Navigation Satellite System (GNSS) Procedures Development.* http://www.dk-export.dk/media/GNSSProposalEAcfrance.pdf.

———. 1999. *East African Community Treaty.* Arusha, Tanzania: EAC.

East African Community Statistics Portal. 2013. "EAC: A Snapshot." http://www.statistics.eac.int.

East African Community Secretariat. 2006. *Report of the Meeting of the 11th Meeting of the Council of Ministers.* Arusha, Tanzania: EAC Secretariat.

Easy Coach. 2013. "Fares Nairobi to Up-Country." http://www.easycoach.co.ke/nairobi-to-upcountry.html.

easyGroup. 2013. "Fastjet December Passenger Statistics." http://www.easy.com/fastjet/3360-fastjet-december-passenger-statistics.html.

Emorut, F. 2012a. "Uganda Tops Africa in Tourism Growth." *New Vision*, September 29. http://www.newvision.co.ug/news/635781-uganda-tops-africa-in-tourism-growth.html.

———. 2012b. "East Africa: Population Growth Worries UNFPA." *allAfrica*, August 11. http://allafrica.com/stories/201208120022.html.

eTurboNews. 2011. "Entebbe Airport Runs Out of Jet Fuel Again." November 30. http://www.eturbonews.com/26650/entebbe-airport-runs-out-jet-fuel-again.

European Commission. 2013. *List of Airlines Banned within the EU.* http://ec.europa.eu/transport/modes/air/safety/air-ban/index_en.htm.

Evans, R. 2011. "New Lease of Life for Kenya's 'Lunatic' Railway." BBC, July 18. http://www.bbc.co.uk/news/world-14151372.

Flight Foundation. 2013. *Aviation Safety Network*. http://aviation-safety.net/index.php.

Fly540 Africa. 2013. "Destinations." http://www.fly540.com.

Gichane, C. 2012. "Kenya Airways Signs Up Afreximbank." Capital FM. June 25. http://www.capitalfm.co.ke/business/2012/06/kenya-airways-signs-up-afreximbank/.

Grail Research. 2010. "Mobile Payment Opportunity in the Middle East and Africa (MEA) Region." Presentation. http://grailresearch.com/pdf/ContenPodsPdf/Mobile_Payment_Opportunity_in_MEA_Region.pdf.

Gwilliam, K., with H. Bofinger, R. Bullock, R. Carruthers, A. Kumar, M. Mundy, A. Nogales, and K. Sethi. 2011. *Africa's Transport Infrastructure*. Washington, DC: World Bank.

Hayter, S., and V. Stoevska. 2011. "Social Dialogue Indicators: International Statistical Inquiry 2008–2009." Technical Brief, International Labour Organization. http://laborsta.ilo.org/applv8/data/TUM/TUD%20and%20CBC%20Technical%20Brief.pdf.

IATA (International Air Transport Association). 2013. "Demand for Air Travel Stays Firm but Regional Variations." International Air Transport Association Press Release, May 28, 30. http://www.iata.org/pressroom/pr/Pages/2013-05-30-01.aspx.

———. n.d. *Fuel Monitor.* http://www.iata.org/publications/economics/fuel-monitor/Pages/price-analysis.aspx.

ICAO (International Civil Aviation Organization). 2009. *ICAO's Policies on Taxation in the Field Of International Air Transport*. Montreal, Canada: ICAO.

———. 2013a. *2013 Safety Report*. http://www.icao.int/safety/Documents/ICAO_2013-Safety-Report_FINAL.pdf.

———. 2013b. *Safety Audit Information*. http://www.icao.int/safety/Pages/USOAP-Results.aspx.

IFC (International Finance Corporation). 2013. *Challenges and Opportunities in Sub-Saharan Africa: Emphasis on Low-Cost Carriers and Their Potential Impact on the Market*. Unpublished presentation, International Finance Corporation, Nairobi, Kenya.

Ihucha, A. 2012. "EAC Civil Aviation Regulatory Body Fails to Get Consent." *The East African*, March 31. http://www.theeastafrican.co.ke/business/EAC+civil+aviation+regulatory+body+fails+to+get+consent/-/2560/1377284/-/255m8oz/-/index.html.

IMF (International Monetary Fund). 2013. *World Economic Outlook Database April 2013.* http://www.imf.org/external/data.htm.

In2EastAfrica. 2011. "Rwanda: Aviation Experts Call for Capacity Building." November 1. http://in2eastafrica.net/rwanda-aviation-experts-call-for-capacity-building/.

ITU (International Telecommunications Union). 2013a. *Core Indicators on Access to, and Use of, ICT by Households and Individuals, Latest Available Data (2008–2012)*. http://www.itu.int/en/ITU-D/Statistics/Pages/stat/default.aspx.

———. 2013b. *ICT Facts and Figures 2013.* http://www.itu.int/en/ITU- http://www.itu.int/en/ITU-D/Statistics/Documents/facts/ICTFactsFigures2013-e.pdf.

Jeppesen. 2013. *Fueling Facilities Kenya, Uganda, Rwanda, Burundi and Tanzania.*

Kagwe, W. 2011a. "Fly540 Connect to MPesa." *The Star*, July 26. http://www.the-star.co.ke/news/article-55817/fly540-connects-mpesa.

———. 2011b. "Shortage of Pilot Raises Concerns in Industry." *The Star*, June 29. http://www.the-star.co.ke/news/article-58901/shortage-pilots-raises-concern-industry.

Kazonta, H. 2012 "Tigo Launches 'Xtreme' Bundles." *Biztech Africa*, July 17. http://www.biztechafrica.com/article/tigo-launches-xtreme-bundles/3556/#.U3Db5_mSySo.

Kazooba, C. 2007. "Uganda: Entebbe Radar Monitors Country Airspace." *The New Times.* http://www.newtimes.co.rw/news/views/article_print.php?&a=1835&icon=Print.

Kenya Airports Authority. 2013. "About Us." https://www.kaa.go.ke/about-us/our-mandate.

Kenya Ministry of Tourism. 2010. *Kenya Tourism Overview 2010.* http://www.tourism.go.ke/ministry.nsf/pages/facts_figures.

Kenya National Bureau of Statistics. 2010. *Reported Visitor's Arrival by Purpose 2001–2010.* http://www.knbs.or.ke/sectoral/tourism/Visitor_Statistics.pdf.

Kenya Revenue Authority. 2013. *The Value Added Tax Act (2013).* Nairobi: Government of Kenya.

Kilimanjaro Airport Development Company. 2013. http://www.kilimanjaroairport.co.tz/.

KPC (Kenya Pipeline Company). 2012. *Annual Report and Financial Statements 2011.* http://www.kpc.co.ke/images/stories/downloads/KPC_2011.pdf.

———. 2013. *Key Achievements 2002 to Date.* http://www.kpc.co.ke/achievements?showall=&start=1.

Lonrho Aviation. 2012. "RNS News Item." Press Release, Lonrho Aviation. June 13. http://www.lonrho.com/Press/News_(RNS)/RnsNews.aspx?id=779&rid=11231504.

Maina, W. 2011. "KQ Sets Sights on Expats to Ease Shortage of Pilots." *Business Daily*, December 18. http://www.businessdailyafrica.com/Corporate+News/KQ+sets+sights+on+expats+to+ease+shortage+of+pilots+/-/539550/1291588/-/5e090w/-/index.html.

Makame, A. 2012. "The East African Integration: Achievement and Challenges." *GREAT Insights* 1 (6). http://ecdpm.org/great-insights/trade-and-development-making-the-link/east-african-integration-achievements-challenges/.

Matschnigg, G. 2013. "Safety: Focus on Africa." Presentation at Annual General Meeting, International Air Transport Association. http://www.iata.org/pressroom/facts_figures/Documents/safety-gunther-agm2013.pdf.

Mbalamwezi, J. 2011. "Tanzania to Upgrade 10 Airports in Infrastructure Project." *The East African*, August 20. http://www.theeastafrican.co.ke/business/-/2560/1222228/-/bc59i2z/-/index.html.

McAuliffe, C., S. Saxena, and M. Zabara. 2012. "The East African Community: Prospects for Sustained Growth." International Monetary Fund Working Paper. http://www.imf.org/external/pubs/ft/wp/2012/wp12272.pdf.

McKormick, D. 2008. *Impact of the Financial Crisis on Kenya.* Institute of Development Studies. http://www.ids.ac.uk/files/dmfile/KENYADorothyMcCormick.pdf.

Momberger Airport Information. 2012. *Who Owns and Manages Privatized Airports.* http://www.air-trans-source.com/linked/manage-bk.pdf.

Muchira, J. 2013. "Uganda Announces $400m Plan to Modernise Entebbe Airport." *Engineering News*, July 26. http://www.engineeringnews.co.za/article/uganda-announces-400m-plan-to-modernise-entebbe-airport-2013-07-26.

Mueller, J., T. Ulku, and J. Zivanovic. 2009. *Privatization, Restructuring and Its Effect on Performance: A Comparison between German and British Airports*. German Airport Performance Project, joint research project of the University of Applied Sciences Bremen, the Berlin School of Economics and Law (HWR), and the International University of Applied Sciences in Bad Honnef, Bonn.

Muhumuza, M. 2012. "CAA in Bed with ENHAS as Airlines Cry Foul." *The CEO Magazine*, April 5. http://www.theceomagazine-ug.com/news/caa-in-bed-with-enhas-as-airlines-cry-foul.html.

Muiri, J. 2013. "State Wants Bigger Say in Running of Kenya." *Daily Nation*, July 9. http://www.nation.co.ke/business/news/State-wants-bigger-say-in-running-of-Kenya-Airways-/-/1006/1910158/-/wmcikuz/-/index.html.

Munyagi, M. T. 2006. *Existing Bi-Lateral Air Service Agreements of Tanzania as of 30 November 2006*. Dar es Salaam: Tanzania Civil Aviation Authority.

Muson, E. 2009. "Rwanda: The Nation Moves to Control Her Airspace." *New Times*. http://www.newtimes.co.rw/news/views/article_print.php?i=13929&a=16671&icon=Print.

Mutegi, M. 2012. "Kenya Airports Authority Doubles Air Passenger Charges." *Business Daily Africa*, May 7. http://www.businessdailyafrica.com/Corporate-News/Kenya-Airports-Authority-doubles-air-passenger-charges--/-/539550/1401486/-/sqng97/-/index.html.

National Institute of Statistics of Rwanda. 2012. *Statistical Yearbook 2012*. http://www.statistics.gov.rw/system/files/user_uploads/files/books/YEAR%20BOOK_2012.pdf.

Ndegwa, N. 2012. "East Africa: EA Aviation Faces Severe Manpower Loss." Capital FM. April 3. http://www.capitalfm.co.ke/business/2012/04/ea-aviation-facing-severe-manpower-loss/.

NEPAD–OECD Africa Investment Initiative. 2008. "East African Community: Overview of Regional Road Infrastructure Projects." Background Paper, Expert Roundtable Investment in Transport Infrastructure. http://www.oecd.org/daf/inv/investmentfordevelopment/41775886.pdf.

News of Rwanda. 2013. "East African Community Aviation Calls for Improved Security." http://www.newsofrwanda.com/english/18963/east-african-community-aviation-calls-for-improved-security/.

New Times. 2013. "Kenya Refinery Seeks $1b to Boost Oil Handling Capacity." May 4. http://www.newtimes.co.rw/news/index.php?a=66591&i=15347.

New Vision. 2006. "Get Tough with Kenya Airways." November 28. http://www.newvision.co.ug/D/8/14/534749.

Ngigi, G. 2012. "World Bank's IFC to Own 7.4 pc Stake in Kenya Airways after Offer." *Business Daily*, April 25. http://www.businessdailyafrica.com/World-Bank-IFC-to-own-stake-in-Kenya-Airways-after-offer-/-/539552/1393786/-/b7kgru/-/index.html.

OECD and WTO. 2011. *Aid for Trade Case Story: The COMESA-EAC-SADC Tripartite Trade and Transport Facilitation Programme*. http://www.oecd.org/aidfortrade/47407250.pdf.

Okulo, L. 2012. "African Airlines to Purchase Fuel Jointly." *The Star*, January 13. http://www.the-star.co.ke/news/article-34322/african-airlines-purchase-fuel-jointly.

Ombok, E. 2011. "Kenyan Internet Usage Doubles over 2010, Ministry Says." *Bloomberg.* http://www.bloomberg.com/news/2011-01-19/kenyan-internet-usage-doubles-over *Aid for Trade Case Story*-2010-ministry-says-update1-.html.

Peterson, T. 2013. "Fastjet to Sell Slice of Dar Stake." *The East African*, June 15. http://www.theeastafrican.co.ke/business/fastjet+to+sell+slice+of+Dar+stake/-/2560/1883826/-/78158w/-/index.html.

Planespotters. 2013. *easyJet Historic Fleet.* http://www.planespotters.net/Airline/Easyjet?sort=dd.

PwC (PricewaterhouseCoopers). 2013. *Doing Business: Know Your Taxes, East African Tax Guide 2012/13.* http://www.pwc.com/ke/en/pdf/2013-east-african-tax-guide.pdf.

Ramah, R. 2013. "East African Community Closer to Common Passport, Tourism Visa." *allAfrica*, July 18. http://allafrica.com/stories/201307190057.html.

Ranganathan, R., and V. Foster. 2011. "East Africa's Infrastructure a Continental Perspective." Policy Research Working Paper World Bank. http://www-wds.worldbank.org/servlet/WDSContentServer/WDSP/IB/2011/10/13/000158349_20111013121848/Rendered/PDF/WPS5844.pdf.

Ratha, D., S. Mohapatra, C. Özden, S. Plaza, W. Shaw, and A. Shimeles. 2011. *Leveraging Migration for Africa: Remittances, Skills, and Investments.* Washington, DC: World Bank.

Rwanda Civil Aviation Authority. 2013. "RCAA Responsibilities." http://www.caa.gov.rw/about-rcaa/rcaa-responsibilities.html.

Rwanda Development Board. n.d. *Highlight of Tourist Arrivals in Rwanda 2010.* http://www.rdb.rw/fileadmin/user_upload/Documents/tourism%20conservation/Arrival_Statistics_2010_Jan-Dec.pdf.

Rwanda Institute of Statistics. 2012. *Statistical Yearbook 2012.* http://www.statistics.gov.rw/publications/statistical-yearbook-2012.

Rwanda Revenue Authority. n.d. *East African Community.* http://www.rra.gov.rw/rra_article199.html.

Rwigamba, R. 2013. "Rwanda's View on Tourism as a Life Changing Experience." *eTurboNews*, July 21. http://www.eturbonews.com/36340/rwandas-view-tourism-life-changing-experience.

Scandinavia Express. 2013. *Scandinavia Express Routes, Fares, Schedules and Charters.* http://www.scandinaviagroup.com/Scandinavia%20Express/index.htm.

Schlumberger, C. 2009. "The Implementation of the Yamoussoukro Decision." Thesis submitted to McGill University in partial fulfillment of the requirements of the degree of Doctor of Civil Law (DCL). http://digitool.library.mcgill.ca/webclient/StreamGate?folder_id=0&dvs=1400678806177~634.

———. 2010. *Open Skies for Africa.* Washington, DC: The World Bank.

Skytrax. 2013. *Airline Travel Rating & Reviews.* http://www.airlinequality.com.

Ssenyonga, J. 2013. "Liberalisation of EAC Air Transport on Course." *Sunday Times*, January 27. http://www.newtimes.co.rw/news/index.php?i=15250&a=13295.

Sskika, E. 2013. "Uganda: No Cheap Fuel When Oil Starts Flowing." *The Observer*, March 12. http://observer.ug/index.php?option=com_content&view=article&id=24163:no-cheap-fuel-when-oil-starts-flowing.

Ssuuna, I. 2013. "New Rwanda Airport Ready for Take-Off." *The East African*, April 13. http://www.theeastafrican.co.ke/business/New-Rwanda-airport-ready-for-take-off/-/2560/1747438/-/oqexn5z/-/index.html.

Tairo, A. 2012. "Rising Jet Fuel Prices a Major Setback to African Airlines." *eTurboNews*, June 7. http://www.eturbonews.com/29622/rising-jet-fuel-prices-major-setback-african-airlines.

Tanzania Airports Authority. 2013. http://www.taa.go.tz/index.php.

Tanzania Civil Aviation Authority. 2013a. *Decision of the Board of Directors on Liberalisation of Ground Handling Services, including Aviation Fuelling.* Decision No. 1 of 2013. http://www.tcaa.go.tz/news_detail.php?news=1876.

———. 2013b. *The Status of Bilateral Air Services Agreements Concluded between the Government of the United Republic of Tanzania and the Governments of Other Countries as at 28 February 2013.* http://www.tcaa.go.tz/files/BASA%20status%20by%2028%20February%202013.pdf.

Tanzania Daily News. 2012. "Tanzania: Tigo Launches SMS Internet Browsing." http://allafrica.com/stories/201210041051.html.

Tanzania Ministry of Natural Resources and Tourism. 2010. *Tourism Statistical Bulletin 2009.* http://www.mnrt.go.tz/index.php/tourism-doc?download=25:tourism-statistical-bulletin-2009.

Tanzania National Bureau of Statistics. 2012. *Tanzania Tourism Sector Survey.* http://www.nbs.go.tz/takwimu/trade/Tourism_Sector_Survey_Report_2010.pdf.

Thome, W. 2010. "Fly540 Takes Over East African Safari Air Express." *Kenya Aviation News*, December 19. http://www.eturbonews.com/20101/fly-540-takes-over-east-african-safari-air-express.

Tierny, M. 2012. "Africa: Modernising Africa's Commercial Aircraft Fleet." *This is Africa*, May 1. http://www.thisisafricaonline.com/Perspectives/Modernising-Africa-s-commercial-aircraft-fleet.

Togan-Egrican, A., C. English, and L. Klapper. 2012. "Credit Cards and Formal Loans Rare in Developing Countries: Informal Loans Most Common in Low-Income Countries." Gallup. http://www.gallup.com/poll/154340/credit-cards-formal-loans-rare-developing-countries.aspx.

Uganda Bureau of Statistics. 2007. *Labor Market Condition Indicators.* http://www.ubos.org/onlinefiles/uploads/ubos/pdf%20documents/2007%20National%20Labour%20Market%20Indicators.pdf.

———. 2010. *Migration and Tourism: Report VI 2005–2009.* http://www.ubos.org/onlinefiles/uploads/ubos/pdf%20documents/migration2005_09.pdf.

Uganda Civil Aviation Authority. 2013. "CAA Profile." http://www.caa.co.ug/index.php?option=com_content&view=article&id=71&Itemid=74.

UNECA (United Nations Economic Commission for Africa). 1988. *Declaration of Yamoussoukro on a New African Air Transport Policy.* Yamoussoukro, Côte d'Ivoire: UNECA.

———. 2004. *La Décision de Yamoussoukro et le transport aérien en Afrique.* Paris: Servedit.

UNWTO (United Nations World Tourism Organization). 2011. "Kenyan President Mwai Kibaki Highlights Tourism's Cultural Benefits upon Joining UNWTO/WTTC Global Leaders Campaign." United Nations World Tourism Organization Press Release, June 27. http://media.unwto.org/en/press-release/2011-06-27/kenyan-president-mwai-kibaki-highlights-tourism-s-cultural-benefits-upon-jo.

U.S. EIA (United States Energy Information Agency). 2011. *Kenya Petroleum Imports.* http://www.eia.gov/countries/regions-topics.cfm?fips=EEAE.

Uwanyiligira, I. 2012. *Rwanda and the Restoration of Rule of Law.* Keynote Address by the Ambassador of Rwanda at The Hague Academic Coalition. http://www.haguecoalition.org/storage/Lecture%20Rwanda%20by%20H.E.%20Ambassador%20Mrs%20Uwanyiligira.pdf.

Vasigh, B., and M. Haririan. 2003. "An Empirical Investigation of Financial and Operational Efficiency of Private versus Public Airports." *Journal of Air Transportation* 8 (1): 91–110.

Ventures. 2013. "Kenya's Lamu Airport Upgrade Nears Completion." January 3. http://www.ventures-africa.com/2013/01/lamu-airport-upgrade-nears-completion/.

Vogel, H. A. 2006. "Impact of Privatization on the Financial and Economic Performance of European Airports." *The Aeronautical Journal* 110 (1106): 197–213.

WEF (World Economic Forum). 2013. *Global Competitiveness Report.* http://www.weforum.org/issues/global-competitiveness.

World Bank. 2005. *East Africa Air Transport Survey.* http://siteresources.worldbank.org/INTAIRTRANSPORT/Resources/514573-1117230543314/050617-East_Africa_Air_Transport_Survey_Revision_2.pdf.

———. 2011a. *East Africa Infrastructure Report.* http://elibrary.worldbank.org/doi/pdf/10.1596/1813-9450-5844.

———. 2011b. "Turning the Tide in Turbulent Times: Making the Most of Kenya's Demographic Change and Rapid Urbanization." *Kenya Economic Update*, No. 4. Poverty Reduction and Economic Management Unit Africa Region.

———. 2011c. *Migration and Remittances Factbook 2011.* http://data.worldbank.org/data-catalog/migration-and-remittances.

———. 2013a. *Doing Business: EAC.* http://www.doingbusiness.org/~/media/GIAWB/Doing%20Business/Documents/Special-Reports/DB13-EAC.pdf.

———. 2013b. *World Development Indicators.* http://data.worldbank.org/indicator/SI.POV.2DAY.

———. 2013c. *Worldwide Governance Indicator Project.* http://info.worldbank.org/governance/wgi/index.asp.

World Bank and IFC (International Finance Corporation). 2013. *Enterprise Surveys: What Businesses Experience.* http://www.enterprisesurveys.org.

WHO (World Health Organization). 2013. *Road Safety Status Report 2013.* http://www.who.int/violence_injury_prevention/road_safety_status/2013/en/.

World Travel and Tourism Council. 2013a. *Travel and Tourism, Economic Impact 2013: Kenya.* http://www.wttc.org/site_media/uploads/downloads/kenya2013_1.pdf.

———. 2013b. *Travel and Tourism, Economic Impact 2013: Rwanda.* http://www.wttc.org/site_media/uploads/downloads/rwanda2013_2.pdf.

———. 2013c. *Travel and Tourism, Economic Impact 2013: Uganda.* http://www.wttc.org/site_media/uploads/downloads/uganda2013.pdf.

———. 2013d. *Travel and Tourism, Economic Impact 2013: Tanzania.* http://www.wttc.org/site_media/uploads/downloads/tanzania2013.pdf.

WTO (World Trade Organization). 2013. *ASAP Analytical Tool.* http://www.wto.org/asap/index.html.

CHAPTER 6

Development Framework for Sustainable Air Transport

The previous chapters of this book outline the characteristics of low-cost carriers (LCCs), their impact on markets, the transferability of their framework to emerging markets, and opportunities and challenges for LCC development in the East African Community (EAC) market—with the objective of examining the role of LCCs in the development of air services in lesser-developed countries and emerging markets. The implied narrower question can be more simply formulated as: "Is the introduction of LCCs into a thin and underdeveloped air service environment the solution to foster growth of air transportation?"

Based on our analysis, the short answer would probably be no. LCCs can only survive and become a catalyst for air transport growth when certain conditions are in place. In essence, the air transport market needs to achieve a certain degree of maturity, become at least partially liberalized, enjoy relatively good governance allowing for undistorted competition, and have a critical mass within a country's population which has sufficient purchasing power to utilize air services. The existence of a significant middle class is particularly crucial for building a market in which LCCs can achieve the highest possible utilization of assets in order to drive costs down. In both the cases of South Africa and Mexico, a substantial middle class was present, which stimulated demand for air travel.

Although developing markets with little traffic and limited economic growth may currently not be suitable for this business model, there are a considerable number of ways to foster the sustainable development of air transport, make air services more affordable for the population, and pave the way for the future development of LCCs. Some of these measures are outlined below.

Access to Markets

One of the key factors in developing air transport is to enable market access and foster competition. LCCs have emerged only when the air transport sector was liberalized and deregulated. As the case studies of Mexico and South Africa show, open competition against key players, such as a state-owned carrier, is necessary to bring down fares and attract new customers. Many developing countries, however, still have a dominant national carrier, be it a state-owned or private carrier, which enjoys anticompetitive advantages.

The first step in liberalizing air service markets is to define a sector policy that is conducive to creating competition. This is of special importance where a dominant national carrier depends on a protected market, and artificially keeps fares high. In order to gain political support for liberalization, it is important to examine the advantages of liberalizing the market, and communicate the expected outcome in terms of economic development to the public. Too often, protecting employment through inefficient dominant carriers is the official or implied reason to oppose the introduction of competition, which could pose a challenge to established players. However, the benefits of increased air services on the tourism sector (to name one example) are rarely clear. They can result in gains in terms of employment, as compared to airline jobs alone.

Enabling market access has to be achieved in an open and transparent manner. This requires the establishment of regulations and laws that set clear requirements for new market entrants. Such regulation must foster an environment without limitations, such as the number of participants or exclusive rights for a given air carrier. Furthermore, any existing market distortions, such as direct or indirect subsidies to select carriers—as well as exclusive rights to serve certain routes—must be eliminated. At the same time, certain subsidies that are granted to fulfill a public service route to remote destinations should be maintained, but only if they are granted following a competitive bidding process and reviewed regularly.

Many developing countries are small, and a large part of their population often cannot afford air travel. The development of air service markets in these countries depends primarily on establishing a competitive international network. As elaborated in chapter 4, access to international or regional markets is traditionally defined and regulated on a bilateral basis. Liberalizing traffic on routes involving more than one government is more challenging than simply opening up the domestic market. Nevertheless, several initiatives to liberalize international air services have been implemented on a bilateral or multilateral basis. On a bilateral basis, many countries have agreed to very liberal air service agreements (ASAs), which do not restrict frequency or capacity of flights and allow for the free setting of airfares. A further step for any government is to establish a so-called "open skies" agreement with another country or a group of countries, for example, as members of a regional economic community (such as the Association of Southeast Asian Nations [ASEAN]). Another effective and rather simple procedure is the adherence to an existing open sky policy agreement, such as the Yamoussoukro Decision in Africa.

It is important that the signing of any liberal ASA, open skies, or multilateral agreement—or even the establishment of a fully liberalized economic environment which includes air services—be implemented and maintained on a transparent and sustainable basis. Too often, governments have announced and even signed important bilateral or multilateral agreements on air services, only to have slow or no implementation for years to come (for example, the Yamoussoukro Decision).

International partners, as well as the industry (for example, aircraft manufacturers), can play an important role in initiating, supporting, and monitoring the process of international liberalization of air services. Support for liberalizing international air services can range from technical advice on existing bilateral air service agreements to fostering the establishment of a regional liberalized air service market. The latter includes the example of the pan-African liberalization of air services, which was initiated by the United Nations Economic Commission for Africa (UNECA), when it actively engaged African countries to agree to the Yamoussoukro Declaration in 1999 (UNECA 1988).

Liberalization of air services is not a one-time event, but rather an ongoing policy that must be monitored and adjusted. Regions that have been, on paper (by treaty), liberalized often have some countries unilaterally depart from their liberal policy and restrict their services. In many cases, such as the West African Economic and Monetary Union, no effective monitoring or compliance body exists that could intervene and correct violations against market liberalization. Institutions, such as regional or global development banks, should initiate policy discussions at high levels of the regional economic communities concerned in order to support adherence to agreed liberalization.

Finally, the private sector, represented by trade organizations such as the International Air Transport Association (IATA) or major industries, such as aircraft manufacturers, must influence decision makers at every opportunity to move toward and maintain a liberal policy when it comes to international air service agreements.

Infrastructure and Physical Capacity

Air transport services, in general, and LCCs, in particular, rely on adequate infrastructure that can handle capacity in a cost-effective and safe manner. As discussed in chapter 4, the sector needs airport infrastructure that can meet traffic demand in terms of capacity and quality, while complying with relevant safety and security standards. In terms of air traffic management, air traffic control infrastructure, which can ensure safety and efficiently manage traffic at peak hours, is critical. Many emerging countries lack adequate airport and air traffic infrastructure. Often these countries do not have sufficient traffic to warrant the modernization of aging airports or communications, navigation, and surveillance (CNS) systems. However, there is a group of emerging states that have seen rapid air traffic growth, while airport or CNS infrastructure lags behind.

In many developing countries, the capacity of airport infrastructure, whether airside or landside, is often not the primary challenge. Whereas at smaller airports, the necessary airside investments, such as tarmac surfacing and the acquisition of boarding bridges, may be required, most airports in developing countries have the necessary capacity to absorb additional traffic. Oftentimes a preliminary measure to handle growing traffic can be simply achieved by working with carriers to schedule traffic more evenly throughout the day. In addition, economic measures such as peak or congestion pricing of airport usage can be temporary solutions before investment in additional infrastructure is undertaken. Nevertheless, both measures have their limits given that carriers depend on many high volume destinations at certain times during the day (for example, early morning or evening).

Similarly, landside infrastructure investments are often not urgent as passengers can be processed temporarily in less adequate environments. LCCs in particular do not need any special amenities or services; basic and efficient installations are sufficient. However, effective maintenance is essential for both landside and airside infrastructure in developing countries. It is crucial in prolonging the infrastructure life cycle and ensuring safe as well as efficient operations.

Yet, oftentimes, the focus of the responsible airport operator is solely on the upkeep of the country's primary entry airport, with little investment or maintenance being made at secondary or regional airports, which are important for domestic and regional traffic development. Even in cases where investments are made, these may not be prioritized correctly due to political or other commercial interests. Political support for a new modern terminal building may be much stronger, rather than for a potentially more urgent airside project or maintenance program, such as an additional taxiway, runway extension, or the hiring of additional maintenance staff. In order to assess the necessary investments in airport infrastructure, an accurate demand forecast and development of an airport master plan is fundamental. Only in this manner can a sustainable airport system be developed and maintained.

Air traffic control installations need to provide reliable CNS services, which allow aircraft to arrive safely and without delay at their destination. However, many lesser-developed countries lack reliable basic services, which can result in constant delays and longer holds on the ground and in the air. Poor communication systems and the lack of positive surveillance installations, such as radar, result in many additional operational procedures, which could otherwise be shortened or eliminated altogether. Examples of such unnecessary procedures include large separations of traffic, as well as the requirement to fly so-called standard arrival and departure routes, or a full approach procedure instead of being directly vectored for a final approach. In addition to delays, poor CNS infrastructure poses a safety challenge, which may hinder development of air services when authorities or carriers limit traffic for safety concerns.

Nevertheless, air traffic installations are comparatively less costly than airport infrastructure. Modern communication systems, even when integrated into satellite-supported networks, cost much less than a new terminal at a major airport. In addition, modern surveillance technologies, such as automatic dependence surveillance systems (ADS-B/C), allow for air traffic surveillance infrastructure at a fraction of the cost of traditional radar-based systems.

Air navigation service providers (ANSPs) need to establish safe and efficient procedures, maintain a high level of reliability, and secure operational maintenance of physical infrastructure. In order to support the development of air traffic, investments in installations and procedures, as well as in maintenance, need to be secured by good management of revenues. Similar to the case of developing airport infrastructure, an assessment of the existing system and a long-term development program need to be prepared. A follow-up implementation program, which includes ongoing maintenance and renovation of the system, would also be required. Like airports, ANSPs need to be corporatized as public or private entities, and must be supervised and regulated by an authority. What is important is that improvements of air navigation services are harmonized on a regional basis in order to avoid disruptions and delays. Coordination between ANSPs is key in achieving this.

Both airports and air traffic control infrastructure require good management in terms of operations and resource allocation. Airport management, in particular, sets many requirements for the seamless handling of arriving and departing aircraft, while safety and security standards are maintained at all times. Many emerging countries experience a lack of adequate staff with necessary technical or managerial skills. The resulting mismanagement can mean delays, waste of resources, or safety and security infringements. Good airport management depends on hiring skilled staff, providing good training, and ensuring constant supervision. The best way to implement good standards is to have airports managed as independent entities, whether as a state-owned entity or as a private sector venture. In addition, airports need to be supervised by a regulatory body, which ensures safe and secure operations, and which may set certain economic boundaries, primarily on usage fees for aircraft and passengers.

Financing of Aircraft and Airport Infrastructure

The financing of aircraft or airport infrastructure poses a particular challenge in many developing countries. The lack of hard currency resources in banks, as well as the perceived or apparent emerging country risk, makes it difficult to finance aircraft or infrastructure locally or by foreign direct investment. This is especially the case in countries with thin traffic, low airport utilization, and a restrictive market policy—all of which prevent a competitive environment.

Aircraft financing depends on a business environment that is conducive to private sector development, which allows companies to freely invest and retrieve funds, and which provides a mechanism for securing and recovering assets in distress. The creation of such a business environment spans over many sectors and public entities of a given country. Emerging countries must take development measures that include regulatory provisions for free capital flows, good governance, as well as laws and institutional mechanisms for asset recovery. For example, an effective bankruptcy procedure, the possibility to cease aircraft operating internationally facilitated by the Cape Town Convention, or a definition of responsibilities with sanctions of the board and management of a company, are relatively easy measures to implement.

Aircraft financing can be provided by a variety of sources and should be complemented, where needed, by international development agencies such as the International Finance Corporation (IFC). However, additional provisions, such as granting an air operator certificate for an aircraft registered in a foreign country, are requirements that need to be in place. One of the most promising initiatives to facilitate foreign direct investments in air carriers, however, is to allow a majority stake for foreign ownership. Despite the fact that most countries have legal requirements that aircraft or air carriers be majority and publicly-owned, a number of smaller nations never adhered to such limitations. Portugal, and countries that were former Portuguese colonies, typically do not limit foreign ownership in aircraft or air carriers. This allowed for the creation of Air Corridor, a foreign-held carrier in Mozambique. Indeed, it is also the reason that all fractional aircraft ownership operations in Europe are conducted by a Portuguese entity with aircraft registered in Portugal.[1]

The scope and feasibility of airport infrastructure financing depends on many factors. First, the dimension and elements to be financed need to be determined. This could range from a simple terminal or a runway, to an entire airport. Second, the source of funds and economic feasibility need to be analyzed. Large airports with several million passengers can usually be financed by commercial banks, and repayment from operational income is relatively secure.

Many airports in emerging countries are on the other side of the spectrum, and struggle to achieve the traffic required for commercial financing. These airports are generally in the public domain, and in many cases their financing and maintenance is provided by the public sector. In between these two extremes, there are is an array of possible financing mechanisms, which range from public funding and ownership, to an entire private airport. In many growing airports around the world, public-private partnerships (PPPs) have become interesting solutions for development. However, they require a certain level of traffic to become financially viable, as well as respective regulation and sufficient governance to attract outside investors.

Safety and Security

The sustainable development of air transport services requires a predictable and stable regulatory environment that sets standards to ensure safety and security. If this is not in place, long-term development of any airline operation is at risk and the traveling public will consequently be reluctant to use air services. Furthermore, financing and insuring aircraft becomes a considerable challenge.

Safety and security requires a regulatory framework that complies with international standards, and which is enforced by an effective civil aviation regulatory entity. In addition, some safety and security measures need financing for equipment, construction, or for training staff of supervisory entities. Most importantly, however, the establishment and maintenance of a sustainable safety and security environment depends on political stability and good governance.

Ensuring safety and security is a priority within all sector operations and entities. For example, airlines need to introduce safety management systems, and should regularly be subject to audits by trade organizations, such as the IATA Operational Safety Audit (IOSA).[2] A similar audit program for airports is currently being implemented by Airports Council International (ACI). Nevertheless, the main responsibility to regulate, enforce, and supervise the air transport sector lies with respective civil aviation regulatory bodies, in most countries, the civil aviation authority (CAA).

As highlighted in chapter 4, the International Civil Aviation Organization (ICAO) is mandated with conducting an audit of the supervisory capacity of a CAA in terms of safety and security. Their audit results provide a good measurement of compliance and oversight with respect to international safety and security standards. However, the establishment of a compliant oversight regime in less-developed countries can entail the creation of an entirely new regulatory and legal framework, the recruitment and training of inspectors, and the preparation of various tools, such as technical libraries, information systems, and inspectors' handbooks and manuals. Many smaller countries do not have the necessary skills or funding, and need support.

Support for establishing the safety and security oversight mechanism can come in various forms. Countries with sufficient income from the sector, for example, through overflight and passenger fees, can use these funds to finance the improvements at the CAA. In this case, development partners may assist by providing policy and technical advice. However, many poorer and/or smaller nations lack the financial and human capacity to provide effective oversight. Regional safety oversight organizations (RSOOs) can prove more viable in such cases. The World Bank, for example, has successfully supported the development of RSOOs in both West and Central Africa, as well as in the South Pacific.

Support should be conditioned on the establishment of good governance. This can be achieved by being fully transparent on financial matters of the sector (for example, by publishing airport income and use of funds), or by disclosing ICAO audit reports on the CAA. It can also be achieved through the release of information on sanctions pertaining to sector participants (for example, imposing a fine on an operator). Development partners can also condition their support to achieving measurable results with respect to safety or security improvements. In this context, the World Bank conditioned the release of a tranche of a Development Policy Loan for Guatemala on the certification of the country by the U.S. Federal Aviation Administration for complying with ICAO standards.[3]

Regulation of Taxes and Fees

Air transportation is a capital-intensive industry with small profit margins. In fact, according to IATA, the global airline industry has been only marginally profitable in 2012, achieving a net profit of US$2.56 billion with revenues of US$228.56 billion (Pearce 2013). Furthermore, for decades, the industry was unable to provide a positive return for investors when profits are compared with the weighted average cost of capital (WACC).[4] These poor returns include some factors that cannot be controlled by the carrier's management, such as a sudden increase in fuel costs. Carriers therefore constantly struggle to keep operational costs as low as possible in order to achieve a positive operational result.

At the same time, aviation has always been an easy target to levy charges, fees, and taxes. Indeed, aviation is a soft target where charges are easy to collect given that only a handful of companies need to remit them. In addition, the voting public often does not know the real amount of taxes paid, as these are mostly embedded in the overall ticket price. Finally, in most countries the traveling public does not have a vocal advocate who lobbies against high charges on air travel, even if these exceed 50 percent of the overall ticket price.

Charging reasonably for services received and costs incurred is a complex issue. User fees for airport usage, including security screening, have increased significantly over the past decade. Airports argue that it is necessary to invest in costly infrastructure for anticipated growth in passengers. In addition, security-related investments and the cost of services have skyrocketed since the terrorist events of September 11, 2001.

The development of sustainable air transport services depends on the affordability of air travel. This is especially true for emerging and developing countries, where income per capita is significantly lower and price sensitivity consequently much higher. In markets where air travel has reached high penetration with large economies of scale permitting low airfares, disposable income is often used to visit friends and families in remote destinations or for tourism. This type of "leisure" travel has become the backbone for most LCCs around the globe. Excessive taxation can act as a major deterrent in such countries.

Therefore, charges for air transport services should be kept at a reasonable level and only cover the cost for services received. However, the determination of reasonable levels of charges can be a challenge, especially in developing countries where passenger numbers are low and where costs of airport usage need to be borne by fewer passengers than in countries with major hubs. In addition, according to Article 15 of the Chicago Convention, there should not be any discrimination between national and foreign carriers. Nevertheless, in many developing countries that operate a national carrier, market distortions and discrimination of carriers can be observed. These may range from simple discounts on airport charges for a carrier to the direct usage of air traffic income paid by foreign operators to settle fees owed by the national carrier to foreign air service providers.

The sustainable development of air transport services depends on reasonable, equitable, and cost-based levies. These charges need to be determined in a transparent manner, preferably in consultation with all concerned stakeholders. They also need to be accessible to the traveling public through detailed ticket prices, as well as listings on official websites. At the same time, governments in emerging markets need to refrain from using the sector as an easy provider for hard currency, and understand that the overall economic benefits of developing aviation services far outweigh the income from such charges. Development support by international organizations should focus on various economic and developmental aspects when advising governments on how to determine taxes and levies on the sector.

Conclusions for Development of the LCC Sector and Role of Development Partners

This chapter has outlined some of the most significant challenges and possible solutions for developing countries to grow their air transport market in a sustainable manner and to pave the way for future LCC entrance. As table 6.1 outlines in more detail, the support of development partners in fostering fair competition, providing guidance on adequate safety and security standards, as well as on reasonable taxation and good governance, is crucial to ensuring the sustainable

Table 6.1 Challenges and Measures for the Development of Sustainable Air Transport Markets in Developing Countries

Challenge	Enabling measures	Support by development partners
Open up access to markets against dominant national carriers (whether state-owned or private)	Privatization of state-owned carrier, granting access to private operators.	Privatization advice; define liberal air transport policy and legal and regulatory changes; study economic impact of opening up access.
Foster a competitive environment	Regulation and laws supporting an open and competitive environment.	Technical support to develop and implement a regulatory environment conducive to competition.
Remove market distortions	Review all direct and indirect subsidies to air carriers to eliminate such distortions, except in cases where a public service obligation is granted on a competitive basis.	Assistance in reviewing and defining which subsidies are to be eliminated, and which should be designated as a public service obligation.
Access to international markets	Negotiate and agree to liberal ASA or open skies agreements or adhere to an open multilateral agreement or to an established open market.	Examination of existing ASAs, and analysis of market potential for liberalization; support for the negotiation of liberal or open skies agreement; initiate, support, and monitor the establishment of liberalized air service areas within existing economic organizations.
Airport infrastructure	Airport infrastructure development planning based on (a) demand forecast, (b) analysis of existing infrastructure, and (c) compliance with safety and security standards.	Technical support for the preparation of an airport master plan, be it on an airport level (case-by-case) or for a national airport(s) master plan, and effective maintenance plans.
Air traffic control infrastructure	Assessment of existing CNS system, and identification of gaps or inefficiencies in service provision; preparation of a CNS development program.	Technical support for the assessment of current CNS systems, and of a development program.
Airport and air traffic control management	Establish independent entities for airport and air traffic service providers; establish an independent regulatory oversight authority; ensure good governance and best practice.	Policy and regulatory advice to establish airport and ANSP entities, as well as to establish regulatory oversight; support on governance and best practice in airport and ANSP provision.
Aircraft financing environment	Establish a private and financial sector that is conducive to domestic and foreign private investment.	Policy and technical support to introduce measures to improve the business environment, including finance/ownership regulation.

table continues next page

Table 6.1 Challenges and Measures for the Development of Sustainable Air Transport Markets in Developing Countries *(continued)*

Challenge	Enabling measures	Support by development partners
Labor force	Provide training for civil aviation authorities, airport staff, air traffic controllers and other relevant staff.	Financing for CAA; airport and airline staff training based on detailed training needs; assessments and training plans.
Aircraft financing	Provision of financing by loans or equity investments.	Direct funding in air carriers through equity or by loans; provision of guarantees for foreign direct investments (for example, political risk).
Airport infrastructure financing	Public or private financing of airport infrastructure by loans or equity investments; facilitation of PPPs through management or concession agreements.	Financing of airport infrastructure works or provision of guarantees for foreign direct investments; establishing regulatory framework for PPPs; advisory services for financing concession agreements in PPPs.
ICAO-compliant safety and security regime	Establishing a regulatory and legal framework; creation of an independent CAA; preparation of inspection materials and training of CAA staff; infrastructure investments in safety and security.	Technical support to assess, determine, and implement safety and security systems for effective oversight; financing of regulatory reform, CAA staff, and required infrastructure improvements.
Taxes and charges on the air transport sector render air travel unnecessarily expensive	Transparent and holistic approach when determining the level of charges.	Technical support to assess and determine levies on air transport services.

Note: ASA = air services agreement; ANSP = air navigation service provider; CAA = civil aviation authority; CNS = communications, navigation, and surveillance; ICAO = International Civil Aviation Organization; PPP = public-private partnerships.

growth of the air transport industry in developing countries. Once these elements are in place, LCCs can be introduced by the private sector, and will commence to catalyze the market further. As such, LCCs are not the solution for initiation, but the catalyst for growth—LCCs are the turbocharger, but they can only become effective once the engine is running smoothly.

In terms of the focus for development of the air transport sector and the role of international development partners, the priorities remain the same. Many basic requirements for LCCs to successfully operate in a given market are the same as for traditional air carriers that need to operate on a sustainable basis without being supported by the public sector. Development partners can assist the sector by providing relevant guidance on policies, regulations, laws, and oversight.

Notes

1. In fractional ownership programs, customers buy a share of an aircraft, rather than an entire plane. The price is prorated from the market price of a full aircraft. Owners then have guaranteed access (for example, 50–400 hours annually depending on share size) to that aircraft. Fractional owners pay a monthly maintenance fee and an hourly operating fee. European fractional ownership programs have owners of many different nationalities, which is not an issue in Portugal where there are no nationality requirements to own an aircraft.

2. The IATA Operational Safety Audit (IOSA) program is an internationally recognized and accepted evaluation system designed to assess the operational management and control systems of an airline. IOSA uses internationally recognized quality audit principles and is designed to conduct audits in a standardized and consistent manner.
3. The World Bank project is Second Broad Based Growth Development Policy Loan (P094897, 2006).
4. The weighted average cost of capital (WACC) is the rate that a company is expected to pay on average to all of its security holders to finance its assets.

References

Pearce, B. 2013. *Profitability and the Air Transport Value Chain*. Economics Briefing 10, International Air Transport Association. http://www.iata.org/whatwedo/Documents/economics/Profitability-and-the-air-transport-value-chain-final.pdf.

UNECA (United Nations Economic Commission for Africa). 1988. *Declaration of Yamoussoukro on a New African Air Transport Policy*. Côte d'Ivoire: UNECA.

APPENDIX A

Carrier Evaluation Methodology

Table A.1 Carrier Evaluation Methodology

Point element	2 Points	1 Point	0 Points
Unit cost per ASK (international dollars)	<6.0 PPP	6.0–7.0 PPP	>7.0 PPP
No (free) frills			
Free on-board meals	No		Yes
Assigned seating	No	Yes, but it is charged as additional service	Yes
Baggage fees (1st bag)	Yes		No
Use of secondary airports	Very high–high	Mixed	Low
Point-to-point services	Yes		No
Internet-based sales (%)	75–100	50–75	<50
High daily aircraft utilization	>11 h	9–11 h	<9 h
Simple fleet structure	Yes		No
High seating density (low seat pitch)	29–30		>30
One-class system (incl. economy premium or similar)	Yes		No

Source: Based on Weisskopf 2010.
Note: ASK = available seat kilometer; h = hours; PPP = purchasing power parity. As some information was not available maximum achievable number of points was set at 21.

Reference

Weisskopf, N. 2010. "Global Expansion Strategies for Low-Cost Airlines." Unpublished dissertation, University of Edinburgh.

APPENDIX B

Database of Low-Cost Airlines Classification

Table B.1 Database Low-Cost Airlines Classification

Airline criteria	Ryanair	easyJet	AirAsia	Southwest Airlines	Air Arabia
Unit cost per available seat kilometer (ASK)	4.36	8.23	4.48	7.96	5.27
Unit cost in purchasing power parity (PPP) international dollars	3.97	7.48	9.53	7.96	4.71
No (free) frills					
Free on-board catering	No	No	No	Yes	No
Assigned seating	No	No	Yes (but at an additional charge)	No	Yes (but at an additional charge)
Baggage fees (1st bag)	Yes	Yes	Yes	No	No
Point-to-point route structure	Yes	Yes	Yes	Yes	Yes[a]
Use of secondary airports	Very high	Low	Low	Mixed	Mixed
Online sales, %	99	n.a.	79	85	Approx. 30
Average daily utilization	8.47 h	9.90 h	12.30 h	11.46 h	14.10 h
One type fleet	Yes (Boeing 737)	Yes (A319/20)	Yes (Airbus 319/20)	Yes (Boeing 737)	Yes (Airbus 320)
High seating density (seat pitch)	30 inch	29 inch	29 inch	32–33 inch	31–32 inch
One-class configuration	Yes	Yes	Yes	Yes	Yes
Total points	20	15	17	13	14

table continues next page

Table B.1 Database Low-Cost Airlines Classification *(continued)*

Airline criteria	WestJet	Jet Blue	Jazeera Airways	Virgin Australia	Vueling	Spirit Airlines	GOL
Unit cost per available seat kilometer (ASK)	8.38	7.12	5.96	9.92	8.34	6.25	7.82
Unit cost in purchasing power parity (PPP), international dollars	8.14	7.12	7.21	8.78	8.77	6.25	15.34
No (free) frills							
Free on-board catering	Yes	No	Yes	Yes	No	No	No
Assigned seating	Yes (but at an additional charge)	Yes	Yes	Yes	Yes (but at an additional charge)	Yes	Yes
Baggage fees (1st bag)	No	No	No	No[c]	Yes	Yes	No
Point-to-point route structure	No	No	No	Yes	Yes	No	No
Use of secondary airports	Mixed	Mixed	Low	Mixed	Low	Mixed	Mixed
Online sales, %	n.a.	ca. 80 percent (2010)	n.a.	n.a.	n.a.	n.a.	n.a.
Average daily utilization	11.90 h	11.80 h	13.00 h	n.a.	8.14 h	12.80 h	12.10 h
One type fleet	Yes (Boeing 737)[b]	No (Airbus 320 and Embraer 190)	Yes (Airbus 320)	No (Boeing 737, A330, Boeing 777, Embraer 190, ATR72, Fokker 50 and 100)	Yes (Airbus 319/20)	Yes (Airbus 319/320/321)	Yes (Boeing 737)
High seating density (seat pitch)	31–33 inch	34–38 inch, 32–39 on Embraer	32–33 inch	30–33 inch	30 inch	28 inch	31–32 inch
One-class configuration	No	No	No	No	No	Yes	Yes
Total points	6	7	4	3	13	15	9

Sources: Compilation based on information from annual reports and presentations; SEC filings, *Air Finance Journal*, and SeatGuru.

Note: Base year 2011/2012 when available. Fiscal year may not be in line with calendar year for each airline and vary in some cases. Data from prior years include Air Arabia unit cost (2011), Aircraft Utilization (2010), Jet Blue online sales (2010), Jazeera Airways unit cost (2008) and utilisation (2009), and Virgin Australia unit cost (2011). PPP exchange rate based on NationMaster. Changes may have occurred since base year. n.a. = not applicable.

a. Air Arabia has used subsidiaries to establish a point-to-point system but still is strongly focused on its hub.
b. WestJet new subsidiary WestJet Encore excluded from analysis.
c. With exception of travelers in lowest fare class without Virgin Australia Membership status.

References

Air Arabia. 2012. "Air Arabia Investor Presentation Q1 2012." http://www.airarabia.com/sites/airarabia/files/styles/square_thumbnail/public/styles/Q2%20-%202012_1.pdf.

———. http://www.airarabia.com/en.

Air Asia. 2013. *Air Asia Annual Report 2012*. http://www.airasia.com/iwov-resources/my/common/pdf/AirAsia/IR/annual-report-2012.pdf.

———. www.airasia.com.

Air Finance Journal. 2014. "The Airline Top 50 2012." http://www.airfinancejournal.com/docs/2013/Airfinance%20Journal/The_Airline_Top_50_amended.pdf.

easyJet. 2013. *Easyjet Investors 2012 Year Results*. http://corporate.easyjet.com/~/media/Files/E/Easyjet-Plc-V2/pdf/media/latest-news/2012/fy-2012-en.pdf.

———. http://www.easyjet.com.

GOL Linhas Inteligentes. *GOL Annual Report 2012 Form 20-F*. U.S. Securities and Exchange Commission. https://www.sec.gov/Archives/edgar/data/1291733/000129281413000979/golform20f_2012.htm.

———. http://www.voegol.com.br.

Jazeera Airways. 2009. *2008 Jazeera Airways Results Summary*. http://www.jazeeraairways.com/AdminControl/J9WebsiteDataFiles/Data/InternalWebPage/InvestorFiles/J9-INV-PACK-FY08.pdf.

———. http://www.jazeeraairways.com.

Jetblue. 2013. *Jetblue Annual Report Form 10-K*. U.S. Securities and Exchange Commission. https://www.sec.gov/Archives/edgar/data/1158463/000115846314000008/a201310-k.htm.

———. http://www.jetblue.com.

NationMaster. www.nationmaster.com.

Ryanair. 2012. *Ryanair Annual Report Form 20-F*. U.S. Securities and Exchange Commission. https://www.sec.gov/Archives/edgar/data/1038683/000119312512323949/d386894d20f.htm.

———. http://www.ryanair.com.

SeatGuru. http://www.seatguru.com.

Southwest Airlines. 2013. *Annual Report 2012 to Shareholders*. http://southwest.investorroom.com.

———. http://www.southwest.com.

Spirit Airlines. 2013. *Spirit Airlines Annual Report 2012 Form K-10*. U.S. Securities and Exchange Commission. https://www.sec.gov/Archives/edgar/data/1498710/000149871013000034/save-20121231x10k.htm.

———. http://www.spirit.com.

West Jet. 2013. *West Jet Annual Report 2012*. http://www.westjet.com/guest/en/media-investors/2013-annual-report/WestJet-Annual-Report-2012.pdf.

———. http://www.westjet.com.

Vueling. 2013. "Full Year 2012 Results Presentation." http://phx.corporate-ir.net/External.File?item=UGFyZW50SUQ9MjA1NjA4fENoaWxkSUQ9LTF8VHlwZT0z&t=1.

———. 2013. "Vueling Results 2012." http://phx.corporate-ir.net/External.File?item=UGFyZW50SUQ9MjA2NzkyfENoaWxkSUQ9LTF8VHlwZT0z&t=1.

———. http://www.vueling.com.

APPENDIX C

Selected Impact Studies

Table C.1 Selected Impact Studies

Title	Author/organization	Year	Key points
Airport Economic Impact Study for Monterey, San Benito, and Santa Cruz Counties	Association of Monterey Bay Area Governments, California	2003	• The study summarizes the economic impact of each of the six airports with regard to jobs, payroll, state and local taxes, and spending. • Aggregate estimates accrue to more than US$1.3 billion in overall economic activity, including US$307 million in payroll, US$11.5 million in taxes, US$1.1 billion in spending, and more than 10,000 jobs.
Clear Skies over Southern Africa: The Importance of Air Transport Liberalization for Shared Economic Growth	ComMark	2006	• Based on two econometric analyses looking at 12 Southern African Development Community (SADC) member states in terms of fluctuations of fare levels and traffic volumes. Price analysis based on cross-sectional data from global distribution system (GDS), survey of national governments and airlines in the region, and two country-city level data sets. • For traffic volumes, data was collected on liberalization events between South Africa and other SADC countries and elsewhere; data was also used from Airport Company of South Africa on the number of passengers arriving at and departing from Johannesburg International Airport every month from 1998 to 2004, quarterly data on trade volumes, gross domestic product (GDP) per capita and population data, and adverse events affecting air travel in relevant countries. • Case studies on specific international and domestic routes, for example, Nairobi–Johannesburg, Johannesburg–Lusaka, and Johannesburg–George. • Study estimates 500,000 additional foreign tourists, spending more than US$500 million and increasing SADC GDP by 1.5 billion South African rand (US$135 million—around 0.5 percent). About 35,000 new jobs in travel and tourism industry alone and a further 37,000 jobs in wider SADC economy if air transport in SADC is liberalized.
The Economic Impact of Civil Aviation on the U.S.	U.S. Federal Aviation Administration (FAA)	2011	• U.S. civil aviation manufacturing industry as top U.S. net exporter. According to 2009 data from the U.S. International Trade Commission (USITC), the U.S. civil aviation manufacturing industry supported a positive trade balance of over US$75 billion. • New research using data from 2008 shows that air transportation enables economic activity in other sectors of the economy through: – Air-traveler spending of US$249.2 billion on goods and services; – Freight valued at US$562.1 billion transported domestically or to other countries; – 10.2 million jobs contributing US$1.3 trillion in total economic activity and accounting for 5.2 percent of total U.S. GDP.
Getting There Fast: Globalization, Intercontinental Flights and Location of Headquarters	Germa Bel and Xavier Fageda (University of Barcelona)	2005	• Study highlighted that the quality of transport infrastructure is one of the major determinants in the location decisions of firms across cities and therefore a major influencing factor on urban economic growth. • Results showed a 10 percent increase in the supply of intercontinental flights resulting in a 4 percent increase in the number of corporate headquarters in major European urban areas. • Moreover, headquarters of knowledge-intensive sectors, which rely more on information exchange, are much more influenced by the supply of direct intercontinental flights than are those of sectors that are not knowledge-intensive.

table continues next page

Table C.1 Selected Impact Studies *(continued)*

Title	Author/organization	Year	Key points
The Impact of International Air Service Liberalization—Country Studies	InterVISTAS Consulting	2006–09	• Study of 12 countries examining the impact of air service agreements (ASA), liberalization on traffic levels, employment, economic growth, tourism, passengers and national airlines. • Includes Australia, Brazil, Chile, India, Mauritius, Morocco, Peru, Singapore, Turkey, United Arab Emirates, Uruguay, and Vietnam. • Example: Singapore—estimated 21 percent in traffic growth, 15 percent reduction in fares, 879 Singapore dollars increase in consumer surplus, 43,900 additional employment, and 921 Singapore dollars in GDP.
The Impact of International Air Service Liberalization	InterVISTAS Consulting	2006	• Traffic growth subsequent to liberalization of air service agreements between countries typically averaged between 12 percent and 35 percent. • Study simulated the liberalization of 320 country pair markets that are not part of open skies agreements today (deregulated). Results indicated a potential traffic growth, on average, of almost 63 percent. This is substantially higher than typical world traffic growth of around 6 to 8 percent. Liberalizing only these 320 bilateral agreements would create 24.1 million full-time jobs and generate an additional US$490 billion in GDP (for example, almost the size of the Brazilian economy).
International Air Transportation and Economic Development	Kenneth Button and Samantha Taylor	2000	• Assessment of the economic benefit of extending open skies agreements. • Empirical evidence showed that in an examination of a relatively large number of U.S. airports, there are links between the economic structures of surrounding areas and the availability of international air services to the European Union (EU) market. • Increasing passenger enplanements by a thousand resulted in an additional 44 to 73 new economy jobs in the metropolitan area.[a] • Impact of additional destinations or services at smaller airports with significant existing service, for example, Boston or Miami.
Air Passenger Linkages and Employment Growth in U.S. Metropolitan Areas	Michael Irwin and John Kasarda	1991	• Air passenger linkages and employment growth in U.S. cities using regression analysis with data spanning a 30-year period. • Focuses particularly on impact in manufacturing and producer services. • Results identified that position within airline network has a considerable impact on metropolitan growth, and changes in position are the cause—and not the consequence—of employment growth. • Study concluded that the reorganization of airline networks in the U.S. has been a critical factor in transforming and integrating the spatial economy of the U.S.

table continues next page

Table C.1 Selected Impact Studies *(continued)*

Title	Author/organization	Year	Key Points
Economic Benefits of Air Transport Country Studies (various countries across globe)	Oxford Economics	2011	• Over 50 country studies including developing countries such as Ecuador, Kenya, Lebanon, Nigeria, and Peru. • Estimating economic footprint of industry (GDP growth and employment) but also consumer benefits, connectivity, and tourism. • For example, in Peru aviation contributes US$702 million (0.5 percent) to Peruvian GDP and supports 51,000 jobs. An average air transport service employee generates US$36,061 in gross value added (GVA) annually, that is, over three times more productive than the average in Peru. The aviation sector pays over US$91 million in taxes (including income tax from employees, social security contributions, and corporation tax levied on profits).
Aviation: The Real World Wide Web	Oxford Economics	2009	• Over 5.5 million workers employed directly in the industry worldwide, with a turnover of more than US$1 trillion. • Aviation, its supply chain and the spending of employees in these businesses, support more than 15 million jobs and US$1.1 trillion of GDP worldwide (including air transport's contribution to tourism, the figures grow to over 33 million jobs and US$1.5 trillion of GDP). • Aviation enhances efficiencies through economies of scale, increased competition, intensified innovation, and access to wider pools of employees. In particular, the benefits to society of research and development (R&D) spending by the aerospace industry are estimated to be much higher than in manufacturing as a whole—every US$100 million of R&D eventually generated an additional GDP of US$70 million year after year. • By 2026, it is estimated that aviation will directly employ some 8.5 million people and contribute US$1 trillion to world GDP. • If Airbus 2007–2026 forecast was estimated at 1 percent lower, the number of jobs supported by air transport would be reduced by 6 million to 44 million, and the contribution to GDP would be reduced by US$600 billion.
Economic Impact 2011, General Aviation in Texas	Texas Department of Transportation	2011	• General aviation activities and expenditures associated with airports, business activities of airport tenants, and visitor spending by itinerant pilots created US$14.6 billion in economic activity in Texas in 2010, supporting over 56,600 jobs paying US$3.1 billion in salaries, wages, and benefits. • Combined, the Texas Airport System Plan (TASP) airports increase economic activity in Texas by US$59.5 billion, support 771,000 jobs, and increase labor income by US$23.2 billion. • Capital spending associated with airport improvement programs from 2006 through 2010 totaled almost US$2.3 billion. This spending created about US$4.7 billion in statewide economic activity and supported over 37,000 job-years of employment.

a. According to the Organisation for Economic Co-operation and Development, the term "new economy" describes aspects or sectors of an economy that are producing or intensely using innovative or new technologies. This relatively new concept applies particularly to industries where people depend more and more on computers, telecommunications, and the Internet to produce, sell, and distribute goods and services.

APPENDIX D

Freedoms of the Air

Table D.1 Freedoms of the Air

Freedom	Description	Example
1st	**First Freedom of the Air**—the right or privilege, in respect of scheduled international air services, granted by one State to another State or States to fly across its territory without landing (also known as a **First Freedom Right**)	Toronto–Mexico City, as a Canadian company, flying over the United States.
2nd	**Second Freedom of the Air**—the right or privilege, in respect of scheduled international air services, granted by one State to another State or States to land in its territory for nontraffic purposes (also known as a **Second Freedom Right**).	Toronto–Mexico City, as a Canadian company, but stopping for fuel in the United States.
3rd	**Third Freedom of the Air**—the right or privilege, in respect of scheduled international air services, granted by one State to another State to put down, in the territory of the first State, traffic coming from the home State of the carrier (also known as a **Third Freedom Right**).	Toronto–Chicago, as a Canadian company.
4th	**Fourth Freedom of the Air**—the right or privilege, in respect of scheduled international air services, granted by one State to another State to take on, in the territory of the first State, traffic destined for the home State of the carrier (also known as a **Fourth Freedom Right**).	Toronto–Chicago, as an American company.
5th	**Fifth Freedom of the Air**—the right or privilege, in respect of scheduled international air services, granted by one State to another State to put down and to take on, in the territory of the first State, traffic coming from or destined to a third State (also known as a **Fifth Freedom Right**).	Bangkok–Kuala Lumpur–Doha, as a Qatari company.
6th	**Sixth Freedom of the Air**—the right or privilege, in respect of scheduled international air services, of transporting, via the home State of the carrier, traffic moving between two other States (also known as a **Sixth Freedom Right**). The so-called Sixth Freedom of the Air, unlike the first five freedoms, is not incorporated as such into any widely recognized air service agreements such as the "Five Freedoms Agreement."	Dubai–Cairo–Paris, as an Egyptian company.
7th	**Seventh Freedom of the Air**—the right or privilege, in respect of scheduled international air services, granted by one State to another State, of transporting traffic between the territory of the granting State and any third State with no requirement to include on such operation any point in the territory of the recipient State, that is, the service need not connect to or be an extension of any service to/from the home State of the carrier.	Kuala Lumpur–Jakarta, as an Italian company.

table continues next page

Table D.1 Freedoms of the Air *(continued)*

Freedom	Description	Example
8th	**Eighth Freedom of the Air**—the right or privilege, in respect of scheduled international air services, of transporting cabotage traffic between two points in the territory of the granting State on a service which originates or terminates in the home country of the foreign carrier or (in connection with the so-called Seventh Freedom of the Air) outside the territory of the granting State (also known as **Eighth Freedom Right** or "**consecutive cabotage**").	Chicago–New York–Toronto, as a Canadian company.
9th	**Ninth Freedom of the Air**—the right or privilege of transporting cabotage traffic of the granting State on a flight performed entirely within the territory of the granting State (also known as a **Ninth Freedom Right** or "**stand alone**" **cabotage**).	Beijing–Shanghai, as an Italian company.

Source: International Civil Aviation Organization (n.d.).

Reference

International Civil Aviation Organization. n.d. "Freedoms of the Air." http://www.icao.int/Pages/freedomsAir.aspx.

APPENDIX E

Major Airlines in EAC

Table E.1 Major Airlines in EAC

Airline name	Ownership	Size of fleet	Type of aircraft (used for regional operations)	Operating base	Type of operation	Financial state in 2012/2013
Kenya Airways	KLM (26.7 percent), government of Kenya (29.8 percent, 42.5 percent public).	43 aircraft	B737-300/700/800, E190 and E170	Jomo Kenyatta International Airport	Domestic/regional/intercontinental—full service	US$92 million (2013) Loss
Air Kenya Express	Consortium (ownership is unclear).	8 aircraft	Twin Otter DHC6-300, Dash 7 DHC 7-100, Dash 8-100, Cessna C208B	Wilson Nairobi Airport	Domestic/regional—commuter	—
African Express Airways	Private (100 percent).	6 aircraft	MD-82, DC9-32, Boeing 727, EMB 120	Jomo Kenyatta International Airport	Domestic/regional—full service	—
Air Uganda	Celestair–Aga Khan Foundation (100 percent).	5 aircraft	Bombardier CRJ	Entebbe International Airport	Regional—full service	—
Eagle Air	Private (100 percent).	7 aircraft	LET L410	Entebbe International Airport	Domestic/regional—commuter—full	— (temporarily suspended in 2008)
Rwandair	Government of Rwanda (99 percent); Private (1 percent).	10 aircraft	Bombardier CRJ, DHC-8, B737-700 Winglets, B737-800	Kigali International Airport	Regional—full service	— (assumed to be loss making)
Precision Air	Kenya Airways (41 percent); various private investors (59 percent).	14 aircraft	ATR42-300/320/500, ATR72	Julius Nyerere International Airport	Domestic/regional—full service	US$0.4 million profit (2012/13)
Zanair Limited	Private (100 percent).	7 aircraft	LET L410	Zanzibar Abeid Amani Karume International Airport	Domestic—full service	—
Fly540 Kenya	fastjet (49.8% percent), Five Forty Aviation (50.2%)—ownership structure still disputed	11 aircraft	Bombardier CRJ, DHC-8, Fokker F28	Jomo Kenyatta International Airport	Domestic/regional—low cost	—
fastjet	Lonrho PLC (49.14 percent); Henderson Global Investors (6.47 percent); easyGroup holdings (3.95 percent); other investors (40.44 percent).	3 aircraft	Airbus A319	Julius Nyerere International Airport	Domestic—low cost	US$56 million loss (including Fly540) (June 2011–Dec 2012)
Air Burundi[a]	Government of Burundi.	2 aircraft	Xian ME60, Raytheon Beach 1900c	Bujumbura International Airport	Regional—full service	—

Sources: Airline websites; Annual Reports, Centre for Asia Pacific Aviation.
Note: EAC = East African Community; — = not available.
a. It could not be confirmed if the airline is still operating services. Some news sources indicated that air services between Bujumbura and Kigali would be reinstated in June 2013, but this could not be verified.

References

African Express Airways. http://www.africanexpress.co.ke.

Air Kenya Express. http://www.airkenya.com.

Air Uganda. *Air Uganda Website*. http://www.air-uganda.com.

CAPA (Centre for Asia Pacific Aviation). 2013. "Precision Air Reports a USD18.9 Million Loss for FY2013 Due to Overly Ambitious Growth." Centre for Asia Pacific Aviation, September 7. http://centreforaviation.com/analysis/precision-air-reports-a-usd189-million-loss-for-fy2013-due-overly-ambitious-growth-127300.

———. 2013a. "Fastjet Posts USD56 Million Loss but Remains Optimistic about African Success." Centre for Asia Pacific Aviation, June 8. http://centreforaviation.com/analysis/fastjet-posts-usd56-million-loss-but-remains-optimistic-about-african-success-113205.

———. 2013b. "Ethiopian and Kenya Airways' Financial Fortunes Diverge in Pursuit of East African Domination." Centre for Asia Pacific Aviation, August 23. http://centreforaviation.com/analysis/ethiopian-and-kenya-airways-financial-fortunes-diverge-in-pursuit-of-east-african-domination-123814.

Eagle Air. http://www.eagleair-ug.com.

Fastjet. http://www.fastjet.com/us/.

Fly540. http://www.fly540.com.

Kenya Airways. http://www.kenya-airways.com.

Kenya Airways. *Kenya Airways Annual Report 2012/2013*. http://www.kenya-airways.com/uploadedFiles/Home/Corporate_Information/Investor_Information/Annual_Reports/KQ%20Annual%20Report.pdf.

Precision Air. https://www.precisionairtz.com.

Rwandair. http://www.rwandair.com.

Zanair Limited. http://www.zanair.com.

APPENDIX F

Fare Comparison Methodology

In chapter 5, a fare analysis was undertaken to compare the level of fares of international and domestic East African Community (EAC) routes with similar routes globally. In order for the comparison to be meaningful, certain criteria had to be identified and applied in the selection of comparator routes. The comparators were identified according to the following criteria: (a) presence of a low-cost carrier (LCC) on that route; (b) similar distance between origin and destination; (c) similar combined population of origin and destination; and (d) similar gross domestic product (GDP) per capita of origin city. Population and gross domestic product (GDP) per capita are two common indicators used as a basis in demand forecasting (see Lyneis 2000; Suryani, Chou, and Chen 2010), and can be used here to assess the size and purchasing power of the potential market.

This approach poses a few limitations, as the GDP per capita of the destination country is not taken into consideration, and could significantly influence demand. However, finding routes fulfilling all criteria (LCC presence, distance, population, and GDP per capita for both countries) was found to be too restricting to obtain an adequate sample. The GDP per capita criteria had to therefore be limited to the origin country. In some cases, countries with a higher GDP than the region's highest GDP per capita, Kenya, had to be chosen to obtain an adequately sized sample. A more detailed analysis should also take into consideration what type of market the route is (business or leisure) information which was unfortunately not available in this case.

The sample for international routes includes the following:

- Dar es Salaam (DAR)–Entebbe (EBB)
- Nairobi (NBO)–Kigali (KGL)
- Nairobi (NBO)–Dar es Salaam (DAR)
- Nairobi (NBO)–Bujumbura (BJM)
- Zanzibar (ZNZ)–Nairobi (NBO)
- Nador (NDR)–Barcelona (BCN)
- Nador (NDR)–Montpellier (MPL)
- Phnom Penh (PHN)–Singapore (SGN)

- Phnom Penh (PHN)–Kuala Lumpur (KLM)
- Chennai (MAA)–Colombo (CMB)

For domestic markets, finding the right set of comparable routes proved to be more difficult. The distance range therefore had to be extended to find a few suitable airport pairs. The sample of airport pairs includes the following:

- Nairobi (NBO)–Mombasa (MBA)
- Nairobi (NBO)–Kisumu (KIS)
- Dar es Salaam (DAR)–Kilimanjaro (JRO)
- Nairobi (NBO)–Eldoret (EDL)
- Dar es Salaam (DAR)–Mwanza (MWZ)
- Buon Ma Thuot (BMV)–Vinh City (VII)
- Danang (DAD)–Hanoi (HAN)
- Danang (DAD)–Ho Chi Minh (SGN)
- Srinagar (SXR)–Sri Guru Ram Dass Jee International (Amritsar) (ATQ)
- Guwahati (GAU)–Kolkata (CCU)

The data for the analysis were gathered from airlines' websites. In order to ensure consistency within the comparison, all searches were conducted on the same date (August 13, 2013) for the same outbound and inbound date (September 11, 2013–September 20, 2013). In some cases where there was no availability or direct connection, traveling dates one day prior to or after were chosen. In order to control for seasonality, two different dates were chosen and compared—but only very small variations were detected.

References

Lyneis, J. 2000. "System Dynamics for Market Forecasting and Structural Analysis." *System Dynamics Review* 16 (1): 3–25.

Suryani, E., S. Chou, and C. Chen. 2010. "Air Passenger Demand Forecasting and Passenger Terminal Capacity Expansion: A System Dynamics Framework." *Expert Systems with Applications: An International Journal* 37 (3): 2324–39.

APPENDIX G

Airports in EAC

Table G.1 Airports in the East African Community

City	Country	Airport name	Airport IATA code	ICAO code	Scheduled services (June 2013)	Operator
Bujumbura	Burundi	Bujumbura International	BJM	HBBA	Yes	Autorité de l'Aviation Civile Burundi
Kitale	Kenya	Kitale	KTL	HKKT	Yes	Government of Kenya serviced by Kenya Airports Authority (KAA)
Kisumu	Kenya	Kisumu	KIS	HKKI	Yes	Government of Kenya serviced by KAA
Nakuru	Kenya	Nakuru	NUU	HKNK	Yes	Government of Kenya serviced by KAA
Nairobi-Wilson	Kenya	Wilson	WIL	HKNW	Yes	Kenya Airports Authority
Malindi	Kenya	Malindi	MYD	HKML	Yes	Kenya Airports Authority
Lokichogio	Kenya	Lokichogio	LKG	HKLK	Yes	Kenya Airports Authority
Masai Mara	Kenya	Mara Serena	MRE	—	Yes	Kenya Airports Authority
Nanyuki	Kenya	Nanyuki	NYK	HKNY	Yes	Government of Kenya serviced by KAA
Ukunda	Kenya	Ukunda	UKA	—	Yes	Kenya Airports Authority
Wajir	Kenya	Wajir	WJR	HKWJ	Yes	Kenya Airports Authority
Amboseli	Kenya	Amboseli	ASV	HKAM	Yes	Government of Kenya serviced by KAA
Lamu	Kenya	Manda	LAU	HKLU	Yes	Kenya Airports Authority
Lodwar	Kenya	Lodwar	LOK	HKLO	Yes	Government of Kenya serviced by KAA
Samburu	Kenya	Samburu	UAS	HKSB	Yes	Government of Kenya serviced by KAA
Nairobi	Kenya	Jomo Kenyatta International	NBO	HKJK	Yes	Kenya Airports Authority
Eldoret	Kenya	Eldoret International	EDL	HKEL	Yes	Kenya Airports Authority
Mombasa	Kenya	Mombasa	MBA	HKMO	Yes	Kenya Airports Authority
Cyangugu	Rwanda	Kamembe	KME	HRZA	Yes	Rwanda Civil Aviation Authority
Gisenyi	Rwanda	Gisenyi	GYI	HRYG	Yes	Rwanda Civil Aviation Authority
Kigali	Rwanda	Kigali International	KGL	HRYR	Yes	Rwanda Civil Aviation Authority
Dar es Salaam	Tanzania	Julius Nyerere International	DAR	HTDA	Yes	Tanzania Airports Authority
Mwanza	Tanzania	Mwanza	MWZ	HTMW	Yes	Tanzania Airports Authority
Zanzibar	Tanzania	Abeid Amani Karume International	ZNZ	HTZA	Yes	Zanzibar Airports Authority

table continues next page

Table G.1 Airports in the East African Community *(continued)*

City	Country	Airport name	Airport IATA code	ICAO code	Scheduled services (June 2013)	Operator
Mtwara	Tanzania	Mtwara	MYW	HTMT	Yes	Tanzania Airports Authority
Kigoma	Tanzania	Kigoma	TKQ	HTKA	Yes	Tanzania Airports Authority
Arusha	Tanzania	Arusha	ARK	HTAR	Yes	Tanzania Airports Authority
Musoma	Tanzania	Musoma	MUZ	HTMU	Yes	Tanzania Airports Authority
Mbeya	Tanzania	Mbeya	MBI	HTMB	Yes	Tanzania Airports Authority
Seronera	Tanzania	Seronera	SEU	HTSN	Yes	Tanzania Airports Authority
Pemba Island	Tanzania	Pemba Island	PMA	HTPE	Yes	Tanzania Airports Authority
Iringa	Tanzania	Iringa	IRI	HTIR	Yes	Tanzania Airports Authority
Lake Manyara	Tanzania	Lake Manyara	LKY	HTLM	Yes	Tanzania Airports Authority
Bukoba	Tanzania	Bukoba	BKZ	HTBU	Yes	Tanzania Airports Authority
Kilimanjaro	Tanzania	Kilimanjaro International	JRO	HTKJ	Yes	Kilimanjaro Airport Development Company
Soroti	Uganda	Soroti	SRT	HUSU	No	Uganda Civil Aviation Authority
Arua	Uganda	Arua	RUA	HUAR	Yes	Tanzania Airports Authority
Entebbe/Kampala	Uganda	Entebbe International	EBB	HUEN	Yes	Uganda Civil Aviation Authority
Gulu	Uganda	Gulu	ULU	HUGU	No	Uganda Civil Aviation Authority

Sources: AZ World Airports; Jeppesen Manuals Airport Information.
Note: IATA = International Air Transport Association; ICAO = International Civil Aviation Authority; — = not available.

Table G.2 Airports in the East African Community: Features

Airport name	Paved/unpaved	Surface	Number of runways	Taxiway/apron	Runway length	Instrument flight rules	Navigation aids	International capability—customs	Fuel availability
Bujumbura International	Paved	Asphalt	1	Yes	11,800 ft	Yes	VOR-DME, NDB	Yes	Yes (jet fuel and avgas)
Kitale	Paved	Asphalt	1	Yes	4,700 ft	No	—	n.a.	No
Kisumu	Paved	Asphalt	1	Yes	6,600 ft	Yes	VOR/DME/NDB	Custom-service but prior notification required	Yes (jet fuel and avgas)
Nakuru	Unpaved	Grass	1	No	5,600 ft	No	—	No	Yes (avgas)
Wilson	Paved	Asphalt	2	Yes	5,100 ft	No	—	Yes	Yes (jet fuel and avgas)
Malindi	Paved	Asphalt	2	Yes	4,600 ft	Yes	—	n.a.	Yes (jet fuel and avgas)
Lokichogio	Paved	Asphalt	1	Apron only	4,200 ft	No	—	No	No
Mara Serena	Unpaved	Unknown	1	Apron only	3,900 ft	No	—	No	n.a.
Nanyuki	Paved	Asphalt	1	Yes	3,900 ft	No	—	No	No
Ukunda	Paved	Tarmac	1	Yes	3,900 ft	No	—	No	n.a.
Wajir	Paved	Asphalt	1	Yes	3,900 ft	No	—	No	No
Amboseli	Paved	Asphalt	1	Yes	3,200 ft	No	—	No	No
Manda	Paved/unpaved	Asphalt/dirt, grass	2	Yes	3,200 ft	No	—	Custom-service but prior notification required	n.a.
Lodwar	Paved	Asphalt	1	Yes	3,200 ft	No	—	No	No
Samburu	Paved	Asphalt	1	Yes	3,200 ft	No	—	No	n.a.
Jomo Kenyatta International	Paved	Asphalt	1	Yes	13,500 ft	Yes	VOR-DME, NDB	Yes	Yes (jet fuel and avgas)
Eldoret International	Paved	Asphalt	1	Yes	11,400 ft	Yes	VOR/DME/NDB	Part-time customs	Yes (jet fuel)
Mombasa	Paved	Asphalt	2	Yes	11,000 ft	Yes	VOR-DME, NDB, PAPI, TXY lights	Yes	Yes (jet fuel and avgas)
Kamembe	Paved	Asphalt	1	Yes	4,900 ft	Yes	NDB	No	n.a.
Gisenyi	Paved	Asphalt	1	Apron only	3,200 ft	Yes	NDB	No	No
Kigali International	Paved	Asphalt	1	Yes	11,400 ft	Yes	VOR-DME	Yes	Yes (jet fuel and avgas)
Julius Nyerere International	Paved	Asphalt	2	Yes	9,800 ft	Yes	VOR-DME, NDB	Yes	Yes (jet fuel and avgas)

table continues next page

Table G.2 Airports in the East African Community: Features *(continued)*

Airport name	Paved/unpaved	Surface	Number of runways	Taxiway/apron	Runway length	Instrument flight rules	Navigation aids	International capability—customs	Fuel availability
Mwanza	Paved	Asphalt	1	Yes	9,800 ft	Yes	VOR, NDB	Custom-service but prior notification required	Yes (jet fuel and avgas)
Abeid Amani Karume International	Paved	Asphalt	1	Yes	8,000 ft	Yes	NDB	Part-time customs	Yes (jet fuel and avgas)
Mtwara	Paved (1)/unpaved (1)	Asphalt/grass	2	Yes	7,400 ft/3,815 ft	Yes	NDB	Custom-service but prior notification required	Yes (jet fuel and avgas)
Kigoma	Unpaved	Gravel	1	Yes	5,700 ft	Yes	NDB	Yes	Yes (jet fuel)
Arusha	Paved	Asphalt	1	Yes	5,300 ft	Yes	NDB	No	Yes (jet fuel and avgas)
Musoma	Unpaved	Dirt	1	Yes	5,200 ft	Yes	NDB	No	No
Mbeya	Unpaved	Graded or rolled earth; grass on graded earth	1	Paved apron but undefined taxiway	5,100 ft	Yes	NDB	Custom-service but prior notification required	Yes (avgas)
Seronera	Unpaved	Gravel	1	Apron only	5,100 ft	No	—	No	No
Pemba Island	Paved	Asphalt	1	Yes	5,000 ft	Yes	NDB	Custom-service but prior notification required	No
Iringa	Paved	Asphalt	1	Yes	5,479 ft	Yes	NDB	n.a.	No
Lake Manyara	Unpaved	Dirt	1	No (turnbay at both ends)	4,000 ft	No	—	No	Yes (avgas)
Bukoba	Unpaved	Dirt	1	No (only very small apron)	3,400 ft	Yes	NDB	No	No
Kilimanjaro International	Paved	Asphalt	1	Yes	11,800 ft	Yes	VOR-DME, NDB	Yes	Yes (jet fuel and avgas)
Soroti	Paved	Tarmac	2	Yes	6,100 ft	Yes	NDB, DME	No	No
Arua	Unpaved	Dirt	1	Yes	5,600 ft	No	—	No	No
Entebbe International	Paved	Asphalt	2	Yes	12,000 ft	Yes	VOR-DME, NDB	Yes	Yes (jet fuel and avgas)
Gulu	Paved	Asphalt	1	Yes	10,200 ft	No	—	No	No

Sources: AZ World Airports (2013); Jeppesen Manuals "Airport Information" (2013).

Note: DME = distance measuring equipment; n.a. = not applicable; NDB = nondirectional beacon; PAPI = precision approach path indicator; TXY lights = taxiway lights; VOR = VHF omnidirectional range; — = not available.

References

AZ World Airports. 2013. "Airport Information." http://www.azworldairports.com/cfm/homepage.cfm.

Jeppesen Manuals. 2013. "Airport Information." Jeppesen Publications.

APPENDIX H

Runway Capacity Estimation Methodology

As highlighted in chapter 4, there are various ways to determine the capacity of an airport. For simplification purposes, the book examines the maximum throughput as the potential number of movements per hour, and estimates the resulting number of passengers based on the average number of seats per operation currently experienced at that airport (Neufville and Odoni 2003). This helps identify any constraints with regards to airside and landside infrastructure.

An average five-minute time lag in between each movement is used for a simple estimation of potential capacity at the region's airports. This is based on the assumption that the airport has a single runway operation—most common in EAC—with separation requirements for an approach based on nonradar navigation (procedural control). In addition, it will be necessary to take into consideration that for some airports, runway layouts can further extend the time required between operations. At Kemembe Airport, for example, the positioning of the taxiway in the middle of the airfield prolongs aircraft movements and consequently impacts the minimum time lag required. The region also has a number of runways without taxiways or aprons, such as Bukoba Airport and Lake Manyara. However, this primarily concerns very small domestic airports with unpaved runways. Taking the above factors into consideration, a 10–15 minute time lag may appear more realistic for the airports chosen for this sample. Estimations also have to take into account the opening hours of the respective airports.

Reference

Neufville, R., and A. Odoni. 2003. *Airport Systems: Planning, Design and Management.* New York: McGraw Hill.

APPENDIX I

Infrastructure Charges Methodology and Detailed Assessment

Methodology

This research used a sample of airports for which charges were available from Aeronautical Information Publications (AIPs), airport websites or directly requested from civil aviation authorities. If possible, multiple airports were chosen for one country to verify if charges differ across airports. Burundi was excluded for domestic operations, as there are no current or foreseeable domestic operations. Because charges vary significantly across aircraft type and weight as well as actual passenger numbers (PAX), a base scenario had to be defined. The base scenario chosen for the calculation of airport charges is as follows:

- Domestic operations
  - Domestically registered ATR-72-500
  - Maximum take-off weight (MTOW): 23 tons
  - Seat Configuration of 74 PAX
  - 80 percent load factor
  - Turnaround time: 2 hours
- International operations
  - Internationally registered ERJ170-100
  - Maximum take-off weight (MTOW): 37 tons
  - Seat configuration of 80 PAX assuming a narrow seat pitch of 29 inches
  - 80 percent load factor
  - Turnaround time: 2 hours

Due to the varying sizes of countries and their infrastructure (for example, runway length), choosing an aircraft type that can be used internationally and for which there is sufficient domestic demand, can prove difficult. This makes a comparison between smaller countries, such as Rwanda and Uganda, with Tanzania and Kenya challenging.

The aircraft chosen for domestic operations allows for the usage of a larger number of airports due to its required runway length (approximately 4,500 feet depending on condition), and is a more fuel-efficient version than other aircraft in its category (for example, the Q400). The aircraft for regional operations was chosen on the basis that it is currently being used for domestic operations by the region's low-cost carriers (Fly540 in Kenya), and is known for its fuel efficiency. The airports included all have the runway requirements (approximately 5,500 feet) for these aircraft. Due to the specific characteristics of the market, it was assumed that airlines operating both domestically and internationally would most likely deviate from the common fleet standardization in LCCs.

For a comparison of charges in domestic markets, the research identifies a number of comparable airports in other developing countries with a similar domestic market to the East African Community's (EAC's) larger markets in Kenya and Tanzania, and a similar gross domestic product (GDP) per capita. Rwanda and Burundi were both excluded from the comparison due to their very small size. Under these criteria, Ghana, Ethiopia, Bangladesh and Nepal were identified as countries suitable for the comparison. These are by no means entirely adequate comparisons, particularly as the geographical size of these countries and their markets differ considerably, but they do give an indication of the overall level of charges in contrast to other countries. For a comparison of charges for regional/international traffic, a comparison of EAC's main airports with airports in Africa and globally in other developing countries with similar traffic volumes is provided herein. Given the significantly higher volumes at Jomo Kenyatta, it was excluded as a benchmark, and the focus was limited to airports with between 1.5 and 2.0 million seat capacity annually. The variable distance measure needed for calculations of navigation charges was set at an arbitrary 500 kilometers, subtracting the given terminal control area (TMA) radius.

Detailed Analysis of Charges for EAC Airports

Following is a breakdown of the aggregated charges displayed in chapter 5. Charges were divided into charges paid for by the airlines, such as landing fees, parking, navigation (approach/terminal and en route), and other charges (for example, aerobridges, communications, and so on), as well as additional charges for night operations, and charges paid for by passengers, such as passenger facility charges (PFCs) or passenger service charges (PSCs), and security charges (either levied from the passenger or the carrier, which are later transferred to passengers). Many countries have additional charges, such as infrastructure development charges, or other charges such as local taxes, duties, and other fees not directly related to the provision of airport services. For the purpose of this analysis, no distinction is made if charges are levied by the airport or the airline, since they are both part of the total travel costs borne by passengers.

Charges Paid For by Airlines

Landing Fees

Landing fees are in most cases dependent on an aircraft's MTOW, but the formulas applied by each airport can vary significantly. For the chosen airports, calculations are based on either a fixed charge per weight category or a variable charge (per ton). In addition, there are different surcharges that airports apply especially for night operations (e.g. lighting surcharges), which are highlighted below. Figure I.1 shows landing fees for the chosen sample of airports. In the sample, Uganda has the highest landing fees for domestic operations, charging US$115 for the applied scenario aircraft. In comparison, at Tanzanian airports landing fees are approximately US$78.

For operations within the region, Bujumbura, previously excluded, shows the highest landing fees for the regional base scenario (see figure I.2). Landing fees in Bujumbura are almost double that of airports in Kenya. Uganda and Tanzania have similar levels of landing fees for regional/international operations.

As noted, airports normally have additional charges for nighttime operations, primarily for the usage of lighting. In figure 1.3, charges for nighttime operations are bundled under lighting charges. Provisions for nighttime operations are charged differently across airports, normally representing a specific percentage of landing charges or a flat rate, but normally charged per movement. In Tanzania, for example, lighting charges are an add-on of 30 percent of landing charges per movement (take-off and landing). In Rwanda and Uganda, this charge is 50 percent of landing charges. Most airports have reduced lighting charges if

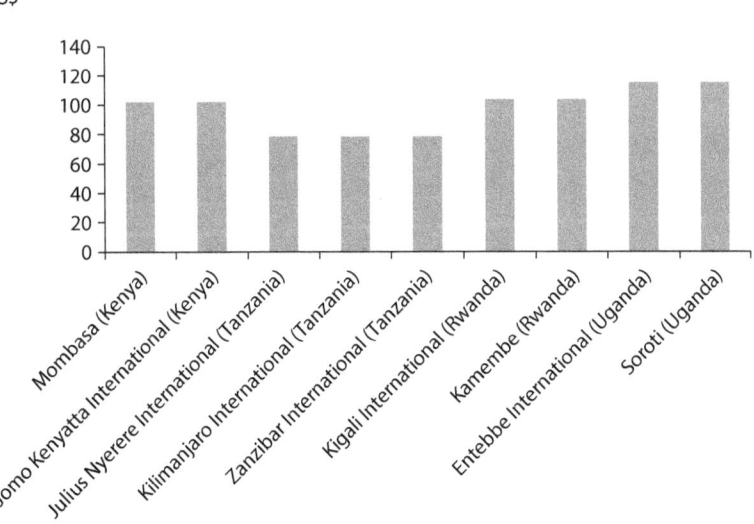

Figure I.1 Daytime Landing Fees for Domestic Flights
US$

Sources: Analysis based on aeronautical information publications of Burundi, Kenya, Rwanda, Tanzania, Uganda, and airport websites.
Note: Domestically registered ATR72-500, maximum take-off weight 23 tons, 74 passengers at 80% load factor, turnaround time two hours.

Figure I.2 Daytime Landing Fees for Regional/International Flights
US$

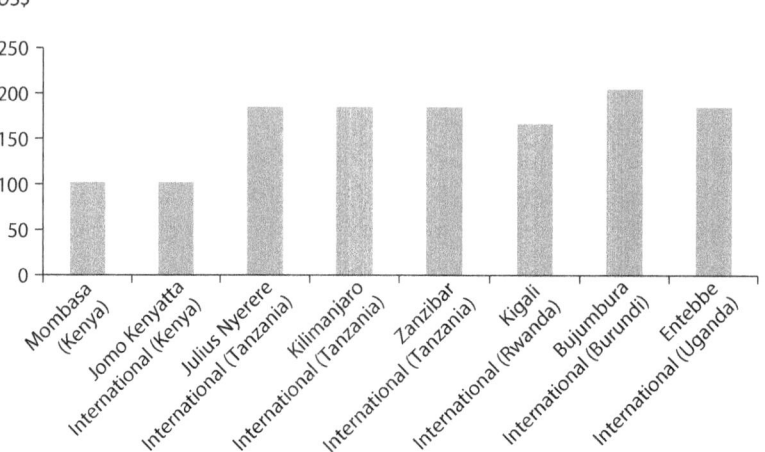

Sources: Analysis based on aeronautical information publications of Burundi, Kenya, Rwanda, Tanzania, Uganda, and airport websites.
Note: Internationally registered ERJ-170, maximum take-off weight 37 tons, 80 passengers at 80% load factor, turnaround time two hours.

Figure I.3 Turnaround (Takeoff and Landing) Landing Fees for Nighttime Domestic Operations
US$

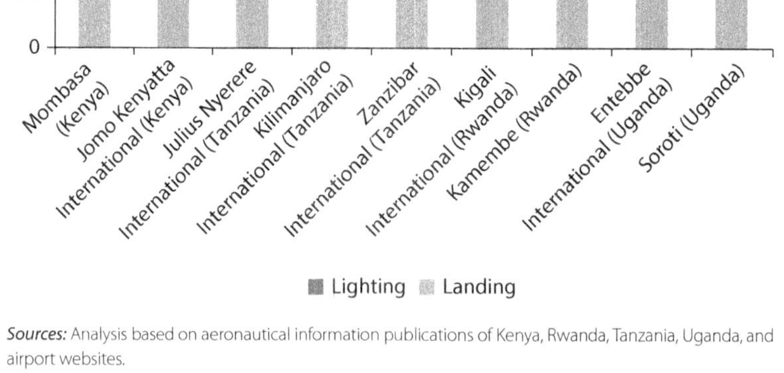

Sources: Analysis based on aeronautical information publications of Kenya, Rwanda, Tanzania, Uganda, and airport websites.
Note: Domestically registered ATR72-500, maximum take-off weight 23 tons, 74 passengers at 80% load factor, turnaround time two hours.

aircraft turnaround is within a short time frame, mostly 90 minutes. With generally higher daytime landing charges and a higher percentage of landing fees demanded for night operations, Uganda has considerably higher total landing fees during nights than all other airports in the sample.

As figure I.4 highlights, for regional operations, Bujumbura has the highest landing fees for nighttime operations, charging a flat rate of US$400 for lighting for turnaround. By contrast, in Kenya or Tanzania, lighting charges are between 20 to 30 percent of landing respectively.

Parking

Aircraft parking fees are both time and weight-based. Most of the airports included in the comparison charge a rate per ton/hour or just a daily charge (for example, Kenya), typically giving a grace period of between two to six hours. Given this grace period, parking charges do not apply for the chosen sample. As an indication, however, parking fees range between US$10/day in Kenya to US$5/six hours for foreign registered aircraft in Tanzania, or US$0.10 per hour per aircraft at Bujumbura International Airport.

Air Traffic Control—Overflight and Approach/Terminal

There are two types of charges related to the provision of air traffic control (ATC) services. The first one is related to approach and departure services

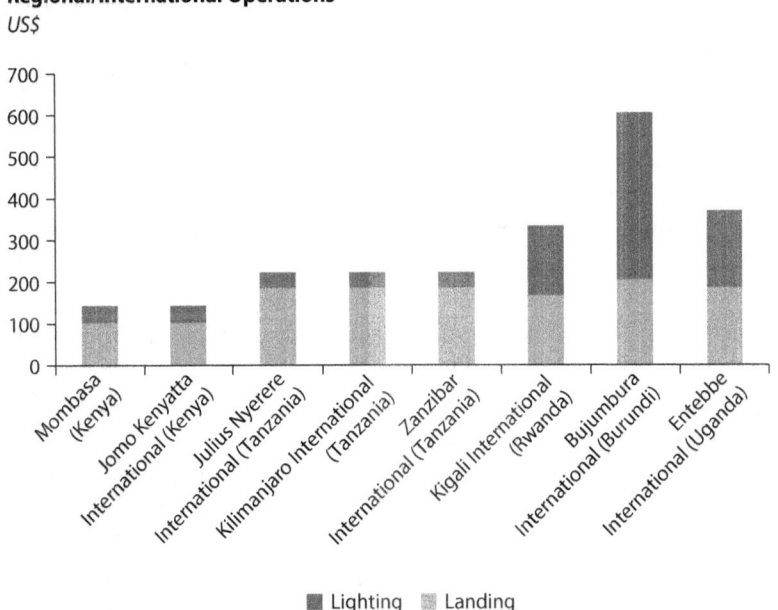

Figure I.4 Turnaround (Takeoff and Landing) Landing Fees for Nighttime Regional/International Operations
US$

Sources: Analysis based on aeronautical information publications of Burundi, Kenya, Rwanda, Tanzania, Uganda, and airport websites.
Note: Internationally registered ERJ-170, maximum take-off weight 37 tons, 80 passengers at 80% load factor, turnaround time two hours.

provided within the airport's TMA, usually delimited by a radius of 20 nautical miles from the airport. In most cases, these are based on the aircraft's weight. The second type applies to all navigation and control services provided to flights from the flight information region (FIR) entry point up to the limit of the TMA, in the case of arriving aircraft (vice versa for departures), or for overflights that transit through a country's FIR. These charges can be more complex in nature and typically involve a measure of distance flown, as well as the aircraft's weight, and varying rates for international and regional flights.

When assessing navigation charges for the chosen sample, only a few countries appear to make a distinction in the charges structure between en route and terminal/approach charges. In the sample, Kenya is the only country that specifically lists en route charges separately from terminal approach charges. In this particular case, a distance approximation is used. For domestic operations in Kenya, this is based on the average distance from that specific airport to destinations in its domestic network. For regional operations, this is more complex. The distance used for Kenya will be an arbitrary 200 kilometers for Nairobi, and 350 kilometers for Mombasa, roughly the average distance from each city to the neighboring borders.

Figure I.5 shows that Tanzania has the highest charges for ATC within their FIR and TMA combined, whereas Kenya (based on the given assumptions) has very low charges for Mombasa and Nairobi on domestic flights.

For regional/international operations, as seen in figure I.6, Tanzania displays significantly higher charges. Considering that charges are combined and do not take into account distances, this appears surprising. The high level of charges is related to the fact that, for the base scenario, a foreign-registered carrier was chosen which is at a considerable disadvantage in comparison to domestically-registered carriers. In Tanzania the air navigation charge for foreign-registered carriers is more than double that of domestically-registered carriers. Bujumbura, which charges a fixed fee for ATC services in its FIR, only levies a small charge, most likely due its size. Although no information could be found, it is assumed that a portion of this is transferred to Tanzania, which manages its upper airspace.

Other Charges

Other charges at the sample airports include, for example, aerobridge charges. Entebbe as well as Mombasa, and Nairobi levy a charge for aerobridges of US$60 and US$75 respectively. Given that LCCs often use simple boarding stairs to reduce costs, this may not be crucial for their operations.

For regional operations, a very small aperture terminal (VSAT) communications charge is raised to support the Southern African Development Community (SADC) and the North Eastern African Indian Ocean VSAT (NAFISAT) networks. Such payment systems ensure the operation and maintenance of the equipment. VSAT charges are levied when crossing from one FIR into another, and are US$9.60 for SADC VSAT usage, and US$10.0 for NAFSAT VSAT usage. Although no VSAT charges are listed in the charges for Kenya, it is assumed that these are levied as well.

Infrastructure Charges Methodology and Detailed Assessment

Figure I.5 Approach and Overflight Charges for Domestic Daytime Flights
US$

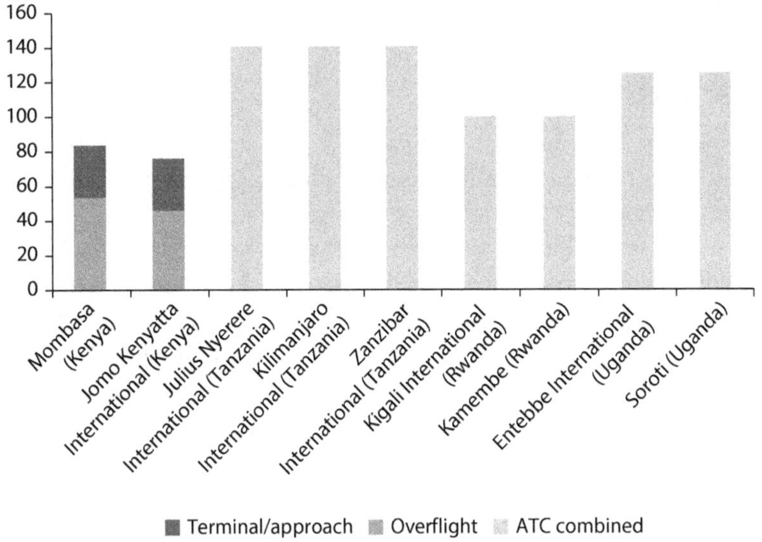

■ Terminal/approach ■ Overflight ▒ ATC combined

Sources: Analysis based on aeronautical information publications of Kenya, Rwanda, Tanzania, Uganda, and airport websites.
Note: Domestically registered ATR72-500, maximum take-off weight 23 tons, 74 passengers at 80% load factor, turnaround time two hours. ATC = air traffic control.

Figure I.6 Approach and Overflight Charges for Regional/International Daytime Flights
US$

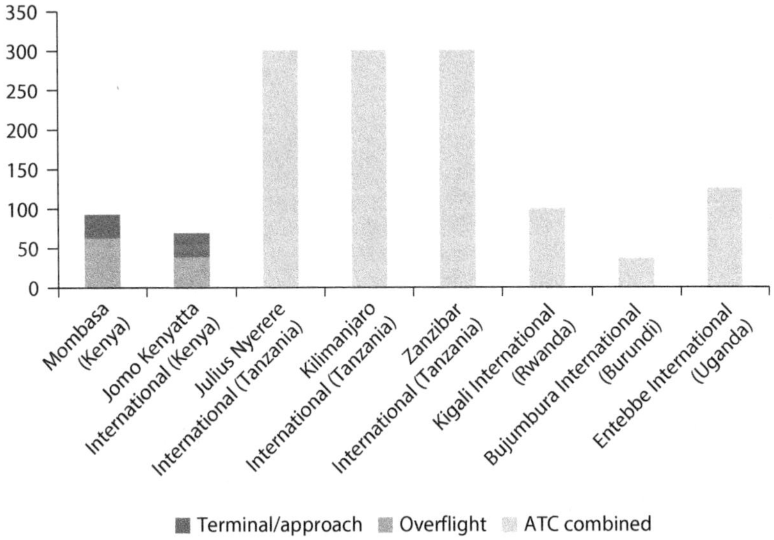

■ Terminal/approach ■ Overflight ▒ ATC combined

Sources: Analysis based on aeronautical information publications of Burundi, Kenya, Rwanda, Tanzania, Uganda, and airport websites.
Note: Internationally registered ERJ-170, maximum take-off weight 37 tons, 80 passengers at 80% load factor, turnaround time two hours. ATC = air traffic control.

Ground handling charges, which have a considerable impact on airline operating costs, could unfortunately not be obtained. As noted previously, however, ground handling charges appear to be particularly high in Uganda and Tanzania.

Passenger Charges

From the sample (see figure I.7), Rwanda is shown to have the highest PSC for domestic operations. Rwandese airports charge a US$8 PSC for departing domestic operations in comparison to approximately US$3 in Tanzania and US$4.60 in Kenya. Rwanda also charges the highest security charge of US$1 per passenger. Kenya appears not to charge any security fees to passengers.

When looking at international passenger charges, the level of charges is more even, with most airports charging between US$30 and US$40 in PSC charges (see figure I.8). Entebbe has the highest security charge at US$10 per passenger. However, these charges are relatively low in comparison to others in the region (see figure I.9).

Passenger charges, although collected by the airports, are often redirected to the treasury of a government. Consequently, they are often used for purposes other than the maintenance and operations of the respective airport. This would define them by nature as a tax, in conflict with ICAO guidelines. In Zanzibar, for example, the passenger service charge levied by the airport goes directly to the Zanzibar Revenue Board. In Kenya, passenger taxes are collected by the Kenya

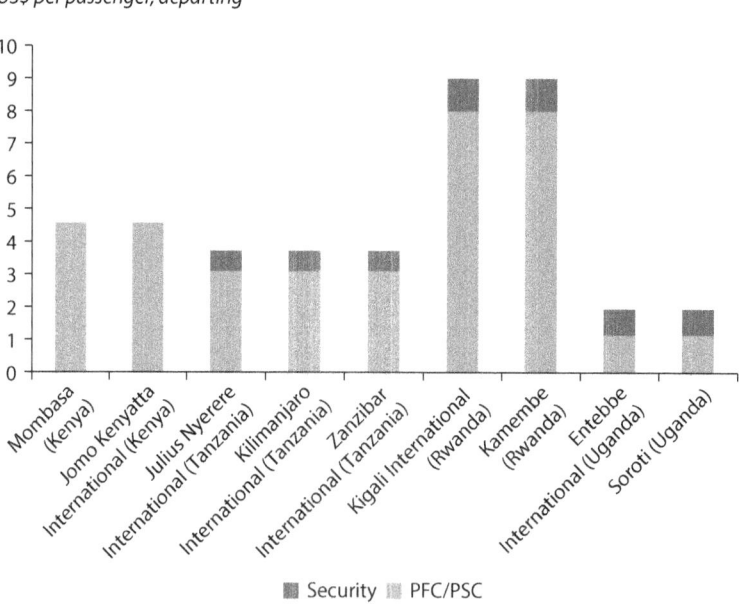

Figure I.7 Passenger Charges for Domestic Flights
US$ per passenger, departing

Sources: Analysis based on aeronautical information publications of Burundi, Kenya, Rwanda, Tanzania, Uganda, and airport websites.
Note: PFC = passenger facility charge; PSC = passenger service charge.

Infrastructure Charges Methodology and Detailed Assessment

Figure I.8 Passenger Charges for Regional/International Flights
US$ per passenger, departing

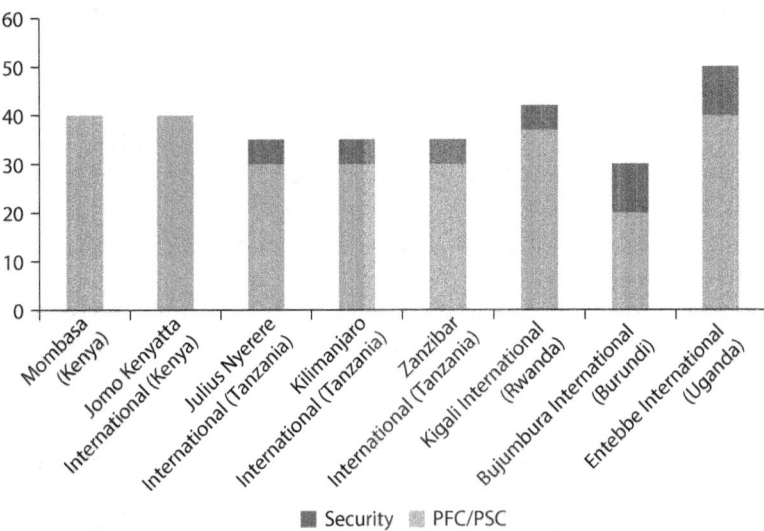

Sources: Analysis based on aeronautical information publications of Burundi, Kenya, Rwanda, Tanzania, Uganda, and airport websites.
Note: PFC = passenger facility charge; PSC = passenger service charge.

Figure I.9 Passenger Charges at Other African Airports
US$, international

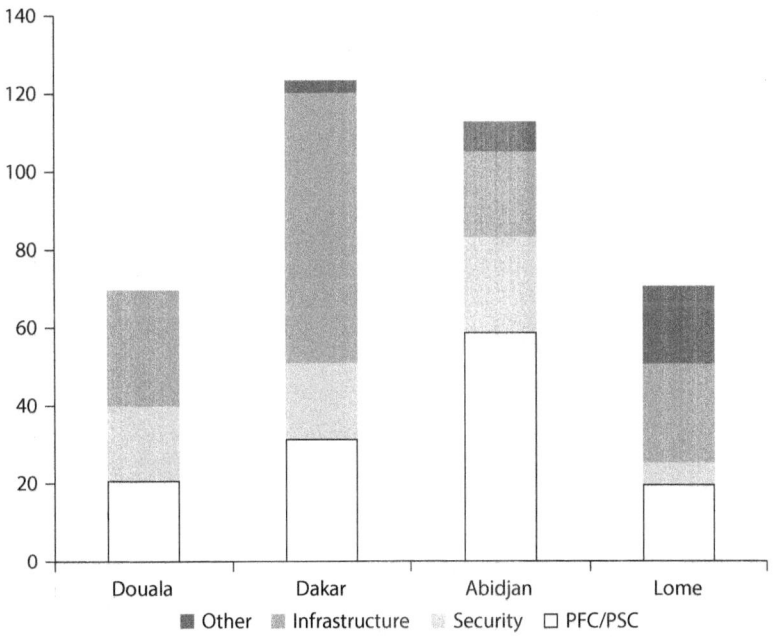

Source: Analysis based on Aeronautical Information Services of ASECNA (Agency for Aerial Navigation Safety in Africa and Madagascar, 2013).
Note: PFC = passenger facility charge; PSC = passenger service charge.

Revenue Authority on behalf of the Kenya Civil Aviation Authority and the Kenya Airports Authority. For this collection a two percent commission is paid (Mutai 2012).

References

ASECNA (Agency for Aerial Navigation Safety in Africa and Madagascar). 2013. "Aeronautical Information Services." Gen-4 Charges. http://www.ais-asecna.org/en/gen/gen4.htm.

Burundi Civil Aviation Authority. n.d. "Aeronautical Information Publication." Burundi Civil Aviation Authority.

Kenya Airports Authority. "Schedules of Airport Charges." https://www.kaa.go.ke.

Kenya Civil Aviation Authority. n.d. "Aeronautical Information Publication." Kenya Civil Aviation Authority.

Mutai, E. 2012. Domestic Air Passenger to Pay More in Levies. *Business Daily Africa*, December 27. http://www.businessdailyafrica.com/Domestic-air-passengers-to-pay-more-in-levies/-/539546/1652274/-/jb6f3i/-/index.html.

Rwanda Civil Aviation Authority. Airport Charges/Fees. http://www.caa.gov.rw/home.html.

———. 2010. "Aeronautical Information Publication." Rwanda Civil Aviation Authority.

Tanzania Airports Authority. "Airport Charges." http://www.taa.go.tz/.

Tanzania Civil Aviation Authority. n.d. "Aeronautical Information Publication." Tanzania Civil Aviation Authority.

Uganda Civil Aviation Authority. n.d. "Aeronautical Information Publication." Uganda Civil Aviation Authority.

———. "Fees and Charges." http://www.caa.co.ug.

APPENDIX J

Accidents (2004–13)

Table J.1 Accidents 2004–13

Country	Date	Aircraft	Registration	Airline	Operated for	Fatalities	Assumed cause
Kenya	01 November 2006	Antonov 12BP	9L-LFQ	748 Air Services	n.a.	0	Abnormal runway contact
Kenya	10 June 2005	Hawker Siddeley HS-780 Andover	5Y-SFE	748 Air Services	n.a.	0	Runway excursion
Uganda	09 March 2009	Ilyushin 76T	S9-SAB	Aerolift	n.a.	11	System/component failure or malfunction (power plant)
Tanzania	19 October 2004	Cessna 208B Grand Caravan	5H-AXL	Air Excel	n.a.	0	System/component failure or malfunction (power plant)
Uganda	08 January 2005	Antonov 12	9Q-CIH	Service Air	n.a.	6	System/component failure or malfunction (power plant)
Kenya	6 July 2007	Beechcraft 1900C	5Y-BTT	Aero Kenya	n.a.	0	Abnormal runway contact
Uganda	28 April 2006	Cessna 208B Grand Caravan	ZS-ADL	King Air Services	United Nations	3	Controlled flight into or toward terrain
Kenya	24 January 2003	Grumman G-159 Gulfstream I	5Y-EMJ	African Commuter Services	n.a.	3	Controlled flight into or toward terrain
Uganda	26 September 2007	Reims Cessna F406 Caravan II	ZS-SSD	Fugro Airborne Surveys	n.a.	2	Loss of control
Kenya	14 October 2003	Cessna 208 Caravan I	5Y-BOY	Air Kenya	n.a.	0	Loss of control
Tanzania	09 April 2012	DHC-8-311Q	5H-MWG	Air Tanzania	n.a.	0	Aerodrome
Rwanda	12 November 2009	Canadair CL-600-2B19 Regional	5Y-JLD	JetLink Express	Rwandair Express	1	System/component failure or malfunction (non-power plant)
Kenya	23 May 2004	Let L-410UVP-E3	5Y-VVD	Blue Bird Aviation	n.a.	2	Midair collision
Rwanda	01 June 2004	Antonov 32	9XR-SN	Sun Air	n.a.	0	System/component failure or malfunction (non-power plant)
Tanzania	01 March 2010	Boeing 737-247	5H-MVZ	Air Tanzania	n.a.	0	Runway excursion
Tanzania	23 March 2005	Ilyushin 76TD	ER-IBR	Airline Transport	n.a.	8	Ground handling (overload)
Tanzania	03 April 2008	Reims Cessna F406 Caravan II	5H-AWK	Auric Air	n.a.	2	Loss of control
Kenya	23 March 2004	Let L-410UVP-E9	5Y-VVA	Blue Bird Aviation	n.a.	0	Midair collision

table continues next page

Table J.1 Accidents 2004–13 *(continued)*

Country	Date	Aircraft	Registration	Airline	Operated for	Fatalities	Assumed cause
Kenya	09 November 2009	Beechcraft 1900D	5Y-VVQ	Blue Bird Aviation	n.a.	1	System/component failure or malfunction (power plant)
Kenya	29 April 2008	Fokker 50	5Y-VVF	Blue Bird Aviation	n.a.	0	Abnormal runway contact
Kenya	07 December 2003	Fokker F-28 Fellowship 4000	5Y-NNN	East African Safari	n.a.	0	Runway excursion
Kenya	27 January 2011	Fokker F-27 Friendship 500CRF	5X-FFD	Fly540	n.a.	0	Runway excursion
Tanzania	13 April 2006	Cessna 208 Caravan I	5H-ZBZ	Mission Aviation Fellowship	n.a.	0	Abrupt maneuver
Tanzania	16 November 2004	Let L-410UVP-E20	5H-PAC	Precision Air	n.a.	0	Abnormal runway contact
Tanzania	17 March 2004	Cessna 208B Grand Caravan	5H-MUA	Regional Air Services	n.a.	0	System/component failure or malfunction (power plant)
Uganda	19 March 2005	Boeing 707-3K1C	9G-IRL	Cargo Plus Aviation	Ethiopian Airlines	0	Other
Kenya	10 April 2006	Harbin Yunshuji Y-12-II	132	Kenyan AF	n.a.	14	Controlled flight into or toward terrain
Kenya	22 August 2012	Let L-410UVP-E9	5Y-UVP	Mombasa Air Safari	n.a.	4	Loss of control
Kenya	08 July 2007	Aérospatiale/Aeritalia ATR-72	5H-PAR	Precision Air	n.a.	0	Runway excursion
Kenya	19 July 2003	Swearingen SA226-TC Metro II	ZS-OYI	Ryan Blake Air Charter	n.a.	14	Controlled flight into or toward terrain
Kenya	13 October 2009	Boeing 707-321C	J5-GGU	Safari Airlines	n.a.	0	System/component failure or malfunction (non–power plant)
Kenya	12 December 2007	Cessna 208B Grand Caravan	5Y-SLA	SafariLink	n.a.	0	Ground collision
Rwanda	28 August 2004	SE-210 Caravelle 11R	3D-KIK	TransAir	n.a.	0	Unknown
Tanzania	01 June 2007	Short C-23 Sherpa	JW9036	Tanzanian AF	n.a.	0	System/component failure or malfunction (power plant)

table continues next page

Table J.1 Accidents 2004–13 *(continued)*

Country	Date	Aircraft	Registration	Airline	Operated for	Fatalities	Assumed cause
Uganda	12 December 2011	Antonov 2			n.a.	0	Unknown
Kenya	10 July 2008	Let L-410UVP-E9	5Y-VVB	SafariLink	n.a.	0	Runway excursion
Kenya	30 December 2006	DHC-5 Buffalo	5Y-SRK	Sky Relief Services	Red Cross	0	System/component failure or malfunction (power plant)
Kenya	10 June 2005	Lockheed L-100-30 Hercules	S9-BAS	Transafrik	United Nations	0	Abnormal runway contact
Kenya	12 December 2007	DHC-5D Buffalo	5Y-MEG	Trident Aviation	n.a.	0	Loss of control
Kenya	29 September 2008	DHC-5D Buffalo	5Y-OPL	Trident Aviation	n.a.	0	Unknown
Tanzania	12 July 2006	Lockheed L-100-30 Hercules	S9-BOF	Transafrik	n.a.	0	Undershoot/overshoot

Source: Based on Flight Foundation (2013).
Note: n.a. = not applicable.

Reference

Flight Foundation. 2013. *Aviation Safety Network.* http://aviation-safety.net/index.php.

APPENDIX K

Doing Business Report: Labor Regulations (2012)

Table K.1 Labor Regulations, 2012
by country

Category	Indicator	Tanzania	Kenya	Uganda	Rwanda	Burundi
Difficulty of hiring	Fixed-term contracts prohibited for permanent tasks?	Yes	No	No	No	No
	Maximum length of a single fixed-term contract (months)	0—Not allowed at all for "our worker" (however, no limit for professionals and managerial cadres)—Sec. 14(1), Employment and Labour Relations Act, 2004.	No limit for term contracts (excluding casual employees)	No limit	No limit	No limit
	Maximum length of fixed-term contracts, including renewals (months)	No Limit	No limit	No limit	No limit	No limit
	Minimum wage applicable to worker assumed in the case study (US$/month)	52.5	111.1	2.7	0.0	2.9
	Minimum wage for a 19-year-old worker or an apprentice (US$/month)	52.5	111.1	2.7	0.0	2.9
	Ratio of minimum wage to value added per worker	0.61	0.89	0.03	0.00	0.08
Rigidity of hours	Standard workday in manufacturing (hours)	9 hours—Sec. 19(2), Employment and Labour Relations Act, 2004.	8 hours (Regulation 5(1) of the RWGO).	8 hours (however the employer and the employee can agree to another limit, as long as it is under 10 hours per day. In addition, there are special rules for shift workers that provide even more flexibility). Sections 52 and 53, Employment Act 2006.	Article 49 of the law fixes the duration per week (45 hours/week) and not per day. Article 3 of the ministerial order n°04/19,19 of Sept. 17, 2009 determining the modalities for application of the weekly working hours in the private sector lets each institution draw up a timetable, indicating hours at which the working period commences and ends. In practice, there is a workday of 8 or 9 hours, depending on whether Saturday is or is not a working day.	8 hours

table continues next page

Table K.1 Labor Regulations, 2012 *(continued)*
by country

Category	Indicator	Tanzania	Kenya	Uganda	Rwanda	Burundi
	50-hour workweek allowed for 2 months a year in case of a seasonal increase in production?	Yes	Yes	Yes	Yes	Yes
	Maximum working days per week	6	6	6	6	6
	Premium for night work (percentage of hourly pay) in case of continuous operations	5	0	0	0	35
	Premium for work on weekly rest day (percentage of hourly pay) in case of continuous operations	100	0	0	0	100
	Major restrictions on night work in case of continuous operations?	No	No	No	No	No
	Major restrictions on weekly holiday in case of continuous operations?	No	No	No	No	Yes
	Paid annual leave for a worker with 1 year of tenure (in working days)	20.0	21.0	21.0	18.0	20.0
	Paid annual leave for a worker with 5 years of tenure (in working days)	20.0	21.0	21.0	19.0	21.0
	Paid annual leave for a worker with 10 years of tenure (in working days)	20.0	21.0	21.0	21.0	22.0
	Paid annual leave (average for workers with 1, 5, and 10 years of tenure, in working days)	20.0	21.0	21.0	19.3	21.0

table continues next page

Table K.1 Labor Regulations, 2012 *(continued)*
by country

Category	Indicator	Tanzania	Kenya	Uganda	Rwanda	Burundi
Difficulty of redundancy	Dismissal due to redundancy allowed by law?	Yes	Yes	Yes	Yes	Yes
	Third-party notification if 1 worker is dismissed?	Yes	Yes	No	Yes	No
	Third-party approval if 1 worker is dismissed?	Yes	No	No	No	No
	Third-party notification if 9 workers are dismissed?	Yes	Yes	No	Yes	Yes
	Third-party approval if 9 workers are dismissed?	Yes	No	No	No	No
	Retraining or reassignment obligation before redundancy?	No	No	No	No	No
	Priority rules for redundancies?	No	Yes	No	Yes	Yes
	Priority rules for reemployment?	No	No	No	No	Yes
Redundancy cost	Notice period for redundancy dismissal (for a worker with 1 year of tenure, in salary weeks)	4.0	4.3	4.3	4.3	4.3
	Notice period for redundancy dismissal (for a worker with 5 years of tenure, in salary weeks)	4.0	4.3	8.7	4.3	8.7
	Notice period for redundancy dismissal (for a worker with 10 years of tenure, in salary weeks)	4.0	4.3	13.0	4.3	13.0

table continues next page

Table K.1 Labor Regulations, 2012 *(continued)*
by country

Category	Indicator	Tanzania	Kenya	Uganda	Rwanda	Burundi
	Notice period for redundancy dismissal (average for workers with 1, 5, and 10 years of tenure, in salary weeks)	4.0	4.3	8.7	4.3	8.7
	Severance pay for redundancy dismissal (for a worker with 1 year of tenure, in salary weeks)	1.0	2.1	0.0	4.3	0.0
	Severance pay for redundancy dismissal (for a worker with 5 years of tenure, in salary weeks)	5.0	10.7	0.0	8.7	8.7
	Severance pay for redundancy dismissal (for a worker with 10 years of tenure, in salary weeks)	10.0	21.4	0.0	13.0	13.0
	Severance pay for redundancy dismissal (average for workers with 1, 5, and 10 years of tenure, in salary weeks)	5.3	11.4	0.0	8.7	7.2

Source: World Bank 2013.

Reference

World Bank. 2013. *Doing Business: EAC.* http://www.doingbusiness.org/~/media/GIAWB/Doing%20Business/Documents/Special-Reports/DB13-EAC.pdf.

Environmental Benefits Statement

The World Bank Group is committed to reducing its environmental footprint. In support of this commitment, the Publishing and Knowledge Division leverages electronic publishing options and print-on-demand technology, which is located in regional hubs worldwide. Together, these initiatives enable print runs to be lowered and shipping distances decreased, resulting in reduced paper consumption, chemical use, greenhouse gas emissions, and waste.

The Publishing and Knowledge Division follows the recommended standards for paper use set by the Green Press Initiative. Whenever possible, books are printed on 50 percent to 100 percent postconsumer recycled paper, and at least 50 percent of the fiber in our book paper is either unbleached or bleached using Totally Chlorine Free (TCF), Processed Chlorine Free (PCF), or Enhanced Elemental Chlorine Free (EECF) processes.

More information about the Bank's environmental philosophy can be found at http://crinfo.worldbank.org/wbcrinfo/node/4.

www.ingramcontent.com/pod-product-compliance
Lightning Source LLC
Chambersburg PA
CBHW060312240426
43661CB00059B/2738